Byzantine Intersectionality

Byzantine Intersectionality

Sexuality, Gender, and Race in the Middle Ages

ROLAND BETANCOURT

PRINCETON UNIVERSITY PRESS
Princeton and Oxford

Published by Princeton University Press,
41 William Street, Princeton, New Jersey 08540
99 Banbury Road, Oxford OX2 6JX
press.princeton.edu

Cover illustrations: Details of figures 4.6, 5.7, 4.8, 4.2, 1.2, 2.1,
5.6, 0.4, 0.1, 5.9, and 5.14 (from top left to bottom right)

First paperback printing, 2023
Paper ISBN: 978-0-691-24354-2
Cloth ISBN: 978-0-691-17945-2

The Library of Congress has cataloged the cloth edition as follows:
Names: Betancourt, Roland, author.
Title: Byzantine intersectionality : sexuality, gender, and race
in the Middle Ages / Roland Betancourt.
Description: Princeton : Princeton University Press, [2020] |
Includes bibliographical references and index.
Identifiers: LCCN 2020010460 (print) | LCCN 2020010461 (ebook) |
ISBN 9780691179452 (hardcover : acid-free paper) |
ISBN 9780691210889 (ebook)
Subjects: LCSH: Byzantine Empire—Social life and customs. |
Intersectionality (Sociology)—Byzantine Empire.
Classification: LCC DF531 .B48 2020 (print) | LCC DF531 (ebook) |
DDC 949.5/02—dc23
LC record available at https://lccn.loc.gov/2020010460
LC ebook record available at https://lccn.loc.gov/2020010461
British Library Cataloging-in-Publication Data is available

This book has been designed and composed in Minion Pro
by Chris Crochetière, BW&A Books, Inc.
Jacket design by Julie Allred.
Printed in the United States of America.

For Dr. Christine Blasey Ford,
Anita Hill,
Monica Lewinsky,
Chelsea Manning,
Matthew Shepard, and
Marsha P. Johnson

I was branded as a tramp, tart, slut, whore, bimbo,
and, of course, that woman . . . When this happened
to me seventeen years ago, there was no name for it.
Now we call it cyberbullying and online harassment.

—MONICA LEWINSKY

CONTENTS

NOTE ON THE TEXT

When available, the author has opted to use the most accessible translations of texts, modified as necessary, rather than using their own translations. Likewise, rather than presenting the full original-language texts, relevant terms and phrases have been transliterated when deemed pertinent to the argument or for added critical nuance. These choices have been done both in keeping with the Press's preferred practices, as well as to enhance the text's readability without impinging on its critical use by both the expert and novice reader. References are provided for the editions of original-language texts, understanding that the majority of these are accessible via open-access resources or databases, such as the *Thesaurus Linguae Graecae* (*TLG*). In the rare instances where a text has been culled from an unpublished (or merely-digitized) manuscript, the full text is reproduced, transliterated.

Byzantine Intersectionality

Introduction

AT THE TURN OF THE SEVENTH CENTURY, an anonymous author from Palestine narrated the encounter of the monk Zosimas with the ascetic Mary of Egypt.[1] This Mary was a sexually promiscuous woman in Alexandria who escaped into the desert to find liberation from her lust and temptations. Earlier sources, however, had described her as a devout woman fleeing the advances of men. The earliest version of her life, from the sixth century, depicts her as a cantor in the Church of the Resurrection in Jerusalem who removed herself from urban life to avoid leading several men, who were infatuated with her, into sin.[2] A similar tale is recounted around the turn of the seventh century, describing an unnamed nun from Jerusalem who fled into the desert because a young man had become desirous of her.[3] In both these cases, Mary isolates herself simply to protect lustful men from sinning—and, as the authors imply, to protect herself from being raped by them.

The Palestinian *Life of Mary of Egypt*, which would become the standard account, alters these narratives. Here, the departure is from her own promiscuous life, sparked by her miraculous conversion at the Holy Sepulcher. After this conversion and wishing to purge herself of her crazed desires for the most debased sex, Mary isolates herself. In other words, her life story shifts from that of a pious woman sacrificing herself in order to shelter and protect erring men to that of an exuberantly lustful woman from whom men need protection.

When Zosimas encountered her, Mary had already spent seventeen years in the Egyptian desert. Her figure was significantly altered by deprivation and the elements: the author describes her as a naked figure with short white hair, like that of an elderly man, and says that her "body was black, as if tanned by the scorching of the sun."[4] Then, the author has her narrate her past for the reader. Filling the text with lurid details, Mary voices her voracious lust, describes how she raped many men, and again stresses her complete bodily transformation through harsh ascetic practices.

What can the story of Mary of Egypt tell us about the ways in which gender, sexuality, and race were construed across Byzantium? My aim in this book is to look at how stories give us a glimpse into the intersectionality of identity in the medieval world, exploring how these various categories overlap with one another—not as distinct identities but as enmeshed conditions that radically alter the lives of figures, both real and imagined. In this introduction, I open my investigation by tracing how these identities are at play with each other in the story of Mary of Egypt. Here, I focus on two main strands of intersection that permeate this book: first, nonnormative sexual practices and sexual consent; second, transmasculine gender presentation and constructions of race based on skin color. In the specific case of Mary of Egypt, we see a literary subject whose identity is not defined by any one of these factors alone but who embodies their intersectionality and the unique conditions of oppression and marginalization. Here, as I do in approaching other figures in this book, I treat Mary of Egypt both as an author's problematic construction and as a potential historical subject in order to give voice to subjectivities neatly purged and expunged from the historical record.

SEXUALITY + CONSENT

While Mary of Egypt is often described in the secondary and primary literature as a sex worker, that title can hardly be applied to the figure portrayed in the anonymous *Life*. Indeed, Mary explicitly rejects the label. As she tells Zosimas, "I was a public temptation to licentiousness, not for payment, I swear, since I did not accept anything although men often wished to pay me. I simply contrived this so that I could seduce many more men, thus turning my lust into a free gift."[5] Placing her beyond excuse for her actions, Mary is made to say that her deeds were justified by neither calamity nor poverty. The author's tactic here is consistently what we would describe today as slut-shaming: a rhetorical practice of criticizing a person's appearance, behavior, or both for failing to adhere to gender-based expectations about their sexuality. Usually deployed against women and queer men, slut-shaming targets a person's real or assumed sexual promiscuity (including premarital or casual sex) and their physical appearance (including attire, makeup, and bodily development). But the practice also relies on a host of other charges, such as accusing or humiliating a person for requesting or gaining access to birth control, engaging in sex work, or for being the victim of sexual assault. In all these regards, the *Life of Mary* effectively produces a character who is both a product and an example of slut-shaming.

In analyzing such stories, we can appreciate slut-shaming as more than just a practice enacted on a single person, group, or class of people. In art and rhetoric, it is a social practice used to generate tropes of women, real or imagined, that are thus cast as sluts. In the Greek-speaking Mediterranean where the author wrote Mary's story, the most vicious and graphic example of this is the mid-sixth-century *Secret History*, the subject of this book's second chapter. Written by the emperor Justinian's historian, Procopius of Caesarea, the *Secret History* contains extensive and repeated attacks on empress Theodora's sexuality. In a text verging on the Byzantine equivalent to revenge pornography, Procopius criticizes and graphically illustrates Theodora's "shameless" behavior, sexual appetites, history of sex work, lower-class upbringing, and reliance on birth control, both contraceptive and abortive. In the *Life of Mary of Egypt*, written just about a half century after Procopius's *Secret History*, we witness the same tropes and tactics of slut-shaming, though given a more demure and censored form in the context of a saint's life. Nevertheless, the scars of slut-shaming as a well-defined rhetorical practice are evident in the author's story.

Aroused by a crowd of Libyan and Egyptian men boarding a ship to Jerusalem, the *Life*'s Mary says (in the first person) that she wanted to go with them so that she "could have many lovers, ready [to satisfy] my lust." But she spares Zosimas more graphic details about her desires, lest she "defile both you and the air with my words." Zosimas urges her to continue, and there the author gives us a prudish glimpse into Mary's lust, as she thirsts over those men on the seashore—"vigorous in their bodies as well as in their movements, who seemed to me fit for what I sought." Later, she states that "there is no kind of licentiousness, speakable or unspeakable, that I did not teach those miserable men."[6] Mary is thus like Theodora, who Procopius accused in meticulous detail of devising new sexual positions and practicing oral, anal, and vaginal sex; the *Life*'s narrative follows such textual precedents to coyly intimate to a medieval audience the various sexual acts in which Mary was engaging with those throngs of Libyan and Egyptian men. The effect of the anonymous author's slut-shaming is twofold: it places Mary of Egypt beyond redemption or compassion, while it titillates the imagination and sexual desires of a presumed cisgender, heterosexual, male audience, familiar with the bawdy performances and slanderous stories popular at the time.

Because the *Life*'s account, like that of Procopius, enacts our current definition of slut-shaming, that term is apt for unraveling the intersection of practices and subjectivities through which women (and also queer men and trans women) were marginalized. These stories also provide an inkling of the various practices connected with sex and reproductive health in which the Byzantines took part, even if the accounts cannot be ascribed to the lived realities of a historical Mary or Theodora. In acknowledging slut-shaming—both as an act by a social group and as a compositional practice by an author—we must be careful not to redeem these historical women by denying the charges. Instead, it falls upon us as readers and historians to call out these male authors for their rhetorical violence against these women, while also ensuring that we do not fall prey to the same politics of "respectability" that sparked the attacks in the first place. In other words, though we must call out the toxicity of the *Life*'s author and of Procopius, we must also provide room for these slut-shamed figures to maneuver within their descriptions. Put simply, we must move past the stigma associated with the sexual acts attached to their names and embrace a sex-positive image of the accounts, allowing a Mary or Theodora to operate without prejudice. At the same time, we can prudently assess the glimpses into medieval sexuality, birth control, and oppressive tactics that these narratives provide.

The anonymous author culminates his multipronged slut-shaming campaign by clearly and precisely accusing Mary of rape. While traveling on the ship to Jerusalem, the *Life*'s Mary repentantly exclaims, "What tongue can declare . . . the acts into which I forced [*ēnagkazon*] those wretched men against their will [*mē thelontas*]?"[7] The author uses the violation of sexual consent as a way to express the extent of Mary's depravity, showing her not only to be licentious in her own voracious sexual drive but also to exceed and impinge on the sexual wishes of others. Thus, her violation of (male) sexual consent is presented as the last straw in the litany of her depravities. Over the course of the two centuries following the *Life*'s composition, Byzantine legal and religious authorities developed clearer and more nuanced language to classify crimes that involved consent, in relation to both sex and marriage.[8] For instance, while Roman law did not unambiguously differentiate between rape, adultery, fornication, and other sexual crimes, in 741 C.E., the law code of Leo III the Isaurian clarified how these sexual crimes and improprieties were designated.

Beyond such codification in law, this period also demonstrated a cultural consciousness that sexual consent was at the very heart of Christian ethics and theology. A telling sign of this importance can be seen in the growing role played by reproductive consent in homilies and narratives on the Annunciation. Writers before Iconoclasm (726–787 C.E., 814–842 C.E.) could be quite careless in their descriptions of when the Virgin Mary conceived Jesus, but, from the mid-ninth century onward, authors deliberately stressed that Mary gave clear verbal consent to becoming the Mother of God before she was impregnated. This emphasis on Mary's consent, which is the focus of my first chapter, underscores the importance given in Byzantine thought to a woman's consent to sex and reproduction. We need to keep this historical context in mind when we consider the author's accusation of rape against Mary of Egypt. Appearing in the final passage before her conversion at the threshold of the Holy Sepulcher, the author's charge pathologizes Mary's sexuality not just as lewd or shameless but also as violent, criminal, and fundamentally inhumane.

I propose further that these narratives present stereotypes of sexual lasciviousness, assault, and violence that are often associated with (and even, at times, praised in) men in Byzantine sources. In staging Mary of Egypt as behaving in a masculine way, the author is impugning not only her moral compass but also her gender identity. Infamously, Byzantine medical handbooks from the sixth and seventh centuries prescribe the trimming of the clitoris for women who seek frequent sexual intercourse, a practice that we today would call female genital mutilation.[9] In his sixth-century gynecological treatise, Aetius of Amida states that an enlarged clitoris is "greatly irritated by constant contact with the clothing and stimulates venery and coitus."[10] A century later, Paul of Aegina expands this observation in his surgical manual, stating that "some women have had erections of this part like men, and also an impulse toward frequent sexual intercourse."[11] These medical sources view incessant sexual desire in women as a masculine characteristic that must be corrected to ensure their femininity. Therefore, we should also read these various slut-shaming tactics as questioning Mary of Egypt's gender by emphasizing her masculinized sexual practices. This is an approach often taken in attacks both on female masculinity and in the broader spectrum of transmasculinity, where a person assigned female at birth identifies more with masculinity, but is nonbinary or not attached to a male identity.[12] We therefore come to the broader intersection of sexuality and gender, and this investigation will lead us further—to the intersection of gender and race.

As we consider the transmasculinity of Mary of Egypt in greater depth, visual culture provides a richer archive than do the textual sources alone. In depicting her great asceticism, painters often produced a transmasculine body for Mary of Egypt that is visually synonymous with that of her male counterparts. For example, compare the image of Mary of Egypt in the sanctuary of the Church of the Panagia Phorbiotissa at Asinou in Cyprus with that of John the Baptist just outside the sanctuary of the same church (figs. 0.1 and 0.2).[13] Both wear a scrappy, tan-colored garment over their emaciated bodies: John's tunic is shredded at its hem, while Mary's is haphazardly tossed over her flesh, wrapped as a himation (a loose mantel-like garment) but without a chiton (the long tunic usually worn under the himation). Her garment, which Zosimas has just tossed to her so that she can cover herself up, is much finer than John's, neither tattered nor torn, with subtle embroidery visible at its hem. As the author details in the text, she had "hair white as wool, and even this was sparse as it did not reach below the neck."[14] In the sanctuary image, Mary's white hair is sparse and shaggy, twisting and turning over her profile and her disheveled pompadour echoes that of John. And though John's body is just as thin and petite as Mary's, her naked chest and back reveal that she is gruesomely famished—her ribs are prominently visible and she has a pronounced hunchback, with thick blobs of paint marking every single one of her vertebrae.

Looking at these two images, we are left with the realization that, by Byzantine standards, John's body is more feminine than Mary's, or rather, Mary's is more masculine than John's. John's hair is longer than Mary's, reaching well past his shoulders, and it falls into locks of thick glossy curls. Mary's tunic falls as flatly over her chest as John's falls over his; a thin swirl of color beside her armpit might allude to withered breasts, a feature recounted in some of the trans saints' lives that we shall see in chapter 3. On her face, the weight of Mary's excess flesh and wrinkles pulls down her jawline. The soft and rounded face of the Virgin Mary, standing next to John, provides a marked contrast: the ascetic has no roundness to her. The streams of paint that contour the ascetic Mary's drooping cheek flow down from the top of her ear and the outer corner of her eye, curving at an angle that echoes her rigidly square jaw. That jaw features a strong and prominent chin, unlike the Virgin's soft and rounded features. The ascetic's brow is furrowed and shadowed, while the Virgin has a serenely elastic brow. John's legs, arms, and feet are covered with body hair, indicated by thin long stripes of black paint. Mary's body is lacerated with similar lines, though thicker and shorter; brownish-red stripes of paint even cover her back, yet notably not the palms of her hands. Her flesh is *also* seemingly covered in body hair. In this ambiguity in representations of scar and hair, the lacerations of asceticism transmute into the secondary sex characteristics of the male body. In the later Western medieval world, though rarely in Byzantine art, Mary of Egypt and her often-conflated counterpart, Mary Magdalene, are both commonly depicted as covered in body hair as if they were beasts of the wilderness. Yet, despite their hairiness, in Western art the women often retain the coded characteristics of feminine beauty, youth, and pallor, making them radically different from the Byzantine Mary of Egypt. In every way, the Byzantine artist has sought to portray Mary as transmasculine.

Is this transmasculine depiction unique? If not, what do such cases tell us about the fluidity and presentation of gender? In the *Life*'s narrative, as Zosimas pursues her, Mary attempts to flee; eventually overtaken, she asks him to toss her his cloak for she is a woman and should not turn around and reveal her nudity.[15] This moment is dramatized in the Theodore Psalter's gloss to Psalm 54:6–8, which reads: "Oh, that I had the wings of a dove! I would fly away and be at rest. I would flee far away and stay in the desert. I would hurry to my place of shelter, far from the tempest and storm." In the marginal illustration, the encounter with Zosimas is captured precisely at the moment that he has tossed the garment toward her (fig. 0.3). The cloth is suspended in midair, having just left his hands. Zosimas looks away, while Mary turns back to catch the fine cloth. As she twists, she exposes her naked chest to the viewer while her right thigh modestly protects her pubic region. When we closely inspect her chest, we again see no indication of breasts, whether full or withered. Rather, her chest is crossed from armpit to armpit by a thick reddish brushstroke, slightly wavy, resembling a wound. It looks more like the mottled dark-red of cauterized scar tissue than breasts.

What do we make of this line? Do we relegate it to a minor painterly gesture, a minute flick of an artist's wrist in a composition? Or is there any possible meaning that we can pull from this detail? Looking at this line with a knowledge of Byzantine medical guidebooks, I perceive a scar that would be in keeping with a mastectomy. According to the medical and surgical handbooks, a mastectomy at the time involved a process of alternately cutting and cauterizing, such as is prescribed in the chapters of Aetius of Amida's sixth-century gynecological treatise that describe the removal of breast cancer. There is no clear evidence to corroborate that this was the artist's intention, and these surgical manuscripts include no illuminations. However, we can compare the scar-like trace on Mary's body to an earlier image of Saint Agatha's torture found in the Menologion of Basil II (fig. 0.4). Here we do have an artist explicitly tasked with depicting the surgical removal of breasts from a Christian saint. The tactics, imagery, and knowledge deployed suggest how artists might have used medical texts in their works.

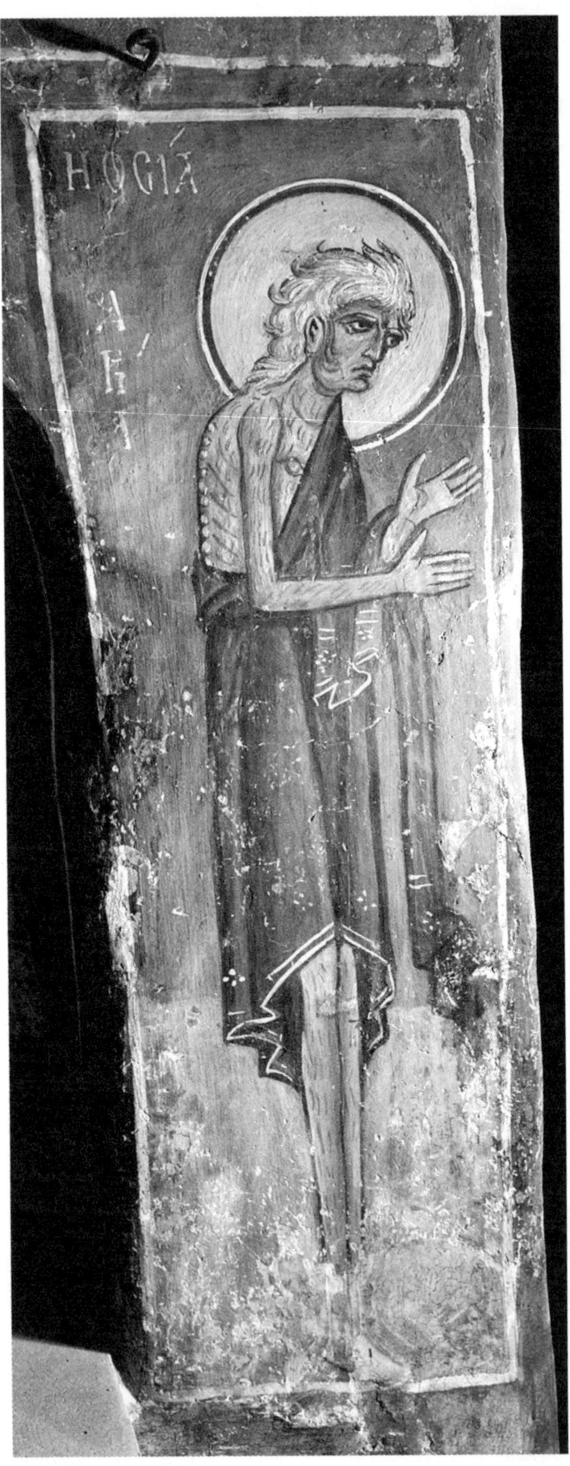

0.1. Mary of Egypt.
Church of the Panagia
Phorbiotissa, Asinou,
Cyprus.

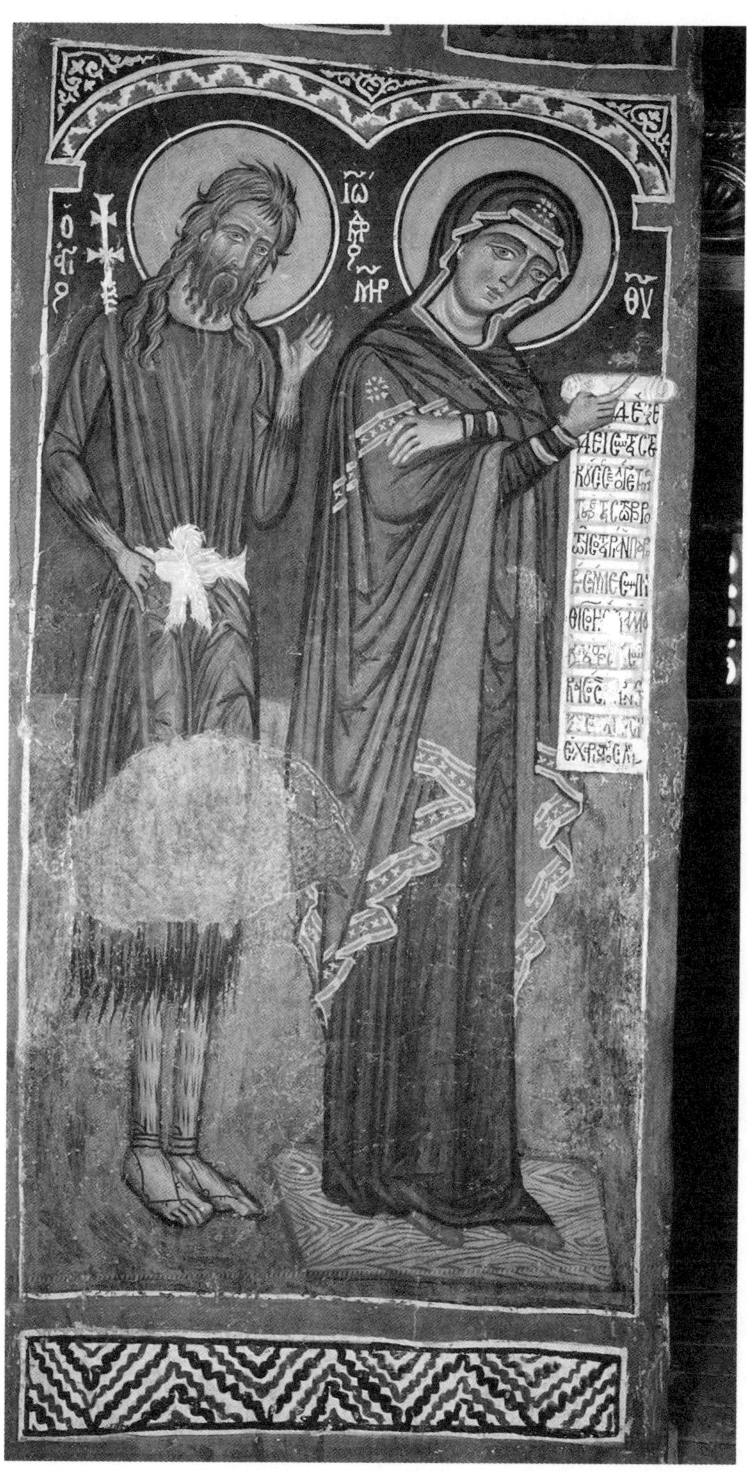

0.2. John the Baptist and Virgin Mary. Church of the Panagia Phorbiotissa, Asinou, Cyprus.

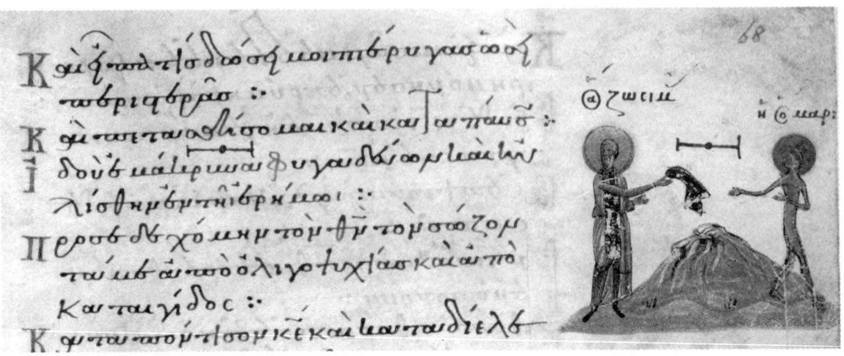

0.3. Mary of Egypt and Zosimas. London, British Library, Theodore Psalter (Add. Ms. 19352), fol. 68r. © The British Library Board.

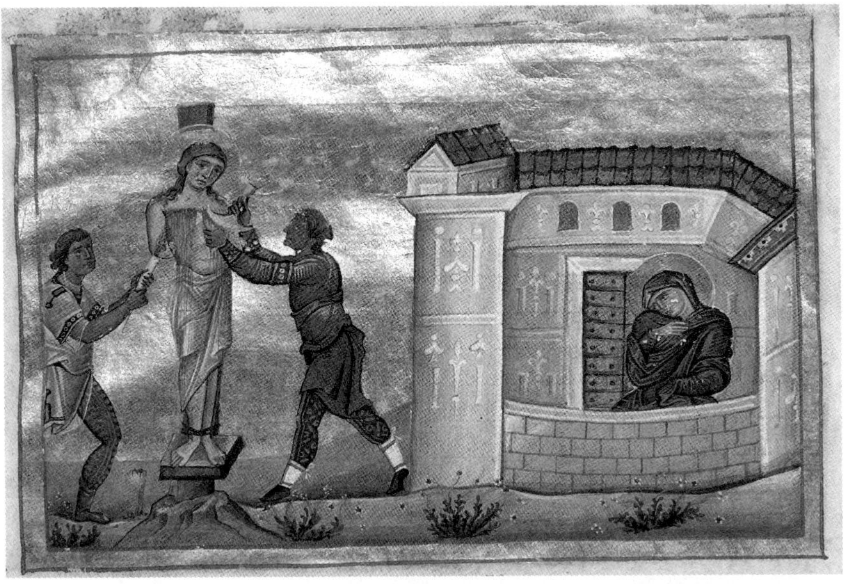

0.4. Martyrdom of Agatha. Vatican City, Biblioteca Apostolica Vaticana, 'Menologion' of Basil II (Vat. gr. 1613), fol. 373. © 2019 Biblioteca Apostolica Vaticana.

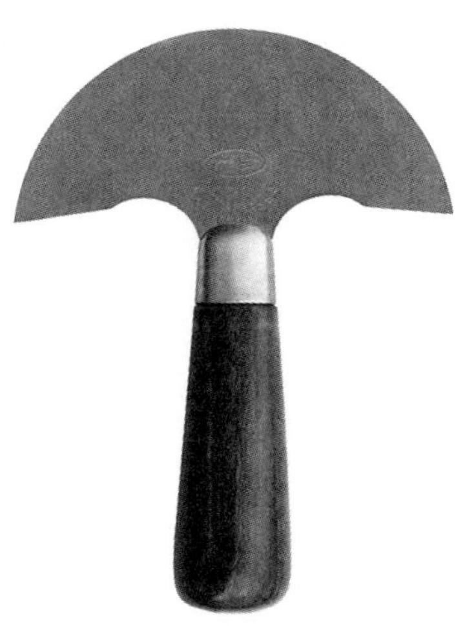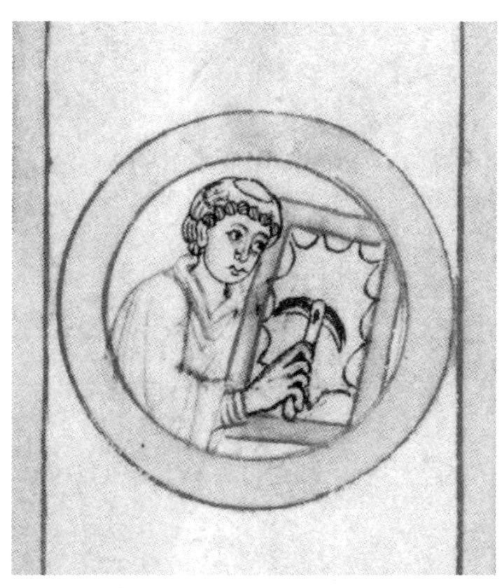

0.5. Modern *lunellum*. Round Knife for leather working by C. S. Osborne and Company.

0.6. Western medieval depiction of monk using a *lunellum* to scrape parchment for manuscript production. Bamberg, Staatsbibliothek Bamberg, Msc. Patr. 5, fol. 1v.

In this depiction, two men are torturing Agatha by cutting off her breasts, using not pincers, as is often shown, but rather a striking half-moon knife. The knife is a *lunellum* (fig. 0.5), commonly associated with the scraping and cleaning of animal skin in the making of parchment (fig. 0.6); it is thus a tool connected with the working of flesh for a scribe and illuminator. In the miniature, Agatha's recently cut-off breast has fallen onto the ground to her right. A man approaches her with a torch that is about to be pressed against the wound where the right breast had been, apparently to cauterize the open lesion. After all, Agatha's torture was not intended to be fatal; rather, she was meant to live on without her breasts. In the composition, this point is stressed by the recumbent Agatha to the right of her torture. Depicted within the walls of a city, she sits with her body contorted, perhaps in pain, as she recovers after the forced mastectomy.

Nuances regarding the proper surgical procedure for mastectomies must be noted here, as these details lead us deeper into the artist's logic. First, an open torch is not hot enough to cauterize such a wound. And, second, we have no evidence that such a lunellum was ever used as a surgical tool. In other words, we are seeing here painters conceptualizing a surgical process through the types of tools and methods with which they would have been most familiar in a manuscript workshop—those used to work,

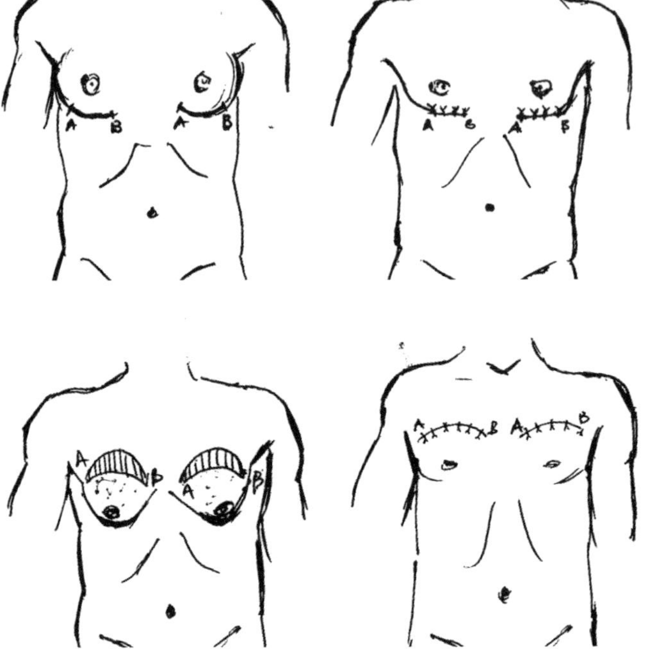

0.7. Reconstruction of Paul of Aegina's surgical treatment for moderate gynecomastia with pre-operative and post-operative lunate incisions.

0.8. Reconstruction of Paul of Aegina's surgical treatment for severe gynecomastia with pre-operative and post-operative lunate incisions.

manufacture, and process animal skins for parchment. Nevertheless, I contend that a familiarity with medical texts is certainly at play here. These patterns of scars and incisions match modern reconstructions of Paul of Aegina's instructions for the surgical treatment of moderate and severe gynecomastia (figs. 0.7 and 0.8).[16] Paul of Aegina's seventh-century instructions for breast-reductions for severe gynecomastia indicate the need for "a lunate incision" (*mēnoeidē . . . tomēn*), which would have naturally led the artist to articulate this "crescent-shaped cut" via the shape of either the cutting tool or, as in other cases, the gash (fig. 0.8). The scene of the Martyrdom of Melasippos, Karina, and their son in the Menologion of Basil II provides an example of such a crescent-shaped wound on Karina's chest, her breasts having been freshly excised (fig. 0.9).

As we compare these images, we can find striking parallels—for example, between the lunate wounds on Karina's chest and the similarly oval form on Mary of Egypt's chest in the Asinou portrait, or between the depiction of Agatha's wound with its height just at her armpit and the curious dark-red undulating line across Mary of Egypt's chest in the Theodore Psalter. Certainly, whether out of cruelty, modesty, or a strong desire to obscure their breasts, these painted figures have had their breasts removed,

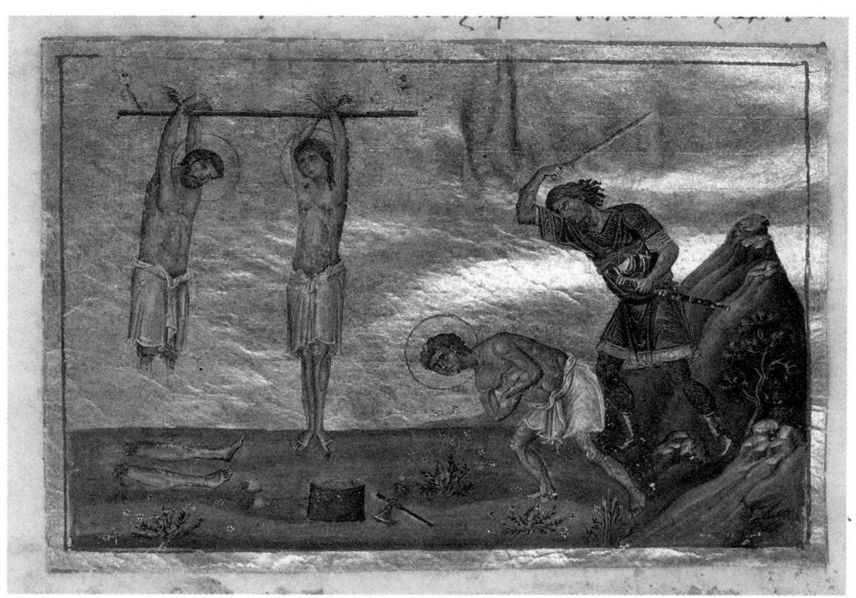

0.9. Martyrdom of Melasippos, Karina, and Their Son. Vatican City, Biblioteca Apostolica Vaticana, 'Menologion' of Basil II (Vat. gr. 1613), fol. 165. © 2019 Biblioteca Apostolica Vaticana.

even showing the scars. This suggests that the visual language of excision and cauterization associated with mastectomies could be deployed to manifest the transmasculine body of Mary of Egypt.

While Mary of Egypt is not explicitly understood as a transgender man or eunuch, as are several of the figures examined in this book (particularly in chapters 3, 4, and 5), her presentation is nevertheless masculinized.[17] Her story and depictions in art also feature several important details that speak to her unsettled gender identity. As we will see, there are several narratives of trans monks who were assigned female at birth but chose to live their lives as male and pass as eunuchs. In those stories, the authors repeatedly make note of how these figures altered their bodies' secondary sex characteristics. The authors comment that these trans men went beyond wearing male garb—they had lost their feminine beauty, their menstruation had stopped, their breasts looked like two shriveled leaves, and their skin had darkened. According to these texts, the figures were unrecognizable to their loved ones; they looked like "Ethiopians"—a reference to the ancient Greek theory of racial difference, stressing that the sun had made their skin "burnt-looking."[18] These details are striking, offering us a host of different factors that not only show ways in which these figures were able to transition but also how Byzantines linked skin color and the attendant assignment of race with gender identity. Medical writers, like Aetius of Amida, associated dark skin with manly women who were hairier and menstruated less than other women.[19] In contrast, Eustathios of Thessalonike praised the emperor Manuel I Komnenos for his dark skin, saying that it spoke to his manliness and his willingness to purge from his flesh all "effeminate paleness" (*thēlyprepēs leukotēs*).[20]

In the *Life*'s text, Mary appears when the monk Zosimas catches a glance of her ghostly shape in the desert, described as "a naked figure whose body was black, as if tanned by the scorching sun."[21] In early Christian and Western medieval texts on the lives of monks and ascetics, black figures often signify the manifestation of demons. At the same time, however, Byzantine sources cast the racial diversity of the empire and its peoples in a positive light, often prizing the diversity of the court and Constantinople; we will return to these matters in chapter 5. But, curiously, the author's Zosimas is ecstatically taken in by the black figure of Mary, writing that "he was inspired with pleasure and, filled with joy at that incredible sight."[22] This narrative simultaneously undoes the aspects of racial prejudice inherent in some early Christian texts and reveals to us the multifaceted intersection of skin color, gender stereotypes, racial identity, and ethnic grouping conceived by a medieval author. The figure of Mary of Egypt as created by an elite author, writing in Greek in the city of Jerusalem in the seventh century, encompasses all these issues. Such stories require new interpretive models that enable us to appreciate the complex entanglements of identity, while understanding the systematics of oppression and marginalization that have all but purged such lives from the historical archive.

BYZANTINE INTERSECTIONALITY

Following the intersectional approach of critical race studies and feminism, this project acknowledges that identity is neither singular nor delimited by neat categories. In 1989, Kimberlé Crenshaw coined the term "intersectionality" to stress that the lived realities of marginalized people do not exist as isolated factors alone but instead come together at the intersection of gender, sexuality, race, socioeconomic status, and so on. Thus, intersectionality looks at how the overlap of social identities creates unique conditions of inequality and oppression.[23] Unlike approaches that study the role of women or foreigners in the medieval world in isolation, intersectionality suggests that a foreign woman, for example, faces a series of challenges that include the struggles of those socially identified as being both foreign and female, yet she is not merely the sum of those parts. This book is titled *Byzantine Intersectionality* not only because it studies the intersectionality of identity across the Byzantine world but also because the pejorative "byzantine" speaks to the inherent queerness of these stories and the empire from which that slur was taken. Intersectional identity is byzantine—it is infinitely complicated, and it is often characterized as devious, deceitful, and corrupt.

For those reasons, I have chosen to use the phrase "the Byzantine world" throughout this book: it serves as a capacious term to encompass the span of the Greek-speaking Mediterranean, as well as the contributions to this world by its closest neighbors and allies.[24] Ultimately, this is a book about the Byzantine Empire, which I define as the Eastern Roman Empire from the foundation of Constantinople in the early fourth century until its conquest in the late fifteenth century. In using a definition that spans the late antique, medieval, and early modern periods, I purposely acknowledge the unbroken tradition of the medieval Roman Empire, which possessed an access to and intimacy with the Greek and Latin heritage of the ancient Greek and Roman Mediterranean and its neighbors.[25]

Intersectionality, however, does more than flesh out the subjectivities of people who experience the overlap of several discriminated against, marginalized, or disenfranchised identities. Intersectionality also alerts us to the subjects whose privilege keeps them away from the public eye. The figure of the abortion-inducing sex worker is shaped by her intersectional identity as a destitute woman of the lowest economic status, yet it also makes us aware that women of privilege would have been spared from such libelous representations in texts, even when performing the same deeds. For example, that an elite medical text would provide detailed prescriptions for abortive suppositories, contraceptive treatments, and late-term surgical methods for terminating a pregnancy demonstrates the privilege of upper-class women's own pursuits of contraception and abortion.

In examining the lives of figures subjected to multiple inequities, we begin to perceive the privileges afforded to some other women, men, and non-binary figures in society. Privilege, and the privacy it often enables, create the greatest lacunae in the historical record. Privacy creates closets that allow certain figures ample room to maneuver, away from the judgment and agency of publics and oppressors. Such figures are usually also safe from the historian's stylus. Thus, in articulating the intersectionality of disenfranchised identities, we will also be outlining the privilege afforded to those persons who might have shared in some of these identities, but whose economic status, social rank, race, origin, and so on spared them from vilification in the historical record—if not from any association with a marginalized identity. Intersectionality makes us keenly aware of all those hidden figures who were able to make choices about their sexual consent, pursue abortions and contraceptives, live as transgender monks, engage in same-gender intimacies, and be black at court, without facing the same degree of invective or libel as their poorer counterparts. This book challenges us to take risks in fleshing out the intersectional lives of the downtrodden, while also providing spectrums of possibility for the identities and freedoms allowed to the more privileged ranks and neglected by the historical record.

Given the historical archive's push toward normative narratives, queer historical tasks such as this require close reading and careful scrutiny of what has been labeled minor. As Elizabeth Freeman has eloquently put it, queer history necessitates "the decision to unfold, slowly, a small number of imaginative texts rather than amass a weighty archive of or around texts, and to treat these texts and their formal work as theories of their own, interventions upon both critical theory and historiography."[26] But, more so, this book struggles with the absences of archives and the potent act of grasping at lives, purposefully and shamefully erased and denied. "To read without a trace," as Anjali Arondekar calls it, is a way of embracing the absences of the archive, the seductions of a retrieval, and the recuperative hermeneutics of accessing minoritized lives and historiographies.[27] It is this intersection of slow unfolding and traceless reading that this book embraces.

The five chapters that follow unfurl a series of *minuscule intersectional histories*.[28] Each history is carefully scaled and delineated to elucidate rich, nuanced, and surprising takes by medieval thinkers and artists on familiar subjects. Sometimes it encompasses a neatly defined trajectory in the evolution of a cluster of ideas; at other times it focuses on a particular person, specific period, or textual genre to generate points of resistance that might otherwise be overlooked or have no place in a broader historical account.

These five chapters will reveal long-standing conversations in medieval thought around matters of reproductive consent, sexual shaming, trans and nonbinary genders, queer intimacies, and racial identity. Chapter 1 traces the evolving emphasis given to consent in treatments of the Annunciation, stressing the important role that Mary's consent to become the Mother of God played in homilies and art after Iconoclasm. Chapter 2 focuses on the practices and tactics that Procopius uses in the *Secret History* to slut-shame Empress Theodora, focusing on his deployment of graphic sexual detail and accusations against her and other women of abortive and contraceptive practices. Chapter 3 surveys saints' lives, medical texts, and the epistolary tradition not only to present evidence for the representation of transgender and gender nonconforming persons in Byzantium but also to elucidate a host of gender affirming practices found in both surgical guides and ascetic action. Chapter 4 examines representations of the Doubting Thomas scene in text and art to reveal potent narratives of same-gender desire and monastic community, stressing the need to include trans, nonbinary, and asexual figures in the history of queer sexuality and intimacy. And chapter 5 places the visual representations of the Ethiopian Eunuch from the Acts of the Apostles in the context of discourses around racial identity, ethnic grouping, and skin color in order to delineate how artists struggled with the figure's intersectional identity as a eunuch, a Christian, and a black African. None of these narratives is comprehensive or exhaustive, but all are sufficient and provocative orientations that require us to think further into these identities and do better as readers, historians, and modern subjects.

My promise to the reader is that I will endeavor (as much as I responsibly can) to treat the figures in my texts and images as *possible* medieval subjects with a past, a present, and—most important—a future. Many of the subjectivities encompassed here have been actively denied, negated, or simply assumed to have not existed in the Middle Ages. I will take their existence for granted and treat them as real, because they were real. Whether Empress Theodora actually carried out the sexual deeds and abortions that Procopius slut-shames her for does not matter, because there were other women in the past subjected to the same—and far worse—rhetorical and physical violence as that imputed against Procopius's literary Theodora. Whether the trans monks discussed in this book actually existed or were simply literary characters is beside the point. The fact is that there were people in the Byzantine Empire who were trans and who, even if they did not have the critical vocabulary to self-identify as such or have their voices recorded, were nevertheless still trans. To deny these realities is to be complicit with violence—both physical and rhetorical—not just in the past but also in the present.

I. The Virgin's Consent

His words, however, which give the impression of being those of a suitor,
prompt me to refuse consent [*synkatathesin*]. For indeed, said the Evangelist,
"seeing *him* she was troubled." Seeing what, and whereof was she troubled?
Seeing the angel looking at her with chaste eyes, yet bringing tidings of a
suitor; *seeing him* attend with a seemly gaze, yet speaking of a marriage
contract. Having heard these bridal words, and seeing the manner of the
conversation to be untouched by the passions, the holy Virgin was troubled
by her conflicting thoughts and, seized by a prudent fear, was amazed by the
strangeness of the salutation.[1]

—*Photius,* Homily on the Annunciation *(modified trans. Cyril Mango)*

IN HIS MID-NINTH-CENTURY HOMILY on the Annunciation, Photius—the
patriarch of Constantinople and a leading intellect in the period immediately following Iconoclasm—describes in intricate detail the climax of
Mary's consent before the angel. Staged as a dramatic narrative between the
archangel Gabriel and the Virgin Mary, and delving into her thoughts and
psychology, Photius's homily has its precedents in fifth- and sixth-century
Syriac *soghyatha* (dialogic liturgical poems) and in a similar homily on the
Annunciation by his predecessor Germanus I, patriarch of Constantinople in the early eighth century.[2] Photius's homily draws from apocryphal
sources, such as the second-century *Protoevangelium of James*,[3] as well as
from the homilies on the Annunciation by Proclus of Constantinople, Andrew of Crete, Gregory Thaumaturgus, Sophronius of Jerusalem, Romanus
the Melodist, and others. But many of these earlier writers are sometimes
careless regarding the exact moment when Mary conceives, thereby implicitly questioning her ability and willingness to consent. Photius, in contrast, eloquently reflects in his homily on her trajectory toward consent. He
shares with his listeners Mary's internal monologue after hearing the angel's words, as she hesitantly reflects. Mary's fear and confusion emerge as
she "pondered what sort of greeting this might be," as the Gospel states. She
has questions not only about the oddity of the virgin birth suggested by Gabriel but also about the very nature of this interaction with a man who has
burst into her chamber and now offers her "bridal words."[4]

Over the course of this chapter, we will consider the increased role that consent played in textual and visual depictions of the Annunciation. As we will see, while early Christian writers laid the foundation for making consent crucial to the Annunciation narrative, this feature was not highly emphasized until the period after Iconoclasm. Coinciding with this shift, in legal and historical sources we witness a greater awareness about sexual crimes and forced marriages. Thus, this chapter first sketches early Christian and pre-Iconoclastic views on the Incarnation, then moves on to consider the tactics used by post-Iconoclastic authors and artists to stress how Mary's consent was vitally important to the salvation of humanity. The following three sections explore the early Christian and pre-Iconoclastic discourses around Mary, including both libel about her rape or adultery and authors' disregard of her consent at the Annunciation. Having established this context, we will then move on to look at Photius's homily in further depth before turning to the legacy of the homily in the works of later writers and artists.

MARY'S PRUDENCE IN EARLY CHRISTIANITY

Throughout the early Christian period, theologians debated the role and nature of the Incarnation around the figure of Mary.[5] One major disagreement centered on the role of Mary in the formation of the Christ. For example, Gregory of Nazianzus in the fourth century, responding to earlier claims, stated that Christ did not merely flow through her "as if through a channel" but was rather formed in her, from her flesh.[6] Debates about the Virgin as the Theotokos, or "God-bearer," articulated the interplay between Christ's humanity and divinity, as well as the structures of this union between humanity and God. The (heretical) Nestorius, patriarch of Constantinople in the early fifth century, claimed that Mary should be called the Christotokos, or "Christ-bearer," because she bore only the Christ and not the Godhead himself. With these two authors we thus see Mary serving as a crucial figure for articulating the identity and Christological doctrine of Christ. An important element was Mary's willing consent. Not only does it distinguish the Christian God's incarnation from the issue of the pagan Zeus's many rapes, but it likewise demonstrates that Mary possessed free will, being fully human and fully conscious of the actions that were to occur.

In stressing her prudence, early Christian writers sought to stage Mary as the antitype to Eve, who hastily consented to the urgings of the serpent and thereby was led astray. Mary's prudence manifested itself as a reluctance to immediately consent. This underscored the importance of that consent; without it she could have easily been deceived and been no better than Eve, a critical distinction for later authors. Mary's confusion and fear before the angel are described already in the Gospel of Luke:

And he came to her and said, "Greetings, favored one! The Lord is with you." But she was much perplexed by his words and pondered what sort of greeting this might be. The angel said to her, "Do not be afraid, Mary, for you have found favor with God. And now, you will conceive in your womb and bear a son, and you will name him Jesus. . . . Then Mary said, "Here am I, the servant of the Lord; let it be with me according to your word." Then the angel departed from her. (Luke 1:28–31, 38)

These qualities demonstrate her purity and intellect as Mary debates and inquires into the good tidings of the angel before assenting to their truth. Writers like Photius would come to emphasize Mary's "superior reason" in the face of the angel's greeting rather than praising her for submissive obedience.[7]

These characteristics set Mary apart from Eve, establishing the latter as her antitype. Eve, as noted by the early fifth-century Proclus of Constantinople, among others, gave birth to evil and caused humanity's expulsion from the garden of Eden with her consent to the serpent's deception.[8] Indeed, Irenaeus had put forth the same idea in the second century, and Justin Martyr before him.[9] The late fifth-century Narsai of Edessa likened the folly of Eve's actions to those of an unfaithful bride whose adulterous pregnancy leads to the "birth of sin," elsewhere noting that the serpent's own verbal tidings "deposited his seed" within Eve's soul.[10] Proclus likened Eve to Mary, with the former undergoing her own (albeit depraved) pregnancy, which for Proclus is literally embodied in the figure of Cain.[11] For these authors, in order to distance Mary from Eve, Mary must resist the angel's tidings. She must be dubious and reserved in her pious and virtuous protection of her virginity and betrothal to Joseph. The need for her to be led willingly to consent thus becomes essential to establishing her character and nature, lest another Eve be unleashed on the world.

Mary manifests her contrast to the deceived Eve through her rigorous inquiry and critical thinking. In one homily on the Annunciation, dubiously attributed to the third-century Gregory Thaumaturgus, the author describes Mary by setting her against her antitype: "She was nothing like the primeval virgin Eve, who, keeping holiday alone in paradise, with thoughtless mind, unguardedly hearkened to the word of the serpent, the author of all evil, and thus became depraved in the thoughts of her mind."[12] Mary, unlike Eve, is persuaded neither quickly nor rashly by the tidings of the angel, who appears to her like a male suitor coming into her midst. Instead, Mary hotly debates with and against him, before being convinced that he is truthful. With a performative speech act she then consents to the Incarnation—"Behold, the servant of the Lord; let it be with me according to your word." This articulation of consent—the moment and act in which Mary conceives—captured the attention of many early Christian and Byzantine writers who endeavored to further flesh out and comprehend the dialogue between Mary and the angel. Specifically, they explored her psychic disposition in this moment, as well as the manner in which she consented and was able to conceive.

In the narrative imagination of many homilists, the presence and visage of the archangel Gabriel present a crucial problem for Mary as she struggles to understand whether this figure of a man is mortal or divine—in other words, whether he comes with true tidings of the Lord or to seduce or violate her. In the sixth century, Romanus the Melodist's hymn on the Annunciation expressed an eroticized tension between Mary and the angel.[13] There, Mary asks herself:

What am I seeing? What shall I think?
An appearance of fire, yet a voice of a man
has the one who has come; he both stirs [*tarattei*] me and spurs [*tharrynei*] me
when he addresses me:
"Hail, unwedded bride!"[14]

In her modesty and chastity, Mary is perturbed (*tarattei*) and encouraged (*tharrynei*), verbs with a sexual undertone that suggests that she is both attracted to the angel's bridal words and reeling back in fear of his advances. Gabriel's appearance is described as fiery, alluding to the heat of passion and the angelic "fiery form" (*eidos pyros*) of his visage. Yet what troubles her mind most is that his voice resembles that of a man, both in the bridal words he speaks and in its outward form and appearance. Thus, the soon-to-be-Theotokos provides a perfect paradigm of virginity—while potentially attracted to the heat of carnal passion, she judges with prudence and discretion what confronts her.

The deference paid to Mary's doubt and debate generated an interesting space for contemplating the manner in which her hesitation dilated time and inverted the power structure of the Annunciation. Romanus the Melodist's Gabriel is caught off guard, flustered, and seemingly perturbed by Mary's continued doubt and cross-examination. At times, it might even seem that Gabriel wishes to lash out and "utter a harsh word to the one giving birth to the Lord," but he restrains himself. Having to stay and answer her questions, the angel appears almost to lose his own ability to consent, stating that "against my will [*mē thelōn*] I am held back," for fear that the Christ might exact retribution on him.[15] In a way, this holding back makes the angel confront the entitlement of the divine to act as they wish, as Gabriel notes that in the past he could act with impunity and silence those who might doubt. The divine appears to be halted in that moment, and time almost seems to slow as Mary cross-examines the angel, debates the tidings, and considers the consent that her assent entails. The angel takes on the role of a spurned suitor.

Writing in the late seventh and early eighth centuries, Andrew of Crete shows a similar tension in his depiction of Mary. In his homily, Mary asks: "Should I deem him to be an angel? But he speaks like a man."[16] Mary expresses uncertainty about Gabriel's identity, viewing him as a suitor in disguise who is contriving this deceitful narrative so as to trick her into consent. Perhaps even more intriguing is the suggestion that Mary experiences some form of attraction to Gabriel.

In an eighth-century homily by Patriarch Germanus, the hesitant would-be-Theotokos says to the angel:

Young man, I see the striking beauty of your elegant form and the splendid
sight of your figure; and I am listening to your words [the like of which] I have
never heard before, and I am rapidly beginning to suspect that you have come
to lead me astray.[17]

Not only does Mary express her seeming attraction to Gabriel's figure and form, but the supposed sexual temptation almost seems palpable in her fearful reproach about his suspected intentions. The scene reads like the flirtatious exchange of two young lovers. Rather than immediately assuaging her concerns, Gabriel in effect changes the subject with a coquettish retort: "Clearly understand and be persuaded that it is rather I who, on perceiving such divinely etched beauty in you, have fallen into amazement." Not until several lines later does Mary return to her concerns: after reiterating her fear of being led astray "like another Eve," she confidently and assuredly denies the suitor's advances by stating that she is not like Eve and cannot be entrapped.[18]

The potentially adulterous flirtations of the Annunciation narrative found in many of these homilies speak to a far deeper and more troubled concern about the virginity and consent of Mary. The implicit equation of her assent to the incarnation with a form of sexual consent might appear to be anachronistic, enforcing contemporary conversations concerning rape culture and a woman's right to choose onto the past. However, the cultural context of early Christian and Byzantine writers makes this association explicit. Not only is Mary juxtaposed to Eve, whose narrative is likened to adultery, but similar charges were also lodged against Mary, as early Christian writers' invectives against such claims attest.

In the gnostic and apocryphal traditions, Eve's misguided actions were seen as connected not simply to the deceit of the serpent but to both metaphorical and literal rape.[19] The gnostic *Apocryphon of John*, written before the end of the second century, depicts the virginal Eve being "defiled" and impregnated by Yaldabaoth, the chief of the rulers (*archones*) of the Demiurge.[20] Similarly, in the third-century *The Hypostasis of the Archons*, the archons lust over Eve and pursue her so that they can forcefully sow their seed in her, a process that causes her to become subhuman, a "shadowy reflection resembling herself," which they "defiled . . . foully."[21] While her deeds were also staged in the later Christian tradition as a form of adultery, these texts suggest a violent and disturbing rape as the source of Eve's crimes against humanity. It is this typology against which Mary must be set, a point that is made clear early on. For example, in the second-century *Protoevangelium of James*, as Mary and Joseph talk after the visitation of Gabriel, Joseph projects himself as a new Adam: "For as Adam was absent in the hour of his prayer and the serpent came and found Eve alone and seduced and defiled her, so hath it befallen me."[22] Here, it is Mary who has been seduced and defiled, as Eve was before her; these parallels are made explicit throughout the Annunciation homilies.

The charge of adultery figures prominently in Joseph's dialogue with Mary in the moments following the Annunciation, as depicted in the *Protoevangelium of James* and in Germanus's homily, among others. In Romanus's hymn, quite startlingly, Mary summons Joseph immediately after the angel's departure and rebukes him for allowing her to have been raped, asking, "Where were you, wise man? How could you *not* protect my virginity?"[23] Joseph marvels as he perceives her newfound radiant form, aptly described through paradoxes—heat and snow, paradise and furnace, smoking mountain and spring, throne and footstool. We must read the loss of virginity as expressed in a similar paradox—Mary has conceived and yet has "no knowledge of the embryo's conception." It almost seems that Mary uses this accusation to shame Joseph preemptively for his potential disbelief, blaming him for her pregnancy if he believes it to be human made. As she states at the end of the hymn: "Who could testify to all this, if not you who protect me?"[24] Thus, Mary's words here have a potent force, not only responding to earlier accusations of adultery or rape but also reworking this slut-shaming invective by blaming Joseph, who, as her betrothed, would have been charged with protecting her from sexual assault.

In his mid-second-century *First Apology*, Justin Martyr addresses the allegations that Mary's divine conception was merely another instance of Zeus's rapes of "those many women whom he had violated [*moicheutheisas*]." Some polemicists suggested, as Justin notes, that this put Jesus in a role akin to that of Hermes, who was begotten through Zeus's rape of his mother Maia in the middle of the night and without her knowledge or consent.[25] In his *Dialogue with Trypho*, Justin responds both to those claims and to Joseph's initial suspicion that Mary had in fact conceived out of wedlock, with another man through sexual intercourse—"that is from fornication [*apo porneias*]."[26] While modern law clearly differentiates between adultery and rape, the distinction, rooted in the question of consent, was developing over the course of the Middle Ages.[27] Thus, medieval writers frequently lacked clarity in their terminology. For example, "fornication" (*porneia*) and "adultery" (*moicheia*) could have various intersecting meanings, though *porneia* often suggested that the woman in question was not married. Nevertheless, both terms could also be used for forms of sexual intercourse in which there was no consent.

Whether the primary sources acknowledge these implications or not, rape is implied when the term "adultery" is applied to Zeus's actions involving victims who did not offer up consent or perhaps were not even conscious, as in the narrative of Hermes's birth. This is relevant to the charges made against Mary, who, according to one narrative—quoted in Origen's response to Celsus—"had been convicted of adultery [*moicheia*] and had a child by a certain soldier named Panthera."[28] Origen goes on to once again use the term "adultery" (*moicheia*) in connection with this libelous story. In modern literature, however, it is often characterized (perhaps somewhat euphemistically) as the rape of Mary, reframing it to emphasize the soldier's violation, not Mary's volition. These accusations of Mary's infidelity or violation have their roots in Jewish critiques of Christianity's origins; Celsus even cast these charges as coming from a Jew. Various permutations of the nonvirgin birth of Christ appear in the manuscripts of the life story of Jesus, the *Toledot Yeshu*, which variously accuse Mary of fornicating with the soldier Panthera or another man, claim she was raped, or say she was deceived into having sex with a man she believed to be her husband.[29]

As late antique and Byzantine writers struggled with the typology set forth by narratives of Eve's rape, both metaphorical and literal, as well as with the charges lodged against Mary's own actions, it is possible to observe the key role played by consent in the Annunciation narratives. In the homilies, ties to the antitype of Eve and the suspected adultery of Mary are ever present, not only as an accusation made against Mary by Joseph but also as a reflection of Mary's own potential deceit.

Pre-Iconoclastic homilies often seem to deny Mary the possibility of consent, troubling accounts that undermine centuries of Christian thought and doctrine. At times the difficulty may reflect the present-oriented setting of the dramatic narrative, which recounts something happening at that moment in the liturgy and the Annunciation as a historical event that has already happened. For example, Andrew of Crete several times uses the past tense to remark on the conception before Mary's assent and describes Christ's incarnation as "having hastened to leap in, he slipped into your belly." Although he quotes Luke, who unambiguously states that Mary "will conceive," Andrew has the angel say that he brings good tidings from the one "who came into your womb before my arrival."[30] Noting the absurdity of such statements, Andrew's translator, Mary B. Cunningham, finds it impossible that the author intended such a meaning; in her view they reveal the dramatic intent of the homily, rather than evincing a particular theological approach.[31]

In his homily, however, Germanus of Constantinople pursues this troubling line of (perhaps poetic) thought, as Gabriel declares:

Cast off your mistrustful opinion, virgin. For behold, it seems to me that my
words have been fulfilled and your womb is beginning to swell. And even
if you do not wish for this, "with God every word shall not be impossible"
(Luke 1:37).[32]

In this deeply problematic homily on the Annunciation, Germanus unambiguously presents a rape narrative. Not only does the angel appear to chastise Mary for her mistrust, but he explicitly states that even if she does not consent the deed will be done. Germanus evinces a total disregard for

Mary's consent, echoing contemporaneous language regarding rape in his glib euphemism, "even if you do not wish for this [*mē boulei*]."[33] What makes Germanus's approach particularly disconcerting is the evidence of his familiarity with matters of rape and sexual coercion. First, later in the homily he depicts Mary asking "how long shall I withhold my consent [*anexomai*]," immediately before she agrees, suggesting an element of coercion.[34] More clearly, in the dialogue between Mary and Joseph, Germanus characterizes Joseph as seeking vengeance for the rape of Mary, citing Deuteronomy 22:28, which explicitly describes the forceful rape (*biasamenos*) of a virgin and the retribution that follows. This passage was often invoked to shape legal definitions on rape suggesting that here, too, it is used as a paradigmatic instance of rape. The same verb was often used in connection with the crime of rape, as in the seventh-century life of Symeon the Holy Fool, where a woman claims that he "raped me" (*ebiasato me*).[35]

Thus, while showing awareness of the laws and regulations concerning rape, Germanus's early eighth-century homily evinces little regard for Mary's consent. These striking tensions within the homily have clear implications regarding rape: they stress an omnipotent God, who may do with Mary as he pleases. Similarly, Romanus the Melodist's hymn shows a mixture of present and past tenses for Mary's conception; for example, it states in one line that "you are about to bear a son" and, in the next, that "you are giving birth to the Lord."[36] Even the latter phrasing takes for granted that she will consent to bearing the child. We may attempt to explain this away by musing on liturgical, homiletic time, which bridges biblical narrative and the present, or by reasoning that the angel operated simultaneously in linear human time and—because of his closeness to God—in a divine temporality outside it. Such rationalizations are ultimately unsatisfying, however. Romanus repeatedly suggests that he knows that Mary does not conceive until after giving verbal consent, but we cannot overlook that the hymn gives her little to no room to maneuver. This portrayal could not be more different from that found in later homilies by Photius and other Byzantine thinkers who, while clearly aware of the style and tropes of the works of Andrew of Crete and Germanus of Constantinople, take a far more nuanced approach to Mary's consent. In the later writings, her path toward consent structures the narrative. Moreover, that consent becomes the story's climax and focal point. This heightened attention may indicate that these authors were consciously seeking to avoid the earlier language that dangerously undercut doctrinal teachings.

While earlier homilies are ambiguous at best regarding Mary's exact moment of conception—suggesting the absence of her full and willing consent—over the course of the post-Iconoclastic period sensitivity to such matters grew. This development appears to be loosely paralleled by an increasingly nuanced approach to matters of consent in various aspects of Byzantine life. Earlier Roman law did not clearly distinguish between rape, adultery, fornication, and other sexual crimes. The Isaurian law code of 741, supported by Leo III and Constantine V, was the first to broadly clarify forms of sexual crimes and improprieties, and its legal definitions would be further expanded and codified in later centuries.[37] At the time, the issue of rape (*harpagē*), understood as abduction with intent to marry or perform sexual intercourse without the consent of both the victim and her family, was extensively debated by canonists and legal writers.[38] In the late twelfth century, canonists were greatly concerned with people being forced to consent to monastic life, for reasons ranging from authorities' desire to reduce a person's political power to the wish to dissolve a marriage.[39] Even within medical circles, attention was paid to the patient's consent to treatment, especially when life-threatening procedures were involved.[40] For instance, in some descriptions of difficult surgical procedures, particularly those performed on high-ranking figures, the patient acknowledges their consent by handing the scalpel themselves to the surgeon, who is thereby freed from any responsibility if the patient should die.

In the narrative and illuminations of John Skylitzes's twelfth-century *Synopsis of Histories*, now in Madrid (known as the Madrid Skylitzes), there is a poignant episode of a woman's attempted rape by a Varangian soldier (fig. 1.1). After sketching out the machinations of the imperial family following the transition of power from Romanos III to Michael IV the Paphlagonian, Skylitzes highlights this rape, thus suggesting the importance ascribed to it by his contemporary audience:

In that year something else worthy of note took place. A man of the Varangians who were scattered in winter quarters in the Thracesion theme met a woman of the region in an isolated place and tempted her virtue; and when he could not get her to agree willingly he tried to rape her, but she got hold of the foreigner's sword and struck him with it through the heart, so that he died at once. When this deed became known through the neighborhood the

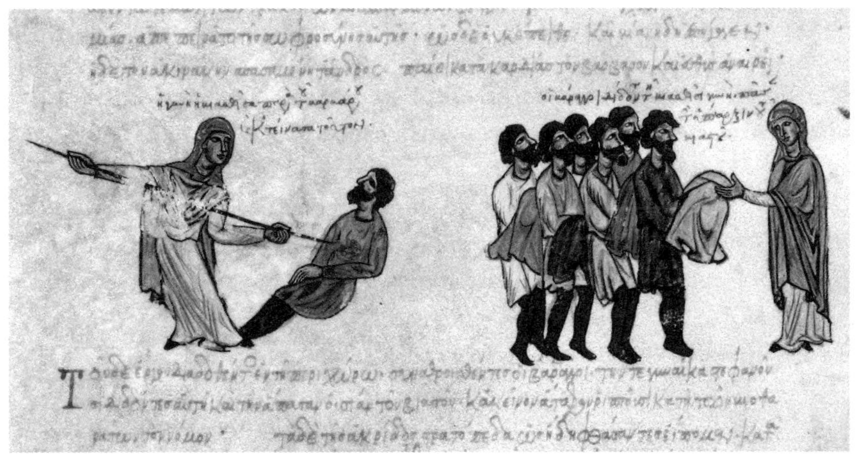

1.1. Attempted Rape of a Woman by Varangian Soldier. Madrid, Biblioteca Nacional de España, Madrid Skylitzes (Matritensis gr. vitr. 26–2), fol. 208r.

Varangians gathered together and honored the woman by giving her all the possessions of the man who had attempted to rape her, and they threw his body away without burial, according to the law about suicides.[41]

Because of the woman's isolation in western Asia Minor, there probably would have been no witness to the crime, no one to hear her cry for help. The legal implications of this circumstance were already recognized in Deuteronomy—there, as Angeliki Laiou notes, "since the external circumstances in which consent might be established are absent, the woman is held to have not consented."[42] While this casts women's right to consent as being inherently social, tied to the authority of family and society, it also presents a paradigmatic instance of rape, one in which consent is fundamentally impossible. The Thracesion woman's virtue is stressed not only by her refusal to consent—even in a space where her ability to do to is prohibited— but also by her ability to forcefully and successfully combat her assailant.

This account may appall modern readers, recalling arguments for "legitimate rape" or narratives that blame victims. It suggests that a woman's virtue is in some part manifested by her ability to prevent her own violation (and that those who do not succeed are somehow inviting the attack). Thus, in the Madrid Skylitzes, the illuminator drew the woman killing the man in the space immediately following the line in the main text that describes the scene (see fig. 1.1). Immediately to the right are depicted the host of Varangians honoring the woman by handing over the rapist's possessions. Yet we see here an inversion of the logic of consent. Much as a patient's handing over of the scalpel is a form of consent, absolving the surgeon of the death that might follow, the would-be rapist who places the sword in the hand of the woman has consented to his own death. Therefore, the law dictates that his body be tossed away without a grave, as is the custom with suicides (*biothanatōn*).[43] That the woman's actions in the text and images are depicted as virtuous speaks to the interest in and sensitivity about matters of sexual consent in middle Byzantine culture. This narrative also makes us intimately aware of the uneasiness created among Byzantines by rape and forced marriages in the context of war, particularly the objectification of women in the plundering of cities and towns.[44]

In Nikephoros Basilakes's twelfth-century handbook of rhetorical exercises, aimed as a Christian supplement to the late antique handbooks for the teaching of rhetoric that were focused primarily on pagan myths, the rape of a girl from Edessa whom a Gothic soldier has deceived and seduced is similarly depicted with military imagery. In the description of the Goth's initial courtship, the woman is objectified as a fortified citadel:

> At first, then, employing sexual desire [*erōti*] as his ally and possessing a siege engine [*helepolin*] for a tongue, he led an assault [*katepestrateuse*] against chastity itself, wishing to besiege [*poliorkēsai*] the acropolis of my virginity and lead a campaign [*katastratēgēsai*] against my chastity. But when his many attempts taught him that these siege towers were not sufficient to topple my chastity, he clothed himself in fox skin and transformed his speech entirely[.][45]

The girl then tells us how this suitor turned to her mother to ask for her hand in marriage, changing his approach from attempted seduction but still seeking the same sexual gratification. The author, using the woman's own voice, fully objectifies her—the descriptions of the sexual offenses of the Goth transform her into a city under siege. The language conveys the actions of a military general, a *stratēgos*, through verbs that speak to his assault (*katepestrateuse*) and campaign (*katastratēgēsai*). The siege engine (*helepolin*) imagery returns, and his actions are described as being poliorcetic, for he strives to besiege her (*poliorkēsai*). The aims of the attacks are clear. This is a strategic assault on her chastity or modesty (*sōphrosynēs*), with the goal of penetrating the walls of her "virginity" (*parthenias*) in order to ultimately conquer (*katastratēgēsai*) that chastity altogether. The verb *katastratēgēsai* implies being wholly overwhelmed by the general strategy, being outwitted by it.

Hence, we see that the Goth wishes to compromise her modesty, have sex with her, and then strip any sense of normative decorum from her. The text offers us not a casual metaphor (as we might think from a superficial reading) but the unfolding of a siege, in gripping detail, that is also strikingly sexual. Note that it is his tongue that is a siege engine—the weapon that latches itself onto her outer walls and breeches her, the actor attempting to penetrate that virginity. The tongue is thus a weapon of seduction, not only a means to remove the defenses but also a sexual actor in persuading her to be penetrated by something more than just his tongue. This sexual innuendo also appears in the previous passage, where the woman discusses her lack of awareness of the dangers she faced, which were "buried in the midst of his handsomeness."[46] Poliorcetics here resembles some form of foreplay, making it possible for foreign soldiers to burst into that acropolis. It is precisely this level of vividness and clarity that rhetorical exercises aim to achieve, accomplished here with striking efficiency through a nuanced deployment of military language.

Strikingly, this text also reminds us of the ethical force of the interchange between objects as humans and humans as objects. Through this mutual objectification, rape occurs. In a sense, Nikephoros Basilakes's text makes clear that the vivid metaphor does more than help us perceive what has befallen this woman: rather, it is because she can be approached through metaphor that her rape is possible. In other words, the process of objectifying her as a citadel—so that she can be assaulted like one—is what enables the forceful violence to which the suitor-turned-rapist ultimately resorts. After all, her story begins with the siege of the city of Edessa as the barbarian Goth arrives. Thus, the Goth is figured as a soldier with siege craft on the mind, displaying how war quickly dehumanizes human actors as objects of assault. The Goth's inability to distinguish between the city's walls and the woman's virginity, the objects of plunder and her humanity, is the most poignant aspect of the story, powerfully told in the first person. In the end, the narrative resolves in her own militarization after the child she bore to the Goth is poisoned by his mistress: "I will become a man [*andrisomai*] for revenge. I will fire back at my enemy with the arrow that struck me, even if I enlist as my helper a child who lies dead before his time."[47] To retaliate she thus becomes a soldier like the Goth was—succinctly captured by the notion that she will be "courageous," or quite literally "will become a man" (*andrisomai*). This verb can be taken metaphorically, but it also manifests in her late antique constructions of female masculinity, as women become guardians against sexual assault and guide an ascent to a higher spiritual state, as will be discussed in chapter 3. In this story, ultimately, violence emerges when no difference can be discerned between humans and objects—violence emerges from the objectification of people. It is such tensions connected with sexual consent that preoccupied Byzantine thinkers from the post-Iconoclastic period onward, across the spectrum of secular and religious writings.

THE ANNUNCIATION AFTER ICONOCLASM: CONSENT, CONCEPTION, AND PREGNANCY

Coming back to Photius's eloquent homily, we can now better appreciate the deep interest in Mary's consent and its nuanced handling by an erudite thinker. Further on in the discourse between Gabriel and Mary, Photius returns once again to Mary's prudent hesitation:

> But what did the most holy Virgin *reply* to this? Was she immediately softened by these words, and having opened her ears wide with pleasure, did she allow her thoughts to give consent [*sygkatathesin*] without scrutiny? Not at all. But what says she? "Now I know clearly that you describe to me conception, pregnancy, and the birth of a son, but you have increased my perplexity all the more. For how shall this happen to me, seeing that I know not a man? For every birth comes from intercourse with a man, while abstention from relations with a man does not so much as permit me to hear of conception.[48]

Once again, Photius reiterates Mary's reluctance to willingly give her consent to bearing a child, as indicated by the term *sygkatathesin*. This word can be understood in the contexts both of cognitive assent and of consent to sexual intercourse or marriage. In the early eleventh century, for example, the prominent jurist Eustathios Romaios comments in the context of a complex case in which a man sought to dissolve his marriage on charges of incestuous abduction and adultery that a woman's character is won more "by flattery than by force"; thus, one seeking to have a woman agree to marriage and sex know that "by kindness he may draw her to consent [*sygkatathesin*]."[49] Photius is evidently quite attuned to the term's sexual and cognitive implications, understanding that, in the case of Mary, impregnation results not from her consent to the physical act of sex but rather from her cognitive assent.

When Mary acknowledges that Gabriel "describes to me conception, pregnancy, and the birth of a son," Photius is subtly punning. The word first used for "conception" (*syllepsin*) has the same resonance here as in English, both intellectual and sexual. Photius then reinvokes conception with the less ambiguous term "pregnancy" (*kuophorian*), which literally means "fetus carrying," and concludes with "birth of a son" (*huion . . . tokon*), thereby referring not only to her pregnancy but also to her identity as the "God-bearer," the Theotokos. The word that Photius uses for "describes," *logographeis*—literally, "word inscribing"—is particularly appropriate, since the Annunciation seeks to inscribe Christ, the Logos. The cognitive actions of perception and cognition's unfolding are here thus restaged as leading to the consummation—the Incarnation of the Word.

In Stoic theories of perception, it was the "cognitive impression" (*katalēptikē phantasia*) that passed on from the senses to the mind, manifesting itself to a person as a self-evident and striking marker of truth that, thereby, "pulls one to assent [*sygkatathesin*]" to the reality it depicts.[50] Photius's play on sensation and perception as analogous to conception is evident in the final line of this excerpt, where Mary demonstrates her virginal chastity by saying that her abstinence "does not so much as permit me to hear of conception." This suggests not only (once again) a connection between perception and pregnancy but also that her mind is as virginal as her womb. That Photius carefully alludes to the notion of her virgin ears is important, for the idea that Mary conceived through the ear became well-established over the course of the fifth century, authoritatively promoted by the works of Proclus of Constantinople in particular.[51] The idea's continued popularity is demonstrated by its appearance in the poetry and sermons of such figures as the sixth-century Romanus the Melodist, Abraham of Ephesus, and Anastasius of Antioch, as well as in the early seventh- and eighth-century works of Sophronius of Jerusalem and Andrew of Crete, respectively.

However, the idea also presented a series of possible problems regarding Mary's consent. That one could copulate nonconsensually through the ear was in fact seen as a possibility in the Coptic world, attested to by a series of hieratic spells specifically intended to prevent rape via the ear.[52] The belief has some precedent in the ancient Greek world; the unwitting pronouncement of sexualized statements during the act of reading aloud might be seen as a form of sexual penetration without one's previous consent.[53] If the question of Mary's consent centers on the point at which she conceives during the course of the Annunciation narrative, then the issue is as much when it occurs as how it occurs. If she conceived by hearing, then one must decide whether she conceived at Gabriel's "Hail" or at some later moment. The play between her heard reception of words and her reception of Christ, the Word of God, was an important trope. Early Christian thinkers proposed various answers to the problem of when she conceived, finding in all the senses metaphors for a conception that occurs without sexual touch. In the Coptic tradition, Pseudo-Demetrius of Antioch suggests that Mary became pregnant from a sweet odor emanating from the angel.[54] Pseudo-Epiphanius and Cyril of Rakote propose that Mary conceived through the mouth, envisioning a conception through taste and consumption.[55] Even vision was seen as a possible medium: for example, in the second-century pseudepigraphal *Martyrdom and Ascension of Isaiah*, Mary saw with her eyes a small child and thus went on to conceive the Christ.[56] All these interpreters seek to use sensation and perception as a model for articulating a form of contact akin to intercourse but with minimal physical contact.[57] The four senses they invoke—sight, taste, smell, and hearing—apprehend external sensory objects without physical touch and are thus the perfect metaphors for a conception that occurred without conventional sexual intercourse.

Given the aurality of the Annunciation and the subsequent Incarnation of the Word of God, hearing provided the most apt metaphor for representing this nonhaptic intercourse. However, because the angel leaves Mary immediately after her spoken consent, she could not have conceived through the literal speech of Gabriel. Furthermore, as his words make clear, Gabriel speaks both of the conception and of its cause—the visitation of the Holy Spirit—in the future tense. Thus, to say that Mary conceived simply by hearing the angel's greeting or other speech alone would preempt the possibility of her giving consent to Gabriel. In Photius's homily, the eventual assent of Mary serves as the climax of the oration, taking center stage in this dramatic narrative:

Such things the archangel was saying, drawing the spotless maiden to consent.
But to this what was the reply of the honored virgin, the heavenly chamber,
the holy mountain, the sealed fountain, kept for Him only who had sealed it?
"Since," says she, "you have clearly explained that the Holy Ghost shall come
upon me, I no longer demur, I no longer object . . . Behold the handmaid of the
Lord: be it unto me according to your word. Let your words be fulfilled upon
me in the act. Let your words be unto me in accordance with the deeds."[58]

Photius's repeated use of the word *sygkatathesis*, with its cognitive implications, to denote her consent is noteworthy, particularly in the context of his earlier play on mental and fetal conception. This language suggests that Mary conceives through the action of consent itself, which manifests not only as her cognitive assent to Gabriel's message but also her consent to be visited by the Holy Spirit. These two forms of assent/consent reach their fulfillment only at the end of the Annunciation when she asserts, as Luke recounts, "let it be with me according to your word."

For Photius, Mary's words enacted the Incarnation, in accordance with the specific terms clearly outlined by the angel, terms that she has virtuously considered at length. By no means was Mary's consent presumed, coerced, or violated by the actions of the angel or the Holy Spirit. This interpretation assuaged contemporary cultural concerns in Byzantium not only with consent itself but also with the importance of consent being arrived at willingly and without coercion, particularly when marriage is involved.[59] Therefore, for Photius, the Incarnation could not occur through any form of sensory contact alone. Instead, congruent with the narrative found in Luke, the moment was manifested through Mary's speech act, which evinces her resolve and the upshot of her careful consideration. This is an important break with the earlier tradition. That the "conception, indeed, was through the sense of hearing,"[60] was confirmed in John of Damascus's mid-eighth-century tome *Exposition of the Faith*, which enjoyed immense popularity throughout Byzantium and served as a source on matters ranging from antiquity's writings on the natural world to the Church's teachings.

THE ANNUNCIATION IN LATER BYZANTIUM: PERCEPTION, CONCEPTION, AND JUDGMENT

At the turn of the thirteenth century, Nicholas Mesarites offers an insightful approach to the matter of Mary's conception through hearing by building on the play between mental and sexual conception, as did Photius before him. In his description of the Church of Holy Apostles in Constantinople, Nicholas turns his attention to the depiction of the Annunciation upon the walls of the church and recounts the various elements of the scene. Contemplating the figure of Mary, he provides an intricate sketch of the process of her consent, staging it as the unfolding of sensory perception:

The word comes to the hearing of the Virgin, and enters through it to the
brain; the intelligence which is seated in the brain at once lays hold upon what
comes to it, recognizes the matter by its perception, and then communicates to
the heart itself what it had understood. The heart is immediately agitated, and
debates begin to rise up to the maiden's heart as she debates, in virtuous fashion, what the greeting means. And she already turns to careful examination of
the greeting; for the Virgin was truly maidenly, not merely in her person but

even in her very thoughts, and she requests the messenger to describe clearly the manner of the conception . . . She yields herself wholly to the conception of the Word, which is beyond thought and speech—for she calls herself a servant, possessing no desire which opposes the fulfillment of the wish of the Lord—and the Word of God at once, as one might say, undergoes the act of incarnation.[61]

In this psychological portrait of Mary's path toward consent, Nicholas puts to use his own nuanced understanding of sensory perception and cognition; his keen grasp of antique and late antique teachings on medicine, physiology, and psychology is displayed throughout his description. In the Annunciation narrative, he regales his reader with a technical explanation of the organs and processes through which the mind comes to apprehend and comprehend the information given to it through sensation.

Compare this characterization of Mary's perceptual process to that espoused elsewhere in the text. Recounting the types of chatter engaged in by medical students in the courtyards in front of the church, Nicholas describes these students congregating in a leisurely way around the stone water trough, where they debate such things as:

whether the power of feeling, in all the organs of sense, gets its strength from the brain, or whether for some objects the seat of the faculty is the brain, which receives the objects of sensation, while for others it is the heart, so that sight and hearing transmit to the brain the first contacts with the objects of sensation, and from it obtain distinction among the objects, while touch and taste and smell refer to the heart sensations as soon as they encounter them, and, when the heart has first made its decision, they themselves are then affected and participate in the sensation along with it.[62]

Looking at these two snapshots of perceptual processes, we see that Nicholas is following antique teachings regarding the unfolding of perception; these are related in a variety of works, including Nemesius of Emesa's late fourth-century treatise *On the Nature of Man* and even John of Damascus's *Exposition of the Faith*.[63] This cognitive process loosely unfolds in five main steps. First, the senses acquire the sensation of a thing, and second, some faculty makes a preliminary assessment of it to discern a given object's identity—as Nicholas says, so as to "obtain distinction among the objects." This step enables one to distinguish, for example, a man from a cow. Third, the imagination visualizes the object; and fourth, thinking makes a judgment to ascertain the truth and accuracy of that visualization, which enables the possibility of assent, as the Stoics described. In the fifth and final stage, these imprints of perception are stored in memory.

Nicholas abridges this process somewhat, choosing to focus more on the physiology behind perception. He argues that the objects of hearing and sight first are processed by the brain to make those initial distinctions between them. Then they are sent to the heart for further judgment, which in turn enables the perceiver to be "affected and participate in the sensation"—a step that seemingly corresponds to the judgment enacted for the sake of cognitive assent. But taste and smell are sensations that go straight to the heart, since they presumably require less scrutiny. Turning to the process undertaken by Mary, we can now appreciate how Nicholas has chosen to stage the narrative of the Annunciation as a drama unfolding within the perceptual processes of Mary's psyche. The focus placed on the heart indicates that the story is mainly rooted in matters of judgment. Her heart, the seat of judgment, is said to be agitated, and debates arise there as she carefully and virtuously investigates the nature of the angel's greeting. When she does assent to its truth and veracity, the Word immediately "undergoes the act of incarnation." Although Nicholas, unlike Photius before him, does not use the term consent/assent (*sygkatathesis*) at any point, his emphasis on perceptual process tells us that Mary's consent occurs at the exact moment that she assents. This consent is certainly willing since the focus on her faculty of judgment underscores that there was no coercion here, and she is understood at the end as "possessing no desire which opposes the fulfillment of the wish of the Lord." In other words, her consent is full and all-encompassing at the moment she acknowledges the truth and veracity of Gabriel's tidings. Though the mechanisms are similar, for Nicholas, the process of perception results not in the depositing of the sensory imprints for future recollection in the storehouses of the memory but rather in the incarnation of that word in the womb.

In staging the incarnation perceptually, Nicholas is able to retain the notion that Mary conceived through hearing—not through the sensation of mere sound but rather through the unfolding of aural perception. The tidings of the angel entered her ear, were received by her brain, and were carefully debated by her heart; and when she assented to their truth, she spoke her consent aloud and "at once" the incarnation occurred. The Incarnation of the Christ occurs through cognition, which began with the sensory inputs of the ear, but neither the mere sound of the angel's voice nor its message alone enacted the incarnation. In other words, Nicholas is able to avoid a potential doctrinal issue raised by the "conception through hearing" thesis by placing the agency of that conception within the realm of Mary's virtuous and keen intellect.[64]

Nicholas's physiological depiction sheds further light on the nuances found within the parallels drawn by Photius between cognitive assent and Mary's consent to conception. By focusing on the human physiology that makes this all possible, Nicholas demonstrates the depth of this parallelism. By putting it in the context of theories on human psychology that stretch back into antiquity and that were widely popular in both the pre- and post-Iconoclastic periods, Nicholas shows that the parallel between cognitive assent and Mary's consent goes far beyond the terminology of assent and consent (*sygkatathesis*) alone.

The broader debate on the precise moment and manner of Mary's conception continued to engross theologians and scholars throughout these centuries. In one case, the twelfth-century theologian Michael Glykas turned his attention to this matter in a work dedicated to explicating the gaps, contradictions, and missing pieces of biblical stories. Michael's argument is based on a close scrutiny of the text of Luke, which speaks to the timing and unfolding of the Annunciation. Michael begins his study by stating resolutely that the conception does not occur at the same time that Gabriel spoke the "Hail"; rather, he maintains that it is only with Mary's "consent" (*synkatathesin*) to the angel's words that she conceives.[65] Using Luke 2:21, which recounts how the angel had called Jesus's name "before he was conceived in the womb," Michael offers further evidence to confirm the careful and precise timing of the incarnation without ambiguity, conception follows Mary's consent and the conclusion of the angel's discourse. Here consent is structured not only as a temporal matter but also as an issue clearly explicated and consistently reiterated throughout the Gospels. Michael chastises those who would place the incarnation before the completion of the discourse and before Mary's consent for not knowing the scriptures and thus diverging from their teachings.[66]

In the fourteenth century, Nicholas Cabasilas provides what is perhaps the most emphatic and developed argument regarding the timing of the incarnation. In his homily on the Annunciation, Nicholas does more than stress that the Incarnation of the Word occurs after Mary's consent—he focuses on the absolute necessity of consent rather than on timing and biblical accuracy. Discussing the salvation of humanity through Christ's Incarnation, Nicholas explains that it would not have been possible "had she not believed and given her consent [*synthemenēs*]."[67] The verb used for consent here is *syntithēmi*, which has the same root as the noun *sygkatathesis* used by the other writers. Nicholas then elaborates: while God descended in the form of the Holy Spirit when Mary sought to learn more regarding her conception, the deed was not accomplished until she was "persuaded and [had] accepted the offer." Further on, Nicholas even adds that the incarnation was not only the action of the Father but also required "the will [*thelēseos*] and faith of the Virgin," whom God made a common "participant concerning this decision."[68]

Nicholas clearly and repeatedly stresses God's respect for Mary's right to choose whether to bear the child. Nicholas's words read like a modern defense of sexual and reproductive consent:

And, thus, God having taught and persuaded her, he makes her a mother, borrows flesh from her with her knowledge and desire; in order that just as he willingly was conceived, it might come to pass for the mother in the same manner: so that she might conceive willingly, and desiring it, become a mother by voluntary decision.[69]

Whereas earlier authors chose to emphasize the temporal importance of the incarnation or the necessity of Mary's consent, Nicholas goes further and insists that this consent is not produced by inevitability, coercion, or force. It is completely voluntary. Beyond the use of the specific term "consent" (*sygkatathesis*), sexual consent in Byzantine sources is more loosely communicated by an indication of a person's willing (*thelein*) or desiring (*boulesthai*) to partake in the act. For example, as noted in the introduction, in the early seventh-century narrative of the life of St. Mary of Egypt, when the saint recounts how in her younger days she used to live a life of sin, she describes forcefully raping men—having sex with them "against their will" (*mē thelontas*).[70] In the homily, Nicholas uses similar terms to stress that Mary is acting with "knowledge" (*eiduias*), that she is "willing" (*hekousa*) and "desiring" (*boulomenes*), that the choice is "voluntary" (*ethelousios*). As a conspirator with God, Mary is said to offer herself, just as Christ offers himself.

Nicholas uses Mary's active role as a co-worker in the salvation of humanity as a springboard to reflect both on the earlier accusations aimed at the primordial Eve's deceitful consent, as well as Mary's own virtuous deliberation as Eve's antitype. Indeed, Nicholas portrays Eve's birth as brought about by a God who did not seek out proper consent. For Nicholas, Mary's birth is tainted by the Old Testament God's use of the unconscious Adam:

On the one hand, Adam concerning his rib, from which Eve was to be built, God did not foretell, nor did he persuade, but removing by force his sensation, then he robbed him of the limb. On the other hand, concerning the Virgin he taught her beforehand, and then waited for her trust, then he proceeded to the deed.[71]

Eve was rash in consenting to the Serpent, but Adam before her was not even offered the opportunity to consent to her creation. Nicholas states that the rib was "stolen" from him after being knocked unconscious by God, struck out of his senses. Nicholas thus reworks the narratives of Eve's adultery or rape found in the gnostic and apocryphal writings, locating the misconduct and the use of force in the actions of God.

God's actions are explicitly depicted by Nicholas as a violation of Adam: God does not warn (*proeipen*) Adam about what he is going to do, he does not persuade Adam (*pepeiken*), and he forcefully makes Adam unconscious (*aphelon*) and robs him (*apesula*). This language is pointed and unambiguous, systematically depicting the rape of Adam—God does not ask for consent, Adam is forcefully placed in a situation in which he is unable to resist, and he is violated, literally stripped of his flesh. The structural parallels of the next sentence, depicting the case of Mary, deliberately rely on the Adam narrative to demonstrate how Mary's story undoes the sins of Adam's creation—God teaches (*didaxas*) her beforehand, crucially waits (*anameinas*) for her consent, and only then proceeds to do the deed. The figure of Mary likewise undoes Eve's narratives by systematically and inversely reperforming the various elements, from the accusations of adultery and rape to her willing consent.

CONSENT AND THE ANNUNCIATION IN ART

Telling counterparts to Mary's consent can be observed in visual culture. Consider, for instance, the exceptional icon of the Annunciation at Sinai from the late twelfth century (fig. 1.2). There, we see Mary seated upon a throne before an architectural setting, spinning wool (as she is often depicted). Gabriel approaches her, his garb and legs rippling and contorting as if he has just arrived upon the scene. The angel's right hand gestures toward Mary in an allusion to an act of speech, indicating the greeting. Mary's arms turn inward, across her body, her left hand grasping her veil in alarmed surprise. Beneath her feet an undulating landscape appears as a microcosm of the land and seas below, filled with creatures of all varieties that seem to be extolling the good news unfolding above. Temporally, the

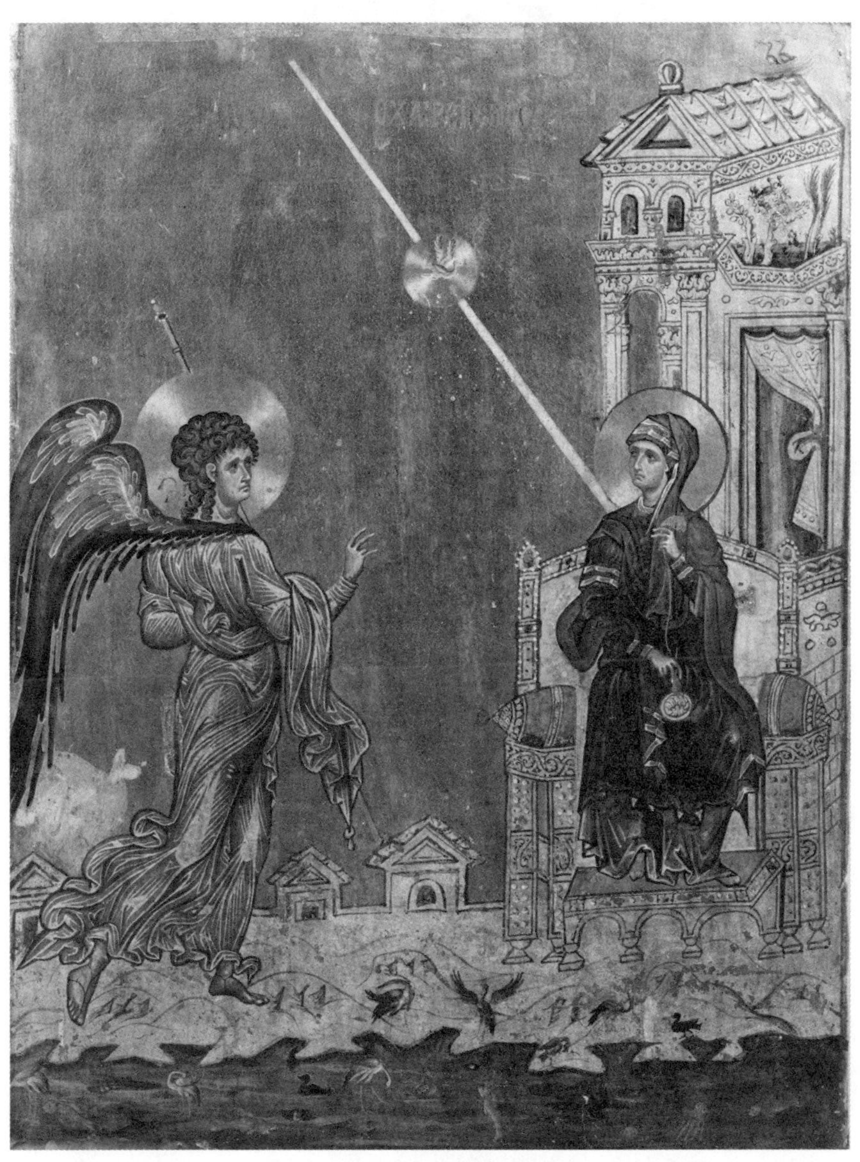

1.2. Annunciation Icon, St. Catherine's Monastery, Mount Sinai, Egypt.

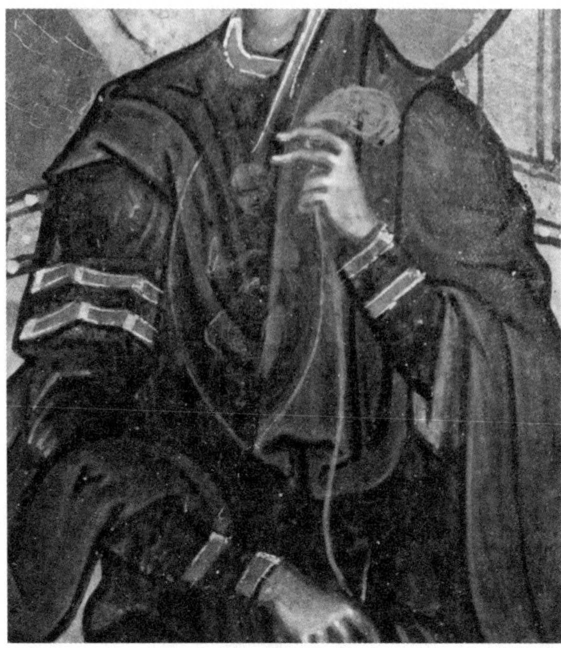

1.3. Detail of Christ in the Womb from Annunciation Icon, St. Catherine's Monastery, Mount Sinai, Egypt.

icon presents its challenges: Gabriel has just arrived; Mary's gestures indicate that she is startled and silent; and yet the Holy Spirit in the form of a dove already is diving down from heaven toward her head, suggesting that she will conceive through the ear by the spirit simultaneously with Gabriel's greeting.

Even more startling is the fact that the Christ child has begun to take form within Mary. Over her womb, in a subtle grisaille nearly invisible to the human eye, we can see a ghostly form (fig. 1.3). Unlike images that present her with the Christ child as an embodied figure, in a sort of medallion over her torso, the fetus here foreshadows what is to occur—a proleptic image of the incarnation that is about to happen. The angel has only begun his greeting, the Holy Spirit is midway through its descent, Mary has not yet offered her consent, and yet apparently a child is already radiating from her womb through her flesh and garb. It would seem that here the challenges of the Annunciation's temporality are echoed in homiletic art, capturing in one instant the narrative whole of the story. Moving from left to right, we can observe the progression from greeting, descent of the Holy Spirit, and incarnation, yet the icon makes no effort to emphasize her consent.

That the Annunciation in art might have implicit associations with rape should not be overlooked. In order to appreciate this connection, we must understand how to identify and define depictions of rape in art. Rape imagery is varied and can be difficult to parse out. For instance, the iconography of rape might involve the forceful grasping of the wrist of the victim, suggesting that they are being carried off without consent.[72] This gesture is usually shown in images of the Levite handing over his concubine to the men of Gibeah. In a late eleventh-century anthology of sermons, a *panegyrikon* now at Mount Athos, the forceful grasping of the wrist is vividly combined with the molestation of the woman's breasts as she is being dragged along (fig. 1.4). Another way of communicating nonconsensual sexual advances, in iconography similar to that of the unwanted grasp, was to represent a figure turning away from their predator with a theatrical contortion. In the late ninth-century copy of the *Sacra Parallela*—the only known illustrated copy of this compilation of theological and ascetic texts associated with John of Damascus—we find two telling depictions of men's unrequited advances toward women who are retaliated against with accusations of immodesty, punishment, and rape.

In one instance, the manuscript depicts the rape of Tamar by her half-brother Amnon (2 Samuel 13; fig. 1.5). In the text Amnon feigns being sick so that she might tend to him and make him food, then demands that she sleep with him; after her refusal he rapes her and sends her home, full of hatred because of her rejection. Here, the *Sacra Parallela* shows him talking to her with his left hand raised in a gesture of speech, while his right hand forcefully grasps her. Tamar's cloak has fallen off her head, revealing her necklace and bound hair, manifesting the rapist's attack on her virginal chastity. Below this episode, the artist has chosen to depict her expulsion from the house. There, Amnon stands in the doorway casting her out, again with his hand raised to indicate his proclamation. Tamar, on the other hand, recoils away. Her head and hands are covered by her veil and her body contorts to gaze back at her youthful rapist, her brows furrowed with grief and hands raised up to her head.

Just a couple of folios later, the artist presents us with another nonconsensual sexual advance—the scene of the nude Susanna bathing in her garden while being stalked by lecherous old men, who threaten to blackmail her unless she has sex with them (Daniel 13; fig. 1.6). After she resists their advances, the old men go on to accuse her of illicitly consorting with a young man. The *Sacra Parallela* depicts these two voyeuristic creeps with long gray hair and beards, peering out from a ditch in the ground where they have hidden themselves; they are shown once again propositioning Susanna after they have emerged from hiding. One of them forcefully grasps

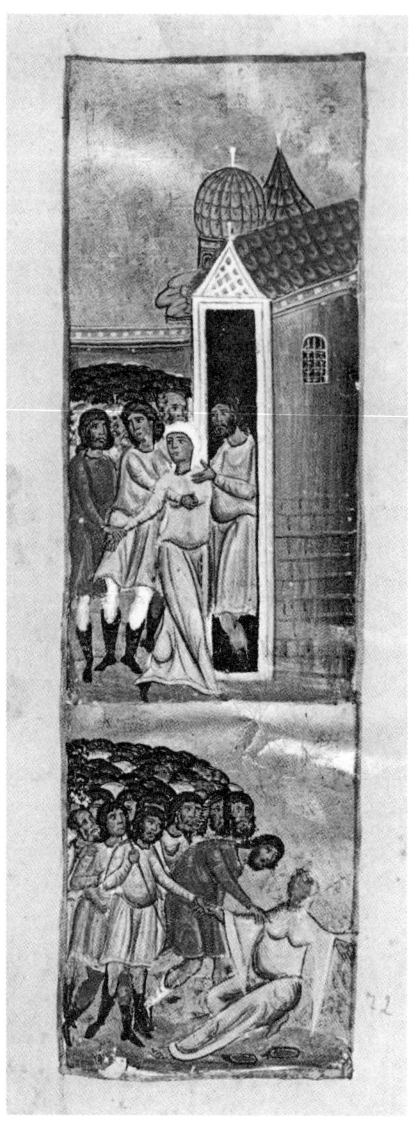

1.4. The Levite Handing Over
the Concubine. Mount Athos,
Esphigmenou Monastery,
Panegyrikon (Cod. 14), fol. 416r.

her right bicep, to her clear shock and alarm. Susanna's face is poignantly
twisted with fear, and the hand of her grasped arm is open as if in reflexive
reaction to this sudden and unwanted touch. She sits upon a golden bench,
turned away from the men but now contorting to look back at them, while
she holds an ivory comb in her left hand. The man's left hand is raised, indicating his lewd and unwanted proposition.

These bodily gestures and contortions, as well as the overall composition of the scene, are reminiscent of the body language and setting of most

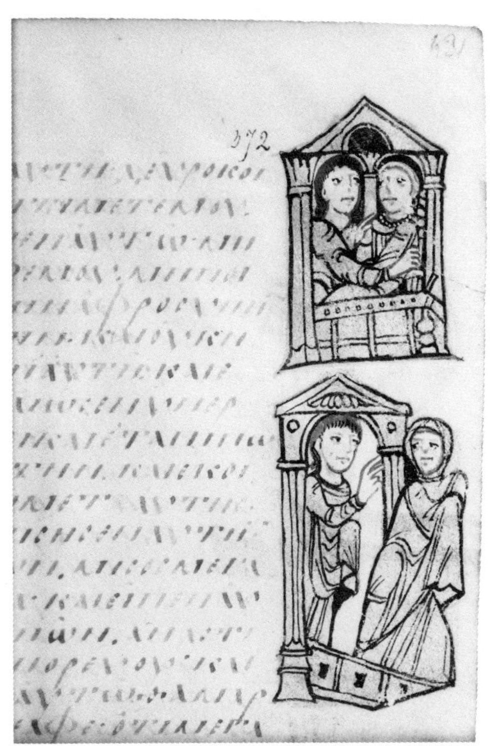

1.5. Rape of Tamar. Paris, Bibliothèque Nationale de France, *Sacra Parallela* (Par. gr. 923), fol. 372r.

Byzantine Annunciation scenes. Over the more than a millennium of Byzantine art, these depictions of Mary oscillate between the serene seated figure facing front, who carefully listens to the angel with calm and diligence (as in the Sinai icon), and her tense and contorted side-facing posture, which articulates her fear and hesitation. In the latter examples, the parallels with the choices made by the *Sacra Parallela*'s artist in depicting nonconsensual advances are striking. To be sure, in the Annunciation scenes there is no forceful grasp or any sort of physical contact between Mary and the angel; that would overstep the bounds of the narrative itself. But the proposition of the angel who comes in unannounced and startles Mary echoes the intrusion of the elders upon Susanna's toilette. Moreover, the anguished postures of both Susanna's sitting and Tamar's expulsion recall the stance of Mary, who is frequently shown turned away from her angel-suitor, twisting back to look at him and often recoiling into herself with a slightly hunched pose. At the arrival of the angel Mary seems to contort the entirety of her body, startled and overcome with fear. That the sudden and unexpected appearance of an unknown male figure in a woman's

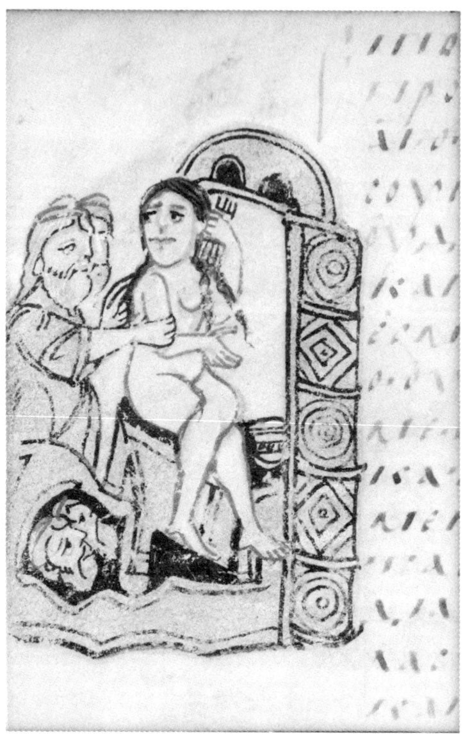

1.6. Susanna and the Elders. Paris, Bibliothèque Nationale de France, *Sacra Parallela* (Par. gr. 923), fol. 373v.

home might have sparked a fear of rape is hardly a point that requires historical substantiation; nevertheless, the point is repeatedly expressed in the various hymns and homilies that we have surveyed here.

THE UNFOLDING OF MARY'S CONSENT IN ART

In a complex enmeshing of word and image, the early twelfth-century homilies of the monk James Kokkinobaphos on Mary carefully articulate her fear and hesitation through an overwrought narrative and the continued repetition of Annunciation scenes until her final consent.[73] James recounts how the angel sneaked into her home before taking on corporeal form, watching Mary without her knowledge as she performed household tasks (fig. 1.7). This hidden gaze echoes the scopophilic gaze of the lecherous elders in the story of Susanna, though here it ultimately extolls the object's virtue and chastity rather than seeking to undo it. Derived from the *Protoevangelium of James* (section 11), the angel tries to not startle Mary; he speaks to her outside before taking on human form in the belief that a voice heard coming from inside the house is more disturbing (fig. 1.8). Yet Mary is deeply shaken and troubled; James describes her as determined to finish

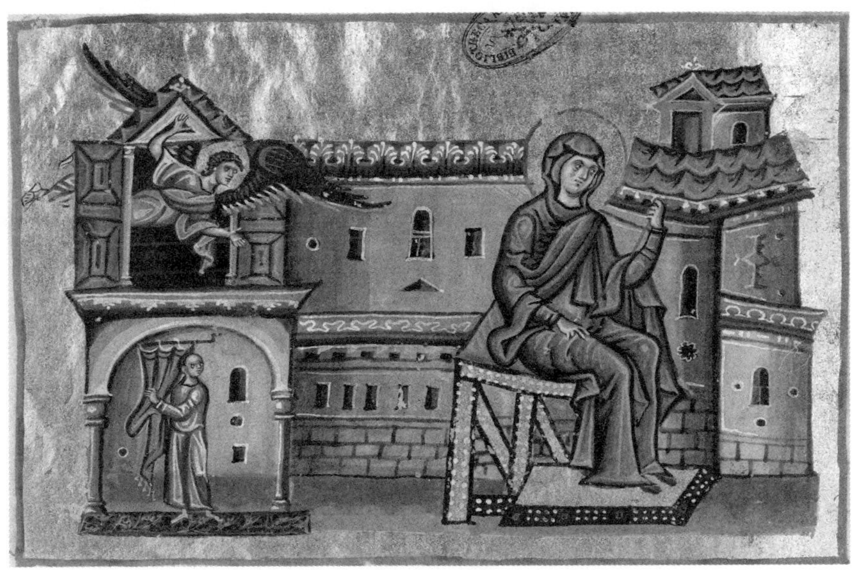

1.7. Arrival of Gabriel. Vatican City, Biblioteca Apostolica Vaticana, Homilies of James Kokkinobaphos (Vat. gr. 1162), fol. 115v. © 2019 Biblioteca Apostolica Vaticana.

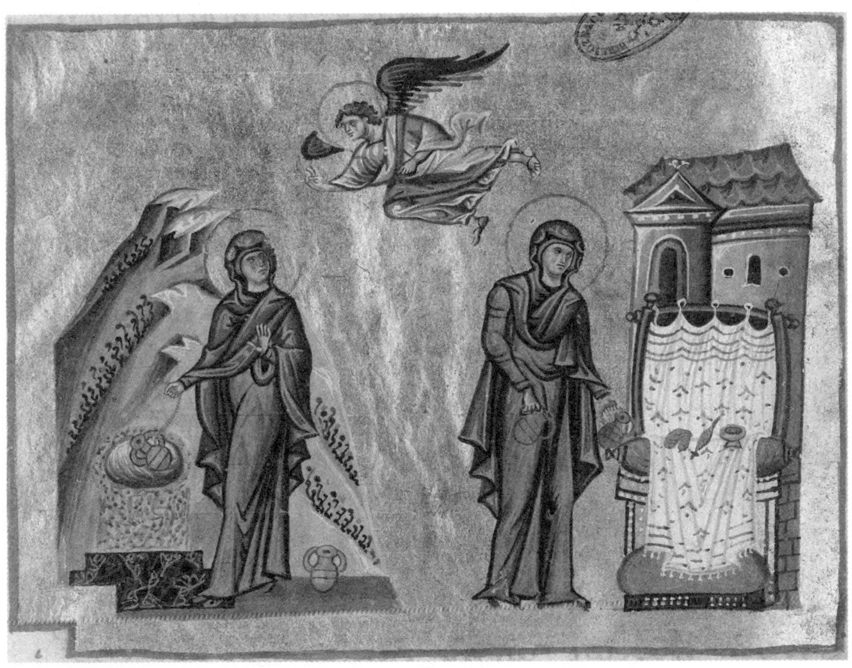

1.8. Mary at the Well and Mary Inside. Vatican City, Biblioteca Apostolica Vaticana, Homilies of James Kokkinobaphos (Vat. gr. 1162), fol. 117v. © 2019 Biblioteca Apostolica Vaticana.

her work with "her heart still trembling and palpitating, with pallor draining her cheeks, and with all her limbs trembling violently."[74]

From here, the reader is lead to the formal beginning of the Annunciation, as described in the Gospel, and encounters the scene of the Annunciation as expected. Thus, the figure of Mary that we find is one that has been visibly disturbed by the angel's intrusion: we see an architectural backdrop before which Gabriel hurls himself toward Mary. She is seated facing away from him, spinning thread with her hand raised, much like Susanna's raised hand holding a comb in the *Sacra Parallela*, and Mary turns to look back at her intruder. Her shoulders recoil away from the angel, and even the stool upon which she sits is curved up as if mystically fleeing his advances. Gabriel's hand, of course, is raised in the usual speech gesture, and it is difficult to ignore parallels with the visual language used to depict Amnon driving out Tamar after raping her. My point is not that the artist was in any way quoting the *Sacra Parallela*, but rather that this visual rhetoric shared across various themes seems to come from their common desire to capture the nonconsensual, violent advances of a suitor. More than likely, the Annunciation served as a prototype for the images of Susanna and Tamar.

The depiction of the Annunciation in the manuscript of James Kokkinobaphos's homilies does not end there, however. Instead, it drags on for many folios as James recounts the unfolding process of Mary's consent. In subsequent instances, the scene is abridged: that is, the architectural backdrop is replaced by gold ground alone, except directly behind Mary, as if the whole world has faded away except for her. Three more Annunciation images follow the first—each one featuring the same scene, as if time has stopped. Mary's raised hand is frozen in space, holding that spun thread, as she looks back at Gabriel. Captions at the top of each folio mark time, moving from (1) "the salutation" (fig. 1.9) to (2) "the demonstration of the truth of the good-tidings" (fig. 1.10), (3) "the doubts of the Virgin on how she is to conceive the Lord" (fig. 1.11), and finally (4) "the releasing of the doubt" (fig. 1.12). Throughout this process, as we have come to expect, Mary cross-examines the angel, inquiring as to the nature of the birth and stressing her attachment to her virginity over the birth of any king.

James's understanding of exactly when incarnation takes place is difficult to parse, adhering as it does to the early writers' conflation of present and future that seems to lessen the force of her consent. In one instance, for example, as Mary draws close to her eventual consent after the final Annunciation miniature, James writes: "and from you the one who is ineffably

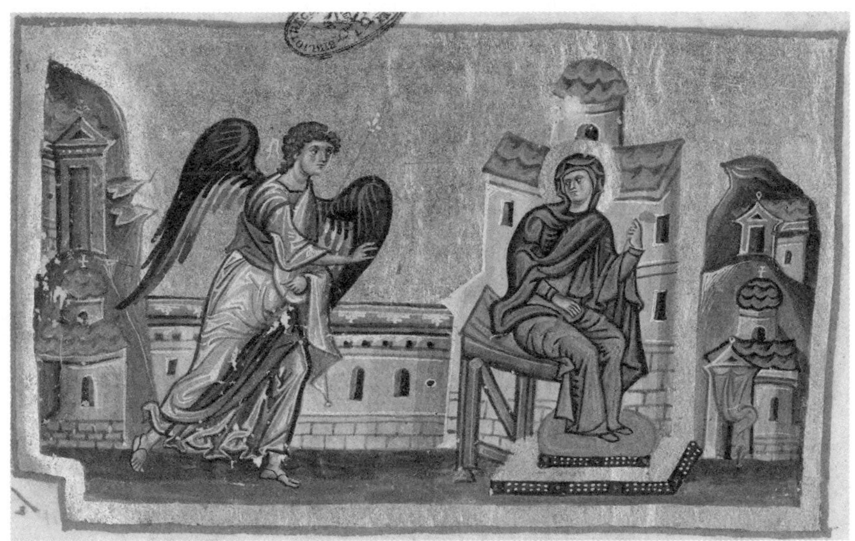

1.9. The Salutation. Vatican City, Biblioteca Apostolica Vaticana, Homilies of James Kokkinobaphos (Vat. gr. 1162), fol. 118r. © 2019 Biblioteca Apostolica Vaticana.

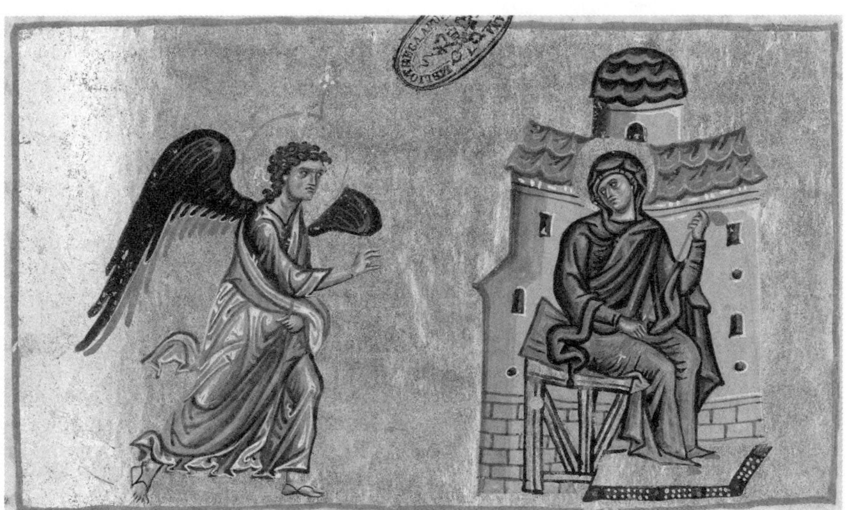

1.10. The Demonstration of the Truth of the Good-Tidings. Vatican City, Biblioteca Apostolica Vaticana, Homilies of James Kokkinobaphos (Vat. gr. 1162), fol. 122r. © 2019 Biblioteca Apostolica Vaticana.

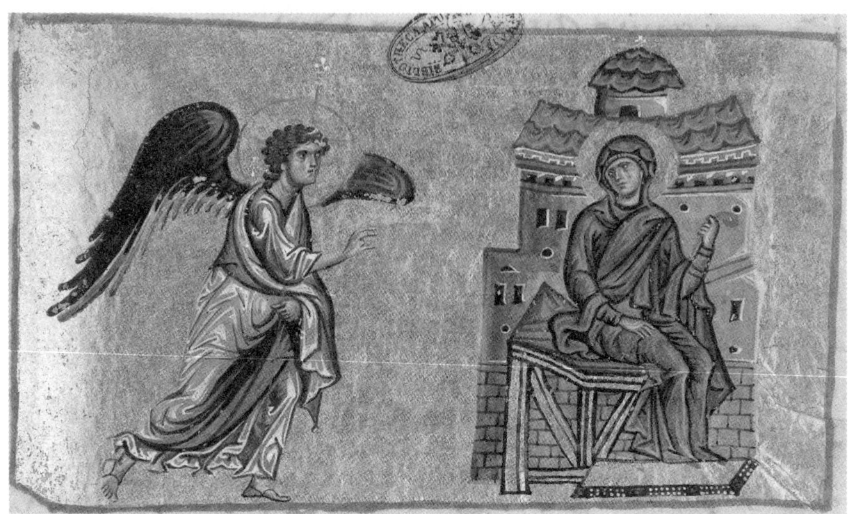

1.11. The Doubts of the Virgin on How She Is to Conceive. Vatican City, Biblioteca Apostolica Vaticana, Homilies of James Kokkinobaphos (Vat. gr. 1162), fol. 124r. © 2019 Biblioteca Apostolica Vaticana.

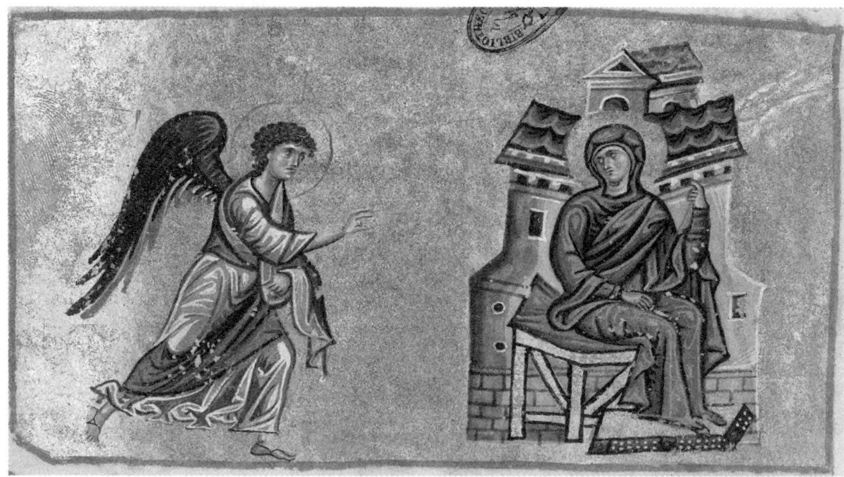

1.12. The Releasing of the Doubt. Vatican City, Biblioteca Apostolica Vaticana, Homilies of James Kokkinobaphos (Vat. gr. 1162), fol. 126r. © 2019 Biblioteca Apostolica Vaticana.

residing in you shall become incarnate."[75] Clearly, there is a strict distinction between Christ's incarnation (*sarkōthēsetai*) and his "encampment" (*kataskēnōn*) within Mary, suggesting a possible nuance to the temporal discrepancy between her pregnancy and Christ's presence within her. Yet, without a doubt, the deed is not completed until Mary consents.[76]

James Kokkinobaphos celebrates the moment in which Mary gives her vocal consent majestically, as the sequence of images of the Annunciation iconography culminates in a miniature captioned: "The prayer and consent [*sygkatathesis*] to the conception" (fig. 1.13). Here, we witness a compression of the same Annunciation setup: the space between Mary and the angel is greatly reduced, occupying one half of the painting, while on the right side the heavenly hosts rejoice at her consent to the Annunciation. The text of the homily that appears after the miniature reads, "The spiritual potentialities were leaping, when they heard the message."[77] Eight angels, aligned in a quasi-zigzag formation, seem to be telling each other the good news, transmitting it up to the heavenly ranks from her lips to the divine. It is clear that without Mary's consent, nothing could happen, and thus the news is received with joy and exaltation.

But note that in this moment, the iconography of the Annunciation scene is again unaltered. This is telling, not only as it represents the culmination of the arduous intellectual process of assent through which readers have made their way over the course of the hymn, but also because it speaks to the temporal expanse encompassed by the Annunciation itself. Looking back at that intriguing progression in the Sinai icon—from the arrival of Gabriel to the descent of the spirit to the incarnation of Christ—we can appreciate that the image of the Annunciation could capture this wide temporal spectrum. Such an icon encompasses not only the salutation but also the entirety of the narrative of the Annunciation from start to finish, which is why it might simultaneously depict the greeting and incarnation in a single moment. This type of simultaneous narrative is seen throughout Byzantine art, expressed more explicitly in scenes such as the Nativity by the repetition of figures, as when the Christ child is simultaneously depicted in his crib and bath. In the Kokkinobaphos homily, we see this duplication in the scene where Mary is at the left drawing water into a jar from the well and at the right entering her home with the same jar (fig. 1.8).

Given this expanse of time, it was imperative for the artist of these homilies to emphasize the temporal complexity of the scene. By repeating the image monotonously, the artist underscores for the viewer-reader the complex unfolding of consent that occurred within the familiar scene. Hence,

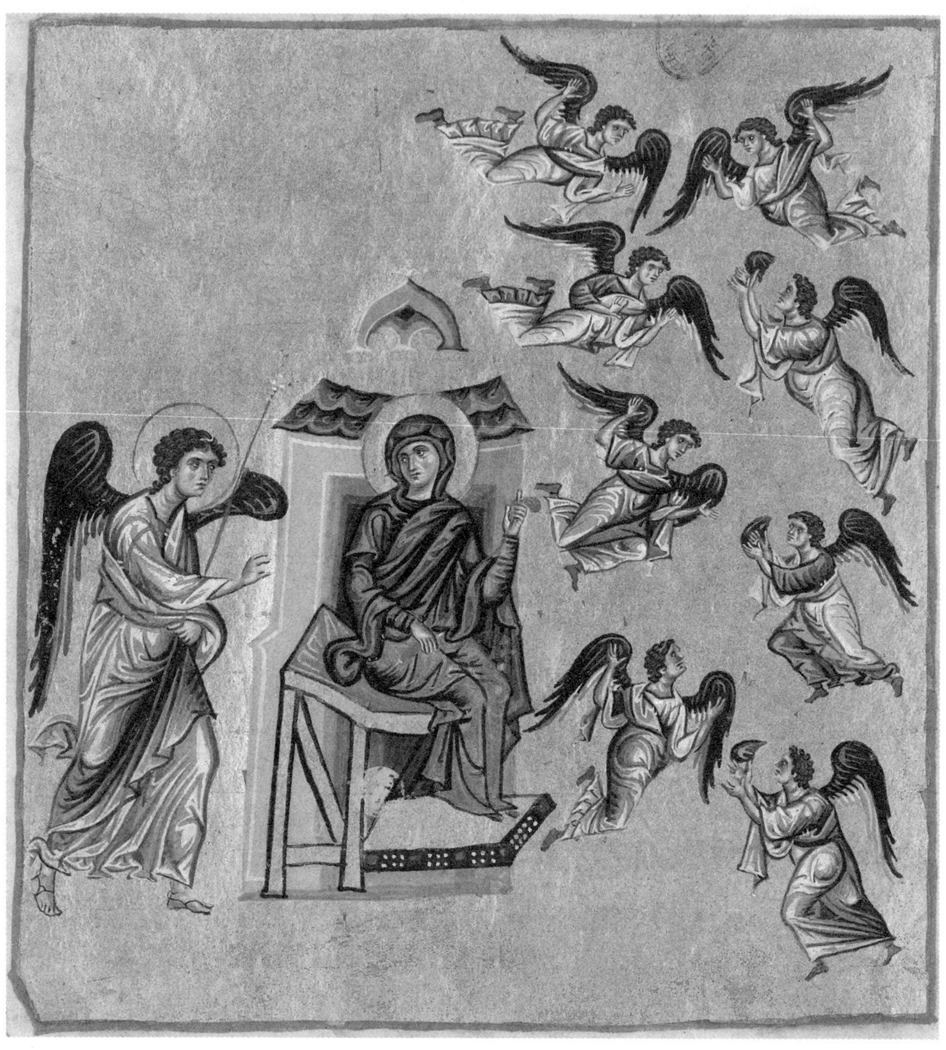

1.13. The Prayer and Consent to the Conception. Vatican City, Biblioteca Apostolica Vaticana, Homilies of James Kokkinobaphos (Vat. gr. 1162), fol. 127v. © 2019 Biblioteca Apostolica Vaticana.

the concluding image of the rejoicing heavenly hosts does the work of emphasizing that only then—after Mary's consent was offered up—was Christ incarnated and the Annunciation scene ended. This stress is made even clearer in the final scene in this homily, which depicts "Gabriel's ascent to heaven" (fig. 1.14). There, the familiar figure of Gabriel who has accompanied Mary for so long now flies past her, ascending into heaven. His size is diminished to suggest he is far away; moreover, he is now to the right of her, as if he has just zoomed past her. Mary remains in her same contorted

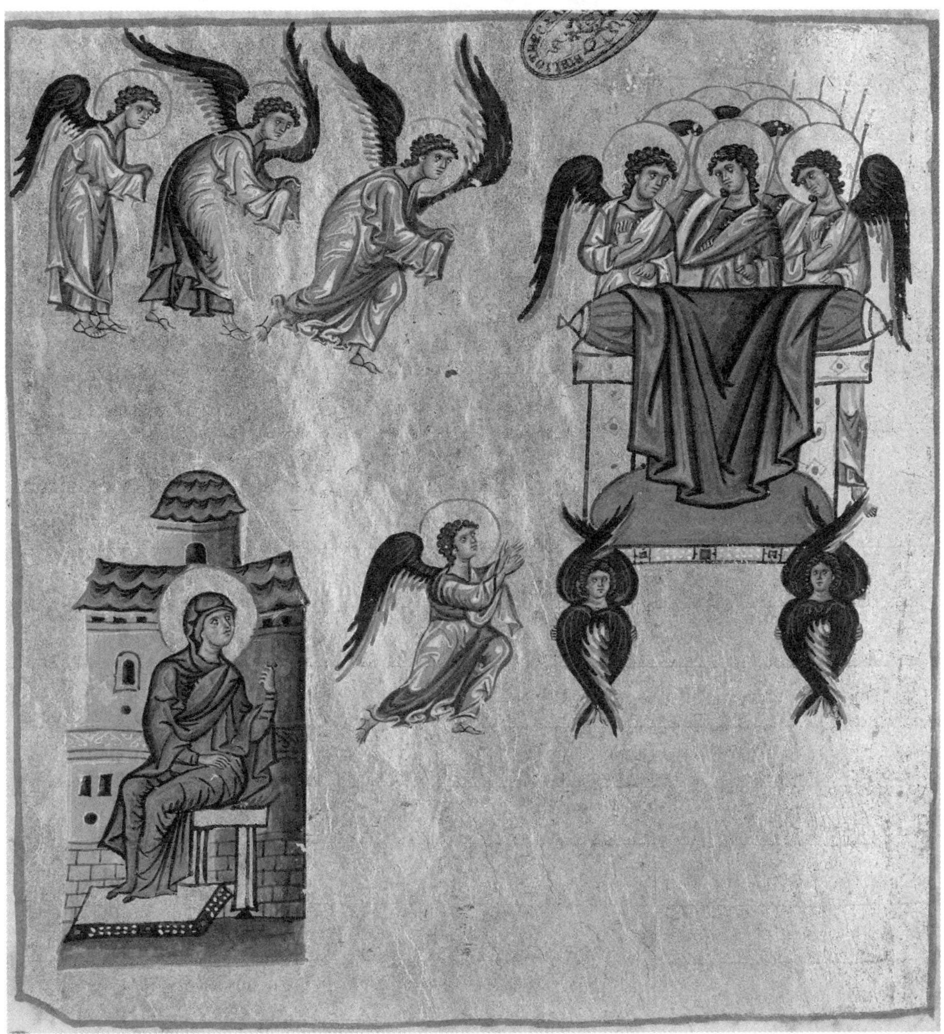

1.14. The Ascent of Gabriel. Vatican City, Biblioteca Apostolica Vaticana, Homilies of James Kokkinobaphos (Vat. gr. 1162), fol. 130v. © 2019 Biblioteca Apostolica Vaticana.

pose, but flipped: rather than looking to the left, where he once was, she now faces to the right of the miniature. Gabriel approaches the throne of God, empty because the Holy Spirit has entered Mary's womb. The ranks of angels stand in adoration before the empty throne, leaving little doubt that God has left to become ensconced within human flesh.

Focusing on Mary's childhood and upbringing, the six homilies of James climax not with the birth of Christ but rather with the Annunciation in the fifth homily and, finally, Mary's response to and vindication of charges of immodesty and rape made against her after the conception. This manuscript was more than likely the commission of a wealthy and learned female patron, specifically *sebastokratorissa* Eirene.[78] Although two illuminated copies from the same workshop exist, we have examined only the one at the Vatican; the two are nearly identical in their iconography and composition, but the copy in Paris is half the size. Their extensive correspondence demonstrates that Eirene had a long-standing relationship with James, and the style, lavishness, and composition of these manuscripts are in keeping with her other commissions. Moreover, the subject and scope of the homilies on Mary emphasize Eirene's position as a well-bred aristocratic woman, as they unfold before palatial settings. While most of the other homilies in the series are found in compilations of patristic sources, the fifth homily appears to have no extant source, suggesting that it is the work of James Kokkinobaphos himself.[79] In other words, this manuscript reaches its peak with a woman's consent and her response to sexual slander and invective, matters that would have certainly been highly resonant for aristocratic women in Constantinople. Perfectly capturing the dynamics discussed here, the Kokkinobaphos manuscript brings together the challenges posed by sexual consent in Mary's story and nudges us toward the lived social dynamics of Constantinopolitan women concerning matters of sexuality, sexual consent, and reproductive choice in Byzantium. Thus, the illuminated manuscript of James Kokkinobaphos's homilies on Mary presents a potent visual representation of the importance of Mary's consent, displaying through a careful progression in iconography not only the unfolding of that consent but clarifying that this process is already condensed within any image of the Annunciation, which, while depicting the greeting, recalls to the viewer the entire salvific history that follows.

In Christian doctrine, the salvation of humanity is marked by three critical moments of consent: God's condescension (*synkatabasis*) to become flesh in the Christ, Mary's consent before Gabriel to the Incarnation, and Christ's consent in Gethsemane to the Passion. While the blood of Christ upon Golgotha seals the deal of salvation, it is these earlier acts of consent that make possible the salvation fulfilled in the Resurrection. When consent is stressed as the source of Christian salvation, we can shift emotional focus from the sacrifice of Christ to the willing actions of Christ and Mary who consent to this suffering.[80] These matters were foundational to Christian thought, which set out a history of salvation that emphasizes the prudence of Mary as she suspiciously questions the angel, before willingly consenting to her impregnation by the Holy Spirit.

Examining the divide between modern and medieval forms of affective piety connected to the Crucifixion, Amy Hollywood notes that the claim that Christ's sufferings at the Passion derive their efficacy from their exceptional nature is "historically, theologically, and ethically untenable." In Hollywood's view, what is exceptional is that Christ "would willingly undergo suffering in solidarity with the suffering of others."[81] In this modern context, the Passion and Crucifixion are testaments of consent that hark back to the actions of Mary in the Annunciation, and even those of God in the decision to take on human flesh. Concerns about the origins of Christ's consent to the Passion are anything but modern, however; nor does this question pertain to affective piety alone, as Christ's willing sacrifice for others resonates emotionally for the worshipper. This issue has implications for the very nature of Jesus's human soul as the medium between the human and the divine will of God.[82]

When Jesus prays in the Garden of Gethsemane, he expresses his human frailty and hesitation in consenting to what is to come. He asks God the Father to "take this cup from me," as recounted in the synoptic Gospels (Luke 22:42; Mark 14:36; Matthew 26:39). In the typology of the sacrificial lamb, Christ is led to be slaughtered for the sins of humanity; but unlike the lamb, he goes voluntarily, and it is precisely his consent to the will of God that cleanses sin. The Gospels do not allude to the internal, psychological tension of Jesus's hesitation and deliberation in Gethsemane as we witnessed with Mary at the Annunciation. Christ nevertheless consents, stating "may your will [*thelēma*] be done" (Matthew 26:42; cf. Matthew 26:39; Luke 22:42; Mark 14:36). As Jesus gives himself over to the will of God, the Gospel text manifests the Passion as having, in a sense, been proleptically fulfilled. After the angel strengthens Jesus and he gives his verbal consent to the execution of God's own will, Jesus continues to pray. Luke writes: "and his sweat was like drops of blood falling to the ground" (Luke 22:44). It is as if, in that moment of consent, the Passion has already occurred—the beads of his nervous sweat are transformed into the drops of blood from his brow beneath the crown of thorns that he will wear. At the moment of Jesus's consent in Gethsemane, the Passion, Crucifixion, and Resurrection are all already immanent. The violations that occurred in the garden of Eden are reworked through the consent that occurred in the garden of Gethsemane.

Critically, Christ's consent to the will of God displays the orthodox resolution to the controversy about *monothelitism*. According to that doctrine, which began to sweep the empire in the fifth century, Christ and the Father possess a single shared will; it was ultimately decreed heretical at the Third Council of Constantinople in 681. The fact that the Christ must consent on his own to the Crucifixion ultimately demonstrated, as Maximus the Confessor wrote, "that with the duality of his natures there are two wills [*thelēseis*] and two actions [*energeiai*] respective to the two natures."[83] What we encounter here is not simply that Christ must consent before he can be led to slaughter, but that structurally the moment of hesitation is required in order to define the two wills of his divine and human natures. In other words, had consent not been necessary or articulated, had there been no hesitation, the perfect humanity and perfect divinity of Christ would have been left unexpressed. Consent thus undergirds the Passion by confirming the divine and human personhood of Christ.

In the covenant of salvation wrought by Jesus, the Passion's bloodshed is merely the signature on the contract, a contract written out through a narrative of consent. In John 19:30, upon fulfilling the typologies set forth for the Passion, Christ's final utterance is "It is finished [*tetelestai*]!" *Tetelestai* suggests less a narrative conclusion or end than a "fulfillment" or "completion." In saying "It is fulfilled," Jesus seals the narrative of consent that fulfills the typologies of the Old Testament, working salvation through the antitypes set forth before. Structurally, the Christological narrative—from the Annunciation to the Passion and Crucifixion—undoes the primordial sin of Adam and Eve. But, as in Nicholas Cabasilas's text, this sin is depicted as arising as much from the actions taken by Eve and Adam before the tree of knowledge as from a creation born without consent. Adam is begotten outside of any possible consent; Eve is stolen from Adam's flesh; and their offspring are said to evidence the traces of Eve's own deceits. If Cain was said to be born, at least metaphorically, from the various infractions of Eve—either hasty consent, adultery, or rape—then Christ comes from the same place as Cain, as Proclus of Constantinople states. However, in a complete reworking and undoing of the flawed or forced consent of Eve, the Christ is unambiguously a product of willing and unforced consent.

Mary's consent and Christ's assent to God's will validate all the other actions of the narrative. Without those actions, their stories would only have echoed those that came before them, and those earlier stories were explicitly and consciously advocated against by early Christian and Byzantine writers in order to draw the distinction. The importance placed on consent grows over the course of the Byzantine period. In a shift from a focus on one's own affective responses to the suffering of Christ—or on Christ's obedient adherence to an omnipotent God—the importance placed on consent enables one to view the Incarnation as rooted less in sacrifice than in willing consent. We can therefore say with some confidence that this history of Christian thought places paramount importance on Mary's ability to consent to her very impregnation and not just on her right to choose to bear the child. These matters are stressed by the language used, which appears to be consciously selected precisely because it is also used in discussing consent to sex and marriage.

As issues of coercion and forced consent became crucial to Byzantine thinking about sexual and matrimonial relations in religious and legal spheres, the focus appears to have had a lasting impact on the narrative around the Annunciation. Consent comes to be necessarily associated with the human soul, tied to matters of will. While the divine need not consent, such consent is necessary because of the human flesh and mind of Mary and the human soul and will of Christ. For Byzantine writers from the post-Iconoclastic era onward, this consent is not confined only to sexual or spiritual matters, but is also a fundamental stage in human perception. Without giving consent to that which is passed along by the senses, as Nicholas Mesarites eloquently suggests, even perception itself would be impossible. Humanity is remade through consent, and consent is fundamental to the nature of humanity itself. While the label "Annunciation" seems to suggest a scene in which the Virgin Mary is merely informed that she will give birth to Christ, in reality the event marks a crucial moment in Christian history. It is the sober and willing consent of Mary that enables the Incarnation of Christ to work the wonders of salvation. The point to take away from this is simple—even God himself asked Mary for consent before impregnating her. To look more deeply into this question of sexual and reproductive consent, in the next chapter we will consider Byzantine approaches to and practices involving terminations of pregnancy and reproductive choice.

II. Slut-Shaming an Empress

One time when she [Theodora] went to the house of a notable to entertain during drinks, they say that when the eyes of all the diners were upon her she mounted the frame of the couch by their feet and unceremoniously lifted up her clothes right there and then, not caring in the least that she was making a spectacle of her shamelessness. Even though she put three of her orifices to work she would impatiently reproach Nature for not making the holes in her nipples bigger than they were so that she could devise additional sexual positions involving them as well. She was often pregnant, but by using almost all known techniques she could induce immediate abortions.

—Procopius, *The Secret History 9:17–19 (trans. Anthony Kaldellis)*

IN HIS NOTORIOUSLY SALACIOUS *Secret History*, the sixth-century Byzantine historian Procopius of Caesarea presents his reader with a vivid pornographic account of the empress Theodora's upbringing and character. Procopius recounts her employment as an entertainer and sex worker, while also suggesting broader sexual proclivities. The same author who provided an intricate, nuanced, and sober purview of the emperor Justinian's military conquests and patronage in his *Wars* and *Buildings* shares here a bawdy vision of Justinian and Theodora's rule as marked by betrayal, brutality, and debauchery.[1] Nevertheless, the importance of this work in medieval history lies neither in its candid image of imperial rule nor in its possible documentation of Theodora's otherwise little-known life (fig. 2.1). Procopius's account is powerful precisely because of how he uses graphic sexual detail to attack Theodora through an imposition of shame, a feeling that he repeatedly and eloquently reminds his reader was not felt by Theodora herself.

Procopius's key rhetorical tactic is what today would be called "slut-shaming," a process intended to shame and socially ostracize a person for their sexual actions, proclivities, or choices. It often includes the leaking and disseminating of incriminating pornographic information.[2] While systemic in the broader culture to police propriety and individuals' assumed sexual and societal roles, the processes of slut-shaming often are used strategically with more specific malicious intentions: the shamer seeks to exact retribution for having been romantically scorned or wishes to out

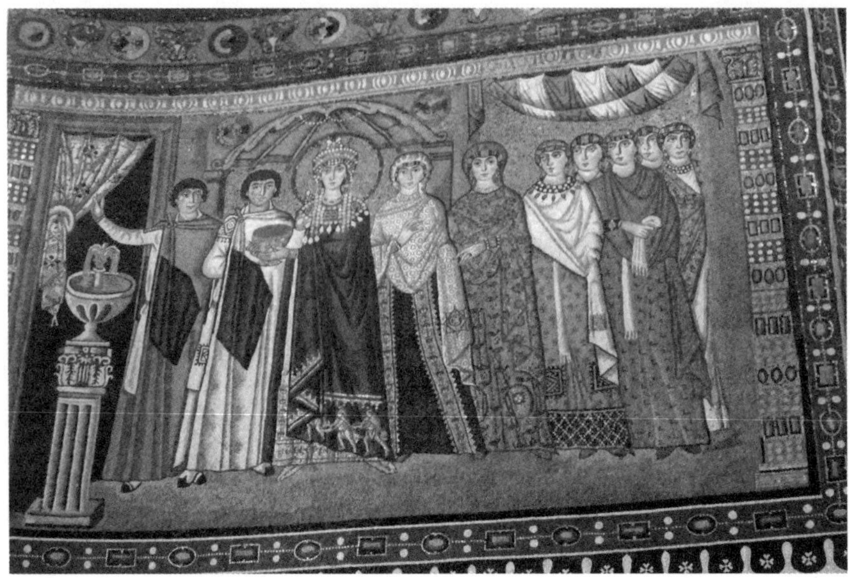

2.1. Theodora and Her Entourage. Church of San Vitale, Ravenna, Italy.

a person's sexual orientation or interests. This process often entails the release and spread of sexually compromising images, a phenomenon commonly referred to as "revenge porn." Here, my aim is to approach the *Secret History* as the medieval equivalent to revenge porn and to likewise understand the nuanced ways in which Procopius uses slut-shaming as his primary rhetorical tactic.

Whether the *Secret History* was read by a large or relatively small audience and whether it has any grounding in truth does not matter, because slut-shaming is a rhetorical practice. It is meant not merely to shame or directly harass an individual but also to corrode their respectability and erode their support networks. These processes can occur on a large scale—for example, the cyberbullying of Monica Lewinsky—or within small communities, as when one person sends nude photos of or stories about another person to their friends. As we will see, Procopius's text offers insight into how sexual shaming was politically deployed, particularly against marginalized subjects; significantly, his text reveals how this was done not only by Procopius himself but also by Theodora, Justinian, and their contemporaries.

In this chapter, I will use the tropes and details in the *Secret History* to consider other contemporaneous nonnormative sexual behaviors and reproductive practices, such as same-gender intimacies, contraception, and abortion.[3] In considering the roles of abortion and contraceptives in the *Secret History* and contemporaneous medical texts, I am seeking traces of the sexual and reproductive choices of Constantinopolitan cis women, activities often suppressed or neglected in the historical record.

THE SLUT-SHAMING OF THEODORA

The accounts of Theodora's sexual activities operated in an established tradition of slander and invective that was grounded on earlier literary tropes of fanciful invention and exaggeration for rhetorical effect.[4] Procopius's text alludes to earlier invective found in ancient authors and, at times, to contemporaneous burlesque performances in late antique Constantinople.[5] For example, the late second-century rhetorical text *On Types of Style* by Hermogenes provides a precedent for the earlier quotation about Theodora's three defiled orifices. In a speech attributed to Demosthenes, *Against Neaira*, the second-century author slanders Neaira with the line "she plied her trade through three orifices."[6] Likewise, the following passage about Theodora's half-naked performance in the theater betrays classicizing elements:

Wearing this outfit [a loincloth], then, she would lie down on her back and
spread herself out on the floor whereupon certain menials, who were hired to
do this very job, would sprinkle grains all over her genitals. Then the geese,
which were trained for this purpose, pecked them off one at a time with their
beaks and ate them.[7]

Procopius seems to suggest that, with this performance, Theodora was pantomiming the mythological story of Leda and the swan, in which Zeus's copulation with Leda in the form of a swan serves as an excuse to have her strip down to a revealing and not-very-effective loincloth while geese consumed grains from her body. Such burlesque performances and pantomimes of mythological tales are found across literary and visual arts—indeed, Juvenal attested to the pantomiming of this very story around 100 C.E.—thus demonstrating their popularity across social groups. Such performances and texts occupied a central place in Constantinopolitan life.[8] By describing Theodora's actions in ways consistent with contemporary literary tropes and popular performances, Procopius increased his attack's readability and thus more effectively associated Theodora with the bawdier aspects of Constantinopolitan life, activities in which some of Procopius's own readers might have happily and regularly engaged. The fact that

Procopius's readers might have (or even probably) found these salacious details quite commonplace and banal is what makes them important—a point that hitherto has been overlooked.

Despite their sensationalism, which has led some to dismiss them, the details of Theodora's sexual conquests are anything but insignificant. The details speak not only to contemporaneous sexual practices but also to Theodora's socioeconomic position, level of education, and origins outside the elite. In other words, the contours of her sexual acts articulate the intersectionality of her subjectivity. Her father was a "bear keeper" (someone charged with keeping the beasts for the amphitheater in Constantinople), and his early death left her, her two sisters, and her mother facing hardships.[9] It is for this reason, Procopius explains, that her mother put them all on the stage when they reached puberty, and Theodora immediately began exploring her sexual interests. Procopius writes:

> At this time Theodora was hardly ripe enough to sleep with a man or to have sex with him in the way that a woman should. So she would offer herself to certain poor wretches who performed that disgusting act on her that some men do with other men.[10]

In this euphemistic account of anal sex, Procopius depicts the corruption of a young Theodora—not even able to perform the proper duties of a sex worker because she is not yet a proper woman, she must resort to unnatural activities. Procopius's later allusion to her "three orifices," suggests that Theodora did not lose her fondness for anal sex. Elsewhere, Procopius observes her penchant for oral sex as well, declaring that she made "it seem that she had genitals not in the place where nature ordained for all other women, but in her face!"[11]

Throughout these accounts, Procopius's Theodora happily continues to practice oral and anal sex, adding vaginal sex when she is old enough. Rhetorically, then, what these various depictions do is to transform her non-vaginal sexual desires into an image of a counternatural body. Not only are Theodora's sexual practices non-normative, but they create a different body, seen particularly in Procopius's account of her three orifices. Theodora's body departs from normal female anatomy for multiple reasons, all tied to her sexual activities: because of her extreme youth, when she cannot perform "as a woman should"; or later because her oral proclivities place her genitals where they are not "ordained for all other women"; or because her anal practices lead Procopius to liken her to male sodomites. In Procopius's text Theodora becomes monstrous, hybrid, and inhuman as her sexual body exceeds what is socially prescribed to her gender and even her humanity.

Furthermore, Procopius endeavors to show that Theodora's promiscuity could not be excused by an appeal to necessity, but was rather a broader moral failure of her character:

> Never has there been a person so enslaved to lust in all its forms. She often went to the potluck dinner parties in the company of ten young escorts, or even more than that, all at the peak of their physical prowess and skilled at screwing, she would bed down with her fellow diners in groups all night long. And when all were exhausted from doing this, she would turn to their servants, all thirty of them if that's how many there were, and couple with each of them separately—but even this would not satisfy her lust.[12]

Procopius underscores throughout the text that Theodora committed acts of violence and debauchery on her own accord; she "never did anything because she had been persuaded or forced by another person," he writes at one point.[13] By maintaining that her actions are done of her own volition, Procopius ensures that the blame and guilt fall on her rather than on anyone else in her circle or on Justinian himself, no matter how depraved any of those people might have also been. Thus, Procopius uses this account of Theodora's orgiastic jaunts with young men to demonstrate that her fundamental nature is unbridled lust. Yet by repeatedly insisting on her self-possessed agency, he makes clear that this lust is not pathological or animalistic lust but rather rooted in Theodora's inherent voraciousness. This is conveyed by his comment about her "toying with new sexual techniques,"[14] which effectively establishes that her sexual deeds are of her own invention. Moreover, through her inventiveness, these sexual acts come to exceed what was known and accepted within the already deviant circles in which she operated. For Procopius, it is important to show not only that Theodora is promiscuous and lustful but also that the sexual practices in which she engages are aberrant and abhorrent even among sex workers.

An apparently passing remark on Theodora's reproductive choices is revealing—"She was often pregnant, but by using almost all known techniques she could induce immediate miscarriage [*exambliskein*]." This is certainly yet another instance in the *Secret History* where Procopius seeks to demonstrate Theodora's immense personal cruelty and depraved agency. These words appear immediately after his comment about her three orifices —and thus seem almost to be a non sequitur, for the anecdote to which it is appended shows that her sexual proclivities were not all reproductive in nature. Yet a sixth-century audience would surely associate this degree of technical expertise regarding methods for abortion and contraception with the knowledge of sex workers. In a much later text from twelfth-century Salerno, an anonymous writer uses a similar phrase in a question for medical students: "As sex workers have very frequent intercourse, why do they conceive only rarely?"[15]

Abortifacients, contraceptives, and more invasive methods of inducing a miscarriage or surgically removing a fetus were understood since antiquity and were well known throughout the Byzantine world.[16] To simply associate this knowledge with those in the sex trade would be a reading in keeping with Procopius's passing mention. However, the reality of the matter is far more complex, and thus we must look more closely at the legal and religious approaches to abortions and contraceptives, as well as consider Byzantine medical knowledge related to these procedures and practices.

LEGAL AND RELIGIOUS VIEWS ON ABORTIONS AND CONTRACEPTIVES

From antiquity on, women and their midwives possessed a great deal of knowledge regarding both contraceptive and abortive prescriptions and methods. Details of this knowledge are preserved in medical treatises and herbals; broader indications of these practices can be found in disparate sources, ranging from a philosophical dialogue by Plato to a homily by John Chrysostom. To any Byzantine reader—man or woman—both at the time of Procopius's writing and for the centuries that followed, Theodora's abortive deeds would not have appeared unusual.

Throughout the late antique and medieval period and despite its ubiquitous presence, abortion was often likened to murder, and it was frowned on by both legal and religious institutions.[17] For example, the civil law compendium of Justinian, the *Digest*, quotes the Roman jurist Ulpian as having said that "if it is made manifest that a female has used force against her own entrails and miscarried a fetus, the provincial government will order her to go into exile." Elsewhere the *Digest* quotes Marcianus (citing Severus and Antoninus) to similar effect, explaining the punishment by declaring that it is "shameful that she could with impunity deprive her husband of children." While abortion was to be punished with exile, a person could be put to death if responsible for more serious malice or harm. For example, the *Digest* clarifies that if a woman loses her life as a side effect of an administered abortifacient, the person responsible would "suffer the extreme penalty"—that is, be executed.[18]

Death is also the punishment for a woman who has aborted a fetus with the malicious aim of altering her husband's lineage. Quoting the jurist Tryphoninus, the *Digest* addresses a case in which a woman was sentenced to death for choosing to deny her husband heirs by aborting the unborn child. However, the *Digest* adds a clarification: if, after a divorce, a pregnant woman should choose to commit the act upon herself, "so as to avoid giving a son to her husband who is now hateful, she is to be punished by temporary exile."[19] Thus, the harshest punishments were incurred if the abortion was deemed to interfere with the rights of the married woman's husband; an unmarried or divorced woman was treated far more leniently. The case of the divorced woman is particularly interesting because the law makes a clear allowance for a single woman's right to choose whether to bear the child of her former husband, against whom she is expected to feel some animosity; furthermore, it does not even set the length of her exile, merely stating that it should be temporary.

Similar prescriptions are found within the context of the Church. For example, a canon from the Council of Ancyra in 314 states that women found to have committed or attempted an abortion on themselves or another were to be exiled from the Church for ten years, revising an earlier rule that they be excluded for life.[20] Echoing this and the juridical opinions of the period, in the mid-fourth century Basil the Great approached abortion as being akin to murder, yet he did not ask that a woman be punished accordingly. In a letter to Amphilochius, Basil writes:

A woman who deliberately destroys a fœtus is answerable for murder. And any fine distinction as to its being completely formed or unformed is not admissible amongst us. For in this case not only the child which is about to be born is vindicated, but also she herself who plotted against herself, since women usually die from such attempts. And there is added to this crime the destruction of the embryo, a second murder—at least that is the intent of those who dare these deeds. We should not, however, prolong their punishment until death, but should accept the term of ten years; and we should not determine the treatment according to time but according to the manner of repentance.[21]

Basil appears to be directly responding to the canons of the Council of Ancyra, which likewise recommended banishment (from the Church) for the same period of ten years. The similarity of the sentences suggests a close connection between church canons and the established prescriptions of Roman law. Unlike Roman law, however, Basil appears to hold out the possibility of greater leniency, hinting that the full ten years need not be served if the woman has properly repented.

Basil focuses on the crime, pointing not only to the harm caused to the fetus, whatever its stage of life, but also to the harm that abortive processes cause mothers, who "usually die from such attempts." He returns to this matter in the letter, stating with no uncertainty: "women who give drugs [*pharmaka*] that cause abortion are themselves also murderers as well as those who take the poisons that kill the foetus [*embryoktona dēlētēria*]."[22] Much later, an artist created a monumental depiction (dated 1291) of a damned woman: she is suspended by hooks, with her legs spread apart, and with an odd pale flux spilling down from her loins and around her leg. This image, in the rural church of Saint John Prodromos in Agios Vasilios, Crete, bears the inscription "She who drinks an herbal potion [*botanon*] so as to not give birth," providing a graphic deterrent against the use of remedies that could have been easily found near the village.[23] This gruesome image was apparently intended to dissuade women from consuming abortifacients by emphasizing the physical risk associated with such drugs, beyond any moral or ethical issues associated with abortion at the time. The woman is shown being tormented for her crime in hell, suggesting that she died before she was able to repent and perform penance; thus, she has been condemned for eternity to atone for her crimes against her unborn infant and against herself—as Basil might have predicted. In a similar vein, other gendered and sexualized attacks on women are found throughout contemporaneous wall-paintings (fig. 2.2), showing women suffering in hell and being humiliated for their promiscuity.[24] These are vivid visual examples of slut-shaming in Byzantine art that merit further attention as such.

The very real dangers of using abortifacients, and the even greater risks that attended the surgical removal of a fetus through an embryotomy, were of immense concern to ancient, late antique, and medieval authors alike. In the famous oath attributed to Hippocrates, abortions are mentioned immediately after the refusal to assist in or recommend euthanasia: "Similarly I will not give to a woman a pessary to cause abortion."[25] While Hippocrates conceivably was showing respect for the life of the fetus, his reservations were more likely grounded in the harm that such drugs often did to women, not only causing severe complications but often, as Basil reminds us, resulting in death. In some cases, as the fourth-century Constantinopolitan physician Theodorus Priscianus explains, abortion is justified to save the woman's life—but he describes those circumstances only after quoting Hippocrates and speaking against abortions in general.[26] Theodora's

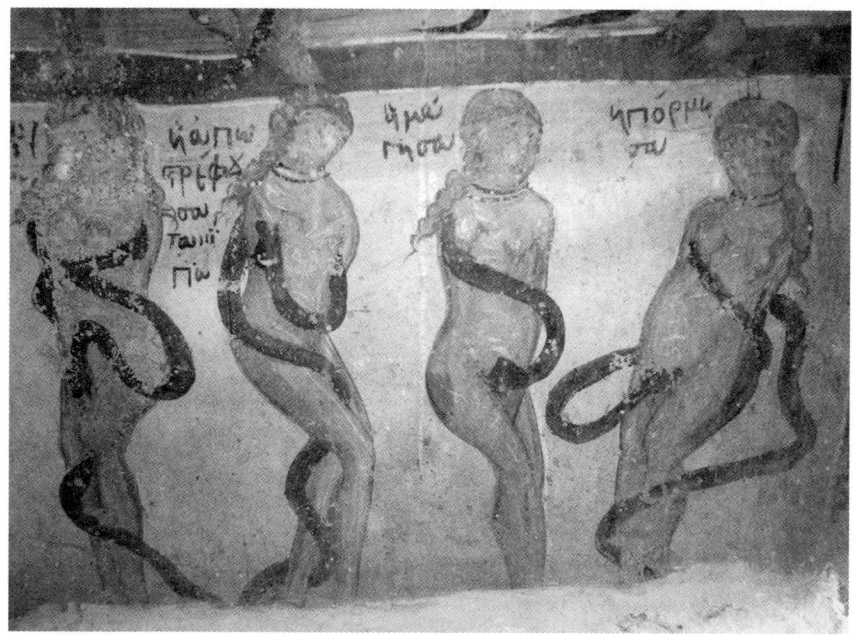

2.2. Female Sinners in Hell, including the Procuress (*hē pornēsa*) and the Abandoner of Children (*hē apostrephousa ta nēpia*). St. Pelagia in Anno Vianno near Heraklion, Crete, Greece.

untimely death might even have been the result of a metastasized uterine cancer related to the abortive drugs and other practices that she had employed throughout her lifetime.[27]

EVIDENCE FOR ABORTIONS AND CONTRACEPTIVES IN MEDICINE

Despite the medical, legal, and religious reservations discussed previously, contemporary medical texts regularly include prescriptions and methods for abortion; indeed, allusions to the process appear in a wide range of sources. Thus, whether approved or not, abortions and contraceptives were evidenced throughout antiquity and the Middle Ages. The second-century medical writer Soranus of Ephesus produced an entire book on gynecology, which devoted much attention to methods of abortion and contraception, even drawing a careful distinction between the two. In his chapter dedicated to the issue of whether and how to use such methods, Soranus explains:

A contraceptive differs from an abortive, for the first does not let conception take place, while the latter destroys what has been conceived. Let us, therefore,

call the one "abortive" [*phthorion*] and the other "contraceptive" [*atokion*].
And an "expulsive" [*ekbolion*] some people say is synonymous with an abortive; others, however, say that there is a difference because an expulsive does
not mean drugs but shaking and leaping.[28]

Under the heading of "expulsives"—a third category—Soranus includes actions that are the opposite of what is recommended for preventing a miscarriage, such as leaping, shaking, carrying a heavy weight, and vigorous exercise. Acknowledging the possible risks and complications that attend the use of such drugs, and recognizing disagreement over whether such methods should be employed, Soranus states that he recommends an abortion only when some complication with the uterus makes the pregnancy especially difficult and dangerous for the woman. But a better course is to prevent conception, Soranus argues, given the dangers associated with methods of abortion.[29]

While recommending abortion in cases of medical necessity, Soranus adamantly opposes the use of abortion to destroy an embryo "because of adultery [*moicheian*] or out of consideration for youthful beauty."[30] This statement sheds light on an important facet of Procopius's mention of abortion to attack Theodora, a woman whom he elsewhere accuses of spending inordinate amounts of time tending to her physical appearance.[31] In his medical texts, Soranus makes no allowance for abortion in the case of adultery or, more broadly, fornication (the term *moicheian* can have both modern meanings). By remarking on her repeated abortions, Procopius is not necessarily depicting Theodora as callous or cruel (as a modern opponent of abortion might) but rather is shaming her for her sexual practices and their consequences. Furthermore, he is suggesting that she is avoiding pregnancy because of her own vanity and desire for self-preservation. In Procopius's account, there is no hint of the dangers that she faced in taking these actions, or in any medical necessity for them.

From antiquity on, sources attest to a concern for the life of the woman. Plato and Aristotle advise that men and women of an advanced age should not bear or rear children, nor should men and women who are unhealthy or ill-suited to do so.[32] In such cases, the authors state that the fetus should be aborted, if conception occurs. In other words, beginning with the classical writers, there is a clear sense that abortion can and should be performed when health is at issue, including instances when the child might be deformed (a practice that may border on infanticide). In the *Laws* Plato even recommends abortions for the purposes of population control, along with fertility stimulants should the birthrate wane.[33]

Regardless of the statements of religious writers and legal opinions, the medical handbooks are unapologetic about including information on contraception and abortion. For example, the sixth-century Aetius of Amida describes the application and removal of one kind of contraceptive, a vaginal suppository, which had been improved since the time of Soranus's text. Aetius adds that, once a woman has removed it, "if she wishes, she may have intercourse with a man [*ei bouloito, androkoiteito*]. It is infallible because of its many trials."[34] Here the text clearly pays attention to the woman's volition (*bouloito*), assuring the reader that this method is tried and tested. Thus, women can use the contraceptive with confidence and resume sexual activities without fear of conception.[35]

Many aspects of these medical texts demonstrate the advanced state of contraceptives in Byzantium, not least being the clear distinction the texts draw between a contraceptive and an abortifacient. Already seen in Soranus, evidence of advanced knowledge continues into later centuries in similar treatises, such as the fourth-century writings of the noted physician Oribasius, the sixth-century text on medicine by Aetius of Amida, and the work of his seventh-century counterpart, Paul of Aegina.[36] Moreover, the same distinction between contraceptives and abortifacients, along with the knowledge of how to concoct and use them, appears throughout the complementary herbals, including Dioscurides's first-century *De materia medica*, which enjoyed a great deal of popularity in the medieval world.[37] Moreover, although such drugs were prescribed mainly to women, anti-fertility agents for men were also known and recommended in these texts.[38]

Over the centuries, this knowledge was not simply preserved and transmitted but actively deepened. Aetius of Amida, for example, provides clear evidence that the recipes for these drugs had been revised and refined. Aetius goes beyond copying Soranus's prescriptions to expand and improve on them, speaking at times to their reliability and effectiveness, as we saw above.[39] A contemporary of Justinian and Theodora, Aetius may have been the doctor treating Theodora and her retinue; as the author of a book on gynecology (within his larger medical treatise), Aetius would have been well-suited to their needs.[40] Aetius's book on gynecology demonstrates the role women played in transmitting this knowledge. It directly cites several women, from the enigmatic figure of Aspasia to a certain "fumigation preparation of the Lady Romula."[41] Aspasia may well have been a physician or midwife, but other women mentioned range from experienced midwives to noblewomen, leaving little doubt that communities of women possessed knowledge about abortions and contraceptives beyond what surviving male-authored texts might only fragmentarily reveal.[42] At times Aetius even defers to the midwives. For example, when discussing births, he only provides information on difficult ones because details regarding a standard delivery "would be superfluous to write down, since, by long usage, these are known not only by midwives but also by other women."[43] Thus, this book on gynecology—a compendium of written sources and word of mouth—is always to be used in conjunction with the practices of women skilled in such health care.

THE PRACTICE OF SURGICAL PROCEDURES

Somewhat surprisingly, an insight into the state of medical knowledge and its practice in the Byzantine world comes down to us from Visigothic Spain. In *Lives of the Fathers of Mérida*, composed in the 630s, Paul the Deacon chronicles the deeds of Paul, bishop of Mérida around 540/550.[44] Describing events contemporaneous to Procopius's writing, the author tells us that bishop Paul performed a caesarian to save the life of a woman whose fetus had died.[45] Caesarians were used in antiquity, but to rescue a child after the death of the mother; some historians herald bishop Paul's as the first done on a living woman.[46] The author tells us that bishop Paul was "a Greek by nationality [*natione Grecum*] and a doctor by trade, [who] came from the lands of [the] East to the city of Merida," thereby indicating that his medical knowledge had roots in the Greek-speaking Mediterranean—probably from education in a major city like Constantinople, given his skill.[47]

Paul the Deacon stresses that the woman's child had died in her womb, but that no Western treatment or medicine was able to expel the dead fetus. Therefore, she and her husband turned to the bishop because of his renowned skill. At first the bishop refuses, claiming that as a holy man he cannot pollute himself by performing such a task and can only advise other doctors. When all this fails, he is all but coerced by the woman's husband to act. The text extols the ability of the Greek doctor:

Placing his hope in God, with wondrous skill he made a most skillful incision
by his cunning use of the knife and extracted the already decaying body of the
infant limb by limb, piece by piece and, with God's aid, restored forthwith the
woman who was on the point of dying and only half alive, safe and sound to
her husband.[48]

While Paul the Deacon lacks medical knowledge, he is clearly depicting an embryotomy as described by Aetius of Amida, citing Philumenos and following Soranus, an operation that is also recounted accurately in Paul of Aegina's seventh-century compendium.[49] Aetius presents the procedure for a late-term abortion, which is to be used when the mother's life is in danger. He details how the fetus's body is to be dissected, depending on its position, and subsequently extracted from the womb through the vagina, piece by piece.[50] Subsequent sections describe the proper removal of the placenta, also attributed to Philumenos, and the proper care for a woman who has undergone an embryotomy, attributed to the woman Aspasia.

The length and specificity of these sections suggests that the material was treated not as a curiosity being passed down but as current surgical practice. The story of bishop Paul, though it does not match the medical texts in its clarity and detail, is evidence for the practice of embryotomy because it alludes to the key elements of the surgical procedures as described by those Greek sources. It is unlikely that the Visigothic author would have had direct access to such texts. Furthermore, the story itself, if we can trust it, shows that bishop Paul had the proper knowledge and experience to (successfully) carry out this procedure. First, the author tells us that the local doctors lacked the ability to undertake her treatment, even with Paul's advice, stressing the difficulty of the task and the need for surgical experience. Second, we see that, after assessing her condition, Paul resorted to performing a fetal extraction via caesarian section, suggesting either that this was a practice known to Byzantine surgeons or that he drew on his familiarity with the procedure to treat his patient.

To those unfamiliar with Aetius's text, this story could seem to be merely an inconsequential exaggeration by a hagiographer attempting to extol the virtues of a holy figure. However, with a grasp of the nuances and details of Byzantine surgical practices, we can to appreciate that the Visigothic author imprecisely captured a procedure known in the Byzantine world, associating it specifically with the Greek eastern Mediterranean. References to the exceptional nature of Byzantine medicine appear across Western sources. For example, in the *History of the Franks*, also from the mid-sixth century, Gregory of Tours tells the story of a eunuch who lived much of her life as a woman. Responding to an inquiry about the eunuch's castration, a doctor comes forward and reveals that he was the one who castrated the youth. As a young boy, the eunuch had suffered from a disease of the groin that no one could cure. Therefore, this doctor performed the procedure "in the way I had once seen physicians do in Constantinople," restoring the child's health.[51] We are thus told directly that a doctor studied a particular surgery in Constantinople and then performed that Byzantine procedure to (successfully) resolve a problem that had baffled Western doctors. Reading the narrative of Paul in Mérida, we appreciate that late-term abortions were not beyond the skill of sixth-century Constantinopolitan doctors and that discussion of the procedure in medical books went further than the copying of ancient texts. This story of a c-section, like the comments on the improvements and alterations to ancient contraceptives and abortifacients, provides further evidence for the use of these medical procedures.

In his early-tenth-century *Life of Patriarch Ignatius*, Niketas David Paphlagon recounts the story of a woman in labor with a breech birth—that is, with the fetus positioned feet downward. She is in immense pain, and Niketas writes that, "in order to prevent the woman too from perishing with her child, doctors attend to operate on the baby and draw it out by cutting it limb by limb [*melēdon*]."[52] Miraculously, the procedure proves unnecessary through the intervention of a wonder-working relic that causes the fetus to turn around and be delivered headfirst without trouble. While, in this case, the procedure for a late-term abortion went unperformed, its mention provides further evidence that its use and knowledge about when to use it continued. Moreover, as in the medical handbooks, the miracle story emphasizes that the procedure is to be used when the woman's life is in danger—whether the fetus is dead, as in the operation performed by Paul of Mérida, or still living.

Significantly, the figures who seek out late-term abortions in these two narratives are not despondent sex workers or entertainers. The women are in no way portrayed as exceptional or in any way marginal. Additionally, in the second narrative, the author explicitly declares that the procedure was about to be used on a living fetus to save the mother's life. We thus should reflect on the role played by aristocratic privilege and power in giving the second woman access to not just adequate but exceptional medical care. As the wife of a wealthy and influential senator, Paul of Mérida's patient has substantial resources to seek out and undergo the operation. Moreover, while invectives might target lower-class women, deriding them for reliance on contraceptives and abortions, the aristocracy would have had recourse to safer and more effective contraceptives and abortive procedures that are not easily accessible in the historical record. Therefore, in order to determine what role abortions and contraceptives might have played in sixth-century Constantinople, we first have to question how we might go about finding reliable information on those practices.

The tone and content of the evidence concerning abortion and contraceptives suggest that both were quite common, even though both were frowned on and punished harshly by legal and religious authorities. In the opening sections of *Secret History*, Procopius suggests another instance of a prominent woman inducing abortions. When shaming Antonina, the wife of Justinian's general Belisarius, Procopius presents her background as similar to that of Theodora, and similarly intimates that she knows about abortifacients.[53] Antonina's father was a charioteer in Constantinople and her mother an entertainer like Theodora, "one of those types who whore themselves on the stage." Following in her parents' footsteps and keeping their associations, Antonina is described as consorting with people "who knew all about drugs [*pharmakeusi*] and had learned from them many things that were useful to her." According to Procopius, Theodora was also familiar with the dark arts, having in her youth "consorted with magicians [*magois*] and poisoners [*pharmakeusi*]."[54] While it is difficult to pin down what knowledge might have been possessed by these *pharmakeusi*, the term encompasses those who trafficked in herbs, poisons, and potions, including the materials needed to produce contraceptives and abortifacients.[55]

This allusion to *pharmaka* is tricky, for the term encompasses a wide variety of drugs—many of which women would have been expected to know about. In sixth-century Constantinople, as was true in earlier periods, as the primary medical caregivers of their households, women would have been expected to have a comprehensive knowledge of the drugs and other remedies available to treat a wide variety of common ailments.[56] The copy of Dioscurides's *De materia medica* in Vienna, commissioned as a gift for the aristocratic Anicia Juliana, includes material not only on tending to wounds, snake bites, and common ailments but also on contraceptives and abortifacients.[57] Anicia Juliana was plausibly the wealthiest and most aristocratic figure in Constantinople during the reign of Justinian and Theodora. In her personal life Anicia Juliana was likely the matron of her house; thus Dioscurides's work would have been suitable for her consultation and use.[58] As Leslie Brubaker notes in a passing remark on this manuscript's entry on the pomegranate, "the pomegranate may symbolize the bounty of the earth, but it was also one of the most common (and effective) ingredients in Byzantine contraceptive suppositories."[59] Beyond the elements of realism, iconography, and symbolism discussed by Brubaker, Anicia Juliana's manuscript provides specific information about the remedies, treatments, and *pharmaka* readily at hand in the gardens or markets of Constantinople, knowledge needed to preserve her household's health, abortive and contraceptive drugs being just a subset.

Therefore, the claim in the *Secret History* that Antonina gained knowledge from so-called *pharmakeusi* should not lead us to hastily conclude that she consorted with sorcerers, witches, or others knowledgeable in poisons. While the term certainly brings to mind sorcery and poison, it could just as likely have applied to—and probably did apply to—people who trafficked in knowledge of medicines as well.[60] As has been repeatedly noted in the scholarship, the lines between magic and medicine were considerably blurred in the Byzantine period—the two fields were not wholly intertwined, but they overlapped significantly.[61] Clearly, Procopius intended to foreground the more unsavory associations and drugs, such as poisons, aphrodisiacs, contraceptives, and abortifacients. Procopius hints at the last when he states that Antonina gained from the *pharmakeusi* knowledge for her own benefit and then, stressing her promiscuity, he suggests that she had borne many children by the time she wed Belisarius. Theodora had a daughter before marrying Justinian, as well as a son whom we are told she tried to abort, evidence of earlier unwanted pregnancies.[62] These details point to the potential unreliability of treatments associated with folklore and superstition, perhaps in distinction to medical prescriptions (though a strict division between the two approaches is a modern one). Procopius intends to shame Antonina by implying that she used contraceptives and abortifacients to cover up her sexual promiscuity, as he did with Theodora. Thus, in that context, Procopius's readers would have understood both women's use of such drugs as shameful. In another context, such as that of bishop Paul's caesarian, any elite, aristocratic Constantinopolitan reader from the period, like an Anicia Juliana, might have understood knowledge of these drugs to simply have been an integral part of a matron's household duties and responsibilities.[63]

This discussion leads to the broader issue of what modern readers might call a woman's right to choose. In the late first/early second century, the Roman satirist Juvenal presents a stinging picture of the factors that affected a woman's right to make choices concerning her reproductive health. Procopius displays familiarity with Juvenal, who is also cited by other sixth-century historians and imperial officials, including John Malalas and John Lydus.[64] In his *Satires*, Juvenal points to the socioeconomic division between poor and wealthy women in Rome:

But at least these [poor] women undergo the dangers of childbirth and put up with all the work of nursing that their position in life forces on them. By contrast, hardly any woman lies in labour on a gilded bed. So powerful are the skills and drugs of the woman who manufactures sterility and takes contracts to kill humans inside the belly. Celebrate, you poor wretch. Offer your wife whatever she has to drink yourself. After all, if she wished to stretch and torture her womb with jumping baby boys, you'd perhaps turn out to be father of an Ethiopian. Soon your will would be monopolised by your discoloured heir—whom you'd never want to see in the morning light.[65]

In a harrowing, if satirical, depiction of intersecting issues, Juvenal confronts a fact that perhaps Procopius would prefer his readers to overlook: those with recourse to safe, reliable, effective, and private abortions were not the wretched lowlifes of the social margins but rather the metropolitan elite. In Juvenal's account, both contraceptive and abortive methods are accessible to the elite, and the drugs are highly reliable and presumably safe enough for common use.

Indeed, in Juvenal's account, the use of such methods was so common among the aristocracy that it is a rarity to see a wealthy woman pregnant— "hardly any woman lies in labour on a gilded bed." This detail helps illuminate Procopius's narrative because, while sex workers may have often resorted to abortive practices, they may not have had access to the most effective drugs and thus their efforts to terminate a pregnancy may often have been futile. In light of this possibility, we should reconsider the possible contradiction between Antonina's cryptic knowledge of *pharmaka* and her bearing of many children, whose existence—like that of Theodora's own two children—suggests that Antonina was not adept, well-trained, or privileged enough to access the proper resources for an abortion. The repeated suggestion in a range of sources that abortion and contraception were relied on by women wishing to preserve their beauty and youth likewise indicates that these methods had established applications well beyond medical need, even if disparagingly attributed to a woman's vanity. Yet the most striking element in Juvenal's satire is the woman's implicit right to choose whether to carry the child to term—"If she wished to stretch and torture her womb." Here, the woman's choice is articulated in terms that reveal traces of the vanity narrative: because her womb will be stretched and tortured, she does not wish or will (*vellet*) to undertake such a physically destructive process. Tongue in cheek, Juvenal remarks that the man himself should be gladly offering up the abortifacients to his wife—"Offer your wife whatever she has to drink yourself"—lest he (presumably a white male) come to father a black, "Ethiopian" son.

The complexities exposed by Juvenal's words are not lost on Procopius, even if he may not wish to spell them out in full for his reader. Later in the *Secret History*, Procopius describes Theodora's unsuccessful attempt to abort a child conceived during an affair:

> It so happened, during the days when she was still on the stage, that she became pregnant by one of her lovers and realized her misfortune late in the term. As usual, she did everything in her power to induce an abortion, but none of her methods rid her of the infant while it was still an embryo, given that it was now close to developing human form. So, as nothing was working, she stopped trying and was forced to give birth.[66]

This passage shines light on the challenge of abortions in the medieval world: in particular, how their timing influences the effectiveness of the methods. While during the early stages of her pregnancy a woman might be able to practice an "expulsive" (*ekbolion*) method, relying on vigorous exercise and activity to expel the embryo, this approach becomes less effective later in the pregnancy.

In Aetius's gynecology, Aspasia's recommendation on when to undertake an abortion is quite strict: in the first month, as already suggested, the woman should endeavor to act in ways opposite those prescribed for avoiding a miscarriage; but, if she does conceive, "the only time to select for an abortion is the third month." Beyond that time, the procedure becomes extremely dangerous for the mother, and it should be attempted only when her life is at risk.[67] Hence, we may reasonably conclude that Theodora's abortion failed because she learned of the pregnancy too late and that her usual methods were thus ineffective. Furthermore, according to Procopius, this pregnancy happened "when she was still on the stage," perhaps hinting that her inability to pursue other procedures, more costly and requiring more skill, was tied to her socioeconomic status at the time. Theodora might have been able to avoid bringing an unwanted child to term later in her life, particularly if she then had access to the knowledge and expertise to which Aetius's medical compendium attests.

The figure of the illegitimate child in both Procopius and Juvenal represents an important concern. Juvenal uses the Ethiopian son to construct a visible difference between the husband and the woman's offspring. By presenting a visible marker of racial difference, Juvenal plays on his reader's assumptions to evoke worries about children conceived in adultery who threaten a husband's patrilineage. Whereas in the case recounted in the *Digest*, a woman performs an abortion to deny her husband a rightful heir, in Juvenal the abortion will ensure that some racially othered child does not inherit the father's name and fortune. A failed abortion, as effectively as a maliciously contrived one, could upset the process of inheritanceand, in both cases, a wife's adulterous actions could jeopardize the man's lineage.

The tension surrounding an illegitimate child is clearly present in Procopius's narrative on Theodora's failed abortion, as he recounts how she handed the child over to his father, who raised him in Arabia. Upon the man's death, the boy returned to Constantinople and made his presence known to Theodora's retinue. Fearing that Justinian might find out about him, Theodora set up a meeting with her son but arranged to have him eliminated; her plan appears to have been successful, though Procopius claims not to know how she made the boy disappear. Here, Theodora's ruthless actions complete the abortion that failed. The explanation of her motive for the murder—"the woman feared lest news of this reach her husband"—is puzzling, however.[68] Procopius has repeatedly declared that, in all matters, Theodora was unmoved by fear, and his statement that "she never did anything because she had been persuaded or forced by another person" has already been cited. It is unlikely that Procopius's Theodora would have been worried simply because Justinian might become angry at her deceit or impropriety. Instead, in light of Juvenal's satire and the countless other legal and literary sources that attest to the challenges to inheritance posed by illegitimate children (at times directly associated with abortion practices), this child may have posed a threat to Justinian and Theodora's empire because of his potential claims of inheritance; this possibility would not have been lost on Procopius's intended readers.

Delving into Procopius's world and the culture of late antique Constantinople, we see that Procopius was shaming Theodora for her seemingly extreme sexual and antireproductive practices. Yet the truth is that Constantinopolitan women—sex workers and aristocratic women alike—engaged in extramarital affairs as well as contraceptive and abortive practices. After relating the story of Theodora's unaborted child, Procopius pivots to attack the moral standing of contemporary Constantinopolitan women in general, thereby pointing to a larger problem:

It was during this time that the morals of almost all women too were corrupted. For they were given full license to cheat on their husbands and no risk or harm could come to them because of their behavior.[69]

This notion of risk-free adultery surely relied in part on access to contraceptives and abortifacients, given this passage's location in the text, that is, immediately after the story of Theodora's disappeared son. But another factor was Theodora's alleged defense of these women, who could launch countersuits against their husbands. These suits, according to Procopius, often left the men destitute after being tortured and imprisoned; thus, as their wives fornicated, men kept quiet out of fear of retribution.[70] What Procopius communicates across these various accounts is that the women of sixth-century Constantinople were acting on their own volition and accord in all matters sexual and procreative, often against their husbands' wishes or knowledge. Moreover, the text strongly implies that the women were either using contraceptives or having abortions, since Procopius in this section makes no mention of children born from extramarital affairs.

Thus, we find in late antique Constantinople and the early Church a grasp, understanding, and promotion of what we might call a woman's right to choose in reproductive and sexual matters. This is not always approved by imperial or religious authorities, nor is it rooted (as it might be today) in notions of individualism. Yet there is certainly an important antecedent for this modern form of thinking. In the fourth century, John Chrysostom addressed the question of a woman's choice to pursue an abortion or to use contraceptives: he condemned the decision, but placed the ultimate blame on the men who copulated with women who did not wish to have children, thus making murderesses out of them. He eloquently writes:

Why sow where the ground makes it its care to destroy the fruit? Where there are many efforts at contraception [*atokia*]? Where there is murder [*phonos*] before the birth? For even the harlot thou dost not let continue a mere harlot, but makest her a murderess also. You see how drunkenness leads to whoredom, whoredom to adultery, adultery to murder; or rather to something even worse than murder. For I have no name to give it, since it does not take off the thing born, but prevents its being born. Why then do you abuse the gift of God, and fight with His laws, and follow after what is a curse as if a blessing, and make the chamber of procreation a chamber for murder, and arm the woman that was given for childbearing unto slaughter? For with a view to drawing more money by being agreeable and an object of longing to her lovers, even this she is not backward to do, so heaping upon your head a great pile of fire. For even if the daring deed be hers, yet the causing of it is yours.[71]

In this damning passage, Chrysostom presents abortion and contraception as crimes so unnatural as to be nameless, "since it does not take off the thing born" but entirely prevents it. Yet his attack is directed at the man, who, by his drunken actions, leads the harlot to commit murder.[72] In his unbridled lust, the man turns the womb from a "chamber of procreation" into a "chamber for murder," and, most crucially, he "arms" or "prepares" (*paraskeuazeis*) the woman for murder.

The reasons why the woman does this murderous deed appear straightforward and accord with those given in other sources: she has an abortion in order to remain beautiful and attract more lovers and—since she is understood to be a sex worker—in order to procure more customers. Remarkably, Chrysostom does not shame the sex worker; indeed, he insists that "you cannot repudiate her for doing this," as it is required by her profession. Thus, he declares in the next sentence, blame ultimately rests with the man: "for even if the shameless act [*tolmema*] is hers, the cause [*aitia*] of it is yours."[73] Chrysostom seems to sympathize with the sex worker's circumstances without condoning her actions. And while he attributes the fundamental cause (*aitia*) to the man, without question it is the woman who seeks out a contraceptive or abortion.

For Chrysostom, the choice results more from male agency than from female empowerment, but regardless, women are left to make the choice and, moreover, know how to perform the procedure. As we saw in the previous chapter, in the Byzantine world considerable attention was paid to a woman's volition in sexual matters, in regard not only to contraceptive and abortive practices but also to the broader issue of sexual consent. In his *On the Nature of Man*, written in the late fourth century, Nemesius, the bishop of Emesa, addresses the question of when various female animals undertake intercourse. He finds it noteworthy that women can decide when to have sex, regardless as to whether they are fertile or already pregnant, precisely because they are not "nonrational" (*aloga*) animals, who seek intercourse only during a determined reproductive period or season. As Nemesius puts it, "[W]omen have their own power of choice [*autexousion*] in sex after conception, just as in other things."[74] Though we are left to speculate what these "other things" (*tois allois*) might be—whether the reference is sexual, reproductive, or something broader—Nemesius's account treats sex in humans as separate from reproduction, emphasizing that the power of choice is what distinguishes humans from lesser beings. Sexual choice is thus presented by this Christian author as the free exercise of reason, rather than as a mindless succumbing to the crude impulses of the flesh.

Using the invective against Theodora in Procopius's *Secret History* as a framework, we have surveyed a range of sources, including legal decrees, popular literature, and epistolary and homiletic religious texts. Throughout these various narratives, while a woman's social position is connected directly to her husband's reputation, fortune, and lineage, the choice as to whether to select and endure abortion or birth appears to have rested firmly (if not solely) in women's hands. As we saw, Juvenal addresses this directly in his satirical depiction of first-century Rome, congratulating the man on his wife having chosen to abort rather than allow her womb to be ravaged by a fetus from an adulterous relationship. Despite legal and religious decrees, canons, and warnings against such methods, the medical guides and herbals all contain detailed information on how to go about producing contraceptives and abortifacients, and even how to surgically remove a fetus, demonstrating a rich and living tradition of medical, folkloric, and magical knowledge on the matter.

In the case of Procopius, behind his attacks on Theodora we sense an uncomfortable truth: contraception, abortion, and adultery were common in his good Christian city, and not just among the lowest ranks of society but also among the aristocratic elite. In her careful and nuanced work on Procopius's representation of Theodora, Anne McClanan explored how the "woman-as-aborter" was a repugnant image for contemporary Byzantine women, noting that this accusation would have associated Theodora with lower-class women.[75] This is surely Procopius's intention and the message he wished to convey to his readers. However, as we have seen, in reality the practice was likely more closely associated with upper-class women—or, at least, there was less socioeconomic distinction than Procopius might have liked. Procopius viewed the women of Constantinople as far too empowered and willing to do as they pleased. While his narrative attempts to decry these behaviors as reflecting untethered lust, moral destitution, or narcissistic vanity, and thus seeks to present Theodora as unnatural and exceptional, he nevertheless (at times unwittingly) provides evidence that the practices are established and widespread.

Yet an important question is left unanswered: why the persistent and gratuitously detailed interest in sexually shaming Theodora and other women of sixth-century Constantinople? Or, rather, from the evidence offered up by the *Secret History*, what role did sexual shaming play in the secular, imperial, and political spheres of the sixth-century city? The use of sexual shaming is central to the *Secret History*'s function as a compromising dossier intended to lay out an alternative history to one presented in the *Wars* and *Buildings*. It is not coincidental, trivial, or merely commonplace that shame is so central to Procopius's rhetoric concerning sexual acts. Indeed, in the chapter's epigraph, Theodora's genitals themselves are reduced to and replaced with "her shamelessness [*akolasian*]."[76] Following her performance with the geese, Procopius declares,

When she stood up again not only was she not blushing with shame but [she] seemed rather proud of this performance. For she was not just shameless [*anaischyntos*]: she was also more accomplished than anyone else at devising shameless acts [*anaischyntopoios*].[77]

This description echoes an earlier description of Theodora:

There was no shame [*ou . . . aidous*] at all in her, and no one ever saw her embarrassed [*diatrapeisan*]. She would provide shameful [*anaischuntous*] services without the slightest hesitation and was of such a sort that if someone slapped her or even punched her full in the face she would crack a joke about it and then burst out laughing.[78]

The subject of similar shaming, Procopius calls Antonina a fearless woman who "never felt shame [*oute . . . aidō*] for anything she did."[79] Procopius portrayed Theodora and Antonina as nasty women who did not know their place and committed egregious deeds;[80] but what seems to have troubled him most was their lack of even a glimmer of shame (*aidōs*).[81]

In Late Antiquity, the rhetoric of sex and shame became a potent tool for shaping early Christian subjectivities.[82] The "shamelessness" that Procopius links to Theodora closely resembles the type most prominently associated in antiquity with the Cynic philosophers. In *Philosophies for Sale*, Lucian's Cynic states: "Do boldly in full view of all what another would not do in secret; choose the most ridiculous ways of satisfying your lust."[83] Theodora may not have practiced Cynicism, but Procopius practiced it on her behalf in the *Secret History*. Like the other established tropes that Procopius deploys, shamelessness fits into classical and late antique stereotypes. Diogenes the Cynic, for example, embodied the image of simultaneous asceticism and shamelessness from the first century onward; he advocated publicly masturbating, defecating, and urinating, as well as incest and cannibalism.[84] Figures such as Origen and Gregory of Nazianzus associated Cynics with cities' marketplaces, and John Chrysostom and Theodoret of Cyrrhus condemned Cynic shamelessness as exhibiting failure to adhere to social norms and codes.[85] Despite these early condemnations, in later centuries the figure of the holy fool and behaviors described as foolishness for Christ would rehabilitate practices of shamelessness into an ascetic method of distancing oneself from the constructs of urban life while critiquing its structures.[86]

Historians of Christianity have attempted to similarly recover shame as a practice. For example, Karmen MacKendrick, Virginia Burrus, and Niklaus Largier explored the pleasures and pain of shame, focusing on the dialectic between shamelessness and the embracing of one's own shame as a site of pleasure, renewal, or arousal.[87] In one thought-provoking study Burrus described how ancient Christians intensified their own shame and transformed it into a site for self-identification. "Martyrdom," she notes, "is the initial site at which shame is converted into defiant shamelessness, giving rise to a performatively queered identity that retrieves dignity without aspiring to honor." Burrus seeks to recover a history of Christian shame by uncovering the inherently queer practices that created such shame-based identities. However, a significant ethical dilemma emerges prominently in her work—the shame-based identities that she discusses are rooted in forms of "self-humiliation."[88]

The literature on shamelessness and shame, often enriched by discourses about sadomasochism, extols the virtues of a shame that is ultimately consensual, self-imposed, or at least self-claimed. But such rehabilitation cannot provide a universal method for dealing with shaming or the shamed, because the ability to construct an identity around shame depends inherently on a certain privilege.[89] Modern studies of slut-shaming and revenge pornography stress that self-harm and suicide by their object often follow. The problem in exalting shame, past or present, is that it misses a simple point: shame also kills. Approaches can extol "self-humiliation," certainly, but surely not the shame that, according to Procopius, Theodora should have felt. To exalt her ascribed shamelessness would validate Procopius's sexual shaming, while simultaneously making Theodora's denuded, sexualized, and shamed body a playground for his heterosexual male viewer's scopophilic imagination. On the other hand, to praise Theodora's shamelessness would do nothing more than treat her behaviors as being akin to those of the Cynic: a deliberate performance intended as a countercultural practice against a modest, shameful society. Such praise again would be complicit with Procopius's assessment that to engage in such sexual practices and choices was to be ridiculous for the sake of being ridiculous. This shame denies the possibility of lived, nonnormative sexual and reproductive practices—which were, in fact, hardly unknown or extreme in sixth-century Constantinople, even though they admittedly defied the prescriptions of imperial and Church authority.

While slut-shaming is endemic to a toxic culture of sexual marginalization, its uses are often political. Procopius's invectives are not merely slanderous inventions or banal rhetorical tropes: he is consciously deploying legal language in order to systematically delegitimize Theodora's political power. Early on, Procopius even shames Theodora for lack of skill in the arts that she ostensibly performed, both elevated and degenerate. Though she may have excelled in all manner at sex, "she had no skill with the *aulos* [a flute], nor could she sing or even perform in the dance troupe."[90] Contemporaneous sources describe two types of entertainers: *thymelicae*, who played musical instruments, danced, and sang; and mimes, who performed burlesque pantomimes and sang crude titillating songs.[91] In this attack, Procopius is further lowering Theodora's social standing by associating her with the latter entertainers. The fifth-century Theodosian Code considered mimes to be the equivalent to sex workers, "who acquire gain by the wantonness of their bodies."[92] Procopius echoed this legal view when, after he criticized her performance, he added that all Theodora had to offer was her youth and "she put her whole body to work for them."[93] Shame in the *Secret History* has a political edge, as it seemingly mirrors contemporaneous deployment of sexual shame as a convenient way to persecute dissenters, competitors, and (perhaps ironically) slanderers.[94]

SLUT-SHAMING AS POLITICAL WEAPON

Beyond shaming Theodora, Procopius repeatedly recounts instances when others in the narrative, including Justinian and Theodora herself, used the revelation or leaking of hidden sexual details to defame a person and destroy their reputation. Procopius was not the only user of slut-shaming; the imperial administration also appears to have employed sexual shaming as a political tactic. For example, Procopius describes the self-serving reasoning behind Justinian's law prohibiting same-gender relations, classified under the complex term of *paiderastia*, usually denoting relations between men and adolescent males:

he issued a law prohibiting pederasty [*paiderastein*], but instead of investigating any incidents that may have been committed *after* the passage of the law he turned on those who had been caught performing this sick act at some point in the past. Moreover, the prosecution of these men was most irregular in that punishment was imposed in the absence of a formal accuser, for example on the word of a single man or a boy, and a slave at that, if no one else happened to be available, even if he had been forced against his will to testify against his master. This was considered irrefutable proof. Those who were convicted in this way had their genitals [*ta aidoia*] cut off and were paraded through the streets in disgrace. At first, however, this atrocity was not inflicted on everyone but only on those who were believed to be Greens or rich or on those who happened to have offended the tyrants in some other way.[95]

Procopius—who clearly does not view same-gender relations positively—uses this story to illustrate Justinian's tyranny and persecution of peoples, noting that the law was in no way equally or fairly applied. Justinian chooses at first to persecute those already found guilty of the deed. Procopius thus implies that Justinian issued the law to go after those who had already been caught and who Justinian knew could be readily ensnared or eliminated by it. Accusations need not even be given willingly; Procopius is clearly outraged that a compelled accusation "was considered irrefutable proof." His outrage is such that Procopius does not rely on his readers' inferences: he explicitly states that Justinian used the law to persecute those suspected of belonging to the opposing faction (the Greens), those with wealth who might potentially compete with or criticize his rule, and those who might simply have "offended" him and Theodora.[96]

Procopius's contemporaries also employed slut-shaming in their attacks on political figures. In his text on the empire's administrative powers, written about 550, John Lydus brutally slut-shames a praetorian prefect named John the Cappadocian, attacking him for having sex with women and adolescent men. One is reminded of Theodora's sexual forays with young men during banquets and picnics when Lydus writes that the prefect:

lived riotously, bathing together with adolescents who were bloomless and not yet masculine-looking because of the smoothness of their body and with licentious harlots, and gratifying his lust both by doing and by submitting.[97]

In its language and vibrancy, the text recalls the *Secret History*, which was also completed in 550/551 and which also reviles John the Cappadocian. The echoes of the *Secret History* in a work that scholars have neither challenged as a historical source nor viewed as whimsical satire underscore the power of slut-shaming in the imperial circles. Furthermore, they hint at the nonnormative sexual and reproductive practices of the Constantinopolitan elite.[98]

In sixth-century Constantinople, exposure of sexual activities and the resulting shame were used as weapons against political figures. Justinian's own actions mirror the approach found in Procopius's *Secret History*. In addition to being castrated, Justinian had those punished for sexual misdeeds paraded through the city afterward. The term for the removed genitals literally translates as "the shameful parts" (*ta aidoia*). Thus, by parading those who by virtue of their shameful sexual act had their shameful parts removed, Justinian created a spectacle of their shame—public, violent retribution for their shamelessness. Procopius details how the slut-shamed Theodora herself used this law against a man accused of slandering her:

She was also furious against a certain Basianos, a young Green of high social status, because he was slandering her everywhere. Basianos took refuge in the church of the archangel, for he did not long remain unaware of her rage. She immediately set loose on him the magistrate in charge of the populace but specified that Basianos was not to be accused of slandering her, but rather of pederasty [*paiderastia*]. The officials pulled the man from the sanctuary and began to torture him with a vicious form of punishment, but when the entire populace saw such misfortune being inflicted on a body that was noble and raised in luxury all his life, they could not bear the sight of it and groaned their lament up to heaven, demanding that the young man be pardoned. But she made his punishment even worse: he lost his genitals and then his life, though without a trial, and his property was confiscated to the treasury.[99]

In this account, shaming engenders shaming. At the same time, the full political force of such sexual shaming is revealed.[100] Even though Theodora could have pursued Basianos for his libel, she demanded that he instead be accused of a crime whose prosecution would defame and shame him—a crime that also featured a public display of humiliation, though here the onlookers begged for forgiveness for the alleged sodomite.

Procopius recounts another story of the same tactics being used against a certain Diogenes because he too was in the Green faction. When Diogenes's popularity helped prevent his condemnation in a public trial, Theodora turned to his best friend, torturing him to elicit a confession. It proved useless in the end, and Diogenes was ultimately acquitted for lack of evidence.[101] Again, Procopius's Theodora resorted to the same tactics of slut-shaming that Procopius used against her in the *Secret History*. For all three—Procopius, Justinian, and Theodora—the goal was to delegitimize the sociopolitical power of the figure in question by revealing intimate details about their sexual proclivities, activities presented as being disgusting and inhuman. Justinian instituted an office specifically charged with persecuting those men "who habitually practiced sodomy, or who had illicit sex with women, along with any whose religion was deviant."[102] Thus, under Justinian's rule we find the simultaneous deployment of sexual shaming and legal persecution to ensure the silencing, torture, and elimination of those who might challenge Justinian and Theodora's reign. In the imperial context sketched by Procopius, sexual shame is less a gendered attack against Theodora than a form of slanderous currency used to silence both men and women whose allegiances, wealth, or outspokenness challenged the imperial hegemony. This toxic culture of slut-shaming targeted the sexual actions and consequent reproductive choices of women and men, who could then be selectively prosecuted.

Modern historians have repeatedly struggled with the question of what exactly the *Secret History* offers as a primary source. While Anthony Kaldellis refers to the text as "our most reliable contemporary source," Stavroula Constantinou and others have dismissed it as "a work of fiction" or the Byzantine equivalent of a comedic and satirical "historical novel."[103] Overall, the text depicts with great specificity the conditions of the empire; its details can often be corroborated in other texts, suggesting that it is one of the more reliable sources for the period.[104] Averil Cameron has pointedly noted that modern male writers have often fawned over Theodora's so-called feminism or feminist actions, such as assisting girls at the court, helping women in distress, and founding a convent for reformed sex workers. These, however, were all deeds that Cameron rightly labels " 'feminine' rather than feminist."[105] In other words, Theodora's so-called feminist actions were rather exactly what one might expect from an imperial woman who, as such, would have dedicated her time to charitable acts and patronage. Though Charles Diehl found in these deeds possible evidence that Theodora had sincerely repented for the actions of her earlier years, or that she perhaps had been a sex worker only by circumstance and necessity,[106] such resolutions offered in modern histories only establish her sexual deeds as inherently shameful and debauched.

Earlier scholarship looked down on Theodora's sinful and immoral acts, while more recent works romanticize narratives of her repentance or misnamed "feminism" in order to depict a historical Theodora that is opposed to the literary depiction of the depraved and misogynistic Procopius. But both these approaches leave untouched the core of the problem: the stigmatization of those nonnormative sexual acts that have persistently drawn the attention of modern readers and saturated the historiographic record and popular imagination for centuries.[107] In her study of the *Secret History*'s typology as an invective against an imperial woman, Anne McClanan concedes that her goal "is not so much to ascertain the sexual virtue of Theodora, a dubious historical enterprise at best," but she does not go as far as embracing the sexual practices that Theodora is accused of.[108]

Averil Cameron has suggested that modern readers have overemphasized the importance of these salacious sections. In her view, they did not have the same hold on Procopius's contemporary readers, "for whom they are partly a literary convention, [and] partly a vivid way of showing the truly exceptional evil of Theodora's nature, whose real sin lay in the harm she had done to the state together with Justinian."[109] Cameron is right in seeing sexual details as merely building blocks in Procopius's case for Theodora's true malice (i.e., her complicity with Justinian and their abuses of imperial power). Nevertheless, this interpretation does nothing to unpack the manner in which the rhetorical deployment of graphic sexual detail was used as a political tactic. Furthermore, it leaves unexamined how, for both modern and medieval readers, nonnormative sexual behaviors and practices were stigmatized, the very process that enabled such behaviors to be wielded as a literary rhetorical weapon by Procopius. Procopius's narrative demonstrates that Theodora's sexual debauchery was only one element of—or a mere symptom of—her and Justinian's "demonic nature." For Procopius, divergent sexual practices function as clearly identifiable markers of this broader evil. With his *Secret History*, he demonstrates the enormous power seemingly banal, salacious, and trivial gossip has in a political state to undermine rulers and dissenters alike—a point underscored by Justinian's own persecution of men performing same-gender sexual acts.

My goal in this chapter has been to understand the rhetorical force of slut-shaming as a practice, whether it is done for a broad audience or only for the perverse pleasure of a small group. In addition, I have shown how slut-shaming deploys not only the expected lurid sexual details but also narratives about contraception and abortion to further shame women as murderers. Ultimately, by closely examining this slut-shaming, we are also able to perceive the immense privilege associated with access to safe reproductive health care, as well as the popularity of these supposedly shameful practices in sixth-century Constantinople. It does not matter whether Procopius's Theodora ever existed or whether anyone beyond a small group read the *Secret History* during her lifetime. An established rhetorical practice since antiquity, the manifestation of slut-shaming reveals much about a culture's practices, prejudices, assumptions, and imaginings about sexuality, gender, and, at times, reproductive choices.

Theodora was slut-shamed, whether she knew it or not, and however she acted. To celebrate her repentance, her charity, her patronage, her contributions to society, or her total innocence without analyzing how slut-shaming operated in Procopius's text—as part of a systematic oppression of nonnormative sexual practice and subjectivities—is neither feminist nor ethical. Instead, it illustrates the use of respectability politics as a form of atonement: celebrating the contributions of members of an oppressed social group in order to suggest that demonstrated excellence, cultural assimilation, and normativity can be reparative. To praise Theodora's shamelessness is not to praise a queer identity; it is to embrace the violent bullying and subsequent marginalization of nonnormative subjects through the imposition of shame. Furthermore, it is to deny the possibility that Theodora could have led a sexually nonnormative life in which her acceptance by fellow marginalized figures allowed her to be free from the horrific violence of shame.

What is necessary is the articulation of an image of a sexually active, promiscuous, abortion-having, orgy-partaking, oral-sex-enjoying, sodomitical Theodora who nevertheless persisted and thrived in the Constantinopolitan social sphere, which included many other figures just like her. This is a celebration of a queered identity: one begotten in the shadows of communities that support promiscuous and shame-free sexual behaviors, and that enable the procurement of contraceptives and abortifacients. Procopius's account offers glimmers of these queer communities in sixth-century Constantinople, found around the theaters and marketplaces, places where a young Theodora or Antonina might learn about all sorts of drugs and pursue various sexual acts free of shame. Regardless of whether Procopius's portrayal of Theodora is at all accurate, it is clear that figures like her did exist in sixth-century Constantinople. The interweaving of law, gender, and medicine by Procopius and the other sources in this chapter provides the foundation for comprehending not only the sexuality of cisgender women in Byzantium but also how gender identity and same-gender desire were conceived and articulated.

III. Transgender Lives

After nine years, they saw that the young girl was beardless and they called her "Hilarion the Eunuch" since there were many such [eunuchs] wearing the habit. For her breasts, too, they were not as those of all women. Above all, she was shrunken with ascetic practices and even her menstrual period had stopped because of the deprivation . . .

The blessed Hilaria, when she saw her lay sister, knew her: but the lay sister knew not her sister, the monk. How should she know her since her flesh had withered through mortification and the beauty of her body had altered, and her appearance, she being naught but skin and bone? Besides all this she was wearing a man's garb.

—*Anonymous,* The Life of Hilarion
  (modified trans. James Drescher)

FROM THE FIFTH TO THE NINTH CENTURY, a number of saints' lives composed in the Greek-speaking Mediterranean detail the lives of individuals assigned female at birth who, for a variety of reasons, choose to live most their lives as monks, usually presenting and passing as eunuchs within male monastic communities.[1] Throughout the ninth to eleventh centuries, more of these stories appeared in the manuscript tradition, suggesting their growing popularity; they were also translated into Coptic, Syriac, Ethiopic, Armenian, and Arabic, as well as Latin and other European languages, fueling the eventual popularity of similar stories in the West.[2] Thirteen of these narratives from the late antique Mediterranean serve as the foundation for the tradition, but in literature from across the medieval world Valerie Hotchkiss has identified no fewer than thirty-four stories of women who dressed as men in some capacity.[3]

The figure of these persons whose sex was assigned female at birth but who later chose to live their lives as men presents a challenge for modern historians attempting to understand their contributions to a history of transgender and gender-variant individuals. This chapter examines how we might not only understand these figures as transgender by contextualizing the narratives within the social, religious, and medical practices that framed their lives but also understand what a transgender Byzantine identity might have looked like in the larger society.

Modern historians usually call these individuals "transvestite" or "cross-dressing" saints, but those labels are problematic for two reasons. First, the term "transvestite" is denounced by all contemporary guides to language on LGBTQ+ matters as a pejorative, suggesting that the practice of cross-dressing is rooted in psychological disorder and eroticism. Second, "cross-dressing" refers to persons who choose, as a form of expression, to dress as but not to live full-time as the "opposite" gender.[4] The term does not apply to the figures discussed here, who lived most of their lives as male eunuchs; theirs were not temporary choices. Terms matter, because they influence the questions we are capable of asking of these sources.

Still, scholars repeatedly have shied away from referring to these figures as "transgender," instead calling them "transvestite nuns," "cross-dressing" saints, or women in "disguise."[5] These pejorative terms, which are pervasive throughout the historiography, negate these subjects' identification as transgender persons. The problem here is less the possible inaccuracy or anachronistic use of the term "transgender" in a premodern context; rather the danger lies in the modern assumptions about a binary gender system and a conflation of sex and gender that the terms "transvestine nuns" and the like imply. As a consequence, in the secondary literature the terms "transgender" and "transsexual" have become synonymous and are used interchangeably. Yet "transsexual" has fallen out of use in contemporary transgender activism and scholarship. This medical and psychological term—often used to describe a person who has or seeks to alter their bodies through hormone replacement therapy, surgery, or both in order to confirm their gender identity—relies on a reductive understanding of gender as biological, binary, and determined.[6] Thus the term is both inappropriate for and unable to cover a gamut of gender expressions.

In contrast, "transgender" is an umbrella term that applies to a variety of gender-variant practices and people, of which "transvestites" and "cross-dressers" are considered to make up an important (but not the only) part.[7] As David Valentine has elucidated in his now classic ethnography on the category of "transgender," as this term came into widespread use by social actors and activists during the early 1990s, many individuals who participated in the transgender community did not always identify as transgender.[8] The label served a key role in structuring a collective community encompassing a range of gender-variant lives and practices, even though at times not all members would have claimed the label for themselves. This tension between self-identification and identification by others is critical, for—as Valentine notes—it draws attention to how the politics of identification are shaped through social power relationships.[9]

While many of the figures discussed here are literary, my goal is to allow them an agency beyond the page that treats them as real and viable possibilities for lived subjectivities. To deny them such agency and plausibility beyond the page would be to continue to deny the feasibility of trans identities in the medieval world and to promote the notion that trans and nonbinary subjects are a modern invention. I therefore will be using "he/him" or "she/her," if those are the pronouns to which the individuals commit in the text, and the gender-neutral singular "they/them" for figures who embrace a gender-fluid or nonbinary identity.

The work of scholars such as David Valentine, Jack Halberstam, and Dean Spade makes clear that we must accept that the category "transgender" encompasses a wide spectrum of gender variation. Furthermore, we must seize its ethical importance for acknowledging and retrieving forms of identification that might not have been available to a person at any given historical moment. Therefore, I apply the term transgender here to figures whose stories tell us that they were assigned female sex at birth but who lived their lives as males, often passing as male-presenting eunuchs. Here I seek not only to consider how we might understand these literary figures as transgender men by contextualizing the narratives within their framing social, religious, and medical practices but also to recognize what other historical transgender identities might have looked like beyond narratives in Byzantium.

TRANS MONKS: THE EXAMPLE OF THE *LIFE* OF MARINOS

The narratives concerning trans monks, whether real or legendary, provide models of what a transgender identity looked like to the Byzantine imagination. To be clear, the extant sources do not provide enough information to support an argument that any of these people felt their gender identity did not match their birth-assigned sex in the way that this subjectivity is simplistically imagined today. Nevertheless, these figures lived most of their lives through a gender expression that did not match their assigned sex, which is more than enough. Many chose to continue living as monks even after their birth-assigned sex had been revealed, while others pleaded that their bodies not be stripped naked at death so that they might retain their gender identities posthumously—though in all the narratives their sex is revealed, often without their consent.

Figures like Hilarion, who appears in the epigraph that began this chapter, suggest ways in which medieval persons constructed a gender identity different from that which they were assigned at birth. Rather than being limited to dress and grooming, the means of transformation affected the very composition of the body, as ascetic practices were understood to wear away the flesh and alter the feminine figure into a more masculine form, into a rougher, darker, and faded beauty. The changes caused by deprivation and malnutrition could include withered breasts and the end of menstruation, as the story of Hilarion suggests. Although many of the transgender monks described in these narratives live their lives and die as men—despite being outed in some way as trans—in other instances, after being outed or forced to out themselves as female, other figures choose to continue their lives as nuns. By analyzing these stories, I explore what differentiates those figures who, after being outed in some way, commit to their identity as men and those who choose to live as cis women.

To explore these matters, we begin by turning our attention to the *Life* of Marinos. His is a typical narrative for a transgender monk, which contains some kind of family crisis, entry into a monastery, conflict, accusation about or outing of their birth-assigned sex, and eventual resolution, usually after the monk's death.[10] In this case, a young child assigned female at birth is raised by his father after his mother dies; once the child has come of age, the father decides that he wishes to join a monastery. Desiring not to be separated from his father, the child asks to have his hair shorn, be clothed as a man, and change his name to Marinos, so that he may continue to share a life with his father. Marinos thus lives his life in the monastery; as is always the case in the Byzantine sources, there the male-clothed female body is understood as being that of a eunuch, an identity that explains his beardless face and delicate voice. Like many of these figures, Marinos is heralded for his great asceticism; he eats only once every other day, a practice that, as I argue below, could have been aimed at stopping menstruation and was believed to reduce the size of breasts. Eventually, Marinos's father passes away, and he is left to bear his truth alone.

One day, Marinos is accused of defiling a nearby innkeeper's daughter; upon conceiving a child after being seduced by a soldier, the young woman blames "the young monk . . . the attractive one called Marinos." Marinos accepts the charges. He says, "I have sinned as a man," embracing the shame of a crime that he did not commit. After he is cast out of the monastery, he lives immediately outside its gates. Once born, the infant is handed over to Marinos, who seeks out milk from some shepherds to feed the child "as its father."[11] After three years, Marinos and the child are let back into the monastery. Eventually, Marinos passes away and is found in his cell. Only then, while preparing to wash the corpse, do his fellow monks realize that Marinos could not have been the one who impregnated the woman. Upon the revelation of this news, the innkeeper is told to repent; his daughter, after confessing her lies, becomes possessed by a demon. When she visits the tomb of the blessed Marinos, the woman is immediately healed of her demonic possession.

In the Menologion of Basil II, an illuminated collection of saints' lives compiled around 1000 C.E., the illustration of this climactic moment collapses the discovery of Marinos's secret and the woman's miraculous healing into a single moment (fig. 3.1). A brother on the far left speaks to the innkeeper at the center, who holds a staff and gazes in judgment at his possessed daughter. She is rushing into the scene; her right leg and thigh are fully displayed to the viewer as she approaches the recumbent Marinos. Her hair stands straight up, electrified, an indication of her demonic possession. The artist has dramatized the moment before the innkeeper's daughter's repentance in front of the deceased Marinos, the act of confession through which this narrative accomplishes its final outing. At the center of the image, Marinos is set on a bier, about to be buried in a female habit. He is thus forcibly returned to his birth-assigned female sex by the artist and narrative alike: the artist and author's implication here is that the miracle all along was Marinos's ability to pass as male.

Consider in comparison the narrative of Matrona of Perge, which features a radically different structure than that of Marinos.[12] Trapped in a physically abusive relationship, Matrona flees her husband and escapes discovery by joining Bassianos, a male monastery in Constantinople, as a eunuch. But, for the entirety of her life, except for the first three years of her monastic career in Bassianos, Matrona lived as a woman. Her story is far longer and more complex than that of Marinos. After the accusation that she is a woman, she spends some years traveling through the Holy Land before eventually serving as the abbess of a convent in Constantinople. In this story, she is outed by a vision that appears simultaneously to the founder of her original monastery—Bassianos—and to another archimandrite at a nearby monastery, informing them that the eunuch in their midst is a woman. Confronting Matrona, the Abbot Bassianos elicits a confession from her as she tells him, "[N]o longer am I thought to be a eunuch, nor to be addressed as Babylas, but am soon once again to be a woman and to be called Matrona."[13] Matrona is then asked to depart the monastery—a

☩ ΤΗ ΑΥΤΗ ΗΜΕΡΑ, ΜΝΗΜΗ ΤΗC ΟCΙΑC ΜΑΡΙΑC ΤΗC
ΜΕΤΟΝΟΜΑCΘΕΙCΗC ΜΑΡΙΝΟΥ ⸪

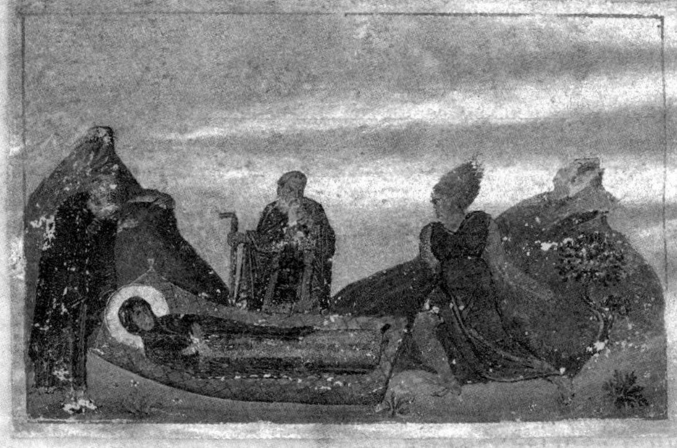

3.1. Entombment of Marinos. Vatican City, Biblioteca Apostolica Vaticana, 'Menologion' of
Basil II (Vat. gr. 1613), fol. 394. © 2019 Biblioteca Apostolica Vaticana.

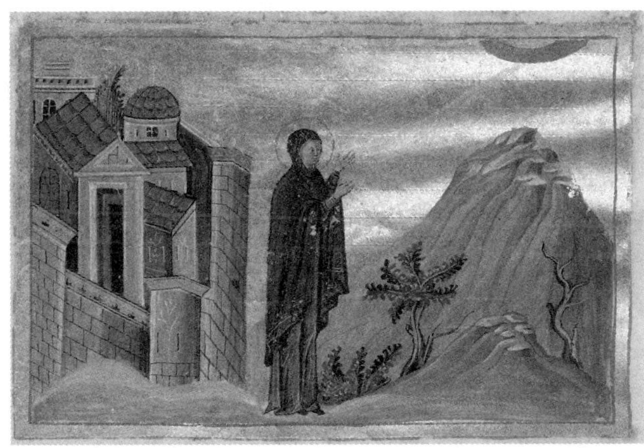

3.2. Portrait of Matrona of Perge. Vatican City, Biblioteca Apostolica Vaticana, 'Menologion' of Basil II (Vat. gr. 1613), fol. 169. © 2019 Biblioteca Apostolica Vaticana.

departure from the pattern in other similar stories, in which fellow brothers help conceal the monk's identity or, alternatively, the saint endures great trials but does not confess to being gender-variant, as in the case of Marinos. Unlike Marinos, in the Menologion of Basil II Matrona is not depicted in any narrative context (fig. 3.2). She is simply standing upright before her Constantinopolitan convent, in the living flesh and wearing female monastic garb, with her hands raised up in prayer to God. Her identity is securely female: there is no climax of outing and deadnaming.

Usually, in these narratives, the saint continues to live as a male eunuch up to their death, even after the revelation of their birth-assigned sex. In the life of Dorotheos, the saint is accused of sleeping with the emperor's daughter and impregnating her. Dorotheos is forced to reveal his breasts to the emperor, who also happens to be his own father, in order to absolve himself of the crime.[14] But, in this case, before his revelation Dorotheos had made his parents promise to allow him to return to the monastery. Dorotheos relieves his sister of her pregnancy—which had resulted from a demonic possession—in an instance of a divinely sanctioned abortion. He then returns to the monastery, dying as a man after he asked his brethren not to prepare the body for burial so that they do not learn about his birth-assigned sex. Comparing the narratives of Marinos and Dorotheos and the story of Matrona, in their different commitments to live and die as men, we begin to perceive the different contours of these figures' gender identities. In another narrative, a figure who has taken on the name Eugenius is similarly accused of being responsible for a pregnancy, but before a public trial begins, the figure reveals her breasts and declares that she is "by nature a woman."[15] Rather than falsely confessing to her crimes or revealing the truth in private so that she might resume her male monastic life, as did Marinos and Dorotheos, she denudes herself and declares her gender identity as female and her name Eugenia.

That Matrona and Eugenia see themselves as women throughout their time in the monastery is a point emphasized by their authors. When asked how she took communion unveiled and how she gave her brothers the kiss of peace on the mouth for years, Matrona replies:

During the divine mysteries I have pulled my cloak halfway over my head, feigning a headache. And as for the symbol of peace and seal of love, I have not shunned it, for I consider that I offered myself not unto human mouths, but unto God's angels and men free of passion.[16]

Matrona's response shows her taking different approaches to two problems created by her gender: a spiritual answer justifies her kissing the other brothers on the lips, but not her taking communion. Instead, she struggles with the fact that she herself felt the need to be veiled as a woman. In the life of Eugenia, we see that during her time at the monastery, she chooses to perform jobs associated with women, such as drawing water from the well, chopping wood for fire, and sweeping the rooms; she "fulfilled all the services of the brethren."[17] These gendered details are not found across all these stories; indeed, often the narrators wish to stress the saints' masculinity even while using she/her pronouns. Moreover, while some saints commit fully to their transgender identities until death, such as Marinos, still others resume their lives as women after a period of time.

TRANSMASCULINITY IN EARLY CHRISTIANITY

To understand the importance of these stories of trans monks in Byzantium, it is crucial to first understand the value of and emphasis on transmasculinity in early Christian piety, even for cis women. In the early Christian world, the emergence of these female-to-male transgender saints can be traced through several possible heritages—from the vestiges of pagan cult practices to the story of Saint Thecla, who in her desire to follow the Apostle Paul said that she would "cut [her] hair off" and sought him wearing "a mantle that she had altered so as to make a man's cloak."[18] Narratives of Christian devotion and piety often evidence a similar cloaking of the female body in a masculine gender expression for the sake of religious pursuit. For example, in the fifth century, Cyril of Scythopolis recounts that a certain Basilina, wishing to visit a holy elder, "planned to put on masculine attire and visit him in the laura." In the *Martyrdom of Perpetua and Felicitas*, in a vision on the eve of her being cast into the arena with the beasts, Perpetua describes her naked body: "My clothes were stripped off, and suddenly I was a man."[19] Here, it is not simply the attire but also the very body of the martyr that becomes male.[20]

This salvific transition from femininity to masculinity has precedent in the roughly early second-century Gospel of Thomas, where Jesus rebukes Simon Peter for suggesting that Mary Magdalene is not worthy of their company:

I shall lead her so that I will make her male in order that she also may become
a living spirit, resembling you males. For every woman who makes herself
male will enter the kingdom of heaven.[21]

The notion that women were to become male is pervasive throughout early Christianity. Since the feminine is seen as entwined with the earthly and sensual desires of the flesh, women should aspire to become like men, unmoved by passions.[22] In the preserved sayings of the desert mother Sarah from the fifth century, we find similar signs that the holy figure's asceticism and triumphs over the demons of fornication and earthly pleasures altered her gender identity. On one occasion, Sarah confronts two male anchorites who sought to humiliate her because of her sex, saying, "According to nature I am a woman, but not according to my thoughts." At another time, when monks came to pay their respects, she "said to the brothers, 'It is I who am a man, you who are women.'"[23]

To become male or to be a man was to conquer the earthly attachment to the flesh and transition from feminine inferiority to masculine superiority. In the writings of the first-century Jewish philosopher Philo of Alexandria, this model of gender transcendence is incisively articulated.[24] In discussing why Moses selected a male sheep to sacrifice, Philo explains that because the sheep is male, it symbolically represents perfect progress:

For progress is indeed nothing else than the giving up of the female gender by
changing into the male, since the female gender is material, passive, corporeal
and sense-perceptible, while the male is active, rational, incorporeal and more
akin to mind and thought.[25]

For Philo, progress is manifested as a rebuking of femininity as such; to become male is to become rational and divorced from the follies of sensual perception. Elsewhere, Philo applies this notion to sense perception itself: he claims that the "ears are more sluggish and feminine [*thēlutera*] than the eyes"—while the eyes anticipate and seek out visible things, hearing involves simply the passive reception of sound.[26] While the statement of Galatians 3:28 that in the kingdom of heaven "there is neither male nor female," all being united as one in Christ, might suggest that an androgynous, dual-gendered body is possible, it appears only as a very basic and rudimentary symbolic formulation early on.[27] As Elizabeth Castelli has cautioned, Philo does not suggest the possibility of any overlap or reciprocity between genders; he only advocates forsaking the feminine in favor of the masculine as a means of transcendence to a higher state of being.[28] Males who condescend to take up the feminine emerge in the Christian tradition exclusively in invectives against same-gender desire, which is taken as synonymous with the feminine identity of a male-sexed body.

This model of gender ascent, from female to male, appears throughout early Christian literature, and this is the context in which the transgender monks are treated by scholars. In reviewing this secondary literature, we find the erasure of possible trans lives and observe a fundamental reluctance to believe in the reality of transgender persons in the medieval world. As Kerstin Aspergen notes in her unfinished study on the ideal of the "male woman," the masculine is not only perfect and good but also virginal, with sensuality and sexuality introduced by the feminine.[29] Attributing the narratives of transgender monks to the Syrian milieu of the late antique Greco-Roman world, Susan Ashbrook Harvey has understood these lives as pointing to a broader and more abstract rebuke of femininity that is in keeping with "the misogynism that had become an integral part of Syrian Christianity, as of the larger church."[30] Caroline Walker Bynum, taking a broader view, understands "cross-dressing" as a "practical device" enabling women to avoid persecution, escape their families, and take on social roles assigned to men alone, while for men it served simply as a "religious symbol."[31]

Jack Halberstam's observations on the modern equivalents of these dynamics help us put the modern historians' responses into context. For instance, Halberstam has noted that female masculinity is often associated with "a 'natural' desire for the greater freedoms and mobility enjoyed by boys," except of course when that masculinity exceeds its bounds and challenges male identity itself.[32] Our evidence for the lives of transgender women is therefore limited, given that men "could have gained nothing socially by it except opprobrium," as Bynum notes.[33] Certainly, it seems inarguable that, as narratives and models of emulation, these stories betray a toxic misogyny in late antique thought and offer proof of the consequential gain to be had by forsaking the feminine. The very fact that the lives of these transgender monks were written, compiled, and widely circulated underscores how positively these stories were viewed.

These transgender saints were thus aspirational models, showing the way for all genders to purge themselves of feminine wiles and weaknesses— but we must not ignore the specific prohibitions against the practices followed by these transgender figures. Cross-dressing in any capacity and in either direction was prohibited not only by biblical tradition but also by Church councils and imperial law codes. Deuteronomy 22:5 states unequivocally that "a woman must not wear men's clothing, nor should a man dress up in women's clothing," both being an offense to God. This edict is reiterated in Canon 62 of the Council in Trullo, held in Constantinople in 692, which decreed that "no man should wear feminine attire, nor any woman that which suits men," particularly addressing such dress in the context of pagan festivals.[34] Earlier, Canons 13 and 17 of the Council of Gangra in 345 prohibited women from wearing male clothing and from cutting their hair, respectively, in both cases specifically rejecting the justification of ascetic practice as pretense.[35] Canon 13 reads: "If any woman, under pretense of asceticism, shall change her apparel and, instead of a woman's accustomed clothing, shall put on that of a man, let her be anathema."[36] Similarly, the mid-fifth-century Theodosian Code states that women who cut their hair "contrary to divine and human laws, at the instigation and persuasion of some professed belief," shall be kept from entering churches, from attending the consecrated mysteries, and from visiting the "altars which must be venerated by all"; and any members of the clergy who allow them to do any of these things shall be found complicit in these crimes.[37] Significantly, beginning with the fourth-century Council of Gangra, these regulations prohibit not just cross-dressing generally, as in Deuteronomy, but specifically cross-dressing by women that has been pursued under an ascetic pretense, as reiterated by the Theodosian Code. In other words, these conciliar and legal decrees demonstrate that the idea of cross-dressing ascetic women in late antique society predates and was not limited to the saints' lives that have come down to us.

These canons and codes suggest that the practice of cross-dressing asceticism by women was more widespread than the textual narratives alone imply, though we are left with a perplexing contradiction between its veneration in later stories and its explicit prohibition. The various laws also underscore that the notion of female masculinity or female masculinization was not simply a rhetorical or symbolic trope in late antique and early Christian literature; instead, the rejection of femininity was manifested in the embodied gender expression of Greco-Roman figures who took on a transgender identity. As the instances surveyed previously suggest, some of these figures presented themselves as men for the sake of their ascetic and devotional pursuits, ranging from access to a holy elder in a monastery to following the teachings of a holy figure—thereby enjoying the social privileges of men, as Bynum noted. However, the texts also demonstrate that some of these figures would come to self-identify and in their bare flesh actually perceive themselves as male, as in the cases of Sarah and Perpetua, respectively. In this context, we must critically examine the implications of taking on the gender expression of a male monastic for a person birth-assigned female, often for the rest of their lives. As the narratives recount, such a person seeks and aspires to fully transform themselves into a man, understood as not just taking on the traits and character associated with masculinity on a psychological level but also physically transforming the appearance of their bodies through dress and fasting in order to effectively pass as male-bodied persons, often, but not always, out of fear of being exiled, ostracized, or harmed by sexual assault.

Adhering to these patterns of male becoming, Basil of Ancyra states in his mid-fourth-century treatise *On the True Purity of Virginity* that, through rigorous ascetic practice, women were to become men; men, in turn, were to join the rank of angels.[38] To become male was, therefore, to become a virginal ascetic: unmoved by sexual desire and the sensuality of the senses, governed by reason and judgment alone. These characteristics were not simply ideated symbols or psychological aspirations but also had an effect on a person's gender expression: both males and females were to avoid any kind of self-presentation that could be understood as feminine. In locating temptation and sexual desire in the feminine, Basil of Ancyra casts virginity not only as pure abstention, but as an active and performative negation of the feminine—both of feminine pleasures in a woman herself and of the pleasures that she might give rise to in men. Basil thus commands that the virgin "must make herself look masculine and her voice hard, and in her walk and generally in every movement of her body constrain the enticements of pleasure." In all respects, her voice, appearance, and movements must be characterized by a firm masculine brusqueness, and her inner emotions must be as dispassionate as if she were an unfeeling sculpted image.[39]

This performance of masculinity is repeatedly staged as being the ideal behavior for a pious Christian woman, even though many of the practices were explicitly restricted by contemporary legal codes that aimed to police and distinguish the dress and behavior of persons according to a strict gender binary. We see here a tension between religious ideals, law codes, and gender identity. The authors of the lives of trans monks were especially adept at playing on and exposing these tensions. In the story of Pelagius, for example, the author infuses the narrative with conflicts in his gender presentation, even when he is passing as a cis woman. In his procession into town, Pelagius, as a wealthy sex worker, presents readers with an ostentatious manifestation of dress and behavior coded as feminine:

This prostitute then appeared before our eyes, sitting prominently on a riding donkey adorned with little bells and caparisoned; in front of her was a great throng of her servants and she herself was decked out with gold ornaments, pearls, and all sorts of precious stones, resplendent in luxurious and expensive clothes. On her hands and feet she wore armbands, silks, and anklets decorated with all sorts of pearls, while around her neck were necklaces and strings of pendants and pearls. Her beauty stunned those who beheld her, captivating them in their desire for her.[40]

Unlike the pure virgin who might work to masculinize her gender expression and remove all form of feminine ornamentation, the figure of the sex worker is allowed an exuberant femininity. The author recounts how the "scent of her perfumes and the reek of her cosmetics" assaulted everyone in the vicinity, while holy bishops sought to avert their eyes "as though she was some sinful object."[41] Certainly, what we are offered here is designed to simultaneously display an excessive femininity (in opposition to his eventual masculine ascetic ascent) and to slut-shame Pelagius for his appearance and garb as a sex worker.

Rhetorically, the assumption of a fundamental opposition between Pelagius's fallen femininity and salvific masculinity is foiled by a telling detail: the author describes sitting in amazement at Pelagius's clothing and the fact that "she went by us with her head uncovered, with a scarf thrown round her shoulders in a shameless fashion, as though she were a man."[42] Loose, unbound hair is often associated with sexually loose women in the late antique Mediterranean, so it would be an apt detail to note in describing a sex worker. But Pelagius's shamelessness seems to be demonstrated more by how he carried that scarf (as a man would) than by his leaving his head uncovered as a sex worker.[43] This detail might be viewed as an instance of foreshadowing or simply another example of his deviant shamelessness. However, the difficulty lies in reconciling this objection to his earlier masculine attire with the later praise for Pelagius's eventual life and death as a male eunuch. Pelagius's life as a sex worker was, by all social accounts, masculine; despite his feminine ties to excessive pleasure and sexuality, he is shown entering as a wealthy figure with a prominent staff and entourage. Transgender monks, like Pelagius, are repeatedly depicted as self-motivated and empowered to seek out the religious life, to break the ties of domesticity, family, or marriage; often, as in the case of Dorotheos, they show precocious devotion to ascetic life from an early age. Thus, we are forced to accept an apparent contradiction: the authors are eloquent in portraying how these figures operated as males in various capacities, including in the fallen state of the highly feminized sex worker, even before they were able to formally transition to monastic life.[44]

THE TRANSMASCULINE BODY OF ASCETIC PRACTICE

Throughout these narratives, from Basil of Ancyra's recommendations for virgins to the extreme ascetic practices of the transgender monks, is a clear and intentional desire to alter one's gender expression and presentation, including the body's secondary sex characteristics. In the case of Hilarion the Eunuch, who appears in this chapter's epigraph, the narrative provides a detailed description of the radical transformation of Hilarion's body as perceived and understood by others. We learn how he was read by others: for example, his "beardless" face caused people to ascribe to Hilarion the gender identity of a eunuch. Hilarion's ascetic actions themselves altered his physical appearance over the years, making him appear more masculine. We are told that his "menstrual period had stopped because of the deprivation," and also that his breasts "were not as those of all women." Hilarion is not unrecognizable simply because of his male garb or haggard appearance: his ascetic practice has directly affected his body's secondary sex characteristics.

That these figures changed their secondary sex characteristics through asceticism and fasting is repeatedly stressed in the narratives; authors particularly point to the reduction of breasts, the cessation of menses, and the alteration of feminine facial features.[45] In the case of Hilarion, the text is not entirely clear as to whether his breasts were "not as those of all women" before he became an ascetic or if his asceticism had changed them, though it seems to lean toward the latter, given both that the passage describes this encounter as occurring "after nine years" and that comments about withered and shriveled-up breasts are found in other accounts, as in the story of Anastasius.

While on his deathbed, Anastasius, who had been living as a eunuch, begs Daniel of Sketis, who knew his life story, to ensure that he be buried with his clothes on so that the other brothers do not discover his birth-assigned sex—a detail found in many of these narratives. As in the other instances, the brother preparing the body for burial is instructed to place the burial garment over what the deceased is wearing. Here, the narrative tells us that, as "the brother was dressing [Anastasius], he saw that on his chest he had women's breasts, looking like two shriveled up leaves."[46] This detail is preserved in both the Greek and Syriac versions, as well as in the Latin, Armenian, and Ethiopian accounts.[47] The Ethiopic text explicitly states that Anastasius's breasts "were dried up from much fasting," thus directly connecting the appearance of his breasts and ascetic practice.[48] The various versions of the story make clear that this brother speaks only to Daniel about what he saw: "Father, did you know that the eunuch we buried was a woman? As I was putting on the burial garment, I felt and noticed that she had breasts hanging down like two withered leaves."[49] He made this discovery only by accident, having "felt" the breasts through the garment; there is no indication in this case that the body was purposely disrobed, against Anastasius's wishes.

How Anastasius's gender identity is constituted from this point forward in the story is revealing. Not only does the brother respect the secret by discussing it privately with Daniel, but Anastasius's identification as a male eunuch is not wholly stripped away. To the brother, Daniel calmly replies: "Yes, my son, I know he was really a woman."[50] Daniel then recounts the story of how Anastasius had been assigned female at birth and raised as a patrician lady in Constantinople whose beauty caught the eye of the emperor Justinian. His romantic interest provoked the jealous wrath of Theodora, and Anastasius turned to asceticism to escape the clutches of the imperial couple. Interestingly, Daniel describes how Anastasius engaged in asceticism along with his monastic brothers, "battering their bodies, and living like angels on earth," even intimating that after ascending from female to male, Anastasius had risen further into the rank of the angels.[51] Daniel concludes his narrative of Anastasius's life with a strong statement:

Let us pray then, my son, that the Lord may hold us worthy of the same course
and way of life, and may we find along with this holy father, mercy on that day;
and together with this father and brother Anastasios the eunuch, may we be
worthy of the kingdom that does not pass away.[52]

Although the author—or perhaps a later writer—appends to this "Now Anastasia was her name," Daniel's words show extreme sensitivity to Anastasius's gender identity, commemorating him not as a mother and sister but as a "father and brother," as well as speaking his male name. Here, the narrative of Anastasius is staged not as a model to be emulated by women but rather as a model for his fellow monks. Moreover, there are clear indications that Daniel, if not the author or a later copyist, wishes to remember Anastasius as a male eunuch, not as a woman.

In narratives that focus on the transformation of the ascetic's body into a masculine form, we also often catch a glimmer of a gender identity that seems to go beyond a mere symbolic or spiritual transformation. For instance, while Pelagius arrived in the story with the display of his femininity as a sex worker, in the later rhetorical inversion of that figure he is radically transformed. In a haunting passage, the former brother of the monastery who assisted in Pelagius's conversion and baptism recounts encountering him much later:

I knocked, and Pelagia, the handmaid of God, opened it. She was dressed in the habit of a venerable man. . . . I failed to recognize her because she had lost those good looks I used to know; her astounding beauty had all faded away, her laughing and bright face that I had known had become ugly, her pretty eyes had become hollow and cavernous as the result of much fasting and the keeping of vigils. The joints of her holy bones, all fleshless, were visible beneath her skin through emaciation brought on by ascetic practices. Indeed the whole complexion of her body was coarse and dark like sackcloth, as the result of strenuous penance. The whole of Jerusalem used to call her "the eunuch," and no one suspected anything else about her; nor did I notice anything about her that resembled the manner of a woman. I received a blessing from her as if from a male eunuch who was a renowned monk, a perfect and righteous disciple of Christ. The holy Pelagia opened her mouth and spoke to me like a man.[53]

This passage clearly describes Pelagius's transition to a male eunuch. Not only is he presented as severely emaciated and fleshless, as one would expect, but the author also uses male stereotypes to underscore the masculinization of his body: his "whole complexion . . . was coarse and dark like sackcloth."

Similarly, in the story of Dorotheos, after spending many years in a marsh his "body became like the skin of a tortoise since she [*sic*] was being eaten up by gnats" and was wasting away from rigorous fasting.[54] Readers would have associated the textures and colors evoked by the descriptions "sackcloth" and the "skin of a tortoise" with the harsh and darkened coarseness of masculine bodies as generally conceptualized. Medical treatises, for example, use similar language to describe women of a masculine composition, whose menstruation is relatedly irregular or absent. As the sixth-century Aetius of Amida writes:

There is a type of woman of mannish traits, dark complexion, strong constitution, robust nerves, with many veins, having thick thighs and big buttocks, broad breasts and shoulders, firm nipples, deep voice, stronger and hairier (than normal). This type of woman menstruates scantily or not at all.[55]

Therefore, we should not read physical characteristics such as described in Dorotheos as being simply indicators of extreme deprivation, fasting, and asceticism—the practices that enabled these figures to pass as male. These physical markers carry meaning with respect to a person's sex. The depiction of Pelagius relies on masculinizing forms of roughness and darkness, and we are told that nothing about his appearance and character "resembled the manner of a woman." Additionally, even though Dorotheos's transformation in the marsh to a rough and dark complexion might be caused by external factors, rhetorically it is this transformation that enables his secondary sex characteristics to be altered in ways consistent with the medical knowledge of the time.

After the physical changes of his body are enumerated, the author repeatedly stresses Pelagius's male gender identity. The brother describes receiving the blessing from him "as if from a male eunuch who was a renowned monk," adding that Pelagius "spoke to me like a man." The latter detail suggests that the character and tenor of Pelagius's voice had also changed. At Pelagius's death, those attending him realize that he had been assigned female at birth. But readers remember how the female-passing Pelagius was introduced into the narrative earlier: even as a highly feminized sex worker, he wore his scarf "as though she were a man." These two appearances—as sex worker and ascetic—though apparently in contradiction to one another, in reality, make legible the outward gender expression of Pelagius's identity and are united by masculinity.

In the end, Pelagius has effectively transformed his body into a masculine form, purging his "astounding beauty" and "bright face"—attributes often associated with feminine beauty. Nevertheless, the masculinity of his garb in a sense has not changed: at the start of the story he wears his garment "as though she were a man" and, in the end, he is "dressed in the habit of a venerable man." In the author's narrative arc, the bodily transformation of Pelagius only completed a path toward masculine gender expression that he had already begun well before his baptism and asceticism. This example hints at a narrative that intimates a monk's gender identity was not solely the result of his asceticism but was to some degree the cause of it—even if that subtle implication would have been legible to a Christian reader only as an indicator of the sex worker's aberrant ways.

GENDER AFFIRMING SURGERY IN THE BYZANTINE RECEPTION OF ELAGABALUS

In sketching out the bodily counterpart to these literary transgender identities, we must consider how medical knowledge shaped notions of gender identity and expression in the Byzantine world—and how medical practices enabled the transgression or affirmation of one's gender. In Late Antiquity, the most detailed narrative of a transgender figure is Dio Cassius's depiction of Elagabalus, who is said not only to have identified as female but also to have actively sought out gender affirming surgery. Elagabalus was a Roman emperor who lived in the early third century and reigned from 218 until her assassination in 222. In his *Roman History*, Elagabalus's contemporary Dio Cassius slanders the emperor's life and deeds. In graphic detail, Dio Cassius recounts horrific and barbaric ritual sacrifices and magic associated with Elagabalus's name, her various marriages, and her lascivious sexual conquests.[56]

Significant for our purposes is Elagabalus's explicit depiction as a trans woman. According to Dio Cassius, Elagabalus "would go to the taverns by night, wearing a wig, and there ply the trade of a female huckster." Repeatedly, she is said to behave like a female sex worker, standing naked in the doorway of the palace while in a "soft and melting voice" soliciting all who went by. In addition, she took on a lover whom she called her "husband" and wished to make a co-emperor, choosing for herself the titles of "wife, mistress, and queen." Only when she sat in judgment of someone in court did Elagabalus have "more or less the appearance of a man, but everywhere else he [*sic*] showed his affectation in his actions and in the quality of his voice." Elagabalus would shave her own face and pluck her hairs out "so as to look more like a woman." She worked wool, wore a hairnet, and painted her eyes. In one particularly disturbing passage, Dio Cassius claims that Elagabalus enjoyed being caught cheating on her husband so that he would violently abuse and beat her, giving her "black eyes," as if suggesting that being the victim of intimate partner violence is a specifically female characteristic.[57]

The figure of Elagabalus confronts us with a slanderous image of an emperor rooted in the tropes of classical and late antique invective—invective that closely parallels what we see aimed at Theodora in Procopius's *Secret History*.[58] Yet, at the same time, Elagabalus's gender expression and conscious self-identification as a woman are unambiguously depicted, even if they are often constituted through her sexual relations with men. In this regard, Dio Cassius's transphobic diatribe may be all too familiar to a modern reader; his description relies on the cruel stereotype of a trans woman that takes a person's gender identity as a by-product of or cover for their own sexual depravity. Nevertheless, through these litanies of so-called depravities, Dio Cassius offers us fragments of historical evidence for a coherent transgender identity and subjectivity, whether or not these were the lived realities of the historical Elagabalus.[59]

Medieval Byzantine historians found the charges of effeminacy and Elagabalus's female self-identification some of the most compelling aspects of her life. The text known as Dio Cassius's *Roman History* is actually a reconstruction pieced together from the writings of a variety of Byzantine historians, most importantly John Xiphilinus in the eleventh century and John Zonaras in the twelfth. The detailed and insightful comments about Elagabalus's gender identity and desires for gender affirming surgery appear in Byzantine sources.[60] In an extant fragment of the seventh-century historical chronicle ascribed to John of Antioch, the author notes Elagabalus's "unmanly adornment" (*anandrōs kosmoumenon*) of herself and her feminine habits. In the early ninth century, George Synkellos describes Elagabalus simply as a "wholly effeminate man, who had turned his character to a feminine one [*epi to gynaikeion ēthos tetrammenos*], adorning himself with and practicing the things of women."[61]

Throughout the Byzantine sources there appears another crucial claim about Elagabalus, at times attributed to Dio Cassius but attested across Byzantine writers: that she not only sought to dress in women's clothing, follow women's grooming practices, and be called by a female name, but also desired to undergo surgical procedures to affirm her gender. In a passing yet telling comment, John Zonaras writes that Elagabalus "carried his lewdness to such a point that he asked the physicians to contrive a woman's vagina in his body by means of an incision, promising them large sums for doing so." A similar request is found in George Kedrenos's twelfth-century

Synopsis of History: Elagabalus, "according to Dio, besought his physician to employ his skill to make him bisexual [*diphuē*] by means of an anterior incision."[62] This detail, whose attribution to Dio Cassius by Kedrenos is plausible, captured the imagination of several other Byzantine writers; the passage is cited verbatim by both the mid-tenth-century Symeon Logothete (also referred to as Leo Grammatikos) and the twelfth-century Michael Glykas in their respective historical chronicles.[63]

Elagabalus's request stresses the desire of this figure (real or imagined) to undergo gender affirming surgery in the late antique world. This point is emphasized by Dio Cassius, who leaves little uncertainty about Elagabalus's motivation. When noting that Elagabalus circumcised herself in order to lead her cult, he writes that Elagabalus "had planned, indeed, to cut off his genitals altogether, but that desire was prompted solely by his effeminacy."[64] These aspects of Elagabalus's gender identity and desire for gender affirming surgery are often the only details provided about the Roman emperor's reign in Byzantine chronicles, a poignant implication for her life.[65]

The salacious details about Elgabalus's sexuality and gender identity were by no means limited to Dio Cassius's work. Similar claims are found in the works of both contemporary and later writers, whose dependence on Dio's *Roman History* cannot be readily assumed. For example, in his *Lives of the Sophists*, Philostratus of Athens tells us that the Roman sophist Claudius Aelianus (a contemporary of Elagabalus) composed and delivered an indignant attack against Elagabalus, called the "Indictment against the Little Woman" (*katēgoria tou Gynnidos*).[66] Several decades later, the fourth-century anonymous author of the *Epitome de Caesaribus* writes that Elagabalus "turned himself into a woman" (*in se convertens muliebri*) and also asked to be called by a female name.[67] The attack by Aelianus referring to Elagabalus as a "little woman" speaks to a widespread perception that the emperor was a trans woman, beyond Dio's account. And while Aelianus's text was long believed to be wholly lost, Steven Smith has convincingly suggested that fragments have in fact come down to us preserved in the tenth-century Byzantine lexicon *The Souda*, providing further evidence that the text was well known and popular in the Byzantine world.[68]

MEDICAL DISCOURSES ON GENDER AFFIRMING SURGERY

While the stories of Elagabalus are unique in their detail and specificity, the notion that surgical procedures could be employed to affirm (or, at times, reassign without consent) a person's gender was not foreign to late antique and Byzantine doctors. Most obviously, they were familiar with the surgical and nonsurgical procedures for the castration of eunuchs in which the testicles were cut out through incisions in the scrotum, crushed, or even dissolved in young children by friction and pressure applied in a hot bath.[69] But, unlike other traditions, such as that of the later Ottomans, the Byzantine process did not involve radical castration: that is, the penis was left intact and eunuchs were often still capable of having erections, posing significant problems for the image of the eunuch in early Christian writings.[70]

Scholars have struggled to understand the gender identity of eunuchs, circling around the realization that they operated in an extremely well-defined gender-fluid category and were staunchly nonbinary. For example, Kathryn Ringrose has proposed that eunuchs functioned in Byzantium as a "third gender," appearing in the writings of figures like Cyril of Alexandria and Basil of Caesarea as "an accursed gender [*genos*] . . . neither feminine nor masculine."[71] Shaun Tougher has added to this conversation by stressing that eunuchs could be considered masculine or feminine depending on the context, particularly in later centuries when eunuchs were viewed with less disfavor in Byzantium.[72] I would suggest that eunuchs served less as a third gender than as embodiments of genderqueer figures. But the most important point is that Byzantine sources themselves consciously and eloquently depicted such individuals as nonbinary and gender-fluid in their bodies, roles, perception, and passing.

Byzantine authors understood castration as feminizing the body and, in a sense, transforming men into women. The more popular writings focused on the psychology, behavior, and appearance of eunuchs. Their character was feminine: that is, it was defined by their inability to control their passions, desires, and appetites. According to Ringrose, Byzantine authors often accused eunuchs of indulging in sexual excess, smelling of musk, weaving webs and trying to ensnare others, having soft and white flesh, possessing high and shrill voices, and, in general, being unable to control their emotions.[73] These are all traits ascribed to women in Byzantine sources. Moreover and significantly, the inverse of these traits appear in the descriptions of the bodies of transgender saints. Basil continued his rant against eunuchs cited previously: "woman-mad, envious, of evil wage, quick to anger, effeminate, slaves to the belly, money-mad, coarse, grumbling about their dinner, fickle, stingy, ready to accept anything, disgusting, crazed, jealous."[74] The eunuch thus powerfully exemplified the malleability of the body's sexes since, as Aristotle wrote, the removal of the genitals alone "results in such a great alteration of their old semblance, and in close approximation to the appearance of the female."[75]

Therefore, while eunuchs were not simply considered to be women as such, and their gender identity could fluctuate between male and female, their body and character were understood to have been transformed surgically into feminine form. In his treatise *On the Nature of Man* from around the ninth century, Meletius the Monk dedicates a passage to distinguishing between the natures of the male and the female. Building upon the work of earlier medical writers such as Hippocrates and Oribasius, Meletius writes:

> And women also have all the same parts as men only internally, not externally . . . Everything else is similar, except in masculinity versus femininity. For while some have masculinity not only in what is called the generative parts [i.e., the genitals], but also in power and intellectual perception, and character and state of health, others have femininity in condition and in physical weakness and in overall constitution . . . And yet some say that masculinity in man is in the testicles, that having cut them off they are made feminine, and come to resemble women, not having a beard, nor having the natural ability to procreate children. Wherefore Gregory the Theologian calls them ambiguous in terms of their "race [i.e., gender]" [*genos*] and they exchange even their masculine voice, and they often perform services like [women].[76]

By presenting the sexes as essentially being one and the same Meletius's text offers a glimpse into theories of sexual dimorphism in the Byzantine world.[77] While he does not fully relinquish the notion of an inherent difference between the sexes, Meletius does emphasize the malleable nature of the human body, of secondary sex characteristics, and of a person's psychological character.

Most interestingly, Meletius expresses the idea that masculinity and femininity are tied not only to a person's genitalia but also to the nature of their character, as in a man who is feminine in "physical weakness and in overall constitution." While peddling earlier stereotypes, Meletius's text captures a sense—closer to our own understanding of the term—that gender exists largely on a spectrum, with the genitals perhaps playing a role in determining it but being by no means the defining factor. In the late eleventh century, Michael Psellus rejoices at the birth of the emperor's son in a letter, expressing their joy that the child has been assigned male at birth but also questioning that response: "What does it matter if the child has been stamped in this way or that, more feminine or more masculine?"[78] In this letter, Psellus's use of the comparatives "more feminine or more masculine" (*thēlukōteron, ē arrenikōteron*) presents sex not as a binary, with only two possible categories, but rather as a difference of degrees. In his study of the passage, Stratis Papaioannou understands Psellus to be describing social gender rather than biological sex, while nevertheless struggling with the verb "stamped" (*diatypoun*), which—because it alludes to material form— suggests that sex is involved.[79] I see instead in Psellus a nuanced under-standing of the exchanges between sex and gender: Psellus is here more acute than our modern scholar in acknowledging that the medicalized no-tion of sex as a biological binary is as much a sociocultural construct as is gender. The various sources, both religious and medical, that we have sur-veyed thus far on matters of sex and gender demonstrate that the two are not understood in isolation and that manly women and womanly men are just as real and pervasive as cisgender men and women. Today, we might say that Psellus is embracing the fact that the child is being assigned male at birth, but that their gender expression and identification might well not align with that assignment. And, as we will see, Psellus did not believe that their own gender identity matched their assigned sex.

Medical handbooks show this nuanced interplay between the catego-ries of sex and gender in the way that they address individuals who have physical characteristics that could be ascribed to the other: namely, women with an enlarged clitoris or men with enlarged breasts (gynecomastia). In both cases, the texts recommend surgical procedures to correct these so-called deformities or improprieties, described as causing shame in those who have them precisely because they cause incongruity with the individ-uals' assigned gender. The seventh-century physician Paul of Aegina justi-fies surgery for gynecomastia as follows: "Since this [condition] carries the unseemly disgrace of effeminacy, it is proper to operate upon it."[80] Thus, gynecomastia is cast as a challenge to the man's gender identity, which is affirmed by an operation to remove his enlarged breasts. Paul gives careful instructions—differing for moderate and severe cases—for how the inci-sions are to be made to remove the excess buildup of fat that is responsible for the problem; his techniques are in keeping with modern surgical prac-tices of breast reductions.[81]

In the case of an enlarged clitoris, the same logic is used to justify what today we recognize as female genital mutilation. In his gynecological trea-tise, Aetius of Amida states that in some women the clitoris reaches a size that constitutes a deformity and thus may "lead to a feeling of shame," but gives no further explanation. The usual reasoning behind surgery is that the clitoris becomes "greatly irritated by constant contact with the clothing and stimulates venery and coitus," thus presenting the condition merely as a problem related to female sexuality and desire.[82] However, Paul of Aegina expands on this matter by explaining that, in some women, the enlarged clitoris becomes unseemly and results in shame, because "some women have had erections of this part like men, and also an impulse toward frequent sexual intercourse." In the preceding entry, which is devoted to intersex persons, Paul notes that some women have what appear to be a man's genitals—"there being three bodies projecting there, one like a penis, and two like testicles."[83] But the entry on an enlarged clitoris contains no suggestion that the woman is intersex. Significantly, Paul states that the clitoris should be trimmed because it behaves like a penis in its ability to have erections and generate sexual desires akin to those of men. It is even possible that in mentioning a similarity with male sexual desire (as does Aetius), Paul is referring not simply to constant or repeated lust but also to a desire for women.[84] Again we see a sense that these operations are intended to affirm a person's gender by surgically altering characteristics of their bodies because those characteristics are associated with the opposite sex. "Shame" here thus appears to be a stand-in term for a sort of gender dysphoria.

As we have seen, there was a gamut of surgical and nonsurgical procedures in the late antique and medieval Byzantine world aimed at altering primary and secondary sex characteristics. In his chapter on circumcision, Paul of Aegina recommends the use of this procedure when the foreskin or glans of the penis is diseased. When the whole glans is affected, Paul instructs the surgeon to cut the penis as necessary and insert "a leaden tube into the urethra" in order to enable the patient to urinate.[85] These directions suggest that the safe removal of the penis was not beyond the skill of Byzantine doctors. Mastectomies played a crucial role in the prescribed cures for breast cancer. Following ancient writers, Aetius of Amida provides instructions for the procedure, primarily for women but also for men "who have large and fleshy breasts," given that they are also susceptible to this ailment.[86] It is doubtful that penectomies and mastectomies were offered electively, but the inclusion of the procedures within medical texts speaks to a host of medical practices associated with Byzantine ideas of gender and its treatment.

Furthermore, medical authorities recommended surgeries for gynecomastia and scrotal *rhacosis* (the presence of excess skin around the scrotum), problems that are neither life-threatening nor physically impairing.

These cases suggest that Byzantines did perform some elective cosmetic surgeries. Various medical writers, particularly the fourth-century Oribasius, provide detailed instructions for a range of cosmetic surgeries, from the removal of varicose veins to the correction and reconstruction of facial defects in the eyebrows, forehead, nose, cheeks, and ears.[87] We cannot rule out the possibility that an elective surgery could have been undertaken to alter the physiognomy of the body so as to adhere to one's gender identity, despite not appearing in the textbook prescriptions that have come down to us.

To my knowledge, there is no extant record of a late antique or medieval doctor performing (or being asked to perform) an operation akin to that requested by Elagabalus. Yet a number of surgical procedures known and practiced in the Byzantine world did seek to alter or confirm a person's gender identity: these ranged from castration intended for a man transitioning to a eunuch to surgeries intended to "correct" the gendered deformities (as they were perceived) of gynecomastia or an enlarged clitoris. I propose that such practices be seen in tandem with the bodily modifications undertaken by transgender monks, who sought to purge the secondary sex characteristics of their female-sexed bodies. As I have shown, the narratives of transgender monks' lives not only provide strikingly precise descriptions of their masculinized female bodies that accord with contemporary medical treatises but the lives also demonstrate that the asceticism of these women might have been practiced to intentionally transform their female bodies into more masculine forms.

NONBINARY AND GENDER-FLUID IDENTITY

In order to perceive any spectrum of transgender persons in the late antique and Byzantine world, we must understand that such individuals could not always present themselves in accordance with their gender. Furthermore, we must move past medicalized notions of gender—even medieval Byzantine ones—in order to acknowledge the gender-queer, nonbinary, and gender-fluid dimensions of trans identities. Therefore, to seek out the hidden trans figures in Byzantium, we must excavate these subjectivities elsewhere. For example, we can consider the gender identity of the eleventh-century court philosopher Michael Psellus, who in their letters repeatedly refer to themselves as being feminine, although birth-assigned masculine. In one instance, Psellus writes that while they have a masculine disposition toward learning, "with regard to nature I am feminine [*thēlys*]," for they are "softened [*malthakizomai*] with respect to natural emotions." Elsewhere,

Psellus observes that "my soul is indeed simply feminine [*thēlys*] and easily moved toward compassion."[88] While this form of feminine identification has precedent in the late fourth-century writings of Synesius of Cyrene, Stratis Papaioannou notes in his careful study of Psellus's gender identification that "what is virtually unprecedented" is that Psellus "does not simply express his [*sic*] emotions. Nor, as it were, does he merely confess the excessively emotional sides of his personality. Rather, he identifies female affects with his unique 'nature' and 'ethos'" and these become a "fundamental feature of the author's persona."[89] Papaioannou refers to this as Psellus's "rhetorical transvestism,"[90] yet I believe that his observation should be pushed further: we should recognize that the case of Psellus offers the schematics for a marginalized transgender identity in Byzantium.

Repeatedly, Michael not only identifies their soul or nature as feminine but also recounts the ways in which they do not adhere to the masculine gender identity that an imperial philosopher should have. Psellus states in a letter that they have always been feminine in their emotional states and interests: "Now if this pertains to a feminine [*thēleia*] soul, I do not really know; at all events, my character [*ēthos*] has been stamped in this way all along," thus comparing their gender to a bit of malleable wax. Almost defiantly, Psellus refuses to be limited to the stereotypes of their assigned gender, explaining in a lengthy excursus that they will behave in ways ascribed to more than one gender. For example, they philosophize while also chatting "with friends in a jolly spirit" and not despising "the women's chamber to indulge in that quarter a bit." Even Michael's surname hints at the rejection of social norms; *Psellos* (gr., Psellus, lat.) appears not to be patronymic, but rather a slur for one who lisps. Psellus concludes with a poetic observation about their gender identity, comparing it to the tuning of an instrument (and possibly playing with notions of masculinity and femininity with the reference to low and high pitches): "For my soul is fashioned to be receptive toward every form of both Muses and Graces. I am not like the strings that are either only high-pitched or in harmony, but contain every melody, now more clear and sweet-sounding, now taut and noble."[91]

Psellus's writings offer a potent comment on gender fluidity in the Byzantine world. This highly learned figure—this court philosopher—contemplates the sociocultural makeup of their profession and assigned gender, which conflicts with their own self-identification as female in matters of emotion, affect, and social behavior. Important for our purposes is that Psellus tests the boundaries of what it means to perceive a transgender subjectivity in the Byzantine world. Their life demands that we look past outward gender presentation alone. In analyzing the past, we can and should look at how authors perceived themselves according to the rubrics of what it meant to be male and female in the late antique and medieval world. But we should not limit ourselves to that binary. We should make use of the evidence that these texts offer us, for they are candid self-assessments offered with all the sincerity of modern-day self-identification as enby (non-binary).

In the encomium for their mother, Psellus recalls an individual with a similarly unsettled gender identity. Suggesting, perhaps, their own emotions, Psellus writes: "the fact that she [Psellus's mother] happened not to be a man by nature [*arrena tēn physin*] and that she was not allowed to study literature freely caused her anguish [*en deinō epoieito*]."[92] Again, we can appreciate how Byzantine figures articulated the suffocating limitations of their assigned gender identity. This desire to participate in aspects of another gender should not be understood merely as women wishing to perform tasks or enjoy privileges afforded to men, as the case of Psellus's mother emphasizes. Instead, we must appreciate Byzantine writers' self-awareness about how unsettled and fluid gender identity was in medieval Byzantium and continues to be today.

In his late twelfth-century history of the empire, Niketas Choniates attributes a similar frustration with assigned gender identity to the early twelfth-century empress Anna Komnene, herself a student of Psellus and known as the first female historian in the Western canon.[93] Choniates recounts Anna's complaints about her husband, the military general Nikephoros Bryennios:

It is said that the Empress Anna was annoyed about the frivolousness of that man [Bryennios] which caused her terribly to rage [*paschousan deina diapriesthai*] and blame nature [*tē physei*] the most, putting the not-small blame on it for spreading and hollowing out in her the opening [i.e., female genital] [*diaschousan to arthron kai egkoilanasan*], while extending and rounding the member [*to morion apoteinasan kai sphairōsasan*] for Bryennios.[94]

Like Psellus's mother, Anna is said to suffer terrible anguish (*deina*), for which she blamed nature (*physei*) because it gave her a vagina and her husband a penis. Beyond this sensationalist complaint ascribed to her by Choniates, however, Choniates's choice of participles to describe nature's molding of their genitalia is provocative. Much like Psellus's comparatives "more feminine or more masculine" (*thēlukōteron, ē arrenikōteron*) when musing about the birth of the emperor's child, Choniates's participles stage male and female genitalia as not finite and fixed. Instead, they are one and the same—in one case having been extended and rounded; in the other, spread and hollowed out. Yet nature is rebuked as having acted in error: for both Anna and her husband, their genitalia did not match the gender identity of their personalities.

The twelfth-century rhetorical exercises of Nikephoros Basilakes provide further evidence that gender fluidity was a noticeable presence in the Byzantine world; the exercises wrestle with the role of "nature" in the assignation of gender when a figure does not adhere to their assigned gender. In an example of a refutation, Basilakes takes issue with the pagan story of Atalanta, the beautiful virgin huntress, suggesting that the story is unbelievable and implausible because of her conflicted gender identity. He writes, "[T]hey make her out to be a woman, but they rob her of the characteristics of a woman, and although they agree that she is female, they praise her for her masculinity."[95] For Basilakes, these elements present an impasse—how can a woman exhibit the characteristics of men? As we read these twelfth-century words, we must keep in mind that Basilakes is writing just as the lives of the various transgender saints were becoming increasingly popular. In the story of Atalanta, we confront not male effeminacy but female masculinity, which all the Christian sources have praised and extolled as the apex of that lesser sex's progress toward the divine. Nevertheless, we find in Basilakes a ferocious attack against such gender fluidity, presumably because in the story of Atalanta what is being practiced is not ascetic endurance but feats of athleticism rivaling the skill of men.

For Basilakes these activities challenge Atalanta's feminine gender identity, for how can a woman still be a woman if she is raised and behaves like a man, and how could her virginity be guaranteed if she is repeatedly exposed to men? In a disturbing turn of words, Basilakes even seems to suggest that a woman who lives a manly lifestyle is making herself likely to be raped:

She spent time with men, and this lifestyle is hostile to virginity. For as soon as one sees a girl, he casts his eyes entirely upon her beauty, and from that point on there is talking and wooing and love gifts; sometimes lust even excites violence [i.e rape] [*bian erōs epēgeire*].[96]

Thus, Basilakes says, "her virginity was not unquestionable." The implication of saying that lust has even aroused "violence" (*bian*) is clearly meant in this context to denote rape. The strong implication is that Atalanta has either succumbed to the wooing of her suitors or, if not, she has most certainly been raped. The text thus shames the victim for her rape, through slut-shaming and by degrading an aspect of her lifestyle. This embodies a perpetuation of a rape culture that understands women who are seen as masculine (owing to their sexual orientation or gender presentation) as valid targets who should be raped as a retaliatory lesson in the virtues of heterosexuality and gender conformity.

In other words, in Basilakes's discussion of the story of Atalanta, we perceive the systematic discrimination to which a gender-nonconforming person was subjected and how it intersected with the female gender-identity ascribed to her. Furthermore, Basilakes states that clearly Atalanta "could not have been beautiful," since she was a hunter and spent all her time in the sun's rays, "which darken [*melainei*] youthful good looks and perhaps would have seriously diminished her beauty." Thus, in addition to critizing her sex, gender identity, and presumed sexual history, he also construes Atalanta as being dark-skinned, with a complexion comparable to the black skin of the "Ethiopian race."[97] As we saw in the narratives of Mary of Egypt, Hilarion, Dorotheos, and even in Aetius of Amida's description of manly women, dark skin was repeatedly associated with masculine women, a connection that added to the realities of their systematic oppression and marginalization: in becoming transmasculine, these figures also are often racialized.

In this attack on gender nonconformity through the figure of Atalanta, Basilakes sets forth his concern about the fluidity of gender and the ease with which a person could transition genders, a process he explicitly describes in those terms. In what is perhaps one of the most lucid Byzantine reflections on gender transition and confirmation, Basilakes reflects on Atalanta's upbringing:

But if she was not raised in the ways of women, then she also transitioned her gender [*to genos parēllatte*]. For one's upbringing confirms one's gender [*bebaioi . . . to genos*], and for the different genders the ways of upbringing are correspondingly different. You tell me that Atalanta's father is Oeneus, and I accept that. You posit that she is a girl [*parthenon*], and I believe you. Then you should also restore to her an upbringing befitting a girl. As you are now molding her female in nature, but male in behavior, then also her paradoxical upbringing throws her gender into doubt.[98]

This account is breathtaking in what it reveals about the perceived fragility of gender in Byzantium. The clarity of the language in discussing gender transition is striking—the term *parēllatte*, or "transitioning," literally means a transposition or alteration; and "confirmation" (*bebaioi*) denotes the act of firmly establishing something or affirming it without a doubt. In a sense, Basilakes's view of transitioning is even more progressive than the modern medicalized notion that relies on a transgender person's ability to confirm that they have undergone a nexus of medical procedures before their gender can be affirmed in matters ranging from legal documents to bathroom access.[99]

For Basilakes, the intervention that modifies a person's gender is their lifestyle and upbringing: these "confirm" the gender that they have been assigned at birth. In the next section, Basilakes highlights the function that gender assigned at birth plays in a person's life, noting that "[a]s soon as an infant is born a woman and goes into the light, at the same time she enters the women's quarter,"[100] where the process of confirming her gender as female unfolds as she is trained by her mother in the conduct of a girl. Once again, we sense the tenuousness of gender identity, for immediately after assigning the child's gender at birth it becomes necessary to begin her confirmation as female. Hence, as Basilakes stated previously, while Atalanta might have been born "female in nature" (*physin men thēleian*), she is wholly "male in behavior" (*tropon de arrena*): that is, in her way of life, customs, and manner of carrying herself.

Yet the most striking aspect of Basilakes's account is that he does not see gender transformation as simply divided between "nature" (*physin*) and "behavior" (*tropon*). Instead, he raises the possibility that Atalanta is a person who while "being female, was made masculine in nature" (*thēlys ousa, tēn physin ēndrizeto*). In this striking turn of phrase, Basilakes demonstrates his consciousness of people whose birth-assigned sex does not agree with their internal gender identity. Admitting that, in theory, Atalanta might have been a man in nature despite "being female," Basilakes vehemently rejects the notion that this identity was possible for the adult Atalanta—not because such a subjectivity does not exist but because it is the role of upbringing to affirm (or, in this case, reassign) one's gender to conform (or not) to what is assigned at birth. Thus, in attacking the claim that Atalanta competed in archery and at the same time displayed virginal piety, Basilakes emphatically writes:

No, for my part I do not see how anyone would believe this. For even if we
were to grant that the girl was like that by nature, surely, how would her
mother—if she did not give the lie to that name—have let her outside women's

quarters and also have released her from her hand, the girl whom she was supposed to train right up to her wedding day?[101]

Here, we see childrearing being treated as a form of gender conversion therapy, particularly in circumstances in which a person's gender identity "by nature" (*physeōs*) does not adhere to their birth-assigned sex. Thus, failure to enforce gender norms becomes the mother's fault. If the mother does not enforce the femininity of their birth-assigned-female child, then she cannot truthfully claim the title of "mother."

Nikephoros Basilakes's words help contextualize the stories that we have examined thus far, throwing light on Michael Psellus's earlier statement about their gender identity. We can see clearly that Psellus was confirming a gender-fluid identity for themselves, flowing between the philosopher's work and the chatter of the women's quarters, the adamantine resolve of thought and the impassioned emotions of human relations. Basilakes's words encourage us to take seriously the claim of a transgender identity for the various trans saints that we have considered throughout this chapter. In his invective against nonnormative gender identity, mediated through a reflection on pagan literature, Basilakes reveals his own hesitations on the fragile divide between binary gender identities, which, he fearfully believes, without indoctrination and policing is easily erased. His text attests to the reality of a relatively well-defined transgender identity that scholarship has for decades assumed did not exist in the Byzantine world. In his condemnation of it, Basilakes has unwittingly demonstrated that the Byzantines understood that there are people who, despite their sex assigned at birth, by Basilakes's own admission, "by nature" do not conform to that gender.

The figures discussed throughout this chapter push against expectations of gender identity in the medieval world and demand a re-evaluation of what transgender identities looked like in Late Antiquity and the Middle Ages. Operating as nonbinary, genderqueer, and gender-fluid figures, eunuchs presented a space for maneuvering around binary gender identities. Eunuchs were also vivid demonstrations that surgical interventions could alter the secondary sex characteristic of the body, as noted by authors from Aristotle to Meletius the Monk. Eunuchs not only allow a space to maneuver for trans monks and other nonbinary identities but also are themselves transgender people of Byzantium—indeed, they present the most visible, prominent, and well-articulated trans identity in the empire.

Rather than struggling with applying modern categories to represent medieval realities, I have repeatedly confronted how the figures discussed throughout this chapter undercut *our own* expectations of gender identity in the early Christian and medieval world and *our own* anachronistic notions of a binary gender construct. If we accept that transgender subjects are not a modern phenomenon—a reality we must accept, lest we deny the lives of trans people today—then we must recognize that these monks and other related figures could have been people that did not identify with the gender they were assigned at birth. At the very least, we must respect that these stories would have offered up effective models with which transgender audiences could have found ways to shape their own subjectivity. There is a longstanding resistance to affirming trans medieval figures. The common premise is that since such language did not exist back then, these persons could not identify as "trans" and therefore cannot be described as trans today. Trans denialism precisely operates by insisting on the "trans-" prefix in order to fundamentally deny, qualify, or somehow input a person's gender. Fundamentally, this view insists on withholding a trans person's gender (past and present) unless it can be somehow qualified. Having read this chapter, I hope that the reader can appreciate the narratives of these Byzantine monks who were assigned female at birth but lived their lives as men as evidence for the complexity of gender variance and nonconformity in Byzantium. But, more importantly, I hope that the reader can respect these figures as men.

These recalibrations in our perspectives of what being transgender means in the Middle Ages reveal a range of sites available to premodern, non-cisgender persons for self-identification: not as queer, abject, and aberrant social figures but rather often within the normative practices of Christian worship, asceticism, and empire. The notion that to be a transgender man in early Byzantium would *not* have been a radical queer practice is deeply powerful. Equally powerful is the simultaneous existence of deeply queer transgender women, whose stories barely come down to us—and only filtered through screeds of transmisogyny when they do. There are two important implications here. First, we need to expand what we understand as a transgender subjectivity in late antique and medieval studies. Second, we need to shift away from an implicitly binary conception of sexuality, abandoning discussions of same-*sex* desire in order to understand the complexities of same-*gender* desire. The historian's work is to perceive these possibilities, express them, and go on to examine how other intersections of identity, like sexuality and race, have contributed to the erasure and preservation of these various lives.

IV. Queer Sensations

Then [Christ] turned His words to the unbelieving disciple [Thomas], and permitted him to feel His hands and side, and graciously showed His bared side, in confirmation of the resurrection, in the very bone and flesh, but free of all fatness, and with an opening which gaped so as to receive the hands of the disciple, which the impact of the spear made as it struck heavily there . . .

But Thomas, as he hears and sees these things is seized by fear, and does not in any fashion dare to draw near the Savior, but indeed trembles and begins to draw back, withdrawing his foot, he who a little while before was bold and contradictory and set himself against everyone; for he does not quite dare to touch the body of the Lord. But the disciples resist him and push him forward from behind, repaying him for his disbelief in them and in the Teacher Himself, and with force they constrain him to approach the Teacher, though he resists as much as he can with his feet. So he, though unwillingly, stretches forth his hand, with his eyes opened to their widest, free from all rheum and flux and murky accretion. The Savior, however, assumes the posture in which He received the wound and bends over and seems almost, so to speak, to fear the touching of the scar. The hand of Thomas enters in at the side of the Savior like some spear stretched out far and pressed against an unresisting body, and it scrapes closely at the wound like some instrument of Paieon, and tries to tear open the wound. The side seems to shrink from Thomas' continued handling of it, and wishes to pour forth blood and water again.

—Nicholas Mesarites, Description of the Church of Holy Apostles *34.2–7*
  (modified trans. Glanville Downey)

THE STORY OF THE DOUBTING THOMAS is one of the more charged plots in the history of Christianity, rooted in the failures of faith that transform into a vocal confirmation of belief. After presumably touching the wounds of Christ as he has been instructed to do, Thomas exclaims, "My Lord and my God!" (John 20:28), attesting to his recognition of the true body of Christ. To this Christ replies, "Have you believed because you have seen [*heōrakas*] me? Blessed are the people who have not seen [*mē idontes*] and yet have believed" (John 20:29). In this moment, the contours of a Christian subjectivity are fleshed out through two simultaneous gestures: Thomas's recognition of the body of Christ as his Lord and God, and Christ's reworking of sensory confirmation and faith. In other words, the Christian subject must have Thomas's emphatic recognition of Christ, yet that recognition must emerge through hearing alone, without the additional confirmations of sight and touch. This narrative embodies and subverts the history of ancient and late antique perception, which, in cataloguing the strengths and weaknesses of each of the senses, generally elevated sight above all, yet considered touching and tasting to be the most adept at countering the potential deceits of vision. The oddity of this subversion is matched by another queerness—namely, the erotic undertones of the scene, as Thomas inserts his flesh into the opening at Christ's side.

In the passage that began this chapter, Nicholas Mesarites, an ecclesiastical official in early thirteenth-century Constantinople, describes the images in the Church of Holy Apostles. His description of the scene of the Doubting Thomas animates the events depicted, conveying the thoughts and responses of the Apostles and Christ. With clear and graphic detail, Mesarites alludes to the dual queerness of the narrative: the penetrative eroticism of this scene between men and the medicalized presentation of sensory perception in this moment of encounter. In this chapter, I suggest that these two threads are intimately entwined: the senses are sexualized in a manner that often structures a queer desire toward Christ, whose image is similarly revealed and validated through the notion of a same-gender union in flesh and spirit. I argue that implications can be drawn between many instances of same-gender desire and a figure's approach through their senses to the body of Christ in an icon or the Eucharist. To begin, we must first contextualize the place of same-gender desire in the Byzantine world, before moving on to consider the associations that could have emerged in this cultural space.

THE QUEERNESS OF BYZANTIUM

Modern historians view Byzantium as very queer in ways ranging from the repeated attacks on the Byzantines' excesses and moral corruptions—rooted in tropes of "the servile and effeminate Greeks of Byzantium" in Edward Gibbon's *Decline and Fall of the Roman Empire* (1776)—to the association of "Byzantine" with queer figures in twentieth- and twenty-first-century popular culture.[1] In the historiography that followed, the empire was maligned and marginalized precisely for the perceived inversion of gender roles that produced effeminate men and manly women. Deeply entwined with Orientalism, the ostensible queerness of the Byzantine Empire offended modern writers and its legacy is with us still. As Leonora Neville recently commented, "Given that most Byzantinists think gender has no bearing on their work, they are likely to be oblivious to the ways assumptions about Byzantine gender play out in their research. We have not begun to confront the reality that the Western denigration of Byzantium is a discourse about gender."[2] But rather than negate or deny the attacks of Western critics and haplessly engage in the futility of respectability politics, my hope is to reparatively recuperate the queerness of the empire and articulate a voice of power from this space of marginalization.

In the historical record, figures such as the emperors Michael III and Basil I have garnered attention for their overly intimate friendship, and the records of their lives suggest possible queer intimacies, often to the surprise (and, at times, disgust) of modern historians.[3] Historians have scrutinized letters of key figures such as Michael Psellus for what they reveal both about the nonnormative gender identities of their writers and about the eroticized interplay between writer and reader.[4] Similarly, same-gender monastic cohabitation and companionship have been central areas of investigation when considering the possibilities that might exist within these experiences of intimacy.[5] Scholars have also sought to explore the broader question of homoerotics in both secular literature and religious writings as an avenue for mining the fantasy of an elusive, yet pervasive, queer subjectivity.[6]

Scholars exploring the history of Byzantine sexuality have particularly focused on the Church rite of *adelphopoiēsis*, or "brother making," a ceremony which bound two people of the same gender in a union of spiritual brotherhood and echoed in some respects the rite of marriage. John Boswell polemically described it as a medieval "same-sex union," at one point glibly referring to it as "basically a gay marriage ceremony for the Greek church." Recently, Claudia Rapp has added nuance to our understanding of the ritual, thereby moving us away from the simplicity of Boswell's thesis.[7] Nevertheless, Rapp's work does not rule out that this rite might have served, at least in specific instances, as a route for achieving a deeper homosocial or even homoerotic intimacy between two men, as earlier studies argued.[8] Consider, for example, that the thirteenth-century Patriarch Athanasius I of Constantinople condemned the rite by stating that *adelphopoiēsis* is a deed "which brings about coitus and depravity [*lagneia kai mochthēria*]" thereby alerting us to the rite's potentially queer uses and manifestations.[9]

Adding to Byzantium's place in the history of queer subjectivities, the *scholia* of the tenth-century scholar Arethas of Caesarea provides the first extant use of the term "Lesbian" (literally meaning an inhabitant of the island of Lesbos) to indicate women with same-gender desires. In his gloss on Clement of Alexandria's *Instructor* (3.3) on "the beautification of men,"

Arethas comments that Clement mentions "women becoming men against nature" in the context of "the abominable 'rubbers' [*tribadas*], which they also call courtesans [*hetairistrias*] and Lesbians [*Lesbias*]."[10] *Tribades* and *hetairistriai* were established terms for women who had some form of erotic attraction to other women. For example, Hesychius's fifth-century Byzantine lexicon defines the related term *dietaristriai* specifically as a sexual "orientation," writing that it applies to "women who are oriented [*tetrammenai*] toward female companions for sex, just as men; such as *tribades*."[11] But Arethas's use of "Lesbian" is remarkable, since the term did not appear until the nineteenth century to describe same-gender female desire. The second-century writer Lucian mentions masculine women in Lesbos, "with faces like men," who were said to consort only with women, "as though they themselves were men."[12] Arethas's *scholion* suggests a use analogous to its modern one being commonly employed in the Byzantine world.

The existence in Byzantium of terms and institutionalized spaces that could have supported homosocial, homoerotic, and same-gender intimacy suggests a world in which gender, sexuality, and, specifically, queer subjectivities, had room to maneuver in certain cordoned-off, private, or homosocial spaces, even if they manifested differently than in our own time. This, of course, is the condition of the closet.[13] But it also captures what it means to be queer, something beyond the limits of sexual identity alone. As Eve Sedgwick puts it in her classic definition of "queer," queerness is that "open mesh of possibilities, gaps, overlaps, dissonances and resonances, lapses and excesses of meaning when the constituent elements of anyone's gender, of anyone's sexuality aren't made (or *can't be* made) to signify monolithically."[14] In looking at queerness historically, we must not only mediate between modern constructions of "gay" or "homosexual" and the continuities and intimacies of same-gender desire and eroticism across time, as David Halperin has noted;[15] we must also struggle with the fact that the archive has often been broken, fragmented, hidden, or missing. Therefore, our aim becomes less to clearly flesh out the existence and contours of specific queer Byzantine identities than to delineate and make perceptible that "open mesh of possibilities." We will start by assuming that, perhaps, not "all Byzantines were straight" and, from there, we can seek to recognize "possibilities rather than identifying certainties."[16]

Various monastic writings attest to a concern about same-gender attraction and how to deal with it. As Derek Krueger has convincingly argued, in "late antiquity and early Byzantium some men pursuing the monastic life sought and achieved enduring and lifelong companionship with other men."[17] Some same-gender monastic relationships could exceed the prescribed bounds of either chastity or intimacy, as was certainly the case with some of those seeking and undertaking *adelphopoiēsis*. The fifth-century superior of the White Monastery in Egypt, Shenoute of Artipe, chastised his monks for their sexual improprieties, accusing some of incest with their sons and daughters; he reprimanded others "who became effeminate among you, and those who sleep with men."[18] Monastic rules often reveal an intense preoccupation with avoiding any possible same-gender eroticism that might emerge as the brothers perform their everyday tasks.[19] In the early fourth-century rule of Pachomius, we find an almost paranoid desire to defuse potential sexual tensions. Expected rules of common decency, such as knocking before entering a cell, give way to prohibitions that appear to be concerned with overintimacy and sexual action. Among the activities banned are oiling one's hands, speaking to one's neighbors in the dark, sitting with another man on a mat, drawing a thorn out of a man's foot, and sitting together with another man on a barebacked donkey or wagon; nor can one "clasp the hand or anything else of his companion; but when you are sitting or standing or walking, you shall leave a forearm's space between you and him."[20] In his mid-seventh-century *Heavenly Ladder*, John Climacus praises those who can sow discord among monks who have "developed a lustful state [*schesin pornikē*] for one another," and are thus able to bring about an end to their "lustfulness" (*porneian*).[21] Across these texts, we can observe a nonchalant acknowledgment of same-gender relationships and intimacies.

FROM SAME-SEX TO SAME-GENDER DESIRE

One of the challenges in articulating the history of queer figures in Byzantium is the conflation of male effeminacy and female masculinity with same-gender eroticism and desire, as we have seen in the previous chapter. In his study of the wide-ranging category of "sodomy" in the Western medieval world, Robert Mills has suggested that the notion of "transgender" is a better fit for the wide spectrum of queer subjectivities in the premodern world, since ancient and medieval authors often attack same-gender desire not as such but as a sign of a person betraying their gender identity.[22] Intriguingly, some of the more unabashed descriptions of same-gender desire in the Byzantine world appear in the lives of transgender saints, where the monks' transgender identity allows authors to forthrightly present these figures as the recipients of both male and female sexual interest.

In the story of Smaragdos, the appearance of the eunuch-passing trans monk in the monastery poses a threat to his brothers, who are overcome with a same-gender desire for the young, beardless monk. We are told that:

Agapius took [Smaragdos] away to his cell because his face was covered with beauty like an emerald. And when he came into the refectory Satan made many to stumble at his beauty, so that they complained against the Abbot, that he had received such a fair and beautiful face into the monastery, and when the Abbot learnt it he called for Smaragdos and said to him, "The fair beauty of your face has occasioned many falls to those who are not well-established. I therefore desire you to dwell in a separate cell at some distance from [the monastery] and you may be quiet and sing hymns there and eat; and do not let yourself be seen by the brothers."[23]

The story does not marvel at what sort of man this monk was who could elicit the desire of his fellow brothers. Instead, the situation is handled calmly and with a clear plan: isolate the monk and limit his contact with others in a highly regulated environment. In fact, the challenges created by youthful, beardless monks were a familiar problem for monastic communities.

In Cyril of Scythopolis's *Life* of the fifth-century Palestinian monastic founder Euthymius, the monk asks his disciples to "take care not to let your youngest brother come near my cell, for because of the warfare of the enemy it is not right for a feminine face to be found in the laura," the monastic community composed of a group of monks' cells. Euthymius similarly suggests to the young Sabas that the youth should not dwell in a laura, urging him instead to seek out the more regulated environment of the cenobium.[24] The threat of a so-called feminine face appears to have been an inescapable concern of monks; Paphnutius was also recorded as stating that he "does not allow the face of a woman to dwell in Sketis, because of the conflict with the enemy."[25] In addition, the acts of the Protaton Monastery on Mount Athos repeatedly warn against allowing beardless young men to come to the monastery to assist with construction or repairs, lest they tempt the monks.[26]

Underscoring the complexity of this same-gender desire, for the monks the object of attraction is the femininity of these individuals. According to these authors, the men ostensibly are attracted not to other men but rather to a transcendent femininity made manifest in certain men's flesh. While a desire for intimacy between these brothers and a trans eunuch or feminine-appearing monk is clearly present, the writers purposely short-circuit the representation of this intimacy by ascribing its origin to the brother's feminine features. By doing so, such intimacies are staged as being rooted only in a heterosexual impulse.

In the narrative of Eugenia, during the brief period when she is living as Eugenius in a monastic community, a similar situation occurs.[27] The saint is deeply mindful of the brothers' attraction and, therefore, refuses to take on the role of abbot, "lest she might cause the minds of the brethren to stumble." Yet this attraction is subverted by the narrative's author when the saint is courted by a woman, Melania, who repeatedly attempts to have sex with the monk. The narrative tells us that Melania "spoke unseemly words" and held Eugenius "without shame and wished to embrace her secretly."[28] While the author's insistence on the saint's female identity allows the revelation of her fellow monks' attraction to be relatively unproblematic, a woman's desire for the saint is doubly understood as a crime: first, it is a same-gender desire of one woman for another; and second, Melania desires to fornicate with a monk.

However, the story makes it clear that Melania made her advances "not knowing that she [Eugenia] was a woman."[29] Hence, it would seem that, while the monks perceive the saint's femininity under Eugenius's masculine gender expression, Melania perceives and is seduced by Eugenius's male appearance. The complexity of sexual desire here forces us to find a more nuanced and capacious language to articulate queer desire in the premodern world. Acknowledging and respecting trans monks as men necessitates that we move away from the language of "same-sex desire" used in the secondary literature. The assumptions underlying the category of "same-sex desire" are fundamentally transphobic; they exclude non-cisgender persons from the possibility of same-gender intimacies. A more encompassing term—such as queer desire—allows us to avoid excluding nonbinary figures from these intimacies—or, even worse, including them by denying their nonbinary gender identity.

To fully elucidate these points, we must also consider same-gender attraction when it is not expressed through sexual desire alone—in other words, when a transgender monk and his brethren form a bond of intimacy and love unmarred by any lust that would pose a threat to their monastic identity. We find one such instance in the story of Athanasius. When living as the wife of Andronicus, Athanasius loses his two children on the same day, following which he and his husband choose to leave behind their earthly goods and join different monasteries. Unbeknownst to Andronicus, his wife (now known as Athanasius) joins a male monastery. Much later the two encounter each other while on pilgrimage to Jerusalem. At this encounter, Andronicus does not suspect anything, because Athanasius "appeared just as an Ethiopian," an indication that his skin had darkened after years of ascetic practice in the desert sun.[30] After their pilgrimage to the Holy Land, the two resolve to not go back to their respective monasteries but rather to find a new home for themselves at a monastery near where they met on the road. Throughout the narrative, until after Athanasius's death, Andronicus remains unaware that this man was once his wife.

During their time together at the monastery, Andronicus and Athanasius live and practice their asceticism together. As a later elaboration of their story puts it:

> From then on he lived with brother Athanasios, living under the same roof, eating together and being known as completely inseparable from him. So, they remained with each other for another twelve years, making little or no account of the body, while providing the soul sensibly in all ways with the service of the spiritual life with all their strength.[31]

This author provides an intimate account of the lives of these two monks, who remained always in each other's company and paid little attention to their bodies—a description understood as referring simultaneously to their great asceticism and celibacy. When Athanasius is on his deathbed, the narratives depict his concern for his loved one and the grief that Andronicus will endure after his death. He instructs the brothers to give Andronicus a letter hidden under his pillow, which will posthumously reveal his identity as Andronicus's former wife.

Ascribing to Athanasius an unwavering female identity, Crystal Lubinsky casts this narrative as a "story of a woman who never ceases to be a loving wife." Similarly, Claudia Rapp, seeking to negate the homoerotic and homosocial valences of spiritual brotherhood, reads it as an exemplar of "chaste marriage and monastic coupledom."[32] This encourages us to assume that their union was chaste, given that the husband remained unaware of his wife's identity until after Athanasius's death and thus it seems reasonable to assume (though we can't be entirely certain) that there was never any carnal consummation of their bond. Nevertheless, what the narrative emphasizes is not the chastity of this couple but the strength of their interpersonal bonds—once shared in their marriage—in which the desires that motivate their reunion and monastic life together are rooted.[33] After all, it is Athanasius, who recognizes Andronicus as his former husband and asks, "Would you like us to live together in a cell?,"[34] thereby reforging their bond of intimacy in monastic terms. The reader knows the identity of both all along and, within the narrative, Athanasius is aware of his husband's identity from the very start. To presume that same-gender desire is rooted only in sex and eroticism, separated from structures of personal intimacy, social relationality, and community, is to play into homophobic narratives that see same-gender attraction as purely narcissistic, antisocial, and death-driven.

QUEER THEORY AFTER TRANS MONKS

In contemporary queer theory writers such as Leo Bersani and Lee Edelman controversially attempt to push against "reproductive futurism," which perceives procreation as synonymous with social contribution. They thus embrace queerness as the refusal of what Edelman calls the "insistence of hope itself as affirmation, which is always affirmation of an order whose refusal will register as unthinkable, irresponsible, inhumane."[35] In other words, Edelman sees the potential of queerness as welcoming the rejection of all those social registers whose very refusal had previously seemed unthinkable—an act that consequently allows the queer, who would have been erased from those spaces already, to ask, "If not this, what?"[36] Ultimately, as we look for the emergence of queer subjectivities in the late antique and Byzantine worlds, what we find in the secondary literature on the queerest Byzantine topics—such as trans monks and *adelphopoiēsis*—is a sublimation of the antisocial thesis by contemporary scholars. They see the queer as inherently only a sexual figure and view antirelationality and the antisocial not as a form of emancipation, as in Bersani and Edelman, but as the inherent quality of the queer. The queer is sexual or it is nothing, it fucks or it does not exist, and when it fucks it dies—whether from AIDS or eternal damnation does not seem to really matter.[37] Relationality and queer utopias are not just denied as possibilities for the queer; they are not even considered as things desired by the queer, by definition.

To make the point less harshly, this outlook could lead one to deny that Andronicus might have had same-gender intimacy with Athanasius that was queer, precisely because it was chaste. Similarly, one might deny that two men bound by *adelphopoiēsis* could have been in a same-gender, queer relationship, even if the relationship was itself chaste. Derek Krueger has been able to sidestep these problems by recognizing and praising the intimacies between monks.[38] Such an approach conscientiously demonstrates the erotic and sexual dimensions of some of these relationships, while not allowing sexual dynamics alone to delimit what constitutes a queer subjectivity in Byzantium. Of course, if, as modern scholars, we overemphasize these chaste intimacies, we run the risk of perpetuating the toxic respectability politics found in our primary sources by presenting a form of queer atonement through celibacy and negation. That is, we must be careful not to praise a person for having same-gender desires but never acting on them in order to conform to prescribed social norms.

In using the language of queer desire, I am also interested in queering desire itself: pushing against the limits of what can be counted as sexual desire with a model of intimacies rather than sex alone. Drawing on the notion of queer intimacy, we can perceive relations beyond "straight" between nonbinary, transgender, and cisgender persons, while understanding that queer desire and intimacy need not always be affirmed or confirmed by sexual intercourse. In this way, we can also count demisexual, asexual, aromantic, and even antisexual subjectivities among queer subjectivities, as we conceive of them today. Medieval history not only has done far too little to grapple with same-gender desire in a way inclusive of a variety of gender identities as well as intimate practices but also has all but erased and ignored asexual subjectivities. With these shifts in terminology, deployed in accordance with an approach that matches modern rubrics, we begin to recognize that the very institution of monasticism—with its self-articulated antisexual, aromantic, and asexual drives—is a fundamentally and inexorably queer practice.

The impulse to see the queer as rooted in radical sociality—the anti-antisocial thesis—has been articulated by contemporary queer theorists, many of them women and persons of color.[39] In the work of José Esteban Muñoz, radical relationality manifests itself proleptically: that is, in a utopia that is envisioned in the future even as its poetics are already becoming clear and vivid in the present. As Muñoz writes in the opening lines of *Cruising Utopia*:

Queerness is not yet here. Queerness is an ideality. Put another way, we are not yet queer. We may never touch queerness, but we can feel it as the warm illumination of a horizon imbued with potentiality. We have never been queer, yet queerness exists for us as an ideality that can be distilled from the past and used to imagine a future. The future is queerness's domain. Queerness is a structuring and educated mode of desiring that allows us to see and feel beyond the quagmire of the present. The here and now is a prison house. We must strive, in the face of the here and now's totalizing rendering of reality, to think and feel a then and there.[40]

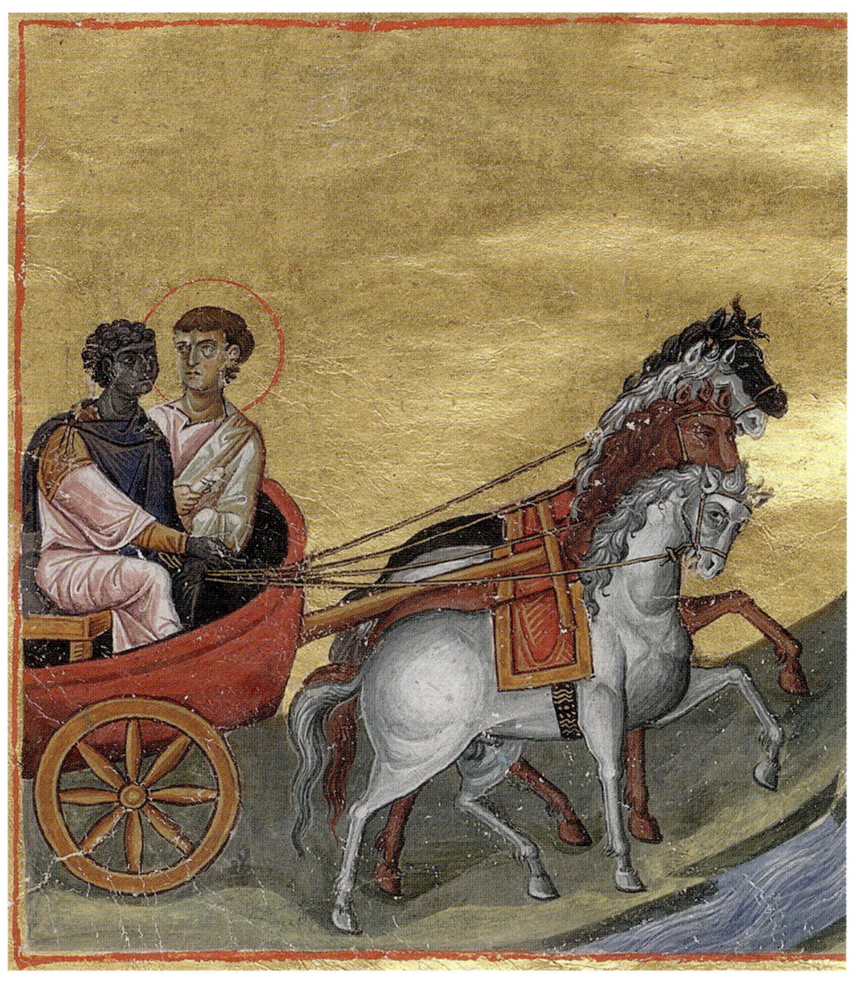

1. Detail of Philip and the Ethiopian Eunuch. Vatican City, Biblioteca Apostolica Vaticana, 'Menologion' of Basil II (Vat. gr. 1613), fol. 107. © 2019 Biblioteca Apostolica Vaticana.

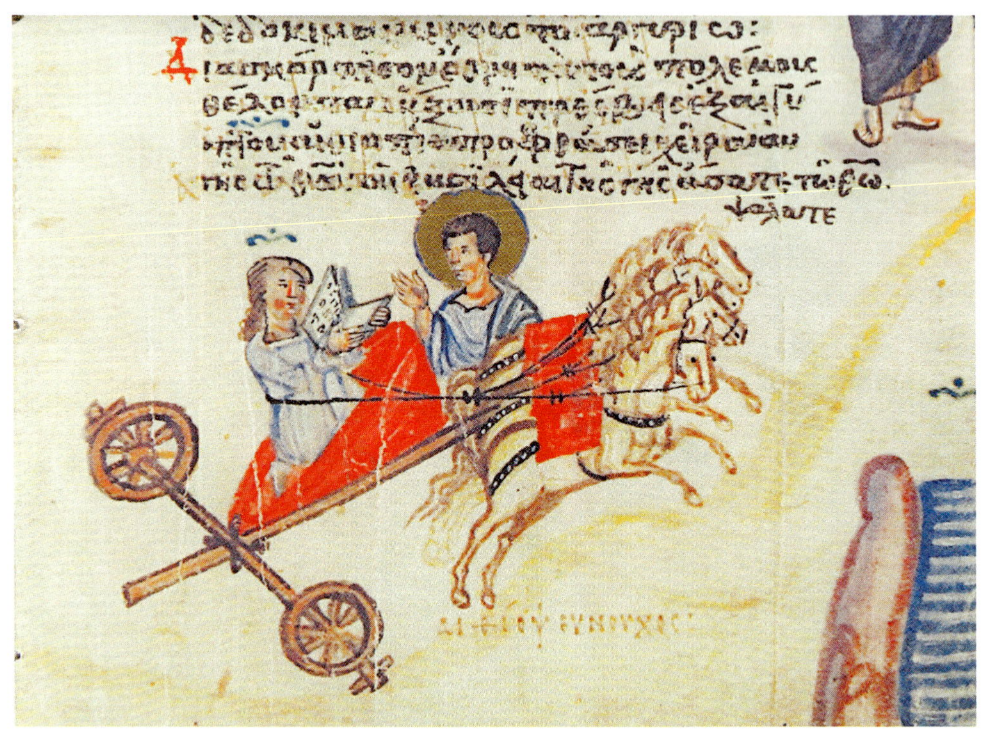

2. Philip and the Ethiopian Eunuch. Moscow, State Historical Museum, Chludov Psalter (ГИМ gr. 129), 65r. © State Historical Museum, Moscow.

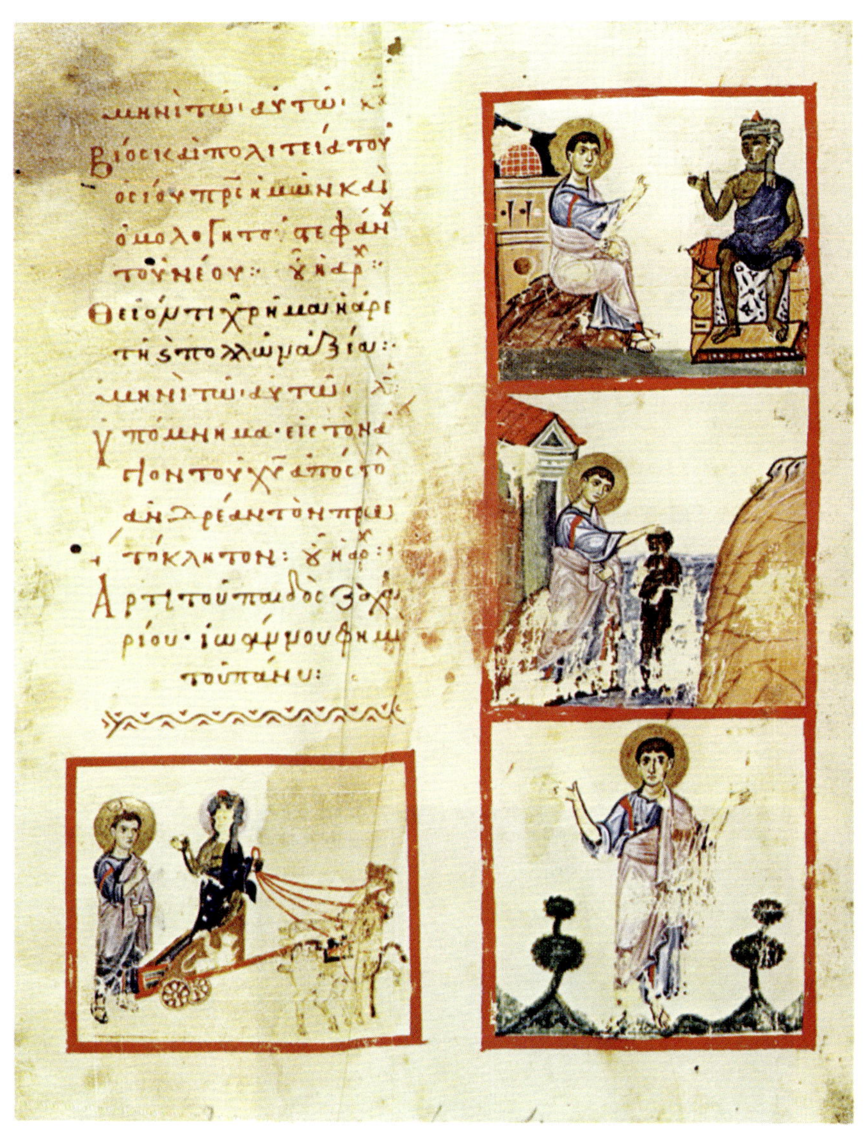

3. Philip and the Ethiopian Eunuch. Mount Athos, Docheiariou Monastery, Synaxarion (Cod. 5), fol. 3v.

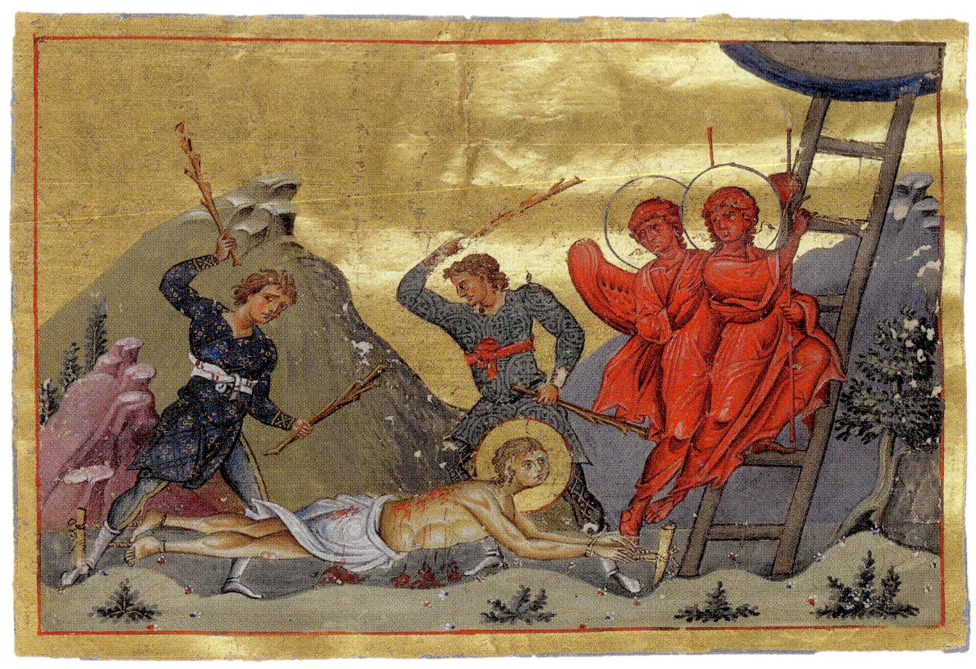

4. Detail of Martyrdom of Ananias. Vatican City, Biblioteca Apostolica Vaticana, 'Menologion' of Basil II (Vat. gr. 1613), fol. 217. © 2019 Biblioteca Apostolica Vaticana.

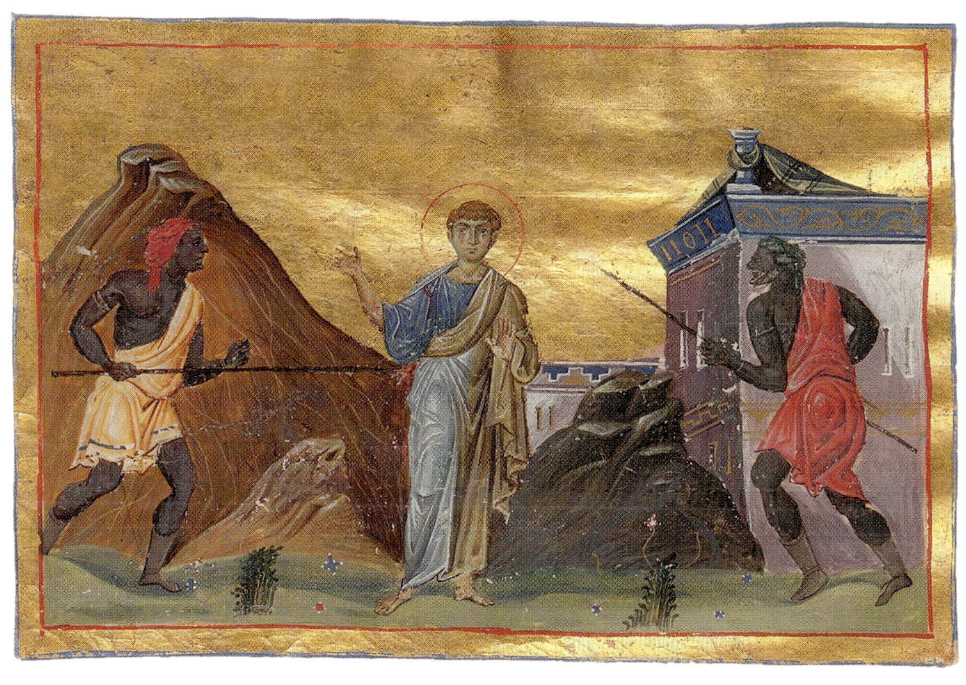

5. Martyrdom of Apostle Thomas. Vatican City, Biblioteca Apostolica Vaticana, 'Menologion' of Basil II (Vat. gr. 1613), fol. 93. © 2019 Biblioteca Apostolica Vaticana.

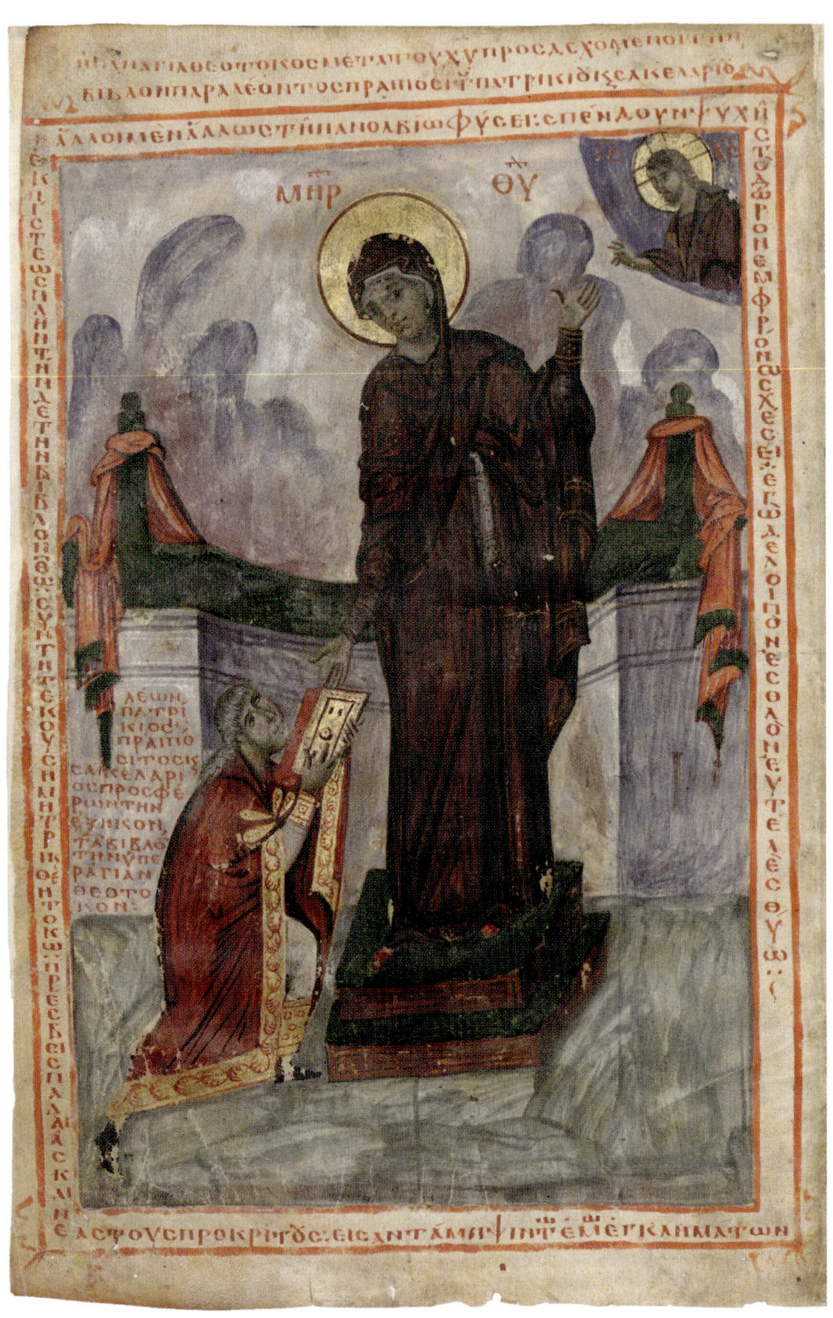

6. Leo *sakellarios* and the Virgin. Vatican City, Biblioteca Apostolica Vaticana, Leo Bible (Vat. Reg. gr. 1B), fol. 2v. © 2019 Biblioteca Apostolica Vaticana.

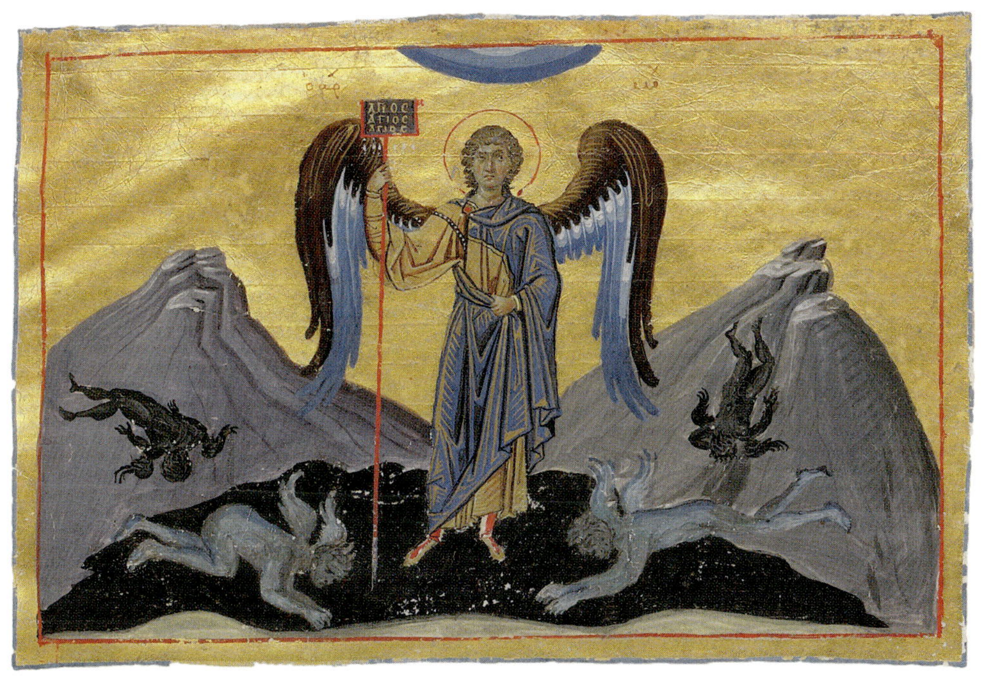

7. Synaxis of the Archangels. Vatican City, Biblioteca Apostolica Vaticana, 'Menologion' of Basil II (Vat. gr. 1613), fol. 168. © 2019 Biblioteca Apostolica Vaticana.

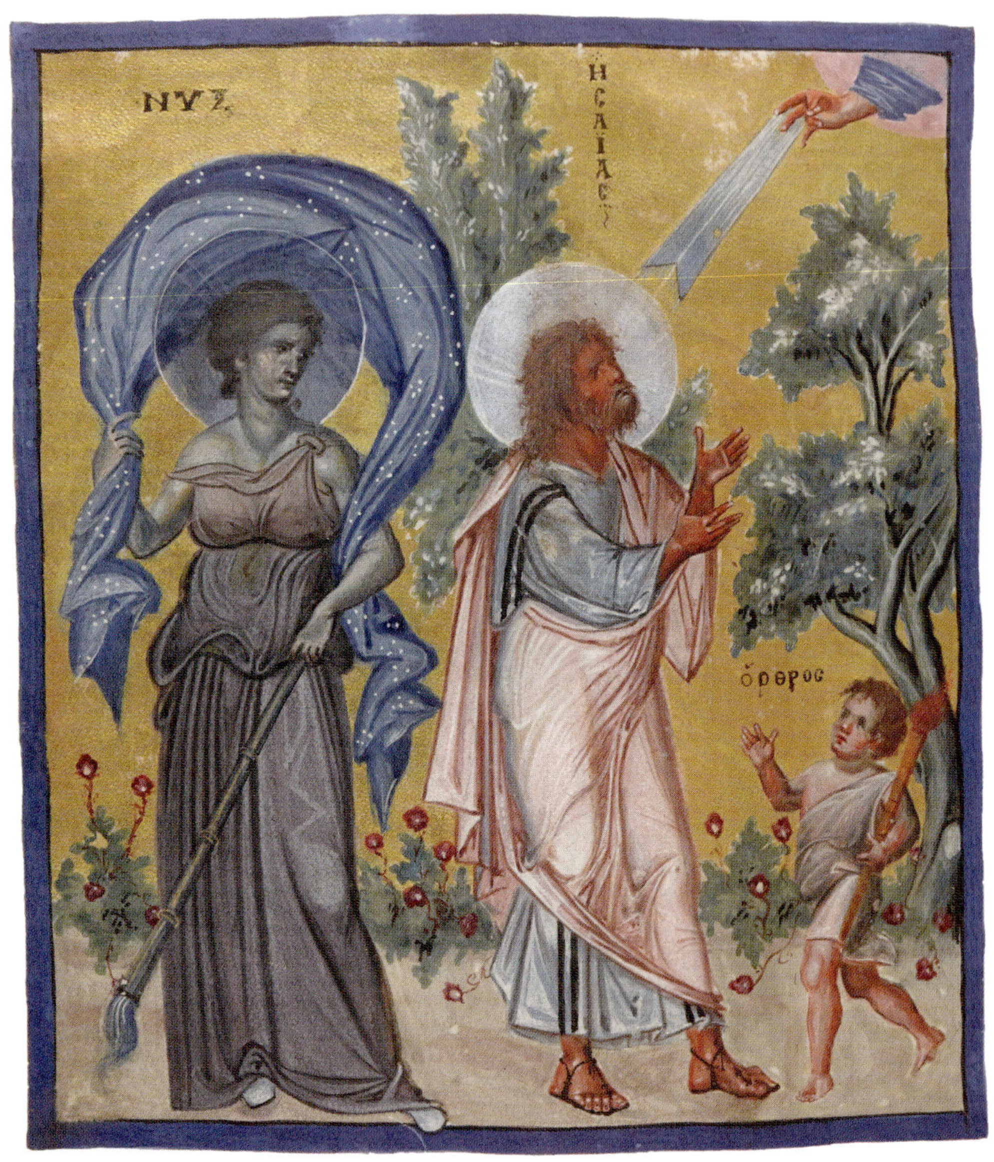

8. Prayer of Isaiah. Paris, Bibliothèque Nationale de France, Psalter (Par. gr. 139), fol. 435v.

There is an eschatological tone to Muñoz's words—not the sadomasochistic penance and sentence of an unclean spirit at the Last Judgment but the ecstasy of a soul welcomed into paradise. With a painful lust not for bodies but for belonging, Muñoz translates this long-standing debate in queer theory into an evocative model that is productive for thinking through early Christian and Byzantine same-gender desire. Moving past the impulse of late twentieth-century scholarship to do the history of same-gender desire as a project of "outing" queer figures, contemporary queer theory reorients us toward the question of orientation itself.[41] "Orientation" is precisely the longing engendered by attraction toward something that is not present, not yet there; queerness is the grit of the utopian communities that emerge in the wake of both these chaste and erotic desires. This is a reminder of what Byzantine historiography has often forgotten: that queers have often loved, but have only sometimes been able to fuck.[42]

THE DOUBTING THOMAS'S TOUCHING QUEERNESS

With Muñoz's reminder that we "may never touch queerness, but we can feel it as the warm illumination of a horizon imbued with potentiality," let us turn back to Nicholas Mesarites's description of the Doubting Thomas in the Church of Holy Apostles in Constantinople. My goal in surveying the known contours of same-gender desire in late antique and Byzantine religious settings has been to contextualize how it was a present reality, manifested both chastely and erotically, in monastic and broader religious life. If Pachomius, for example, does not even allow a brother to "clasp the hand or anything else of his companion," then how would the monumental depiction of the Doubting Thomas scene in churches and monasteries be read by their own communities? A modern viewer who accepts the fact that same-gender erotic desires existed in Byzantium will be dazzled by the elements of Mesarites's description. The language is charged with sexual potential. Christ is pronounced "free of all fatness" thus indicating he is free of all base materiality, earthly grossness, or density, as the term *pachytētos* is variously translated. After displaying "a gaping opening [*chasmatōdē kektēmenē diastasin*] so as to take in the hand of the disciple . . . the Savior assumes the position in which He received the injury [*eschēmatismenos ton traumatian*] and sinks toward Himself and seems almost, so to speak, to fear the groping [*anaskaleusin*] of the wound." Fisting the side wound, the entire "hand of Thomas enters through the side of the Savior," reperforming the violence of the lance and "wishing to tear open the wound" (*bouletai to trauma anaxanein*) once again, through his "extensive handling"

(*sychnēs epaphēs*) of it. Thomas's hand is compared to a medical scalpel—
"like some instrument of Paieon," the ancient Greek physician god—as it
cuts into the wound. The event is initiated by the homosocial hazing of
Thomas's fellow Apostles, who, angered at his initial skepticism, "resist him
and shove him from behind, retaliating [*amynomenoi*] against him for his
disbelief."

This translation is suggestively sexual, stressing the violence of a forceful penetration of the side wound. Similar sexual implications are found in
the Greek text. Consider, for example, how the Apostles force Thomas to approach and place his hand into Christ's side: "with violence they coerce him
to approach the Teacher" (*kai bia proseggisai tō didaskalō katanagkazousi*).
This is the charged language of coercion and rape—*bia* (violence) is one of
the terms that, since antiquity, has denoted rape, specifically, rape involving
violent force.[43] As discussed in chapter 1, *biasamenos* is used in Deuteronomy
22:28 in the context of the forceful rape of a virgin. As we have seen, the terminology around rape is not clear or direct, and thus any interpretation must
deal with a host of related terms denoting anything from a lack of consent
to the claim of adultery. On a literal level *bia* simply denotes violence. However, in Mesarites's text this term is deployed alongside the verb *katanagkazousi*, suggesting that this violent force is being used to "coerce" a person to
do something: namely, to "approach" (*proseggisai*) Christ. Most importantly,
beyond its literal meaning *proseggisai* is associated with violently attacking
or accosting someone—and is also used euphemistically to connote sexual
intercourse.[44] Thus, the layers of these three terms suggest that Thomas is
molested through the touch and intercourse that Christ has welcomed and
that the Apostles coerced him to perform, despite his protestations.

Within Byzantine art, the homoerotics of the Thomas narrative are most
vividly manifested in a wall painting in the main church of the Chilandar Monastery on Mount Athos from around 1321 (retouched in 1803/04;
fig. 4.1). The scene of Thomas's incredulity is dramatized with a startling
eroticism. Christ raises his right arm, palm turned outward to expose the
mark of the nail, while his left hand pulls open his garments on the side
in order to expose his flesh to Thomas. Christ's index and middle finger
are ever so slightly parted to form the shape of a V, drawing attention to
the wound that lies just beyond them and adding an eye-catching and elegant tension to his hands as he holds his parted garb. Christ's eyes are fixed
on the viewer, inviting them to touch his side as well. Meanwhile, Thomas
peers in and closely examines the wound, approaching its flesh with his index finger. Unlike other renditions of this scene, which seem to depict the

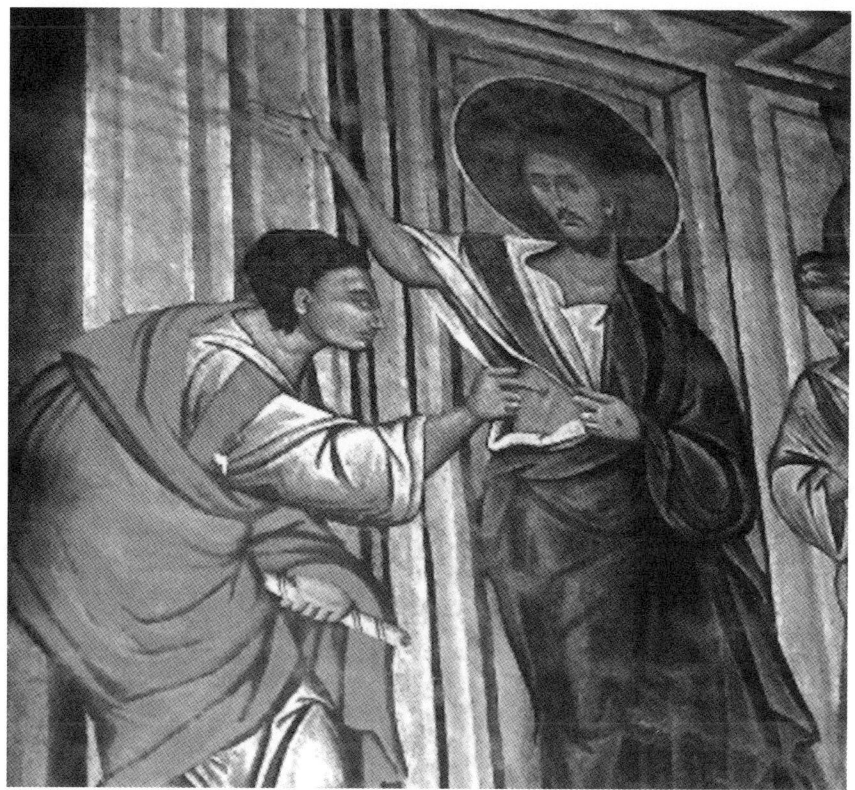

4.1. Doubting Thomas. Chilandar Monastery, Mount Athos, Greece.

instant after Thomas molds his hand to the side of Christ, this image shows us the moment just before contact with the flesh. Thomas's hand fades into Christ's body, his fingertip about to not only touch but also enter Christ. Thomas is youthful and beardless, with a rounded face, unlike the oval, angular, and bearded faces of Christ and the rest of the Apostles. Thomas is thus purposely feminized as he approaches to enter Christ.

The Chilandar wall painting adds a curious detail in Thomas's left hand: a scroll. In Byzantine art, scrolls often are used to represent a spoken text—here, presumably Thomas's impending declaration, "My Lord and my God!" (John 20:28). We see a similar placement of a scroll in the scene at the Church of San Marco in Venice, but there the scroll is unfurled, displaying to the viewer its Latin text: "Dominus meus et deus meus" (fig. 4.2). As in the Chilandar painting, the scroll in the Church of San Marco scene is positioned before Thomas's pelvis, but less suggestively because it is unrolled. In the Chilandar example, in contrast, the scroll is tightly wound

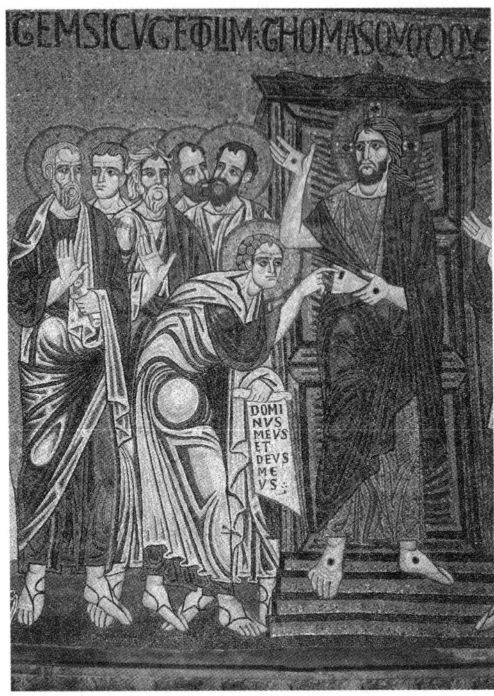

4.2. Doubting Thomas.
Church of San Marco,
Venice, Italy.

and apparently even tied up with a cord wrapped around it. The scroll is grasped awkwardly, held tightly against the body; it is clearly phallic in look and placement, stiffly pressed into Thomas's loins and terminating in a rounded tip. Thomas's speech act is deferred in the rolled-up scroll, which we expect to explode open to proclaim him coming to recognize and know Christ. There is a sexual tension to that string that binds the words about to be spoken. The prodding finger is symbolically displaced onto the erectness of the scroll, where finger and penis are conflated.

HYMNOGRAPHY AND HOMOEROTICISM

The interplay between finger and penis in experiencing the body of Christ appears in other Byzantine writing. In his hymns from the mid-eleventh century, Symeon the New Theologian contemplates his approach to the divine, understanding the mutual union between his earthly body and the divine body of Christ as entailing all of his bodily members becoming one with Christ. Symeon provocatively writes:

And so thus you well know that both my finger and my penis [*balanon*]
    are Christ.

Do you tremble or feel ashamed?
But God was not ashamed to become like you,
yet you are ashamed to become like Him?[45]

Here, Symeon observes that, if Christ became fully human and fully divine, then humanity itself has been fully divinized by Christ's actions. This view manifests in Symeon's devotional practices rooted as they are in a mystical vision of the divine through a form of eros and conveyed through an erotic and nuptial language with a strong undercurrent of homoeroticism. Symeon speaks of marriage, consummation, sexual intercourse, and so on with God, yet as Derek Krueger has noted, Symeon retains the male monastic's masculine gender, choosing not to produce a heteronormative model of divine erotic union but instead ascribing a "cross-sex and same-sex desire to God."[46] Symeon, who elsewhere calls himself a "sodomite by deed and choice,"[47] presents an image of the monastic self in his hymns that is unabashedly rooted in a same-gender longing for a union with Christ. Though Symeon the New Theologian represents an extreme, he also provides precedent for understanding the moment of fleshly union with the resurrected body of Christ depicted in the image of Thomas at Chilandar and elsewhere through a divine eros.

Earlier, in the sixth-century homilies of Romanus the Melodist, we find an intimate portrait of Thomas's inner thoughts at his confrontation with Christ.[48] Here, the erotic undertone of Thomas's prodding finger is more subdued, yet the text reveals the significance of the union between hand and side wound:

Who then preserved the disciple's palm unmelted
when it approached the fiery side of the Lord?
Who gave it daring and gave it strength to handle
bone to flame? Only that which was handled;
for had not the side given the power
how could a hand of clay have handled
wounds which had shaken things above and things below?[49]

Romanus is focused on the fiery union of human hand and divine flesh. While there may be no obvious eroticism here—certainly nothing as explicit as in Symeon—we nevertheless observe a meditation on what it means for the human to be divinized through a penetration of Christ's body. Contemplating how it might be possible that a human hand could touch that fiery Christ and remain "unmelted" (*achōneuton*),[50] Romanus focuses on a metaphor of materials that is ultimately left unresolved beyond divine intervention. Yet those in the homily's audience are left to consider how Thomas's material composition is altered by his handling of the wound. Like the finger and penis in Symeon, both equally divinized protruding extremities of the body, for Romanus, the "right hand of clay" (*pēlinē dexia*) is inflamed in the "fiery side" (*pyrinē pleura*) of the Lord.[51]

Romanus manifests the sensual erotics of Thomas's privileged contact with Christ's body through a Eucharistic play on the side wound and the blood. Later in the homily, Romanus evocatively imagines Thomas's saying to Christ:

"Stay gentle, that I may take my delight in you, Lord.

Satisfy me, who am yours. You were patient with strangers;

be patient too with your own and show me your wounds,

that, like springs, I may draw from them and drink.

Do not burn me up, O Savior, for you are fire by nature,

but, by your will, you are the body which you became.

Hide yourself, then, just a little, I beg.

Accept me, my Savior, like the woman with the issue of blood.

It is not the hem of your garment that I seize, but you I touch,

saying, 'You are our Lord and our God.'"[52]

Sounding more like a lover or suitor, with these words Thomas skirts the edge of sexual desire. He asks Christ to remain "gentle" (*hēmeros*), a word that would be homophonous in pronunciation and accent with *himeros*, which denotes sexual longing, lust, and yearning. Thus listeners, who would not have had a written text of the hymn before them, would hear not simply "Stay gentle" but also "Stay lusting, that I may take my delight in you." This interpretation would have been strengthened by the term "delight" (*katatryphēsō*), which, when used in religious texts, describes delight in God, but also implies being insolent and behaving wantonly in one's excessive desires.[53] Furthermore, "satisfy [*plērophorēson*] me,"—literally, to fill repeatedly—denotes complete satiation. This resembles the language of Symeon the New Theologian who describes himself as being "filled" (*emphoroumai*) with God's love and beauty.[54] Romanus's hymn also evidences the association between fire and sexual yearning found in other ancient texts. In his study of Romanus's depiction of the Virgin, Thomas Arentzen shows the interplay of erotic desire and fire in Romanus's hymn on the Annunciation.[55] The language is quite similar to what we see in the hymn about Thomas: when Joseph gazes upon the newly impregnated Virgin, he begs that she not "melt him" (*chōneusē*), as he yearns for her beauty and newfound fiery radiance.[56]

In the hymn about Thomas, the erotic language gives way to the pains of the Crucifixion and of Thomas's repenetration of Christ's flesh; Thomas asks Christ to be "patient" (*anaschou*), as he was with others. A difficult term to translate in this context, *anaschou* suggests to undergo something or bear a difficulty or put up with something. As in Mesarites's text, there is the notion that Christ will suffer once more when Thomas's hand enters the wound. Romanus stresses that the sacrifice of Christ will be reperformed at that moment by shifting to Eucharistic language. In requesting that Christ show his wounds so that Thomas may draw from them like springs and drink, Thomas recalls the act of communion.

Significantly, Romanus then returns to the idea of Christ's fiery nature, which Thomas fears will burn him. During communion in the Divine Liturgy, the Byzantines add hot water to the chalice of wine, a practice known as the rite of *zeon*.[57] This is done so that the consecrated wine becomes the image of Christ's blood even in its temperature. While there are some suggestions that the rite existed as early as the mid-sixth century, and thus contemporaneous with Romanus's compositions, the evidence is tenuous at best.[58] Nevertheless, given the enduring popularity of Romanus's hymns, these liturgical associations and interpretations would have been clear to the hymn's audiences in later centuries. A liturgical commentary from the late eleventh century known as the *Protheoria* as well as a poem derived from it make the association between heat and communion explicit. Both texts tell us that the water is mixed with the wine so that we may drink it "just as we received it from the Holy Side."[59]

The *Protheoria* anthropomorphizes the chalice as it describes how in communion one drinks Christ's blood just as it came from the side wound— "filled with warmth" and taken from "the nipple [*thēlē*] of the chalice, just as if touching the life-giving side itself."[60] Here we have a direct connection between Thomas's drinking from the fiery side wound and the liturgical rite in which one would have drunk Christ's hot blood, just as it came out from the wound. Moreover, as the *Protheoria* recounts, the recipient in effect touches and handles Christ's side wound through its manifestation in the chalice. Furthermore, the act of drinking from the chalice renders the blood fleshy and feminine, and the side wound of Christ is feminized as the teat from which one may nurse and suckle. The word *thēlē* denotes this nursing nipple through an association with the female sex, *thēlys*. Hence, in the *Protheoria*, composed by a male monk, the body of Christ in the chalice becomes feminine in communion. As a result, the space of a heteronormative model of sexuality (within which one suckles on the teat as either the offspring of heterosexual lovemaking or as a lover) gives way to a space in which same-gender desire can arise. In other words, in feminizing Christ, the male author is able to allow for a same-gender desire for Christ by ascribing to his image feminine qualities, just as a feminine monk was believed to spark the lust of his brethren.

The Eucharistic proximity to Christ in the Romanus hymn is rooted in male privilege. Thomas begs Christ to conceal himself from him, "just a little," so that he might not be overwhelmed by Christ's full presence. But ironically, it is the male Thomas who has full and unimpeded access to Christ; in contrast, in an earlier encounter with Mary Magdalene at the tomb, Christ tells her, "Do not grasp me" (*mē mou haptou*; John 20:17). Indeed, Romanus's Thomas relishes his privilege, comparing himself to the woman who healed herself of years-long bloody hemorrhages by touching Christ's garment without his consent (Mark 5:25–34); Thomas boasts that, unlike her, it is not "your garment I seize [*kratō*], but you I touch [*haptomai*]." This side, Thomas goes on, is "the side which as I grasp, I enjoy."[61] It is the male disciple of Christ, not the female, who is afforded the privilege to intimately touch Christ. That a suggestive image depicting this encounter is found in the church at the Chilandar Monastery, an all-male monastic community, powerfully underscores that the Doubting Thomas story manifests the privileged access of a male figure to the male divinity.

Ultimately, Christ chastises Thomas in Romanus's hymn—"You, by handling me, have come to know my glory, / while they, by reason of a sound of words, worship me."[62] While Thomas comes to believe through the intimacy of same-gender touch, it is those who believe without touching Christ, such as Mary Magdalene and the other Apostles, whom Christ extols. I do not wish to dwell any further here on the potentially homoerotic details of this specific text and image, or of the Doubting Thomas scene more generally. To be sure, the possibly homoerotic trope of the denuded body of a fit Christ being penetrated by another man through the wound in his side may be able to generate an understanding of queerness rooted in sexual identity and sexuality. However, to embrace the full queer potential of the Doubting Thomas in Byzantine art and literature requires that we now focus on the critical role the story plays in shaping ideas about perceiving the divine through the bodily senses. Thus far, we have considered how the tension between sight and touch is eroticized in these religious writings and images. Now, we must assess the interchange between hearing, sight, and touch foregrounded in the story of Thomas.

TOUCHING AND SEEING AS CONFIRMATION AND AFFIRMATION

In the Doubting Thomas narrative, Thomas hears a story that he does not believe and therefore demands further sensory proof. The notion that words or images might require further sensory confirmation has been a well-established trope since antiquity, particularly in ancient thinking about the arts. Pliny the Elder's *Natural History* provides an example in the competition between Parrhasius and Zeuxis. In a contest as to who was the better painter, Zeuxis exhibited an image of "some grapes so true to nature that birds flew up to the wall of the stage," but Parrhasius won by painting a curtain that fooled even Zeuxis himself (who demanded that it be drawn to reveal the painting). Zeuxis admitted that Parrhasius had surpassed him by deceiving not merely the birds but a painter.[63] Similarly, in Philostratus the Elder's *Imagines*, it is uncertain "whether a real bee has been deceived by the painted flowers or whether we are to be deceived into thinking that a painted bee is real."[64] In these stories, humans and animals are left uncertain as to whether they are viewing artifice or reality.

The Stoics struggled with the question of cognitive "consent" or "assent" (*synkatathesis*) to the presentations of the senses. Diogenes Laertius offers a story about the philosopher Sphaerus, who is deceived into thinking that wax pomegranates are the real thing. When the king ridicules the philosopher for having given assent (*synkatatetheisthai*) to a "false presentation," the philosopher responds that he assented not to their veracity as pomegranates but to their verisimilitude: "I assented not to the proposition that they are pomegranates, but to another, that there are good grounds for thinking them to be pomegranates. Certainty of presentation and reasonable probability are two totally different things."[65] In this way, Stoic thought distinguished between what is absolutely certain and what is plausible or probable.[66]

In the fourth-century treatise *On the Nature of Man*, Nemesius of Emesa struggles with how we make judgments about what our senses tell us:

For if an apple is not identified by colour and shape alone, but also by its smell
and its characteristic taste, sight knows that it is an apple not by grasping these
as well, but [because] the soul calls up the memory gained from smelling and
tasting and, at the time of observation, attends to these along with shape and

colour. So when we believe that an apple made of wax is a real apple, it is not sight that is deceived but thought. For sight was not mistaken about its specific objects of sense; for it recognised both the colour and shape.[67]

This passage follows Nemesius's argument against the idea that sight can sense the heat of a fire; he reasons that our knowledge that fire is hot (gained from previous tactile experiences with it) is what enables us to perceive the heat of a flame in our mind when its visible form is seen by our eyes, which certainly cannot sense temperature. In the discussion of the apple, Nemesius applies the same logic to explain an error: sight has rightly assessed the outward visual appearance of an apple, but thought has erred in hastily consenting to believing that the wax apple is real based on visual appearance alone without confirming this fact through the other senses; thought has forgotten that an apple is not defined by color and shape alone (i.e., the qualities of objects conveyed by sight).

Therefore, the thought experiment of the wax apple demonstrates the need to always use the other senses in tandem with sight and hearing. This is particularly true of art and literature whose goals are often to deceive their viewers and listeners:

So sometimes sight needs additional evidence from the other senses, when what is viewed is crafted in order to deceive, as is the case with pictures: for what painting does is to deceive sight with non-existent projections and hollows, if that is the nature of the thing. Hence for discernment there is need of grasping, especially by touch, but sometimes also by taste and smell, as in the case of a waxen apple. But sometimes sight by itself vividly presents things seen, when it sees them from not far off.[68]

To be sure, sight can err on its own under certain circumstances; perhaps the object is far away, moving quickly, or viewed through something that obscures it, such as mist, water, or smoke. Yet Nemesius places the responsibility to discern on the mind, which should not be distracted, as distraction too can cause thought to misinterpret or miss the impressions of sight. Unlike a speech, which requires us first to imagine its words, judge them with sober attention, and only then assent to their truths, sight communicates so vividly that it often elicits our immediate assent. At times, however—owing either to poor viewing conditions or to the deceits of art—we must seek out confirmation beyond outward appearance. Thus, we must use our other senses, particularly touch and taste, to differentiate, say, a wax apple from a real one, or honey from honey-colored resin.

In the story of the Doubting Thomas, touch confirms the appearance of the risen Christ as not simply some phantasmagoric deception of sight.[69] Touch also affirms that Thomas's fellow Apostles neither spoke with intentional deceit nor had mistaken another man for the risen Christ. The doubt expressed by Thomas was not about Christ but about the truth of his own perceptions of hearing and seeing. Mesarites's account stresses this point, as Peter tells Thomas that the figure they had seen earlier on the road "was not an illusion of the sight, no phantom of the midday brightness."[70] Mesarites indicates that, by sight alone, Thomas was satisfied that the figure before him was the risen Christ. It is his fellow Apostles who keep him to his earlier hyperbolic demand to touch Christ, however, forcing Thomas to handle the side wound.

At the moment of contact with Christ, Mesarites vividly describes Thomas's clarity of sight: "his eyes opened to their widest, free from all rheum and flux and murky accretion."[71] At the instant of this touch in Christianity, Mesarites chooses to highlight Thomas's eyes and unobstructed vision. The medical language of "rheum [*lēmēs*] and flux [*epirroias*] and murky accretion [*lignyōdous episymbamatos*]" not only speaks to Mesarites's interest in medicine but also, and more importantly, suggests that Thomas's intellect has not been compromised: severe and life-threatening fevers could be diagnosed by the accretion of "rheum" (*lēmas*) in the eyes.[72] In other words, Mesarites speaks to Nemesius's concern that, even when an individual sense accurately conveys a perception, the intellect may err in hastily assenting to what has been brought before it. The Christ that Thomas perceives is not some feverish dream; nor, as Peter attempted to communicate, was the Christ they saw some "illusion of the sight." While Glenn Most has noted that the Gospel text never tells us that Thomas touched the Christ, in the Byzantine tradition, as in the modern understanding of the scene, that touch is inescapable, even when Thomas doesn't want it.[73] In the narrative of the scene, hearing leads to seeing, and seeing leads to touching.

That sight inevitably leads to a temptation to touch is an idea familiar to Byzantine viewers. In his Homily 16 on Genesis 2:25, John Chrysostom recounts the taunting of the serpent in Eden, who gives voice to humans' desire to touch all that lies within their sight:

What is the advantage of life in the garden when you are not free to enjoy
the things in it, but are even worse off in incurring the more intense pain of

having sight of things but missing out on the enjoyment that comes from partaking of them?[74]

Sight is therefore the perfect sensory medium for contemplating both the acts of salvation through veneration and also the damnation that comes from unbridled lust, that is, the desire to go beyond sight and actually touch with the hands. Elsewhere, in a homily on adultery, John Chrysostom makes clear that sight's temptations toward touch could be construed as sexual and sinful, even without sexual consummation: "Even if you have not touched [*hēpsō*] them with your hand, you have handled [*epsēlaphēsas*] them with your eyes."[75] In a monastic setting, then, the Doubting Thomas scene could be as much a site for homoerotic arousal as a reminder (as intended) for the viewer to not be a Thomas—that is, exhorting the monks to not be attached to the confirmations of the flesh, urging them to deny the impulse to touch and instead to believe and love through hearing (and seeing) alone.

The figure of Thomas confirms the Gospel for himself and for all who follow. He spares humanity from the impulse to touch: because he has touched Christ as a risen body, all others have partaken in that touch. After completing his description of the Doubting Thomas image in the Church of Holy Apostles, Mesarites asks:

And in the picture, these are the things that the side of the Lord suffers. But
you who are revealing it, why are you still delaying and shrinking back, and
why do you not in a loud voice proclaim Lord and God, as [Thomas did] before, and now being handled by you, why do you not make manifest to us the
things that have been mysteriously revealed to you from the truthful touch?
But you will not give heed to us, and rightly so, for the things which we see
and which are described in this discourse are not among the living but among
the soulless and painted things. One would say, however, that though silent
you are in agreement and that you approve what we say and assent and that
though not speaking, you express the same opinion.[76]

In this turn to the viewer, Mesarites proposes that the viewers themselves are the ones touching Christ and, through that contact, they unveil the sufferings of the side wound. We are reminded of the gaze of Christ in the Chilandar fresco, staring directly at the viewers and inviting them to touch his side along with Thomas. In fact, Mesarites chastises the viewer for not exclaiming in a loud voice their own confirmation of their faith, "My Lord and my God!" as Thomas did then. Those viewing the scene of Thomas thus are urged to identify with Thomas and share in his experiences. Accordingly, the viewer handles Christ once again (*hypo sou psēlaphōmenon*) in the present, and Mesarites exhorts them to tell us what they have mysteriously uncovered through that "truthful touch" (*alēthous epapēs*).

The conceit is that in seeing Thomas touch Christ, we have touched Christ, and thus must believe as Thomas did. But Mesarites immediately turns this conceit on its head, approving of the viewer's silence and reticence. They have not touched Christ; what they see is painted matter that is not "living"—literally, "ensouled" (*empsychois*)—but rather "soulless" (*apsychois*) and "painted" or "written" (*graphais*), as Mesarites alludes both to image and text. Hence, Mesarites agrees that we should keep silent, just as the things depicted are themselves silent; nevertheless, we "assent" (*synkatatithesthai*) to that which they show. Here, the complex term *synkatatithesthai*, with all its implications of mental cognition and sexual consent, affirms the sensory confirmation of Christ's resurrection. Although the Byzantine viewer could not, like Thomas, handle the side of Christ, the viewer could, through hearing and seeing, "assent" (*synkatatithesthai*) to the bodily resurrection of the Christ.

Therefore, the queerness of Thomas emerges not from the homoerotic valences of the scene's details but from the queering of sensation itself. Thomas operates in the Byzantine world as a personification of the sensory experience of the body, a foil to the expectations and needs of a Christianity rooted in assent through faith alone. The Doubting Thomas is a personification of the lowly senses approaching the embodied image of God. As noted earlier, Thomas himself is often feminized in his depictions, and his youthful face and characteristics connect him with humanity's faculties of sense perception. Bearing in mind Philo's description of the "female gender" as "material, passive, corporeal and sense-perceptible,"[77] thus connecting the feminine with the sensory, we see in Thomas and his physical need to confirm through sight and touch a manifestation of humanity's feminine characteristics. And since, as Philo states, the "ears are more sluggish and feminine [*thēlutera*] than the eyes,"[78] to masculinize perception we must move from hearing to sight, and onward to the active touch.

THE EFFEMINACY OF PERCEPTION

For Byzantine writers, the understanding of sensation as feminine persists. It is most eloquently elaborated in Michael Psellus's play with the feminine gender of the word "sensation" (*aisthēsis*) in one of their letters:

As for my sense perception [*aisthēsis*], how might I describe her experience with any precision? When she dashed against the beauty of your writing, when she saw the flowering of your words, discerned your composition of the parts of speech, and understood that everything had been composed according to the science of harmony, she cried aloud as much as she could. Like the most intense and skilled of lovers [*erastōn*], she poured her self [*sic*] entirely over the letter, touching [*epaphōmenē*] the words, the composition itself, embracing the letter's each and every word and utterance, placing it into her heart.[79]

Psellus presents sensation as a woman receiving the letter that Psellus themself now reads; this woman is overcome with emotion, just as Psellus is overcome in processing the sensations of reading the letter. After seeing the written text and vocalizing it while reading, sensation is finally compelled to touch (*epaphōmenē*) the words of the letter itself. Stratis Papaioannou notes the erotic tones of the passage, casually calling it the "only medieval Greek representation of female climax."[80] Sensation's communication of sensory impulses to the mind is seemingly staged as an orgasmic scream—*aisthēsis* "cried aloud as much as she could" during perception.

As in Mesarites's description of the Virgin's conception discussed in chapter 1, Psellus's feminine faculty of sensation processes sense data from the world in a sexualized manner that results in that which is perceived being impressed on and confirmed by the heart. Just as Mary conceives Christ through perception, in this letter perception is a feminine sexual act with which Psellus identifies as they read. The description recalls Psellus's claim that Constantine IX Monomachus was such an ardent lover of their prose that, not knowing from where exactly his great pleasure came, he would hang on Psellus's every word and often "would almost kiss" their lips.[81] Throughout their letters, Psellus captures the erotics of reading as words are offered up to the senses to be seen, heard, touched, tasted.[82]

Whereas Thomas is a manifestation of sensory perception, a lowly and feminine character, Christ is the lofty image that Thomas regards, seeking to touch, kiss, and embrace it as one would a Byzantine icon or as Psellus's feminine sensation approaches the letter. In the early eleventh-century scene of Doubting Thomas found in the narthex of the main church of the Monastery of Hosios Loukas, we find a fairly typical depiction (fig. 4.3). Christ stands before the Apostles while Thomas approaches the wound, just about to penetrate the hole in Christ's side, which is the perfect shape and size to receive his finger. As is typical in the Byzantine tradition, this narthex image is labeled not with a description of the action—for example, the

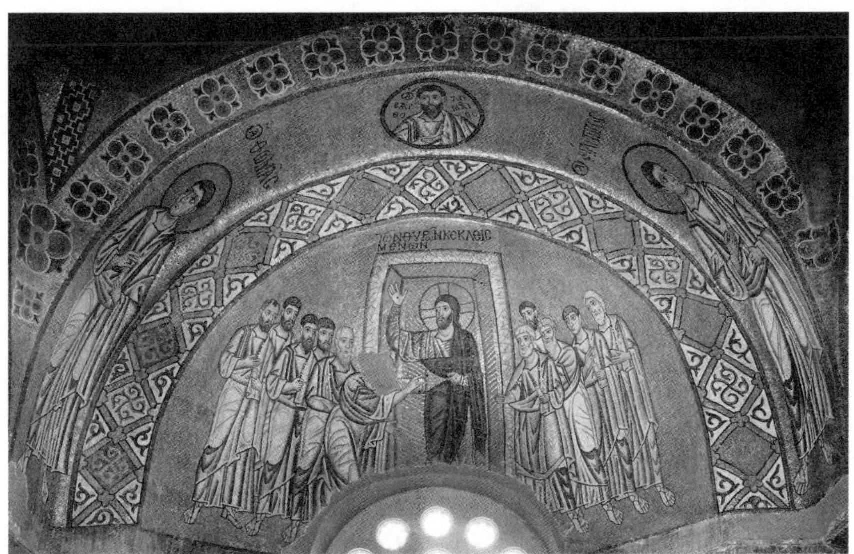

4.3. Doubting Thomas. Narthex, Church of Hosios Loukas, Greece.

Doubting Thomas or the Incredulity of Thomas—but with the words "the doors having been closed" (*tōn thyrōn kekleismenōn*), quoted from John 20:26 (cf. John 20:19). This phrase refers to Christ's miraculous entrance into the room, as he is simultaneously corporeal and tangible to Thomas, yet also immaterial and intangible in penetrating the closed doors.

The language of closed yet penetrable doors appears prominently in Marian hymnography, often describing Mary's pregnancy and paradoxical inviolate virginity;[83] it alludes to the line in Ezekiel 44:2 that "the gate will be shut [*kekleismenē*]," yet God "has entered [*eiseleusetai*] by it." In the Doubting Thomas scene, the paradox of Mary's miraculous pregnancy is reiterated in Christ's manifestation before the Apostles. In his hymn on the Annunciation, Romanus the Melodist seems to draw from the Thomas story, subtly citing John 20:19 and 20:26. Mary describes to Joseph the appearance of the suitor-angel Gabriel:

His form [*morphē*] filled the entire chamber,
and me at the same time: For the doors having been closed
   [*tōn gar thyrōn kekleismenōn*] he appeared to me.[84]

In this way, Romanus stages the Annunciation as a foreshadowing of the Doubting Thomas narrative. In both instances, human perception is pushed past its limits as it confronts the image or form (*morphē*) of Christ. Just as this form filled Mary and the chamber at the Annunciation, it now once again fills the locked chamber after the Resurrection. Just as Mary, by perceiving, cognitively conceives and then bodily conceives the Christ—assenting to the Annunciation and consenting to her impregnation—so Thomas perceives Christ in mind and body, as Christ consents to be touched and Thomas assents to the realization that indeed this is "My Lord and my God."[85]

The closed doors in both instances manifest the limits of human flesh, that of the womb and of the senses, which Christ penetrated without violating when he became tangible at the Annunciation and at Thomas's incredulity. In other words, these closed-yet-penetrated doors are the site before which Christ becomes visible and tangible, beyond the merely verbal news of his resurrection. As we saw in the Chilandar and San Marco examples, the Doubting Thomas scenes are often depicted in a rich gold that frames the Christ figure. Such framing plays with the duality of Christ in the image; he is a depiction of the narrative and a representation as an icon. The gold-ground frame, which resembles the gold background of Byzantine icons, makes it seem as if Thomas is genuflecting and touching an icon of Christ. Thus, Christ is simultaneously depicted as corporeal and as painted matter.

In the Theodore Psalter from 1066, we find a series of depictions of Christ within an icon, as supplicants pray to him for his intercession in earthly matters (for an example, see fig. 4.4).[86] At times, such as in the image here, angels are shown below doing the bidding of Christ as he answers the prayers of the faithful. Christ is shown in an image on a gold background at the top of the page. That physical icons are being portrayed is emphasized by the details included, such as a metal ring from which the icon would have been hung. Yet the Christ in this icon is not a soulless painted image but rather an animate and living being as he responds to prayers. In some instances, as shown here, his hand violates the boundaries of his painted icon, going beyond the image's frame; in this way, he is shown to be simultaneously painted and corporeal.

In a Doubting Thomas scene found in the crypt of the same church at Hosios Loukas, we again see Christ before the closed doors, which are painted with a marble-like beige border around golden doors that match Christ's golden halo (fig. 4.5).[87] As in the Chilandar image, Christ pulls away his garment with the parted fingers of his left hand, revealing his abdomen. Yet, here his right hand forcefully grasps Thomas's wrist, drawing him into the wound as the Apostles watch. In so doing, the icon-like Christ transcends its limits, much as the animate Christ icons in the Theodore Psalter go beyond their painted nature. This gesture of Christ forcing

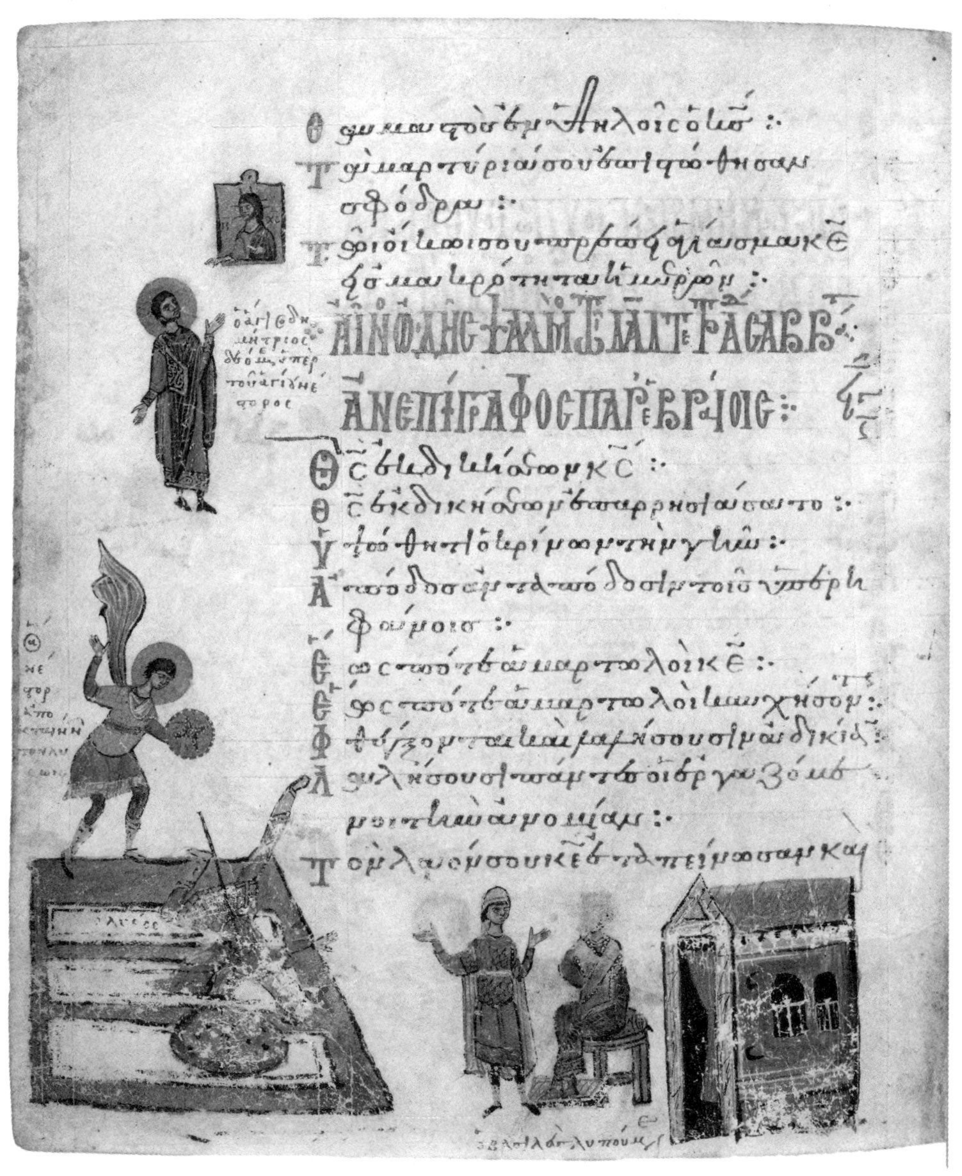

4.4. Demetrius with an Icon of Christ. London, British Library, Theodore Psalter (Add. Ms. 19352), fol. 125v. © The British Library Board.

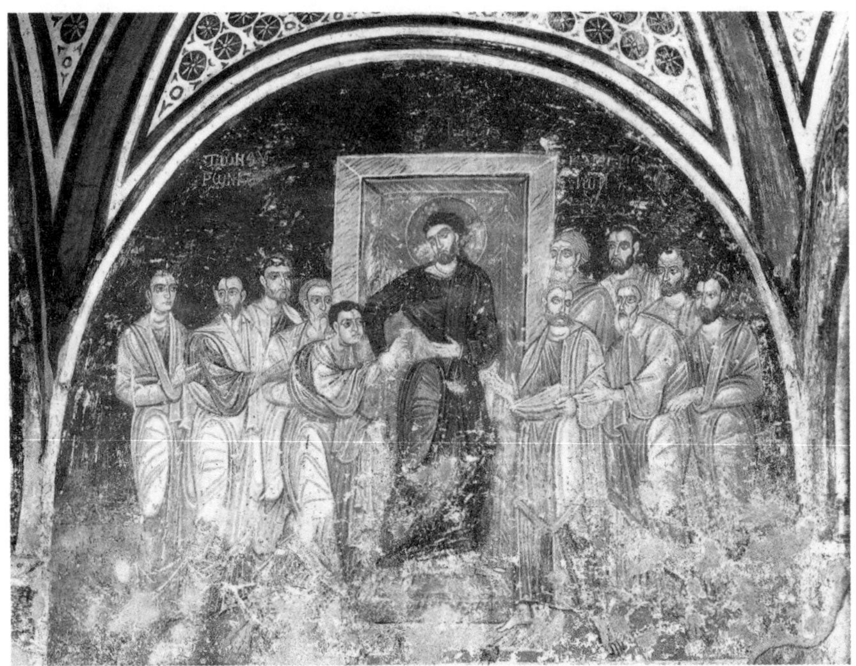

4.5. Doubting Thomas. Crypt, Church of Hosios Loukas, Greece.

Thomas to touch him captures the scene's violence, in Mesarites's telling, as Thomas is coerced into touching Christ. The rest of the Apostles gesture toward Christ with open hands, pushing the viewer's gaze toward the center. Thus, the scene in which Thomas doubts the risen Christ serves as a space in which to contemplate one's sensory access to Christ via the icon. As Mesarites makes clear, the image reminds the viewer of their own identification with Thomas and assent to the narrative of Christ's resurrection. But, likewise, the scene is a meditation on what it means for a viewer to approach the icon of Christ, being unable in the present to touch him and, in the case of the narthex mosaic, also unable to touch his image, which is placed high on the wall. Thomas is doubly an image of humanity's approach toward the risen Christ and humanity's approach to Christ in the icon.

THE EROTICS OF SENSATION

A late fourteenth-century icon from the Monastery of the Transfiguration in the Meteora includes a startling addition in the scene of the Incredulity of Thomas: the figure of a female patron, Maria Palaiologina (fig. 4.6). Maria commissioned the icon to commemorate her late husband, the despot Thomas Preljubović, who is also is depicted in the Gospel scene (staring

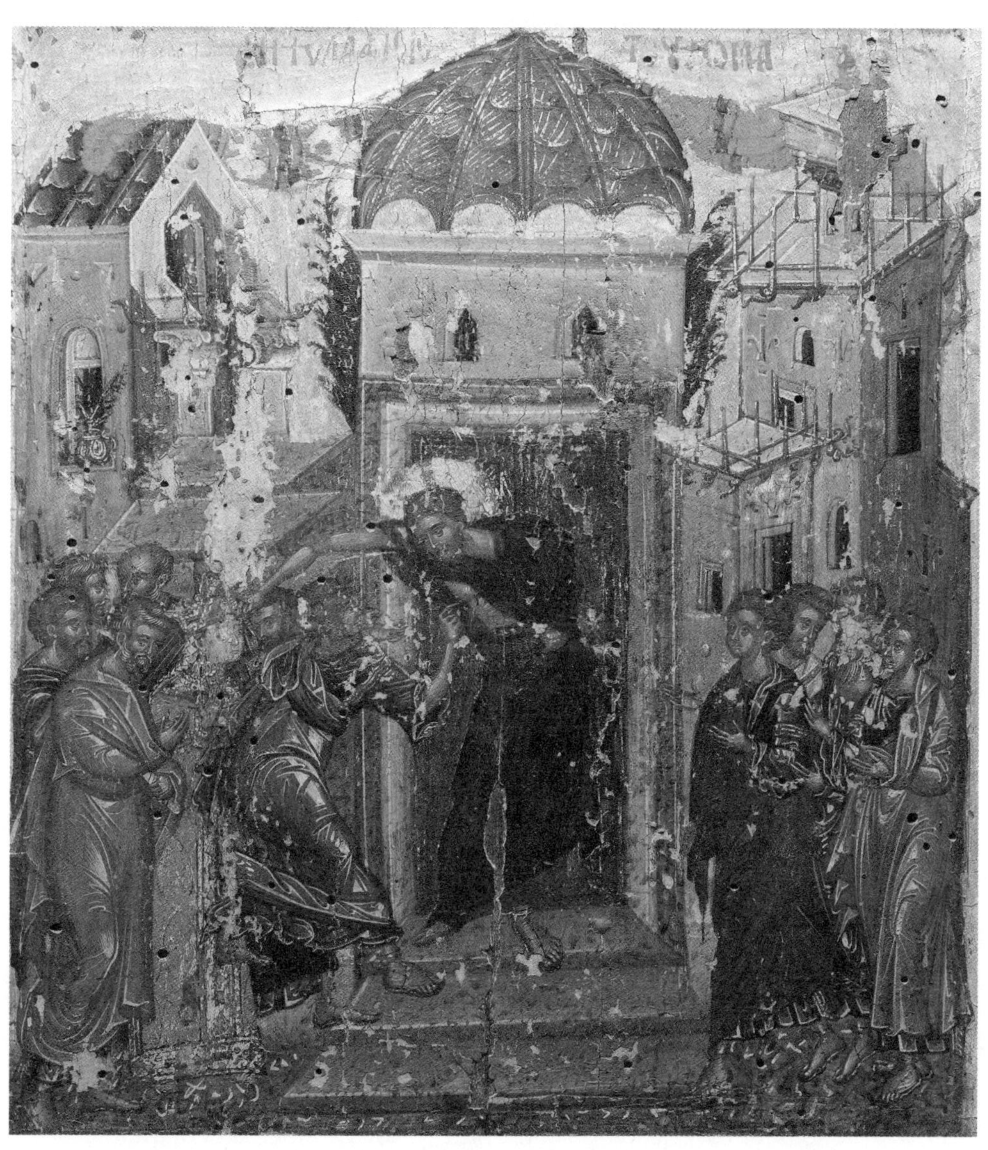

4.6. Doubting Thomas Icon, Monastery of the Transfiguration, Meteora, Greece.

out at the viewer between Thomas and Maria).[88] While patrons are at times depicted in Byzantine art on the margins, this insertion of Maria and her husband directly (and centrally) into the Gospel narrative is unique. It is striking that Maria is wearing contemporary clothing. Even more suprising is that, while Thomas touches Christ's side, Christ ignores that touch and reaches out awkwardly over both Thomases to touch Maria. Unlike other depictions of the scene, which are simply labeled "the doors being closed," this one is labeled "the touching of Thomas," thereby drawing even more attention to the act that it downplays. Various readings of the scene have been proposed. For example, Nancy Patterson Ševčenko has suggested that it emphasizes the importance of faith for those who have not seen and touched Christ, as the Gospel explicitly states: "Blessed are they that have not seen, and yet have believed" (John 20:29).[89] In effect, the insertion of the patron subverts the discomfort inherent in the Thomas story.

Using Thomas as a foil to proper Christian piety and faith, Maria rebukes the need for sensory confirmation. In this image she receives the grace and touch of Christ in a gesture akin to a coronation scene, but her identity both as a woman and as a contemporary figure in an ancient scene highlights that she in fact did not see and touch. Thus, the icon serves as a corrective to the desire of the senses to confirm, attempting to discipline the temptation to disbelieve, see, and touch. It is she, not the Apostle Thomas or her late husband Thomas, who receives Christ's touch—a touch that was denied even to Mary Magdalene. In diverging so prominently from other depictions of the scene, this icon raises an objection to the erotics of sensory perception and to the assumption that there is a fundamental need to confirm and affirm belief through sight and then touch.

The paradox of the Doubting Thomas's place in art, hymns, and homilies is the episode's function both as an exuberant depiction of fleshly, carnal congress with Christ and also as a troubling meditation on the danger of this desire and the need for a religion rooted in faith in what cannot be perceived with the bodily senses. In the interplay between these two approaches, we find the erotic dynamics of sensory perception in Byzantine thought. In the eleventh-century *synaxarion*—a liturgical calendar with instructions for the celebration of the liturgy—of the Monastery of the Theotokos Evergetis in Constantinople, the monastic community is instructed to read John Chrysostom's homily on the Doubting Thomas the Sunday of Antipascha, the first after Easter.[90] Centering his homily on John 20:24–21:14, Chrysostom begins by musing on Thomas's incredulity and approach to Christ through the earthly senses. Chrysostom notes that it is just as much a crime to "believe carelessly" as it is to "be beyond measure curious and meddlesome." Echoing the praises of the Virgin for her proper deliberation on the angel's words—rather than hastily assenting as did Eve before her, as discussed in chapter 1—this homily then reflects on the inverse of such deliberation, the pursuit of a "gross understanding" (*pachytatēs dianoias*).[91]

The language of grossness, materiality, or fatness suggested by *pachytatēs* is difficult to translate; we have already seen it in Mesarites's description of Christ's body as "free of all fatness" (*pasēs apēllagmenēn pachytētos*). The term denotes a certain earthly materiality, which Christ does not participate in, even while becoming tangible. The reason that Christ could take on a tangible form was his "condescension" (*sygkatabaseōs*): that is, his consent to become fleshy and fat, fully human. Yet, in Chrysostom's homily, it is Thomas's perceptive faculties that are accused of this grossness and, in this regard, too, Christ is said (this time by Chrysostom) to be "free of all fatness" (*pachytētos pasēs apēllakto*). But Thomas "sought proof from the grossest of the senses [*aisthēseōs tēs pachytatēs*], and would not even trust his eyes." Thus Thomas, earthly and gross, is attached to the materiality of the basest of the senses—touch.

Chrysostom stresses Thomas's unbridled desire: in his account, not only was Thomas overcome by desire but Christ delays encountering him precisely so that by continuing to hear the Apostles' stories, "he [Thomas] might be inflamed [*ekkaēnai*] to more eager desire [*pothon*]." When Christ appears to Thomas, he does not even let Thomas speak but immediately "wherefore his desire, he fulfilled" (*haper epethymei, plēroi*).[92] Throughout the homily, Chrysostom emphasizes the need to orient one's desires and love for Christ, as if they were directed at loved ones who are gone. If one is always oriented with love toward those who are missing, then the temptation of the earthly pleasures is removed—replaced by the pleasure of longing for and looking at those whom one desires. "For such a thing," Chrysostom writes, "is *erōs*." Every day a person is to imagine their loved ones and, in so doing, one is chained to that desired object and thus free from earthly desires, which then seem like nothing more than "a shadow, an image, a dream."[93]

This, according to John Chrysostom, is where the pious Christian should put Christ: as the object of their *erōs* and desire. Thus, Chrysostom's homily is a manifesto extolling the role of perception, demanding that his listeners imagine and long for the Christ they desire, never consummating that experience so that it may continually fuel their yearning for him. The image of the Doubting Thomas is meant as a temptation: it is intended to taunt the viewer with the delusion that they might clasp Christ and then immediately deny that possibility, since sight cannot touch. Like the hymns of Symeon the New Theologian or Romanus's play with longing and lust, Chrysostom's scene of the Doubting Thomas was intended to incite and kindle a desire for the touch of Christ's risen body, inflaming that desire by tantalizing the eyes yet denying that touch to the hand.

Rooted in erotics, such worship in the Byzantine world was fueled by the icon, which offers visible images of holy figures who nevertheless remain beyond the viewer's palpable grasp. In the context of Byzantine art, Ivan Drpić notes, desire (*pothos*) is "the name for loving desire generated by a feeling of lack and separation."[94] Because it appears so often in religious texts, some have attempted to set *pothos* against the carnal love of *erōs* and sexual desire, but both in their usage and definitions the two terms overlap considerably in secular and religious writings. A consistent difference, however, is that, while *erōs* often refers to that which is present, *pothos* is preferred to articulate the longing, desire, and lust for that which is absent.[95] Thus, *pothos* articulates the "erotic component of devotion"; but, rather than viewing this simply as an "outpouring of the self toward a divine or saintly Other," as Drpić puts it,[96] I suggest that the erotics inherent in Byzantine sensation and perception are deeply tied to a lust for consummation, with all the sexual resonances inherent in that word. I do not mean by this that all veneration was pornographic in its imagination, even if many writers do tend toward that language, but rather that veneration operated via a similarly structured yearning for carnal presence and consummation. Beginning with early Christian rhetoric, theologians gravitated toward a language of love, desire, and *erōs* to articulate matters of bodily and divine union, even when attempting to avoid carnal knowledge and praise abstinence.[97]

FROM SEEING TOUCH TO RITUALIZING TOUCH

In art and ritual, the desire for sensory confirmation plays an erotic role in suturing the divide between sight and touch. The dynamic between touching and seeing is given material form in pilgrimage flasks from the Holy Land depicting the scene of the Doubting Thomas. As Gary Vikan notes, such flasks, or *ampullae*, were unlikely to have been tied to a site or relic associated with the Thomas narrative.[98] Instead, just like many other *ampullae*, these probably contained oil that had been sanctified by contact with the True Cross or the tomb of Christ. In one example from between the

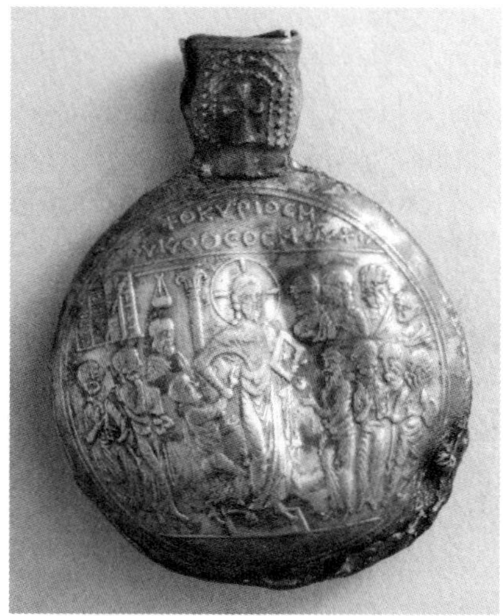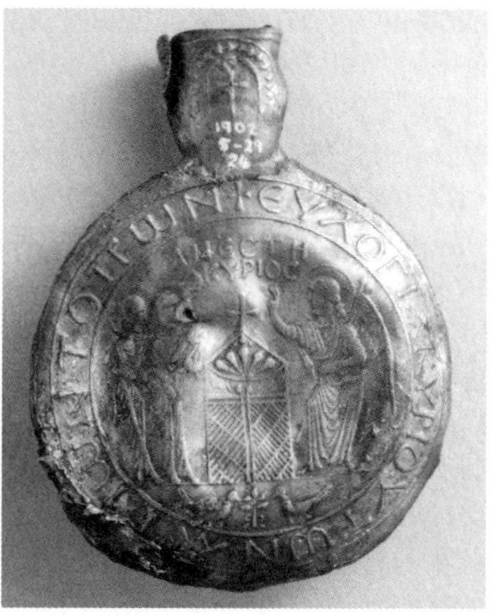

4.7. Pilgrimage Flask with (*left*) Doubting Thomas and (*right*) Women at the Tomb of Christ with Angel. London, British Museum, Ampulla (no. 1902,0529.24). ©Trustees of the British Museum.

eleventh and thirteenth centuries, now at the British Museum, the Doubting Thomas scene is depicted on one side (fig. 4.7 *left*), while on the other side is an image of the tomb of Christ with the angel announcing his resurrection to the holy women (fig. 4.7 *right*). Between the angel and the women is the phrase, "The Lord is risen," and the scene is surrounded with an inscription stating that this is a "blessing of the Lord from the Holy Places." The inscription announces the blessing that the owner has received by visiting and touching the holy places of the Christ's resurrection—namely, the Holy Sepulcher, which is depicted in the scene.

When we turn the flask over, we encounter the familiar scene of the Doubting Thomas with Christ at the center and the Apostles surrounding him. Thomas extends his arm to Christ as Christ grabs him by the wrist and inserts his prodding finger into his own side. Unlike the monumental wall paintings that label the scene "the doors having been closed," the pilgrimage *ampulla* captures the scene by referring to its resolution. "My Lord and my God!" is inscribed above the scene, announcing the tactile confirmation of the Resurrection simultaneously for Thomas and for the pilgrim, who has also touched the traces of the risen Christ with this object.[99] Christ grasps Thomas's wrist, just as the pilgrim now grasps this object, thereby confirming the risen Christ, just as Thomas is doing in the image. Conflating the act of pilgrimage with the narrative of Thomas, the iconography of these *ampullae* often diverges from the scene's depiction elsewhere, choosing to stress the validating touch that comes with pilgrimage. Interestingly, the crypt at Hosios Loukas was also an important site of pilgrimage, where the ill came to be healed by the relics of the saint it contained. Thus, this image's stress on Christ touching Thomas as Thomas touches Christ seems to suggest a self-reflexive use of this iconographic variant in sites associated with pilgrimage, where the faithful came, saw, and touched in order to partake in the miraculous deeds of Christ.

A number of scholars have noted the mimetic qualities of the images in the narthex of Hosios Loukas and related monuments, drawing attention in particular to how the monastic community would have liturgically reperformed the narratives that they depict in and around the spaces where they are displayed.[100] In the case of the Thomas image, it is likely that a set of doors was originally a part of the construction below the image, though now a window's frame crudely breaks into the image's center.[101] In this case, the doors not only would have echoed the closed doors depicted in the image but also likely would have served as the site where the monks congregated after the Eucharist and before heading over to the nearby refectory.[102] Having confronted the body of Christ in the Eucharist, they would then confront the image of Thomas's encounter with the body of Christ as they went through the doors, newly opened in an action symbolic of the reopening of Paradise through Christ's passion and resurrection.

The image of Christ washing the feet of the Apostles is opposite the Doubting Thomas scene in the Hosios Loukas narthex, a common placement for the former scene in contemporary churches (fig. 4.8). Though the exact location varies, both the *Typikon of the Great Church* and the monastic typikon of Kecharitomene prescribe that the commemoration and reenactment of this Gospel scene occur in the narthex of the church on Holy Thursday.[103] During this event, the abbot of the monastery imitates Christ by washing the feet of twelve monks substituting for the Apostles; the Kecharitomene typikon specifically directs that the rite be performed near an image of the scene. Thus, as has been noted by other scholars, this mosaic would have had a direct mimetic resonance with the ritual on Holy Thursday.[104] Whereas the Doubting Thomas scene eroticizes and denies viewers a penetrating touch with the body of Christ, the washing scene and its ritual commemoration expressly fulfill and enact that touch, both visually and physically. Despite the various warnings and prohibitions found in monastic rules against gratuitous (or even necessary) touching between brothers, the events memorialized in this scene provided a sanctioned moment in which the brothers could publicly and communally touch in an

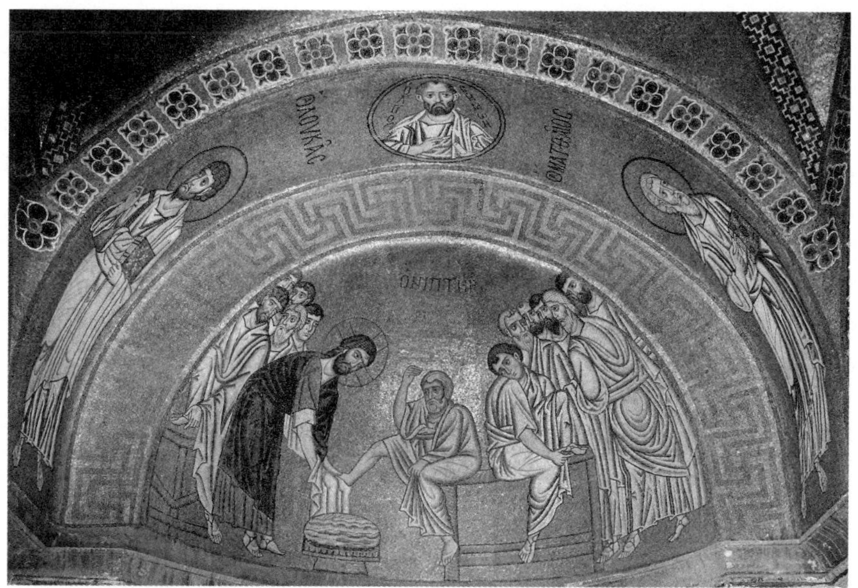

4.8. Washing of the Feet. Narthex, Church of Hosios Loukas, Greece.

intimate fashion. After this rite, the brothers would proceed on to the refectory, passing through the doors beneath the Doubting Thomas scene and again reminding themselves and grappling with the desire for touch and consummation with Christ that the washing would have stirred.

In the mosaics at Hosios Loukas, the gaze of the Apostles varies strikingly in these two scenes. Whereas the Apostles' gaze appears incredulous in the Doubting Thomas scene, in the mosaic of the washing they all look to one another. The gazes of the twelve men crisscross with a frantic energy: some look directly into the eyes of the man standing beside them, while others look over to catch the gaze of a man across the way, and some observe the others in these acts of looking. This multiplicity of gazes communicates both a longing voyeurism and an uncomfortably aroused energy, as if the Apostles are each (self)conscious of their exposed intimacy in the washing narrative. There is a pronounced sense of queer conviviality and community. And, while such a composition of glances is common in Byzantine art, the contrast with the incredulity mosaic is striking: there, none look to one another, no one looks to Thomas, all are fixed on Christ himself. Here, in contrast, it is not simply that most of them look to one another but that none look to the focus of the scene: Christ washing the feet of Peter. The youthful man who sits behind Peter, undoing his own sandal, looks intently at the scene unlike those behind him, eagerly awaiting Christ's touch.

The artist has highlighted that this man is next. He sits on the bench as if about to slide over and have his feet washed. Christ is not simply washing Peter's feet but also drying them, so there is a sense of urgency in the youth's action of stripping off his own sandals. The way that Peter's hand releases his forehead is also significant. In other scenes, the gesture of Peter clutching his head is meant to communicate the Apostle's discomfort and shock at Christ's submissive desire to wash his feet. These details stress to viewers that they are encountering the scene at the end of Peter's wash, and the other man is thus placed in relief. The youth's face tenderly rests on his own shoulder, his red cheeks blooming, as he looks back. Yet he looks not to Christ, not to Peter, but directly at Christ's clothed hand caressing Peter's right foot. In other words, this youth acknowledges the focus of the scene and longingly wishes to be touched by Christ next. He is the figure with which a monk might associate as he prepares himself to be washed by the abbot.

Given his round and beardless face, blushing red cheeks, and short hair, this figure can plausibly be identified as the young Apostle Thomas. A comparison between this man and the one depicted in the labeled portrait of Thomas to the left of the Doubting Thomas mosaic (see fig. 4.3) makes the association with Thomas all the more likely, for their facial characteristics are identical. Compositionally as well, this figure mirrors in location and gesture the figure of Thomas on the other side of the narthex in the incredulity mosaic: both are looking westward, heads inclined toward the touch of Christ. Thus, we can sketch the interplay between the mosaic of the washing and that of the Doubting Thomas—in both, Thomas plays a crucial role as the one about to partake in Christ's touch.

While the washing of the Apostles serves as a manifestation of Christ's humility and humanity through his submissive touch, the scene of the incredulity serves as just the opposite: Christ has begrudgingly condescended to be touched by Thomas. That the figure of Thomas serves as foil in this scene is telling. Unlike Peter, who initially shows reluctance at Christ's request to wash his feet, Thomas eagerly and longingly accepts the opportunity to touch Christ. The two mosaics may work to educate and discipline the monks about faith and congress with Christ, but in Thomas they could also have identified with a queer figure, who in both scenes oversteps the proprieties of faith in his desire for confirming and consummating a communion with Christ. Together, the mosaics of the narthex in Hosios Loukas tie Thomas to the erotics of sensation, as the monks themselves participated in parallel acts of touching and seeing. Interestingly, the only other figure beside Thomas that looks to Christ in the feet-washing scene is Luke (on the far left), who is identifiable by his labeled portrait just outside the mosaic on the left as well (see fig. 4.8). As the namesake of the monastery, his gaze represents the monastic community's own partaking in the re-performance of this scene in the narthex. The manner of this public and ritualized moment of touch between men is rife with erotic tension, even if it is just the cursory titillation of being intimately touched as a monk. As modern subjects, we might be inclined to underplay this reading were so many monastic rules not so verbose, explicitly cautious, and suspicious about these types of queer intimacies and the pornographic desires they could easily stir up.

THE QUEERNESS OF MONASTIC COMMUNITY

Throughout this analysis of the Doubting Thomas scene, we have witnessed a repeated concern with the operations and limits of sense perception in approaching Christ. The issues of consent and assent (*synkatathesis*), addressed in chapter 1 and again here, reveal the interweaving of sexual intercourse and cognition, and the crucial role that both play in making Christ perceptible to humanity even when our senses fail us. It is at this intersection of sensation, sex, and assent that the Doubting Thomas scene finds its true queerness, beyond the incidental homoerotics of the scene and its depictions in literature and art. I do not mean to disregard the potency of its homoerotic potential, particularly in all-male monastic communities where various forms of same-gender intimacy, both erotic and otherwise, would have been given room to maneuver. Indeed, this additional substratum of male same-gender desire is precisely what gives the narrative its particular poignancy. Yet, to return to Muñoz's evocative words, we "may never touch queerness, but we can feel it as the warm illumination of a horizon imbued with potentiality."

Thomas's incredulity opens up this queerness "as an ideality that can be distilled from the past and used to imagine a future," as Muñoz continues. This imagined future is one of radical conviviality, staunchly positioned against the "no future" of the antisocial thesis. In other words, this is a queer theory invested in the utopian communities that emerge in the face of persecution, providing a place of respite for the maltreated. This is a queerness neither constructed on the embracing of shame as an identity, as Virginia Burrus has suggested, nor one rooted in a closely related attachment to the *jouissance* of the death drive, as Lee Edelman has advocated.[105] Here, the shut doors—closed, as the text of John 20:19 tells us, when the

Apostles first saw Christ in that room (that is, without Thomas) "because a fear of the Jews" (*dia ton phobon tōn Ioudaiōn*), and closed again eight days later when Christ appears to Thomas and the others—become particularly salient. This element of the story moves us beyond the problem of perception and assent that the Doubting Thomas tale foregrounds, drawing our attention instead to the context in which the issues play out: namely, the secretive congregation of like-minded men, who are in hiding from those seeking to persecute and oppress them. In this instance, the Apostles are queer in all respects—queer subjects at the margins of their own society and queer in their choice to embrace the safety that lies in communities of men behind closed doors.

The Doubting Thomas exhorts the Apostles and the Christian subject to examine and revise their denials of Christ, working through fear to find community in their shared assent. That this prototypical closet opens the way to the formation of a Christian identity should not be viewed as trivial. For the male monk, the narrative must have served on some level as a model of and model for a homosocial way of living together in the Christian faith. In his hymn on the Doubting Thomas, Romanus captures this queer utopia as a radical site for proud and shameless self-identification, as Thomas exhorts his fellow disciples:

"Announce to all the people what you have seen and heard.

Disciples, do not hide the lamp under the measure.

What you are saying in the dark proclaim in the light.

Stand openly outside with confidence.

You are still in the lair, yet you act boldly.

You speak out loud—while the doors are shut!

Cry out, 'We have seen the Creator in secret.'

Let it be shown to all, let creation learn,

let mortals be taught to cry to the Risen One,

'You are our Lord and our God.'"[106]

In this command to embrace a queered identity, Thomas orders his fellow Apostles, in Muñoz's words, "to think and feel a then and there" for the unveiling of their identity. Thomas literally asks that the Apostles come out— out of their closet as Christian subjects—saying to them, "Stand openly outside with confidence." I do not mean to suggest that there was a late antique or early Christian conception of the closet connected to same-gender desire or other nonnormative sexualities. I am instead grappling with how we construct other closets, other systems and structures of concealment and confinement that generate spaces within which individuals can maneuver openly, given the challenges posed by their intersecting identities in the outside world. Closets, in this sense, are created for our own protection against the failures of our brethren; in the course of their construction, such closets enable us to find new "brothers," monastic or otherwise, different from those in the families into which we were born.

This is the practice of queerness: to find refuge amid likeness; to seek, uncover, encounter those who, like you, have been marginalized and oppressed, and to set out together to construct spaces for the inclusion of others who are placed in opposition to the normative forces of a monolithic political, religious, social, or sexual majority. In this refuge amid likeness, there is the recognition of the self in the other. To be sure, in that recognition we sometimes make contact with another's flesh, like Thomas's finger prodding against a resistant body. Yet that fleshy handling is not necessarily prescribed, and it emerges from the fundamental and inalienable intimacy of a shared community.

In Maximus the Confessor's scholia on Pseudo-Dionysius the Areopagite's *On the Divine Names* from around the turn of the sixth-century, the author observes that God is the prime cause of love (*agapē*) and desire (*erōs*), which unifies all things.[107] This erotic attraction, in both rational and irrational souls, is what draws us all to community. There exists a "law of affection" (*philias nomos*), and this "desire" (*erōta*) in irrational creatures, rooted in "sensual affection" (*aisthētikēn philian*), brings about conviviality. As the late antique author writes:

For from this erotic faculty [*erōtikēs . . . dynameōs*], winged creatures fly in flocks, just as swans, geese, cranes, crows, and other such things. And, similarly those that go on land, like deer, cattle, and the like. And those that swim, like tuna, mullet, and the like. And those not belonging to a herd are moved toward a partner of the same kind as one [*homostoichōn sunodon*] from that cause.[108]

Structuring community as an "erotic faculty" across living animals, the author intimates that, on some level, a form of erotic, sexual attraction is responsible for the desire of beings to live together. Indeed, in those animals who do not congregate into a flock, this *erōs* leads individuals to be moved to find a "companion" (*sunodon*)—literally, a traveler on the road with one—who is of one's "same rank" or "same kind" (*homostoichōn*). Thus, the erotic faculty that structures community and that is synonymous with God's love leads one to desire a companion who is like oneself, structuring a community or personal bond of likeness through *erōs*.

The radicality of early Christian community in the late antique world is thus paradigmatic of queerness, as defined by world building. Same-gender desire and consummation are only a small facet of that queerness as a radical cohabitation. Yet it is important to remember that, when over time queerness becomes itself complicit and synonymous with power and normativity, as sometimes happens, we must begin to look elsewhere for glimmers of that once-queer utopia. Therefore, while the refuge offered to men with same-gender desires within monastic communities captures the ethos of the conviviality of Thomas's touch, the monasticism of later centuries is not the same as that of its nascent days, when it operated in society's wildernesses and deserts. Then, it is the women denied their right to consent to sex (unlike the Virgin) and childbearing, the prostitutes of the ilk of Procopius's Theodora, the transgender men living their life as eunuch monks, the effeminates of Cyril of Alexandria's invective, and the monks finding companionship in the cell of a beloved brother who come to occupy the queerness conveyed in Romanus's depiction of an open Christian subjectivity. Queerness is captured in the paradoxes "You speak out loud—while the doors are shut!" and "You are still in the lair, yet you act boldly," which manifest a community that is simultaneously out and cloistered, persecuted and proud, just as the doors manifested the simultaneous tangibility and incorporeality of the risen Christ. The Doubting Thomas thus confronts us with the possibility of Christian queerness as the process of learning to live together—with intimacies that sometimes include those of the flesh.

V. The Ethiopian Eunuch

THIS CHAPTER FOCUSES ON A SINGLE IMAGE, the figure of the Ethiopian eunuch in the Menologion of Basil II (fig. 5.1), a text commissioned for the Byzantine emperor around the year 1000.[1] In this painting, we glimpse two episodes in the life of the Apostle Philip, who is being commemorated in the scene. On the right, we encounter the elderly Philip, who as the text above the image tells us would eventually become the bishop of Tralles in Asia Minor. On the left, we encounter a scene from the Acts of the Apostles (8:26–40)—the moment Philip encounters a powerful eunuch who served as the treasurer of Queen Candace, the ruler of the Ethiopians (plate 1). The eunuch is sitting on a chariot reading the prophet Isaiah, while on pilgrimage to Jerusalem. Hearing them read from Isaiah, Philip joins the eunuch. They ask Peter to be their tutor, showing them how the words of the prophet became manifest in Christ, and together continue on the eunuch's pilgrimage to Jerusalem. Upon encountering a source of water on their way, the eunuch asks to be baptized. Philip agrees, and after doing so, Philip is swept away by the spirit of God and continues on his own to Asia Minor.

One of the most striking details of the manuscript is its depiction of the eunuch as a black person. The artist, a man named Georgios (identified by the inscription to the left of the image), has chosen to depict the moment when Philip agrees to baptize the eunuch. There is an intimacy between the two figures as the eunuch stares intently into Philip's eyes. Philip looks back with a gaze that seems slightly awry, apparently captured as he is in the midst of considering the eunuch's request for baptism. In his right hand, Philip carries a tied-up scroll that intimates his impending response and speech act, commanding the chariot to stop so that the eunuch may be baptized. Note the way that the eunuch's right hand rises from the reins and gestures toward the stream before them, while the other hand almost seems to pull at those reins, suggesting Philip's command to stop the chariot. The horses' front left legs are raised, while the right ones are firmly planted on the ground and their back left legs are bent, all indicating to the viewer that

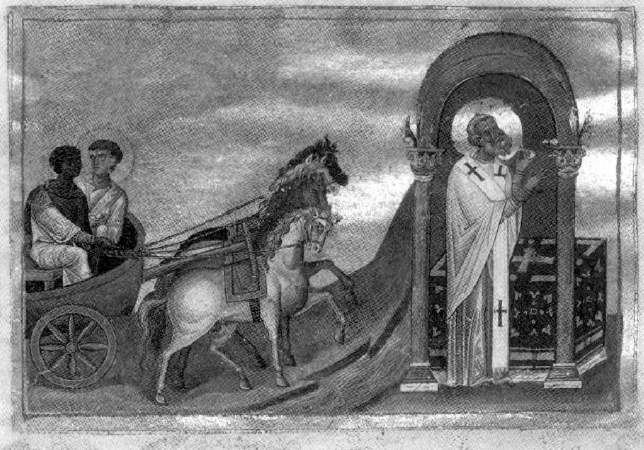

5.1. Philip and the Ethiopian Eunuch. Vatican City, Biblioteca Apostolica Vaticana, 'Menologion' of Basil II (Vat. gr. 1613), fol. 107. © 2019 Biblioteca Apostolica Vaticana.

the horses are abruptly stopping in their tracks. The gray horse closest to the viewer captures our attention, the only figure in the scene to stare directly at the viewer while also anchoring the center of the composition. The drama of the Ethiopian's conversion and baptism is thereby heightened though the image is dedicated to the life of Philip; the eunuch demonstrates the success of the Apostle's evangelical mission to Ethiopia and the conversion of its people to Christendom.

While it is impossible to use a term like "race" uncritically in the context of the premodern world, we must nevertheless ask how skin color operated in the late antique and Byzantine worlds. Relevant questions include: Can we perceive any systematic oppression of people whose skin color was noted as different? Do we observe the use of skin color in art and literature to code figures as other? And, more broadly, how and when does skin color manifest itself as a form of identity? In other words, given that geopolitical, cultural, and social identity are often not directly tied to variations of skin color in the ancient and medieval worlds, in what cases do we find skin color used as a marker of identity or as a site for self-identification? Obviously, these are matters that merit an entire study of their own, particularly because too brief an inquiry risks perpetuating skin-based definitions of race. Nevertheless, I will use these questions to consider how these issues intersect with the other identities already discussed in this volume. My goal is to bring out the ways in which race thus far has quietly entered into these various intersectional identities and, furthermore, to consider how the texts evidence a certain degree of racial fluidity.

THE DEPICTIONS OF THE ETHIOPIAN EUNUCH

The image of Philip and the Ethiopian eunuch most commonly appears in Byzantine art in the context of the Psalms—notably in conjunction with Psalm 68:31 (67:32), "Ethiopia shall soon stretch out her hands unto God," understood as foretelling the deeds of Philip in the Acts of the Apostles.[2] In such instances, we see a similar iconography: a youthful, boyish eunuch with a beardless face sitting in his chariot with Philip nearby. Subtle variations across the manuscripts change the exact moment depicted. For example, in the late ninth-century Chludov Psalter, we see a long-haired youth with large rosy cheeks standing in the chariot and wearing a simple blue tunic, while Philip greets them from beside the chariot (plate 2). This illustration thus dramatizes the moment that Philip overhears the eunuch reading from Isaiah, initiating the series of events that culminate, on the right side of the page, in the eunuch's baptism. The same moments are depicted in the

Pantokrator Psalter, also from the ninth century (fig. 5.2). In the Theodore Psalter from 1066, the scene is similar, featuring both the chariot and the baptism, though here the artist stresses the education of the eunuch (fig. 5.3). An open text is displayed, suggesting Philip's tutelage, while neither of them pay any heed to the road. An elaboration of the scene is also shown in a wall painting from 1327 to 1335 in the Dečani Monastery in Serbia (fig. 5.4). There, Philip and the eunuch are intimately seated on the same bench, poring over the open codex on the eunuch's lap, while carriage attendants lead the chariot, which has become a sort of horse-drawn cart. The eunuch once again has long streaming hair, as in the earlier examples, but they wear a white turban and unique tunic with golden hems. These details make the figure seem exotic in contrast to Philip's traditional Roman tunic, but because the overall style of the eunuch's garment matches the attire worn by the carriage attendants, Philip appears to be the foreigner in this scenario.

Significantly, in all the Psalter images and in the Serbian wall painting, the eunuch is invariably depicted as white. Despite the literal meaning of the term "Ethiopian" and its usage to denote black Africans, this Ethiopian eunuch has been repeatedly depicted with white skin. Depictions of Ethiopians as white are by no means rare among Byzantine artists. For example, in the Church of San Marco in Venice, the Byzantine mosaicists depicted King Aeglippus of Ethiopia, his family, and his fellow countrymen all as white at the king's baptism, their alterity marked by their pointed hats and turbans, similar to what we find later in the Dečani image (fig. 5.5). In the case of the white Ethiopian eunuchs, the youthfulness of their faces, the effeminate locks of hair, and their rosy cheeks (as in the Chludov Psalter) stress their identity as a court eunuch. Despite being Ethiopian, the eunuch's identity as a eunuch was dominant, and thus they were rendered with eunuchs' stereotypical characteristics: ghostly paleness, flushed cheeks, thin long hair, and feminine features.

Indeed, the Menologion of Basil II is highly unusual in its depiction of the Ethiopian eunuch as a black person. The Menologion, whose name is a misnomer, is technically a synaxarion, since it provides brief narratives of the saints being commemorated in calendrical order, in this case from September 1 to the end of February. This detail is worth noting because one of the only other appearances of the eunuch as black in Byzantine art is in another synaxarion—one from the Docheiariou Monastery on Mount Athos, which shows Philip standing alongside the eunuch in the chariot (plate 3). There, the eunuch is brown-skinned and wears a turban, details to which we will return. If we look closely at the image in the Menologion

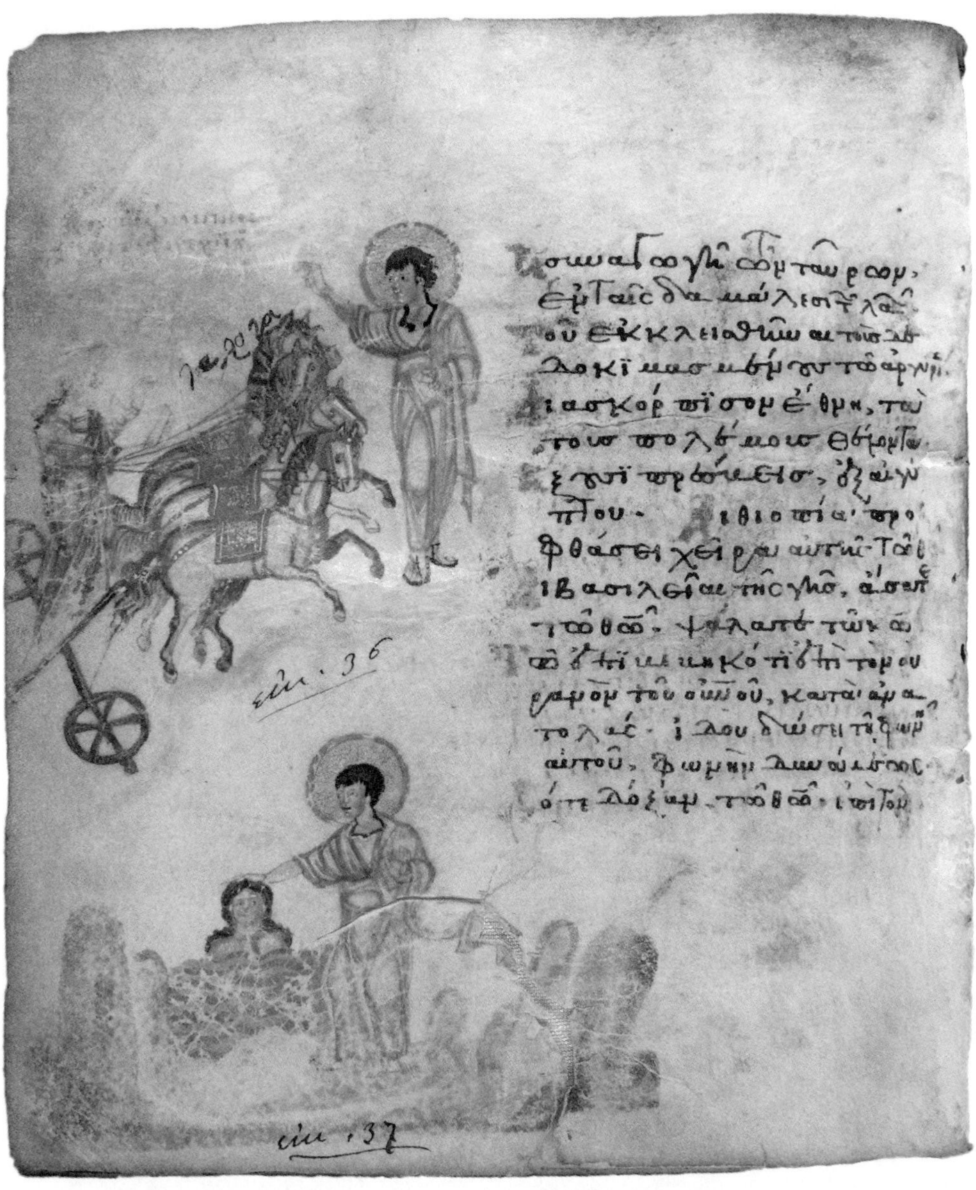

5.2. Philip and the Ethiopian Eunuch. Mount Athos, Pantokrator Monastery, Psalter (Cod. 61), fol. 85v. © Pantokrator Monastery, Mount Athos.

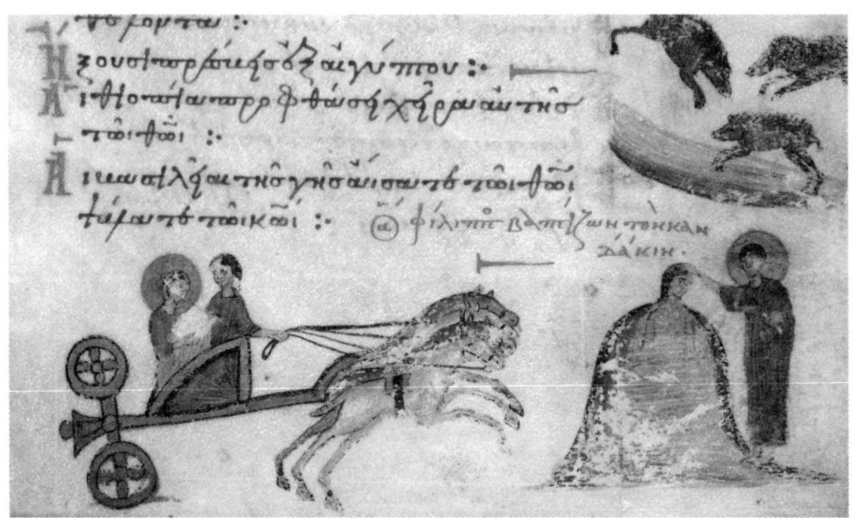

5.3. Philip and the Ethiopian Eunuch. London, British Library, Theodore Psalter (Add. Ms. 19352), fol. 85r. © The British Library Board.

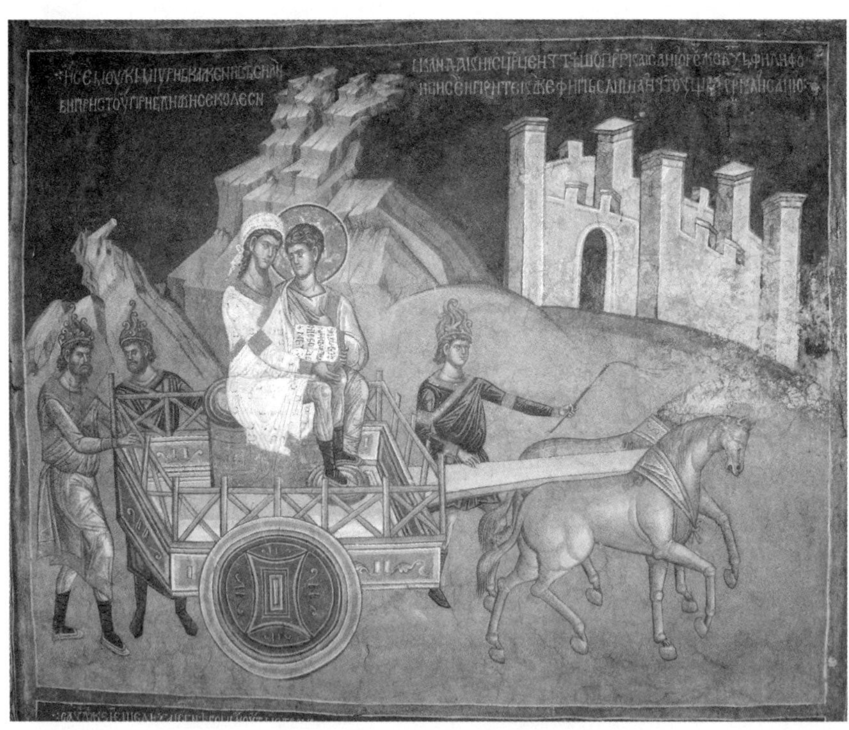

5.4. Philip and the Ethiopian Eunuch. Nave, Dečani Monastery, Serbia.

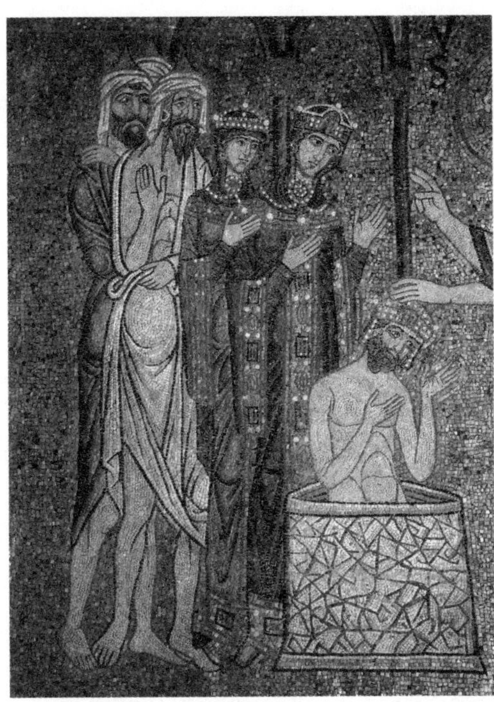

5.5. King Aeglippus of
Ethiopia, His Family,
and Fellow Country-
men. Church of San
Marco, Venice, Italy.

of Basil II, an imperial commission of the highest quality, we observe that
the facial features of the eunuch are comparable to that of the youthful
Philip and the eunuch's curling, undulating hair resembles that of other
figures in the manuscript. Unlike many ancient representations of Ethiopians, which deploy grotesque stereotypes analogous to the infamous blackface of nineteenth- and twentieth-century minstrel shows, the Menologion
eunuch is depicted no differently than the rest of the saintly subjects in the
manuscript—except, of course, his face, hair, and hands are painted in a
grayish black.

In the Docheiariou synaxarion, the darkness of the Ethiopian eunuch is
transmuted into a racialized blackness intended to communicate an ethnic alterity. A youthful and pale Philip approaches the chariot wearing a
pink himation over a light blue chiton. The eunuch gestures back while the
Apostle speaks to him, and they are caught in conversation. The eunuch
wears a rich, dark blue himation-like tunic; they have a dull, mottled brown
skin and a turban upon their head. In other words, the eunuch's iconography closely resembles that of the Menologion's Blemmyes, Saracens, or Indians (Indians were understood as being very closely related to and at times
were even confused with Ethiopians). In a sense, this image recognizes real

skin tone, beyond a stereotype of blackness: Ethiopians are a group of people with as much variance in skin color as the Byzantines themselves.

Such variation is clearly displayed in the Byzantine mosaicist's depiction of Egyptians in the Church of San Marco in Venice: in the dome featuring the Pentecost scene, various groups of people are included and labeled according to their identity. The Arabs are dressed in loose white togas, wear turbans, and have a pale white skin (fig. 5.6). Only the Egyptians, who wear the same white tunics and turbans as the Arabs, are shown as having dark skin (fig. 5.7). However, the two Egyptians are not depicted uniformly. Indeed, the skin tones of the two figures are markedly different: on the left, the skin of the figure is a grayish-black, whereas the right figure's skin is a rich brown with highlights of ocher. In this way, the mosaicists acknowledge the variety of hues in Egypt, shattering any notion of a monolithic comprehension of race or the assumption that, for Byzantine artists, racial darkness simply meant "black."

In the Docheiariou manuscript (plate 3) the figure of the eunuch is articulated as a foreigner in appearance and garb. In the second scene, on the top-right corner of the folio, the two figures are repeated, showing Philip's education of the eunuch. Indicating their imperial associations, the eunuch sits on an imperial gold throne with a lofty red cushion, embroidered textile, and a bejeweled footstool; in contrast, Philip sits on a boulder. Compared to Philip, the eunuch is stripped down: while they wear a blue tunic, there is no chiton underneath, so their flesh is clearly revealed. This himation also resembles a knee-length tunic rather than the more classical himation of Philip. Immediately below, in the baptism scene, the eunuch has been wholly denuded, turban and all, revealing to Philip their brown flesh as they are baptized in a stream between a building and a cliff. The sequence of images shows the eunuch abandoning their earthly garb and becoming wholly naked before God. The accoutrements of their royal filiations and foreignness are all stripped away, leaving behind only the color of their skin. They are thus a model of Christianity as its own group or race, a *genos* that wishes to transcend race and ethnicity.[3] In other words—and I am by no means suggesting that this is some "postracial" ideal—the brownness of the Ethiopian eunuch's skin stands as no impediment to baptism or conversion. They are also not black, as a demon might be represented, but rather brown. They do not shed their skin, but they do shed the garb of their past life and with it, ultimately, their foreignness.

Returning to the Menologion (fig. 5.1), we find Philip in a pink chiton under a crème-colored himation in the style of late antique figures, as the

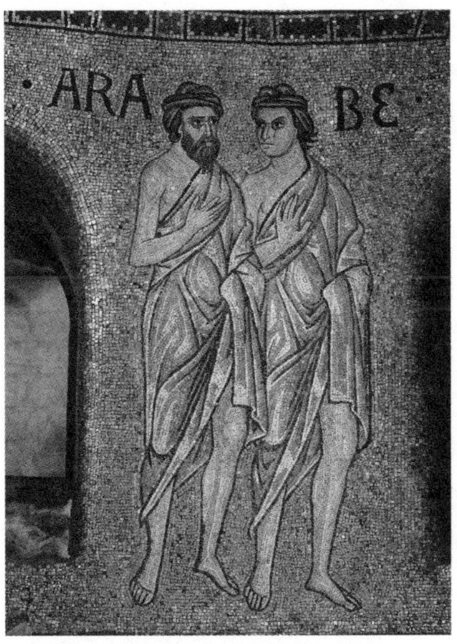

5.6. Arabs from Pentecost Dome. Church of San Marco, Venice, Italy.

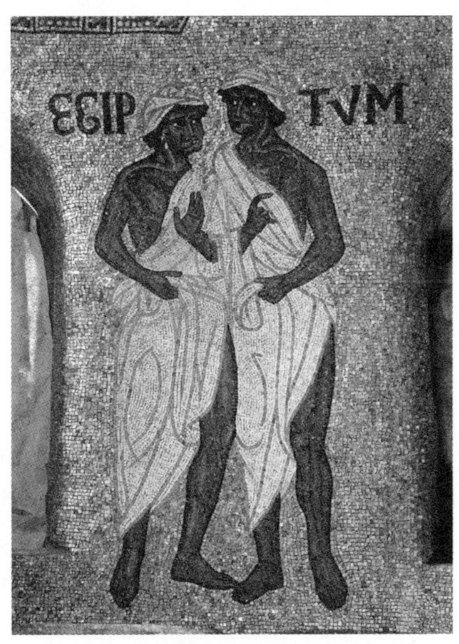

5.7. Egyptians from Pentecost Dome. Church of San Marco, Venice, Italy.

Apostles are often shown. However, the Ethiopian eunuch is dressed as an imperial subject from the time of Emperor Basil II, corresponding to the text's commission.[4] Like Philip, the eunuch wears a pink tunic, but their tunic is cuffed with gold bands and features a gold-ornamented epaulet on their shoulder. This is in keeping with Byzantine imperial attire, with the addition of the short military tunic, an overgarment known as the chlamys.[5] The eunuch's chlamys is fastened by a bejeweled fibula over their shoulder, attire wholly in keeping with the garb of a Constantinopolitan court eunuch. Thus, despite the eunuch's dark skin, the viewer is not encouraged to read them as other, foreign, or different. In fact, in this image, it is the eunuch who looks like a contemporary Constantinopolitan subject, not Philip. We are left with the image of an imperial Constantinopolitan eunuch who happens to be black. We will focus here on why this is the case and how this matter is explored in the Menologion of Emperor Basil II.

CONSTANTINOPOLITAN COSMOPOLITANISM

In order to understand the context in which the image of the Ethiopian eunuch would have been received, we must appreciate how epidermal racial difference was understood in the diverse space of Constantinople and, specifically, within imperial circles. In his oration for the emperor delivered on

Epiphany in 1174, Eustathios of Thessaloniki praised the diversity of representation in the court of Manuel I Komnenos, calling these various peoples "living pearls and stones." Eustathios presents this range of humanity as a sign of the emperor's magnanimous rule and worldly renown that brought envoys from many lands:

I will marvel at these living pearls and stones, chosen from the whole earth, and the other materials of similarly great worth, these first-fruits of great nations, which encircle your crown. Oh, the varied nature of their garments! Oh, the different tongues! It seems to me that all of the dispersed nations are represented here. And I have come to know the Scythian, and he is not a stranger to my sight, and the Paionians and the Dalmatians and everything that neighbours these peoples as well, and these men are accustomed to be fellow-slaves, but there are not a few who are enrolled among our own slaves, whom you yourself, after acquiring them as prisoners of war, have honoured with servitude. I know well also the son of Hagar, the fleshy weighty one, and the man from among the Armenians who knits together his eyebrows and shows his inner depths with a treacherous kind of look, and the Indian too, slightly tinged with black, and the Ethiopian with his whole skin burnt dark, and those dainty ones from among the Franks, the lordly ones, and the others, over and above them, of all kinds. The Italian race is a proud one; and I know these men from experience; but that envoy of a different kind of speech confuses me, and the one after him and the one after that. And there are numerous others of this kind, themselves an unusual race of a different tongue, a strange sight, like nothing we are accustomed to, causing amazement by the novelty of their garments and attracting the attention of the listener by the alien nature of their language, and fixing the gaze of the viewer upon them because of the novelty of the sight, these men who have come from the outermost part of the earth, and from unexpected places, for whom the business of addressing them cannot be achieved without every tongue stumbling on account of strangeness and the twittering sound of their names. Nor would an interpreter readily be found to assist in suggesting the purpose of the embassy.[6]

Unlike Western medieval myths of monstrous races, Eustathios's oration embraces the various groups. After beginning with a lament that he was not able to accompany the emperor on his military campaigns, Eustathios turns to that which he knows well: the imperial court. What is fascinating about this oration is not simply the range of peoples it describes but the rhetorical force of its allusions to outsiders. Eustathios details with intimate familiarity the peoples who populated the Byzantine court as either temporary envoys or more permanent fixtures.

It is worth exploring the designations and identities of the peoples Eustathios mentioned.[7] "Scythian" is a term used by Byzantines to denote any nomadic group of the Eurasian steppe or Black Sea, in this period most likely the Cumans. "The Paionians and Dalmatians and everything that neighbours these peoples" refers to the Hungarians and their Slavic neighbors, including the Serbs. "The son of Hagar" was a common term in the period for Muslims generally, applied to both the Turks and the Seljuks. "Armenians" is relatively self-explanatory, denoting the people of the kingdom of Lesser Armenia in Cilicia. After mentioning Indians and Ethiopians, the author moves on to western Europe and the Franks, whom Byzantine historians somewhat confusingly called *germanoi* (referring to the Germanic tribes as *alamanoi*). "The Italian race" may well refer to the Normans, given the degree of the Byzantines' recent contact and strife that with them; it may also mean the Latins more broadly, which is how Eustathios uses the term in his later Epiphany oration from 1176.

For our purposes, the references to Indians and Ethiopians are particularly important yet difficult to parse, since two terms could be used interchangeably. Direct contact with India had ceased in the seventh century after the Arab conquest, but mediated trade and exchange continued. While the same is true of Ethiopia, ties to that region remained stronger, and the Byzantines often distinguished political groups in that region, such as those in Nubia and Axum. Nevertheless, the two terms are often used as racial markers to convey the relative darkness of people, just as we see here. The sixth-century chronicle of John Malalas provides an earlier glimpse into contact with the Indian subcontinent, a space that, while often geographically conflated with Ethiopia, was clearly identified through the trade in spices, incense, and precious stones.[8] Malalas mentions in passing that in the year 532, "an Indian ambassador was sent with gifts to Constantinople."[9] Malalas also recounts an Indian king's extravagant ceremonies as witnessed in 529 by an ambassador sent from Constantinople to warn the Indian king of Persian transgressions.[10] With a description strikingly similar to the Ethiopan eunuch's depiction in the Docheiariou manuscript, Malalas recounts how the ruler is partially nude, wearing a gold-threaded linen cloth below his waist and a gold-threaded turban on his head. Malalas describes the lavishness of the imperial ceremonies, which echoed and rivaled those that we might associate with contemporary Constantinople.

But he never mentions skin color, nor does Malalas treat this figure in any way as a gaudy barbarian or uncultured foe. By all accounts, Malalas's depiction is one of relative equals, as the Byzantine envoy comes to warn the Indian king of the Persians' warmongering.[11]

Eustathios's oration is interlaced with telling details that flesh out for the emperor and his larger audience the identities of the figures described. He uses demonstrative pronouns to pick out the Muslim as "this" fat and serious one, while "that" Armenian has a unibrow and fraught gaze. There is a sense that Eustathios is speaking not simply about abstracted types but rather about specific people with whom the emperor and his court would have been familiar. More importantly, these figures do not contour the limits of the known world. That is, they do not serve as liminal figures whose race, ethnos, or physique labels them as other. Instead, the space on the borders of the world is reserved to a nameless class of people, whose strange tongue and appearance amaze all around them. Eustathios himself trips over the "twittering sound of their names," and it seems that, unfortunately, no interpreter could be found to assist in communicating with such envoys.

In other words, in the people Eustathios named, we find not a mysteriously foreign other but rather an intimately familiar one. The lack of clear representation for the nameless throng of others underscores the familiarity of the rest, for whom, we presume, interpreters and translators were available. Eustathios finds no novelty in the appearance of the named peoples, merely praising them for their "different tongues" and the "varied nature [*poikilou*] of their garments." Variety (*poikilia*) is a particularly sought-after quality in Byzantine art and prose; because the word captures the variegation of light and color, it is particularly well-suited to describe the effects of a myriad of courtly attires from around Byzantium's spheres of influence.[12] In other words, the diversity of Constantinople was one that came to exceed the empire's direct acquaintances.

In the previous century, we find similar praise of Constantinopolitan cosmopolitanism. In a letter to Patriarch Michael Keroularios written in the 1050s, Michael Psellus boasts that they had attracted students from both west and east, from the Celtic, Arabian, Egyptian, Babylonian, Persian, and Ethiopian worlds:

But I have made Celts and Arabs yield to me, and on account of my fame they
regularly come down here to study even from the other continent; and while
the Nile irrigates the land of the Egyptians, my speech irrigates their souls.

And if you ask a Persian or an Ethiopian, they will say that they have known
me and admired me and sought me out. And now someone from across the
boundary of Babylon has come to drink from my springs through an insatia-
ble desire of his.[13]

While Psellus is certainly guilty of bravado when it comes to extolling their
work and renown as a teacher, this claim appears plausible. Some scholars
have even endeavored to identify Psellus's foreign students, naming George
and John of Petritzos from Georgia.[14] To doubt the accounts of Psellus and
Eustathios is to cling to a denial of the diversity of medieval Constantinople in the face of ever-mounting evidence. Psellus may be boasting of their
own renown here, but if the presence of an Ethiopian in eleventh-century
Constantinople were either noteworthy or mythical, its mention would not
have been so casual, or Psellus's Constantinopolitan contemporary, Keroularios, would have been wholly skeptical of the claim. Byzantine writers
were clearly proud of the ethnic and racial diversity of the empire, its subjects, and the citizens of Constantinople.

Notably, in his oration, Eustathios reserves the most disdainful treatment for the white Europeans. For example, Eustathios points to the excessive luxury and daintiness (*habrous*) of the Franks. In ancient literature
the term *habrous* can mean "beautiful," but it also carries the negative connotations of a dainty and stubborn person living in excessive luxury, and is
associated with charges of effeminacy.[15] Eustathos also mentions the pride
(*gauron*) of the "Italian race," using an adjective primarily understood
as meaning disdainful, arrogant, and haughty.[16] These subtle resonances
could have been prudently removed in the translations of interpreters for
any Europeans that might have been in the oration's audience. Thus, Eustathios's oration contains the perfect double entendres for a political speech,
with the Europeans as the ones who are treated with contempt.

WESTERN PERSPECTIVES ON RACIAL DIFFERENCE IN CONSTANTINOPLE

Byzantine writers are often largely silent about racial diversity, which either
goes unnoticed or is disregarded as meaningless (as we can see in the white-
washed depictions of the Ethiopian eunuch in art). Yet, the racial diversity
of Constantinople often is observed by visitors from western Europe, who
are both struck by the diversity of people in the city and also note that the
Byzantines themselves did not always pass as white.

In the early years of the thirteenth century, the chronicler Robert de Clari
recounts the visit of a Nubian king to Constantinople while on pilgrimage

in 1203. The king appeared before Isaac II Angelos, Alexius IV Angelos, and the Frankish barons:

And while the barons were there at the palace, a king came there whose skin was all black, and he had a cross in the middle of his forehead that had been made with a hot iron. This king was living in a very rich abbey in the city, in which the former emperor Alexius had commanded that he should be lodged and of which he was to be lord and owner as long as he wanted to stay there. When the emperor saw him coming, he rose to meet him and did great honor to him. And the emperor asked the barons: "Do you know," said he, "who this man is?" "Not at all, sire," said the barons. "I'faith," said the emperor, "this is the king of Nubia, who is come on pilgrimage to this city." Then they had an interpreter talk to him and ask him where his land was, and he answered the interpreter in his own language that his land was a hundred days' journey still beyond Jerusalem, and he had come from there to Jerusalem on pilgrimage . . . And he said that all the people of his land were Christians and that when a child was born and baptized they made a cross in the middle of his forehead with a hot iron, like the one he had. And the barons gazed at this king with great wonder.[17]

No Byzantine source recounts this event, which has captured the attention of a Frankish writer. While the identity of this king has been debated, he is thought to be Lalibela from Ethiopia, a king of Makuria, or one of the lesser Nubian rulers.[18] The text communicates the ignorance of the Frankish dignitaries, who are shamed by Alexius for being wholly unaware of who this important figure is—a figure who, the chronicle tells us, has been lavishly and warmly welcomed into Constantinople with an indefinite invitation to stay in and lord over one of the city's wealthy monasteries.

As we read this account key details come into focus. First, the visiting king explains that his people are Christians, making his own pilgrimage seem to be less unusual than it first appeared. Second, Robert de Clari notes the king's blackness and the branded cross on his forehead but makes no mention of his attire, an omission that suggests that it must have been in keeping with that of the Byzantines, or simply not worth mentioning. And, third, there is the matter that the Nubian king "answered the interpreter in his own language" (*tant qu'il respondi as latimiers en sen langage*).[19] This phrase is difficult to parse, given the ambiguity of the text's pronouns, but it appears either that a Constantinopolitan translator knew Old Nubian or, more likely, that the king himself spoke Greek to the translator; the latter seems more likely given that Greek was used as a lingua franca by the Nubian kings from the sixth through twelfth century.[20] In Robert de Clari's telling, these details seem to startle the Frankish envoys for whom the Nubian king's prominence and pilgrimage serve as foils, making their own pilgrimage to Constantinople seem petty and small, while at the same time revealing to them the broad expanse of Christian empires beyond their grasp and imagination.[21]

We must acknowledge that because the Byzantines were Mediterranean subjects drawn from a variety of lands across the region, we can by no means presume a single, monolithic ethnicity or skin color when we speak of the Byzantine Empire or Constantinople itself. A telling instance of racial tension unfolding in Corfu, involving not the Byzantines but marauding gangs of Venetians, appears in the early thirteenth-century chronicle by the government official Niketas Choniates. In 1149, after a street fight with the locals, a group of Venetians seized the imperial barge of Manuel I Komnenos and performed a mock coronation of a Byzantine emperor.[22] Calling the Venetians "barbarians," Choniates describes their egregious actions:

They stole the imperial ship, adorned the imperial cabins with curtains interwoven with gold thread and with rugs of purple, and placed on board an irritating manikin [*andrarion epitripton*], a certain black-skinned Ethiopian. They acclaimed him emperor of the Romans and led him about in procession with a splendid crown on his head, ridiculing the sacred imperial ceremonies and mocking Emperor Manuel as not having yellow hair, the color of summer, but instead being blackish in complexion like the bride of the song who says, "I am black and beautiful, because the sun has looked askance at me."[23]

The Venetians sought to ridicule the failure of Emperor Manuel I Komnenos to adhere to European standards of whiteness. The "black-skinned" (*kelekrōta*) Ethiopian becomes a stand-in for the emperor, who is mocked for not having blond locks and for "being blackish in complexion" (*hypomelainomenon tēn morphēn*). This example of racial shaming, in Choniates's view, demonstrates the full barbarity of the Venetians—it is even worse than their brawling violence that had preceded it. The text attests not only to the presence of black people in Byzantium but likewise to a certain discomfort toward dark skin felt by Westerners, which the Byzantines clearly did not share.

In a strikingly similar account, Liutprand of Cremona, a bishop from northern Italy who undertook a mission to Constantinople in the mid-tenth century, ridicules the skin color and appearance of Emperor Nikephoros II Phokas:

He is a monstrosity of a man, a dwarf, fat-headed and with tiny mole's eyes;
disfigured by a short, broad, thick beard half going gray; disgraced by a neck
scarcely an inch long; piglike by reason of the big close bristles on his head;
in colour an Ethiopian and, as the poet [Juvenal] says, "you would not like to
meet him in the dark"; a big belly, a lean posterior, very long in the hip considering his short stature.[24]

The invective continues in similar fashion. Liutprand engages in every possible form of shaming, deriding the emperor's intellect, skin color, pro-
portions, weight, height, and so on. His "monstrosity" is associated with
disability, as he is called a "dwarf" (*pygmaeun*), with the suggestion that
his bodily features are ill-formed. Notably, Liutprand labels him "in color
an Ethiopian" (*colore Aethiopem*), with a cutting citation of Juvenal. Such
accounts of racial difference do not appear in Byzantine texts; racial difference is seldom commented on—and when it is, the comments are rarely
disparaging. Yet, for Westerners, the racial othering of the Byzantines was
a repeated trope in both texts and actions, and one thing is clear: some
of the Byzantines were not white in Westerners' eyes, even in the highest
ranks and echelons of society.

The othering of Manuel I and Nikephoros II Phokas because of their
dark complexions could not happen within the Byzantine sphere. Thus, to
consider how prejudice rooted in skin color might have operated in the
Byzantine world, we must first acknowledge that imperial privilege did not
mean that the Byzantines were white Europeans. While they frequently
praise the white, feminine skin of women, Byzantine texts also evidence
a wide spectrum of complexions, often with little prejudice against darker
skin. For example, in an eleventh-century poem praising a schoolteacher in
the Sphorakiou quarter of Constantinople, Christopher of Mytilene com-
mends his erudition and eloquence. Christopher casually describes the
teacher as "handsome, with stately nose and curly hair, agreeable eyes and
dark skin, well-bearded."[25] Here there is not a hint of prejudice; in fact, as
we will see, in Byzantine sources men were often praised for their dark
complexion. Only when they are understood as also belonging to another
ethnic group do we perceive examples of prejudice and racism based on
skin color; even such instances are moderate in comparison to that found
in the works of Western writers and artists.

Across these various snippets from the sixth, tenth, eleventh, twelfth, and thirteenth centuries, we become aware of contact with peoples who are noted as being different because of their skin color—namely, Indians and Ethiopians. At the same time, however, skin color does not always appear to be used as a marker of these people, and there is no observable prejudice against the people who are being in some way racially othered. Scholars have often observed that in Byzantium, as in the ancient world, divisions between a Byzantine (or Roman) identity and that of the foreign other were often reflected in ethnic affiliations between people instead of the color of their skin.[26] In other words, a person's geopolitical and cultural origins were the factors used in constructing notions of "barbarians" or others; skin tone often appears as merely a cursory descriptor with little depth or elaboration that would constitute a congruent identity. For example, the term "Ethiopian," which in Greek literally means "burnt-face," generally referred to any black person, often with little regard for their geographical origin. Indeed, the tenth-century *Suda Lexicon* defines "Ethiopian" as simply a "black person" (*ho melas*), while the related "Ethiopia" is listed as a country or land (*chōra*).[27]

The lack of precise terminology that aligns with our own modern constructs of race is merely one of the impediments to our understanding how skin color and difference might have operated in the Byzantine world. It is also extremely difficult to determine the role played by black Africans in ancient and medieval Europe. In a 2004 book focused on the invention of racism in antiquity, Benjamin Isaac went as far as to say that black people "did not form much of an actual presence in the Greek and Roman worlds"; he excluded Ethiopians from "systematic treatment" in his study because "they are clearly mythical and this study deals only with people whom the Greeks and Romans actually experienced."[28] Though not without its merits, this book contributes to the systematic erasure of black people in antiquity despite their obvious presence across literature and art. At the other extreme is Frank M. Snowden, Jr., whose work praises how black Africans were represented in ancient and late antique culture, finding in the sources little evidence of racial prejudice in antiquity and suggesting that Christianity provided a space for a postracial culture in which race was irrelevant.[29]

As is often the case, the truth is more subtle and lies somewhere in between. In recent years, scholars have turned their attention to the study of race in the late antique, early Christian, and medieval worlds.[30] Denise Buell, for instance, has demonstrated how early Christian thinkers advocated for Christian peoples as a unified race (*genos*), deftly navigating through the imprecise definitions of race and ethnicity across the modern and late antique worlds.[31] Currently, scholars are attempting to employ more capacious and nuanced definitions of race to encompass both modern and premodern uses of the term as well as the identities and problems it seeks to call out and describe. Geraldine Heng, for example, proposes to define race as "a structural relationship for the articulation and management of human differences, rather than [as] a substantive content."[32] This definition alerts us to the necessity and utility of thinking about race in the medieval world, as well as to thinking about race beyond definitions that rely exclusively on colorism to demarcate differences and essentialized groups. Heng's work focuses instead on the various areas of interaction and intersection that place race dynamically in action as a category and reality.

Yet, to date, much of this scholarship has all but ignored the Byzantine world, acknowledging it exclusively through Western sources or focusing only on its late antique and early Christian foundations. My goal here is to continue exploring how race manifested itself in the Byzantine sphere, putting it into dialogue with its critical early Christian roots. More particularly, I wish to focus on where colorism fits into Byzantine discourses of race and ethnicity in order to further inform the depictions of the Ethiopian eunuch as white and explore more deeply the nuanced complexity of the eunuch's depiction in the Menologion.

BLACKNESS AND DEVIANCE

A popular way in the Byzantine world to describe futile acts was a phrase drawn from Aesop's fables—"to wash an Ethiopian" (*Aithiopa smēchein*).[33] In her historical chronicle, after mentioning a series of futile political tasks, Anna Komnena ends by saying that, alas, "the Ethiopian has never been made white [*eleukaineto*]."[34] She is clearly using the term *smēchein*, meaning "to scrub or wash," pejoratively in associating Ethiopic blackness with dirtiness.[35] The immutability of skin pigmentation similarly serves as a metaphor for authors wishing to capture the unchanging nature of a person's character. Speaking about the heretical Arius, in the fourth century Basil of Caesarea writes to Theodotus that "neither will an Ethiopian ever change his skin, nor a leopard her spots, nor is a man who has been nourished on perverted doctrines able to rid himself of the evil of heresy"—a line elaborated from Jeremiah 13:23.[36] Such adages may be neutral observations of differences in skin color, as the comparison with the leopard suggests, but we must not ignore that they are often associated with resistance to desired change: either the attempt to whiten the Ethiopian is futile or the immutability of one's character is associated with wicked doctrine.

In the case of the Ethiopian eunuch, the notion of the immutability of skin and nature presents an interesting challenge. The futility of being unable to "wash" the Ethiopian creates a possible impasse for those urging conversion and baptism. In matters both of race and beyond race, we are left to wonder whether the eunuch's character is mutable. Perhaps the pink tunics worn by both Philip and the eunuch suggest that these two figures of different skin tones somehow share a nature, already and before the baptism. If whiteness and light are equated with the divine, then it is certainly worth investigating whether the same was read onto skin color in the Byzantine world.

In this investigation, we are inevitably led to the association between blackness and evil in early Christianity.[37] In Byzantine art, demons are invariably depicted as gaunt and winged black figures with hair that stands on end as if it were electrified. Demonic forces, as we will see later in the miniature for the Synaxis of the archangels in the Menologion (see plate 7), are depicted as black figures in art. In the twelfth-century Sinai icon of the ladder of heavenly ascent, monks piously make their way up the rungs of a ladder at whose top is Christ, who welcomes them into heaven while angels above and their brethren below watch their ascetic climb toward the divine (fig. 5.8). These men, however, are harassed by black demons, who attempt to ensnare the monks and drag them off their pious course. The monks are variously shot with arrows; pulled with ropes around their hands, necks, and hair; and stabbed with lances.

In literary and hagiographic accounts, demonic forces are not simply described as dark or black but are specifically embodied as Ethiopian. Ethiopian figures were repeatedly said to haunt monastics during the course of their ascetic practices, attempting to lead the religious astray, as the Sinai icon portrays. In the literary sources, David Brakke observes that these demonic forces are described as Ethiopians and they were often sexualized and feminized, tempting monks in ways that carried sexual undertones.[38] In *The Sayings of the Desert Fathers*, the life of Heraclides contains the story of a brother who sought the renowned monk's advice about combating demons. When the brother went to lie down on his mat to sleep, he "saw an Ethiopian lying there who gnashed his teeth at him"; he told Abba Heraclides that "on my bed I saw a black Ethiopian, as I was going to sleep."[39]

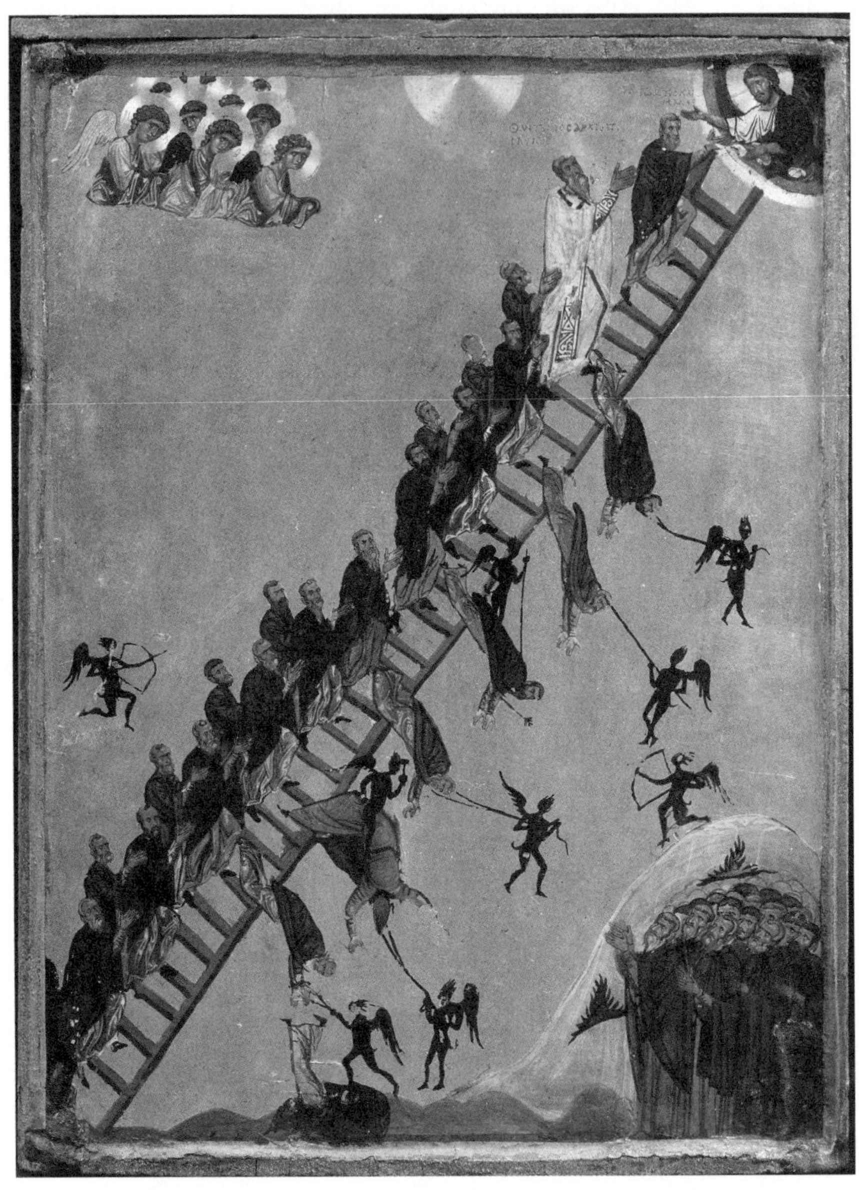

5.8. Icon of the Ladder of Heavenly Ascent. St. Catherine's Monastery, Mount Sinai, Egypt.

This episode echoes Pachomius's rule forbidding monks to "sit two together on a mat or carpet."[40] That the threatening Ethiopian joins the monk on his mat makes clear that Pachomius's prohibition was targeted at whatever same-gender desires might have led to such intimacy.[41] As Brakke puts it, this demon's appearance on the mat presents a "homoerotic possibility that troubles the homosocial monastic bond."[42]

In other words, the hypersexuality of these Ethiopian demons opens a space in which the same-gender desires and homoeroticism of monastic life can appear, since as demonic forces they can shamelessly express any unbridled desires buried within the monks. Thus, the Ethiopian figures in each of these instances, whether attacking in the Sinai icon or appearing on the mat, are less a manifestation of a demonic other than an externalization and mirror of the monks' faults and lusts. We have already seen the same forces at work in the figures of transgender saints, who provide a rhetorical space in which the same-gender desires of monks can be openly displayed, particularly when directed toward the youthful and feminine faces of these transgender men passing as eunuchs. In the story of Eugenius, when the townswoman Melania attempts to sleep with the monk, the author is able to reveal another iteration of same-gender desire, which only the reader and the protagonist can recognize. Chastising her for attempting to sleep with a monk, Eugenius tells her: "Justly wert thou called Melania, for a heavy blackness and a putrid filth wells up with thee."[43] The author thus plays on the Greek meaning of *melania*—"blackness"—to emphasize the evil and corrupt nature of her soul.

Throughout these late antique sources we see the recurring metaphorical language of blackness, inherited from the ancient world and associated with evil and demonic agency. Furthermore, blackness is again associated with an unbridled hypersexuality, which in the story of Eugenius is construed as doubly wrongful, since it is both directed toward a monk and, ultimately, understood as being directed toward the same gender. The intersectional force of these stories is that, while Melania suffers divine retribution for her attempt at fornication (as does the innkeeper's daughter who accused Marinos of impregnating her, as discussed in chapter 3), the monk-tempting Ethiopians are reduced to nonhuman demonic agents. This serves as a sharp reminder of the inequities of an intersectional identity. In some capacity, race unites with these metaphors of blackness. The various rhetorical figures are treated entirely differently: the nonblack would-be fornicator suffers punishment, but the black would-be fornicator is made into a demon, who (as the proverb went) could never change their skin color or character.

EPIDERMAL RACISM IN EARLY CHRISTIANITY

Negative associations with blackness are inherited from antiquity, but Eastern Christianity seems to grapple with these tensions and to attempt to eliminate their causes. The approach to dark skin generally appears to be that it is in some way ugly or unseemly.[44] In the Song of Songs, the line in the Greek Old Testament (1:5) uttered by Solomon's bride, "I am dark and beautiful" (*melaina eimi kai kalē*), would be translated into Latin in the Vulgate (1:4) as "I am black, but beautiful" (*nigra sum sed formosa*). This change racializes the statement and underscores the presumption that beauty and blackness are mutually exclusive. In the context of the Western Church, for example, the fourth-century Spanish bishop Gregory of Elvira reasoned that this statement must be metaphorical, since "it is not possible for what is dark to be beautiful."[45] Such statements were not expressed as explicitly in the Church of the eastern Mediterranean, however.

In the writings of the early Christian thinkers, this verse was generally taken to reveal a person's inward beauty in their love and faith in Christ. Origen expands on the Song's words to mean "I am indeed dark—or black —as far as my complexion goes . . . but, should a person scrutinize the features of my inward parts, then I am beautiful"; similar views are reiterated by several figures.[46] Elsewhere, Origen proposes that humanity looks "like the soul of the Ethiopian at the beginning—then we are cleansed so that we may be more bright."[47] In the mosaics of the Genesis cycle in San Marco in Venice, we see the first-formed body of Adam as a black-skinned figure (fig. 5.9).[48] This representation presumably alludes to Genesis 2:7, which states that God formed man from the "dust of the ground" and then breathed life into him, an action depicted in the next vignette of the decorative program. Yet, in the second scene, Adam is white (fig. 5.10). The implication is that the inanimate, proto-plastic human is black until they are in some way whitened by the spirit of God.

Eastern writers, however, show a growing desire to comprehend metaphorically this casting of the virtues or defects of the soul as white and black. Moreover, they also work to counter the prejudices against dark-skinned individuals that accompanied the Church's expansion. In the fourth century, Gregory of Nyssa treats the darkness as a metaphor for corruption that is reformed through the light of Christ, but his tone turns pentecostal in his description of the city of God. There, "Babylon is domiciled and

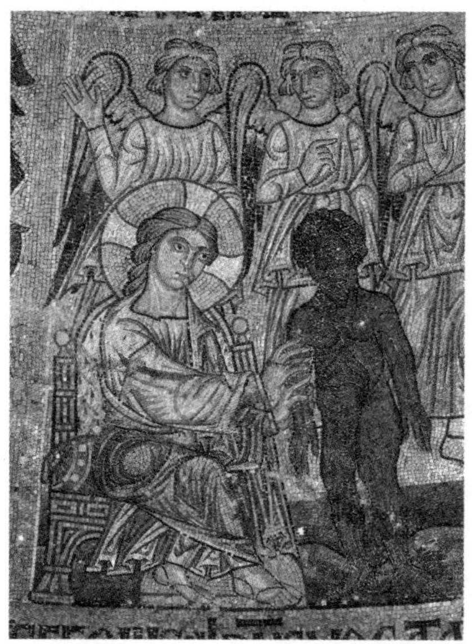

5.9. Formation of Adam. Baptistery, Church of San Marco, Venice, Italy.

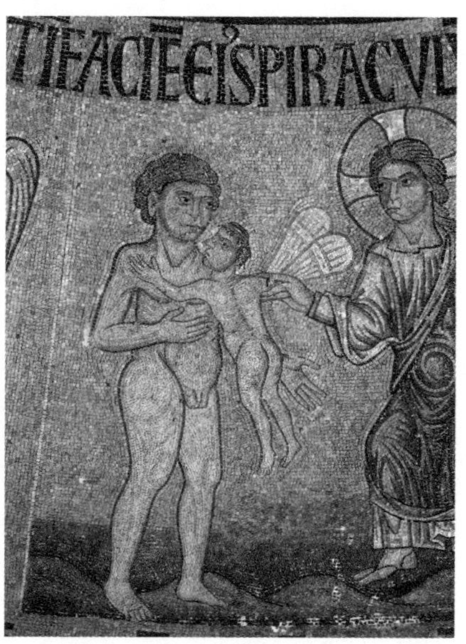

5.10. Inspiration of Adam. Baptistery, Church of San Marco, Venice, Italy.

Rahab the harlot is named, and there are foreigners within her, and Tyre, and the people of Ethiopia . . . For there strangers become fellow tribesmen of the city, and the Babylonians become Jerusalemites, and the harlot a virgin, and the Ethiopian bright [*lamproi*]."[49] Playing on "dark" rather than simply "black," Gregory uses the the word *lamproi* to suggest a nonracialized brightness, not synonymous with whiteness but instead shining or radiant. Furthermore, the entire premise rests on the unification of peoples within the city of God, as a community of virtue rather than one of exclusion or oppression. We should not ignore or become apologists for the systematics of racism, yet we must acknowledge the nuanced inclusivity that the text seems to aim for.

We can compare the earlier words of the Spanish bishop Gregory of Elvira to those of one of his contemporaries in the East, the early fourth-century Theodoret of Cyrus. Theodoret expands the phrase in the Song of Songs. After listing the figure's many corrupt deeds and her reformation in Christ, Theodoret ends with the following reflection:

So do not reproach me for my black color, nor bring my former vices to the fore: I am black, I admit, but beautiful and pleasing to the bridegroom . . . I too am Ethiopian, then, but the bride of the great lawgiver, daughter of

a Midianite priest, an idolatrous man. I forgot my people and my father's
house—hence the king desired my beauty.[50]

Here, Theodoret presents her as a pagan convert who has abandoned the
practices of her people and the wrongful deeds of her past life, which were
responsible for her spiritual darkness. Theodoret grapples with the identity
shaped by her skin color, turning around the prejudices against her skin
color by pointing to the exceptional purity of her soul. There is almost a
sense of pride in her monologue, as she acknowledges herself in the face of
racial ridicule to be both an Ethiopian and a Christian who, no matter the
color of her skin, radiates virtue.

These statements, while by no means free of a pattern of social prejudices against black people, apparently attempt to dialectically counter contemporary disdain for black skin and its associations with ugliness. These
texts can each be seen as different responses to the proverbial "washing of
an Ethiopian," indicating that darkness of skin is in no way an impediment to brightness of spirit. One such response to racial prejudices can be
glimpsed in the life of Moses the Ethiopian, a desert father in the monastic community at Sketis, who is described as "a big black man."[51] Like the
female ascetics and anchorites discussed in chapter 3, Moses is at times
treated with contempt, yet he keeps his composure. In one council held at
Sketis, Moses's character is tested when a father questions whether he belongs in the community, asking derisively, "Why does this black man come
among us?"[52] The brothers marvel at Moses's resilience and silence in the
face of such scorn.

While not unique in the experience of monks and ascetics, this hazing
of Moses is striking and at times difficult to read. Another instance occurs
after he has been ordained:

It was said of Abba Moses that he was ordained and the ephod was placed
upon him. The archbishop said to him, "See, Abba Moses, how you are entirely
white." The old man said to him, "It is true of the outside, lord and father, but
what about Him who sees the inside?" Wishing to test him the archbishop said
to the priests, "When Abba Moses comes into the sanctuary, drive him out,
and go with him to hear what he says." So the old man came in and they covered him with abuse, and drove him out, saying, "Outside, black man!"
Going out, he said to himself, "They have acted rightly concerning you, for
your skin is as black as ashes. You are not a man, so why should you be allowed to meet men?"[53]

The words of the archbishop suggest that it is indeed possible to whiten an Ethiopian, a point that is clearly not lost on Moses, who responds that it is "true of the outside . . . but what about Him who sees the inside?" Moses parries the racist comment, not by praising the cleanliness and whiteness of his spirit but by agreeing that he is indeed fully white on the outside, referring to the color of his garments at his ordination. At the same time, he suggests that his soul remains darkened as he continues in his ascetic struggles. As a former slave who lived as a robber in Nitria, Egypt, the darkness of his soul concerns Moses. Thus, Moses has inverted the racial comment by accepting the external whiteness put on him by his ordination, whose high worth he acknowledges while also pointing to its limitations.

In Abba Moses's story, the demons that torment the monk are not spectral black figures from the desert but rather his fellow brothers. Moses's ordination is made poignant by the hazing and the internalized self-hatred that the hazing reveals. Moses's abuse and expulsion from the sanctuary dehumanize him, for it is connected to the color of his skin being "black as ashes." He assents to the notion that he is subhuman and thus closed off from the mysteries of the sanctuary, as well as the community of his brethren. While elements of such monastic hazing can be found in the Doubting Thomas scene—specifically in the Apostles' treatment of Thomas (as discussed in chapter 4)—the racist dimension of Moses's story is impossible to ignore. Taking it together with the associations between blackness and ugliness or demonic agency, we see Christians struggling with ancient and late antique racial prejudices while purportedly attempting to construct an inclusive apostolic community.

THE BLACKNESS OF THE ETHIOPIAN EUNUCH

Returning to the Menologion of Basil II, we must consider the tactics and methods used in the manuscript to depict other forms of perceived racial difference. In so doing, we find that the Ethiopian eunuch's representation differs from the manuscript's other efforts to communicate alterity. In his depictions of the eunuch, the artist Georgios appears to be attempting to produce an image that embraced racial difference without playing into colorist prejudices that might cast the eunuch as a foreigner. A number of questions are thus raised by the unique elements of Georgios's portrayal of the eunuch: Is the eunuch's body deprived of whiteness and light as if they were standing in shadows, or has it been blackened and darkened as if burned by the sun? And what difference, if any, would the answer make?

If whiteness is assumed to be the norm or foundation onto which nonwhite, racialized skins are overlaid, then we might read the image as something like an imperial eunuch in blackface. The ancient environmental theories of racial difference, which treated a dark complexion as a darkening by the sun, might partially support such a reading. But, according to those same racial theories, both Scythian whiteness and Ethiopian darkness are extremes mirroring the extreme conditions of the two homelands—racial whiteness thus cannot be the default or normative, as twentieth-century eugenics might have argued. Thus, the artist must confront the challenge of constructing a notion of Ethiopian blackness in which the skin color is presented positively and not as the signifier of a foreigner or demon who tortures and kills Christian martyrs, as we see in other appearances of racial difference in the manuscript.

We should note that the Ethiopian eunuch is not just black but radiates darkness from their skin (fig. 5.1 and plate 1). Consider another image in the Menologion painted by the same artist. As Ananias of Persia is being martyred, he prays to God and is rewarded with a vision of a ladder rising to heaven (plate 4). Upon that ladder, Ananias witnesses two "fiery-looking men" (*pyroeides . . . andras*) leading him up to the heavenly city, as the text of the Menologion tells us. Georgios has chosen to portray these men iconographically as two angels, as shown by their wings, the binding of their hair, the standards they hold, and the simple tunics they wear. Yet, they strikingly diverge from usual depictions of angels: seeking to capture their fiery appearance (*pyroeides*), Georgios makes their flesh, hair, garments, and standards radiate a rich and flaming-red hue. In Byzantine manuscript illumination, the sun—a fiery body—is often depicted with this burning red, at times tinged with orange. Throughout the Menologion, the blazes of fires are consistently rendered in the same pigment. On the body of the martyr, the freshly oxygenated blood of his open wounds glows with the same shade of red, contrasting with the coagulated and darkened blood that has dripped onto the ground.

Formally, we see striking similarities with how the eunuch's flesh is handled by Georgios. For both the angels and the eunuch, their entire bodies radiate a single color, with no distinction between hair and flesh. Because these figures are composed of a single color—red and black, respectively— the artist must take a different approach in delineating the body's flesh than the technique used for the other figures. Facial features cannot be articulated through the use of ochres, greens, browns, and whites, as we saw in the figure of Philip, for example. For the eunuch and the angels, three-dimensionality is achieved instead with varying strokes of black and white pigments. The division between hairline and face in the angels is shadowed by thick black sinuous lines, just as we see in the eunuch. For the latter, each curl is outlined in this way, and they are given individual texture through the white highlighting of their swirls, which echo the bound and rippling hair of the angels. The protrusions of the eunuch's brow, chin, nose, and cheeks shimmer with delicate white strokes. Finally, the eunuch's skin, accentuated by the rich blue cloak, radiates with what can best be described as a dark light, comparable to the brilliance of the angels.

THE DEPICTION OF OTHER RACES IN THE MENOLOGION

The eunuch is depicted quite differently from other people of color in the Menologion, such as the dark-skinned Indians who martyr the Apostle Thomas (plate 5). The figure on the left has a striking profile, with a pronounced nose and pointed chin. His flesh is dull, a blackish brown with hints of redness, contoured with swaths of gray down his sternum and rib cage, forearms, thighs, and shins. The figure on the right is darker but has similar facial features, with a trimmed grayish beard. His skin is just as dull but blacker, and a similar mix of pigments gives life to his arms and legs. Other persons of color throughout the manuscript are essentially portrayed using the same artistic technique as that employed for the white figures, with considerable detail in contouring achieved by mixing various color shades. For example, this approach can be observed in the martyrdom of Theophilus the Younger by a Saracen (fol. 359) and of the monks of Mount Sinai by a tribe of Blemmyes and a group of Saracens (fols. 315, 316, and 317; fig. 5.11). In these images the men have different skin tones, indicating that a shared ethnic identity or grouping never entailed identical skin coloration. The two Indians differ in shade and the groups of Saracens and Blemmyes range from a purplish-brown to a grayish-black, showing subtle variations of these shades. Though these various miniatures are not made by the same hand—the artists include Nestor, Pantoleon, and Michael of Blachernae— these figures of color are consistently handled the same way, as might be expected in a manuscript renowned for its uniformity.

The eunuch's black skin, in contrast, displays a striking regularity of color, as do the fiery-red angels. This use of color makes the figures seem to glow off the parchment with a radiant, crisp, and refined appearance. Philip, with his mottled pigmentation, looks far earthier than does the Ethiopian eunuch, whose pure radiance has more in common with the gleaming personifications of Night than with the Indians, Blemmyes, or Saracens who

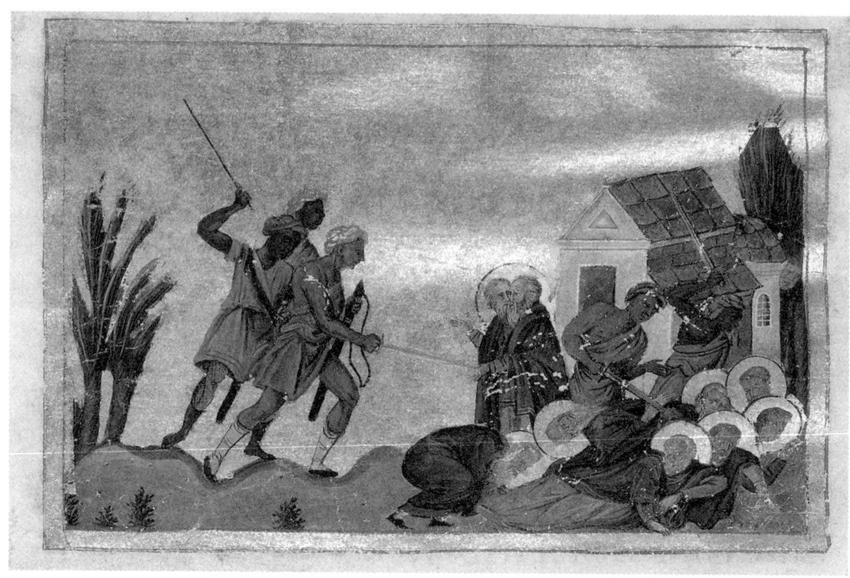

5.11. Martyrdom of Monks of Mount Sinai by Blemmyes. Vatican City, Biblioteca Apostolica Vaticana, 'Menologion' of Basil II (Vat. gr. 1613), fol. 317. © 2019 Biblioteca Apostolica Vaticana.

often were clustered together with a vague geopolitical concept of Ethiopia. I believe that the eunuch's Ethiopian darkness is construed almost as an allegorical or personified image of darkness. This darkness is not conceived as the dull absence of light but rather a shining, almost glowing darkness. Georgios has chosen to depict flesh that radiates darkness. Why?

Over the course of his rule, Basil II was known for his many military triumphs and conquests. He led campaigns that would eventually annex Bulgaria and much of the Balkans, making Serbia and Croatia dependencies of the empire; he acquired western Armenia and Georgia, as well as the islands of Crete and Cyprus; he fought against and signed a treaty with the Fatimid caliph in Egypt; and, late in life, he planned campaigns against Sicily and western Europe.[54] His brutal assaults on the Bulgarians would earn him the epithet "Basil the Bulgar-Slayer" in later centuries.[55] In a Psalter for Basil II, roughly contemporaneous and closely associated in style with the Menologion, a portrait of the emperor in the manuscript's frontispiece sheds light on the tenor and aims of the Menologion itself (fig. 5.12). Prostrated below Basil II is a series of men, seeming to encompass the span of the empire's lands and representing both those liberated by and those subjected to Byzantine rule through his conquests; assigning a specific identify to each is difficult.[56] Because this form of prostration (*proskynesis*) is a

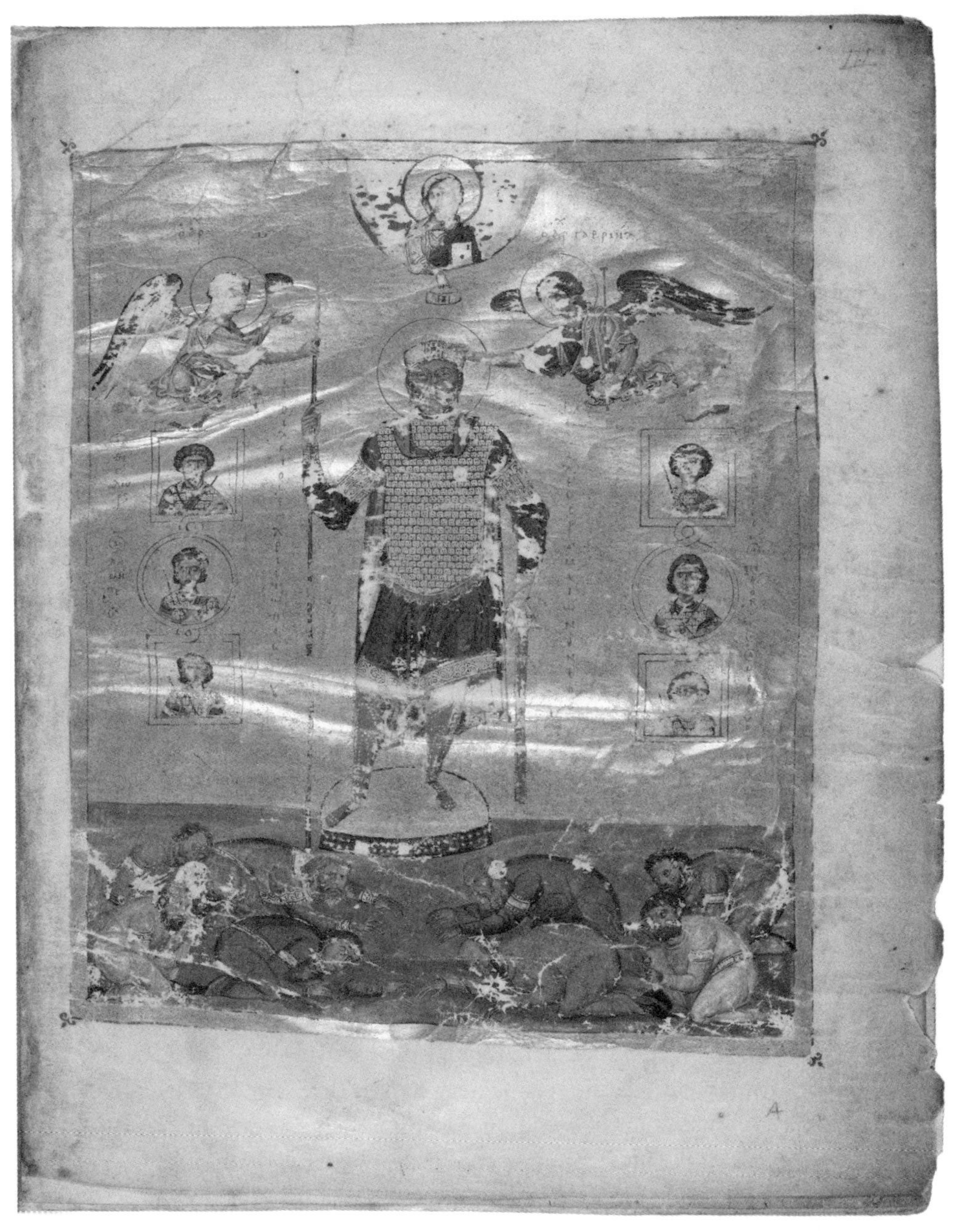

5.12. Frontispiece of Basil II. Venice, Biblioteca Marciana, Psalter of Basil II (Marciana gr. 17).

practice of obeisance and respect, it should not to be understood in purely negative terms. Furthermore, the details that at times have been interpreted as intended to signify barbarian peoples—such as the earrings or the arm-cuffs on the dark-skinned figures—can be found inside the bounds of the empire. Thus, we should see this image as a general representation of the union of the various people brought into the empire and not as the con-demnation of others as barbarians.

The adjacent poem describes the emperor's image, offering a meditation on his divinely sanctioned coronation with all his accoutrements of war. Icons of martyrs and military saints hang beside him, while subjects cower at his feet. As the final lines of the poem tell us, "The martyrs are his allies, for he is their friend. They throw those down [*riptontes*] lying at his feet."[57] "Throwing down" (*riptontes*) suggests that the prostrate individuals are be-ing forced into the position. The general tone of the poem is militaristic, with an implied ambivalence between subjugation and veneration, suggest-ing that the prostrate figures represent those peoples Basil is bringing into his empire through its expansion. They may be conquered peoples, but they have come to recognize his magnanimity. With the martyrs as "his allies," the contemporaneous Menologion becomes a sort of companion to the Psalter, manifesting in its pages all those martyred allies of the emperor. The opening poem of the Menologion alludes to this relationship: "In those whom he has portrayed in colors, may he find active helpers, sustainers of the State, allies in battles, deliverers from sufferings," and so on.[58] In other words, for Basil II, the Menologion served as a potent site of contemplation for his military craft as well as a validation for the imperial brutality that he undertook against neighboring lands.

The Menologion contains exceptionally graphic violence and gruesome depictions of martyrdom. There is a fascination with the suffering of the Christian saints. As we have seen throughout this volume, artists drew on wide-ranging medical knowledge to vividly limn the sufferings of these fig-ures, echoing mastectomy techniques and distinguishing between freshly spilled and old blood, for example. Figures appear disemboweled with their intestines spilling out of their abdomens, while dismembered figures offer up their parts bit by bit, suggesting that their fingers, palms, wrists, fore-arms, and so on have been hacked off piecemeal so as to demonstrate the cruelty of these people.

Reviewing the depiction of Indians and other foreigners in the Menolo-gion of Basil II, as well as the eunuch's handling in the Docheiariou syn-axarion, we realize the uniqueness of the Menologion's Ethiopian eunuch.

Unlike the "ethnographic" treatment in the Docheiariou manuscript, which seeks to represent the eunuch as belonging to another *ethnos*, in the Menologion the Constantinopolitan-like imperial eunuch proclaims their social and cultural placement within the empire's center. Their complexion and overall body appearance seem intended more as a personification of the Ethiopian's darkness than as an ethnographic sketch; thus, the eunuch is placed outside the militaristic economy of the Menologion and of Basil's rule. Ethiopia is depicted as an ally rather than a foreign power; not knowing how to depict the alleged epidermal alterity of that friend, the artist constructs it as darkness itself. "Ethiopian" becomes an adjective modifying the hues of their identity as a court eunuch.

Unlike the other depictions of racial difference in the Menologion, therefore, the Ethiopian eunuch is not othered or marginalized but rather is a subject and protagonist in the deeds of the empire. While Byzantines themselves are happy to describe each other as either of dark or light complexions, they show some hesitation when discussing the dark skin associated with a foreigner or other, hesitating to make the figure appear alien. For example, a popular twelfth-century romance recounts the deeds of Digenis Akritis, a hero born of an Arab emir and the daughter of a Byzantine general. The protagonist's name means "the Frontiersman of Double Descent" (literally, "born of two races"). But when his Arab father is introduced, he is described in ways that make him seem as Byzantine as possible—he "knew the Roman language perfectly" and he was curly haired and "not black like the Ethiopians but fair and handsome."[59] Thus, the Arab father retains a sense of a foreign ethnic identity, while the author Romanizes the son and attempts to place the color of his skin well within the spectrum of a Byzantine identity. A similar, albeit less extreme, tactic is at work in the Menologion. Ethiopians are not one of the many neighboring foes of Basil II, and the eunuch is his servant and companion. Hence, the Ethiopian eunuch in the Menologion subverts our expectations, caught between the whiteness associated with their gender identity as female and the necessity for them to be dark as an "Ethiopian." The artist therefore produced an image that oscillates between these possibilities, a representation that ultimately articulates the eunuch not as a foreigner but as an imperial official.

THE GENDERED COLOR OF SKIN

As noted earlier in this book, blackness—associated with the loss of youthful beauty—appears in the lives of desert ascetics as a clear marker of virtue and self-discipline. When Zosimas first caught a glimpse of Mary of Egypt in the desert, what "he saw was a naked figure whose body was black, as if tanned by the scorching sun."[60] The lives of transgender monks likewise often mention a bodily transformation through ascetic practice that leaves a physique blackened by the sun. For example, when Athanasius's former husband encounters him on the road to Jerusalem, the life tells us that the husband did not recognize his former wife because he "appeared just as an Ethiopian."[61] Athanasius's being read as an Ethiopian causes no tension in the narrative; he certainly is not treated as some demonic apparition or as an object unworthy of regard. There is a sense, however, that the former wife has transitioned not only in gender identity but also in racial identity. In the story of Theodore of Alexandria, we learn that the trans monk has been "hardened from the burning of the sun" (*ebaphē apo tēs hēliakēs kauseōs*), a phrase indicating the transformative darkening of his complexion through his ascetic deeds.[62] Similarly, as discussed in chapter 3, the lives of Pelagius, Hilarion, and Dorotheos, and even Aetius of Amida's description of masculine women, all associate a roughened and darkened complexion with masculinity.

Let us return to the figure of Manuel I Komnenos. At opposite ends of the spectrum, Manuel is both the emperor that the Venetians shamed for his skin color, as Choniates recounts, and also the emperor for whom Eustathios of Thessaloniki wrote the Epiphany oration praising the diversity of his imperial court. In the funeral oration commemorating Manuel, Eustathios provides insight into Byzantine perceptions on the intersection of gender and skin color:

And the quality of his complexion matched the dignity described thus far. His face did not display an effeminate paleness, but was instead suitably part of a manly mixture, a face right out of ancient history, weathered by exercises and other labours, not least by the sun. For he did not conduct his affairs indoors, in the shade, since he cared not for a soft and easy life. Instead he exposed himself to the elements, from which his skin drew its manly colouring, having aspired to an appearance that one does not find on womanly or soft people, but such as might adorn a heroic austerity.[63]

The funeral oration's description of Manuel presents his dark complexion as a manifestation of his masculinity—a "manly mixture" (*andrōdes ekekrato*) with a "manly coloring" (*andrias . . . chroian*). This appearance was a byproduct not only of his deeds in the sun but also his desire to avoid "effeminate paleness" (*thēlyprepēs leukotēs*).

This text uses language that is transphobic and homophobic in order to distance Manuel from "womanly and soft people" (*tous gynaikias kai malthakous*): "womanly" (*gynaikias*) communicated not only effeminacy but also weakness and cowardice, while "soft" (*malthakous*) carried similar connotations and served as a derogatory descriptor for those practicing same-gender sexual acts. *Malthakos* even became a technical term in late antique medicine to pathologize same-gender desire, particularly for men acting as the passive partner in such acts.[64] Therefore, we understand that Eustathios is purposely emphasizing Manuel's skin color both to demonstrate his heroic deeds and labors in the sun and to assert his cis male gender identity and sexuality. That Manuel had aspired to his appearance (*opsin pephilotimēmenos*) places not only his skin color but also his gender identity in his own hands, as if his dark skin were part of a gender affirming program.

A similar trope, though suffused with vitriol, is found in Nikephoros Basilakes's twelfth-century description of Atalanta, the mythical hunter and maiden—a figure who, as discussed in chapter 3, demolishes gender conformity. Basilakes finds the pagan myth implausible, arguing that Atalanta's masculinity and her alleged beauty are contradictory:

Even if one should grant that the girl was skilled at hunting, still she could not have been beautiful. She was a hunter; she spent most of her life in the mountains; she passed her time on lofty hills; and she was continually struck by the sun's rays, which darken youthful good looks and perhaps would have seriously diminished her beauty. The Ethiopian race is the result of the sun's rays striking people excessively, and one sees that women from the city are whiter than the mountain-bred women in the countryside.[65]

In the lives of ascetic saints, the process of epidermal transformation demonstrates the conquest of the corrupt and earthly flesh—particularly for female bodies, which allegedly are thereby removed from a heteronormative sexual economy. Yet, in Basilakes's attack we glimpse the opposite perspective, one that derides how this transformation withdraws the feminine from the desirous male gaze. There is no admiration, such as we found in descriptions of the transgender saints, for the way in which Atalanta achieved both virginal chastity and masculinity. Instead, the claim of both in a single person is what leads Basilakes to dismiss the story as unconvincing. Yet, once again and despite Basilakes's condemnation, the story of Atalanta reveals that the masculinization of the female body entails a quasi-racial transformation as well. Basilakes makes this explicit, not by directly comparing Atalanta to an Ethiopian but rather by appealing to classical racial theory to explain her darkness.

Historians often refer to the ancient theory of race as the "environmental theory"; it divided the known world into climate zones and regarded racial difference as a by-product of the exposure of both skin and humors to the sun.[66] In this theory gender plays a crucial role in how racial difference is conceived and understood. In his *Airs, Waters, Places,* Hippocrates examines the ways in which environmental factors affect people's skin, natures, and characters. For him, the Egyptian and the Scythian are alike since both are assaulted by extremes of temperature—hot and cold, respectively. Unlike the Egyptians, it "is the cold that burns [the Scythian's] white skin and turns it ruddy."[67] Pliny the Elder declares in his *Natural History* that "it is beyond question that the Ethiopians are burnt by the heat of the heavenly body near them, and are born with a scorched appearance, with curly beard and hair," while the opposite is true in regions that are cold.[68] The same logic persists throughout the Byzantine world, where a sun-darkened skin is likened to that of an Ethiopian.

According to this theory, environmental conditions affected more than the outward appearance of a person's skin; it also influenced their nature and character, including their gender identity and sexual character. Hippocrates, for example, states that the harsh environment of the Scythians makes them feeble and effeminate, noting that the men are even said to "become eunuchs, do women's work, live like women and converse accordingly."[69] Thus, beginning in these early texts, we find a theorization of an intersection of race and gender.[70] The quasi-racial transformation of a transgender saint from an ostensibly white woman into a dark or Ethiopian male, albeit a eunuch, likewise is visible in the story of the Ethiopian eunuch. Moreover, the eunuch's depiction in the manuscript tradition as a light-skinned youth with long hair strongly suggests that, in a sense, their gender identity was privileged over their racial identity.

BETWEEN GENDER AND RACE, BETWEEN NIGHT AND DAY

When we compare the image of the court eunuch Leo *sakellarios* in the Leo Bible, kneeling before the Virgin (plate 6), with that of the Ethiopian eunuch in the Pantokrator, Theodore, and Chludov Psalters, we see that the iconography adheres to that favored for the depiction of eunuchs. In a sense, gender identity has won out over racial identity. Yet I would go further and suggest that there is no easy division between race and gender.

Instead, since a eunuch tends toward being feminine, their racial identity also is seen to tend toward being white. As a well-kept and sheltered imperial eunuch, accustomed to the fineries of an urban capital, the Ethiopian eunuch and treasurer of Queen Candace is white precisely because of their gender identity, just as "women from the city are whiter" than their rural counterparts, according to Basilakes.

Understanding the complex ways in which Byzantines saw gender identity, sexuality, and racial identity as intersecting, we can now better appreciate the artist's nuanced and unique approach to the figure of the Ethiopian eunuch in the Menologion (figs. 5.1 and plate 1). One of the most striking details is the apparent flickering between the eunuch's skin and their dark-blue chlamys. Looking closely at the garment, we notice thick jet-black pigment outlines it, thus giving body to the cloth's folds. Muddy-gold high-lighting makes the chlamys look almost gray when given a cursory glance. Hence, the jet-black contouring lines, blacker than the Ethiopian's skin, make it appear as if the dark blue of the chlamys is almost the same shade as the ash gray of the eunuch's skin. This blue, like the night sky tinged with silvery moonlight, can be compared to that used in the scene of the Synaxis of the archangels (plate 7). There, the archangel wears a similar chlamys of blue with gold highlights, but the blue is lighter and the gold radiant. Only in the Synaxis image's darker shading do we encounter the same hues as those found in the eunuch's chlamys. In the scene of the archangel, our eye is immediately drawn to the fallen angels—the demonic creatures entering the gaping dark underworld at the archangel's feet, who are depicted as either jet-black or a grayish light-blue. Comparing the two images we see that our eunuch's appearance is somehow caught between light and dark, between night and day.

In Byzantine art, personifications of night and day are featured in the Genesis cycle, where they portray God's separation of the light from the darkness (Genesis 1:3–4), and in instances in which the artist is seeking to personify nighttime as a means of informing the viewer of the time of day when the scene is unfolding. In the Vatican Octateuch, which contains the first eight books of the Old Testament, the separation of night and day is depicted with a light-gray and soft-blue figure holding a tapered torch, who personifies light (fig. 5.13). God reaches out of the heavens toward the figure in a gesture of speech, commanding light into existence and thus separating the light from the darkness. On the left side of the scene, we encounter a ghostly figure hidden in the muddy depiction of shadow, whose dark blue-gray form represents the darkness. We observe here a uniform color

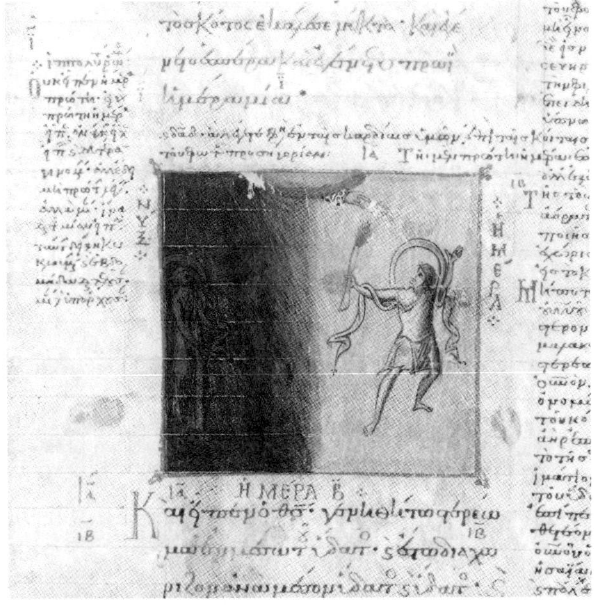

5.13. Separation of Darkness and Light. Vatican City, Biblioteca Apostolica Vaticana, Vatican Octateuch (Vat. gr. 747), fol. 15r. © 2019 Biblioteca Apostolica Vaticana.

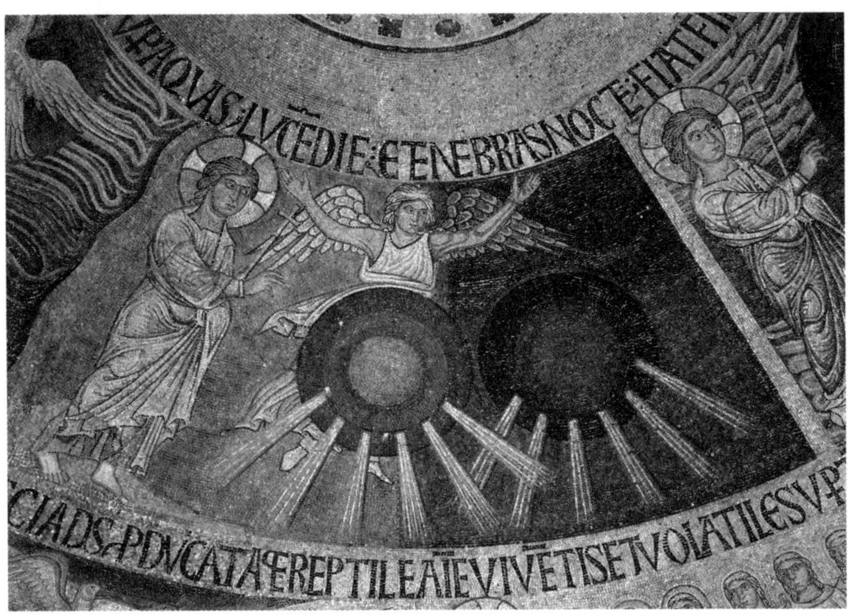

5.14. Separation of Night and Day from Genesis. Church of San Marco, Venice, Italy.

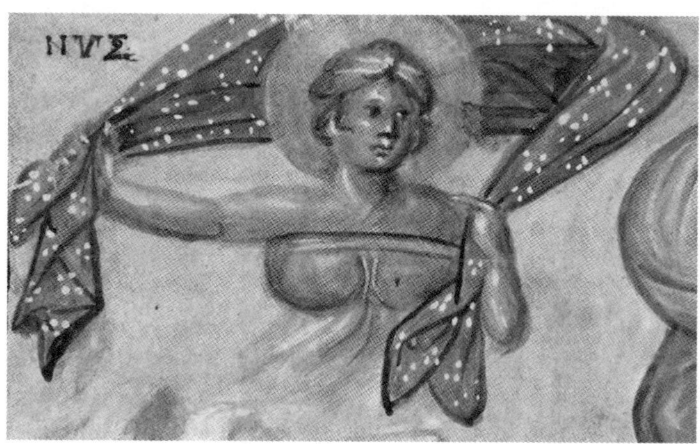

5.15. Detail of Night from Scene of Moses Parting the Red Sea. Paris, Bibliothèque Nationale de France, Psalter (Par. gr. 139), fol. 419v.

palette, differing only in the shade of hue: in this way dark and light are shown to be the same, simply varying in degree. The depiction is almost racialized in the image of the angel dividing night from day in the Genesis cycle in San Marco (fig. 5.14). There, the angel separates two gleaming orbs representing light and darkness, while the portion of their figure that lies in the darkness—that is, their arm and wing—is a bluish-gray, as if that darkness had altered their skin tone.

Two of the more lavish representations of night and day that come down to us are found in the mid-tenth-century Paris Psalter: first, in the miniature of the parting of the Red Sea, where the personified Night (*Nyx*) is depicted as a bust-length bluish-gray figure in the scene's top left corner (fig. 5.15); and second, in the representation of Isaiah's prayer to the Lord from Isaiah 26:9–21 (plate 8). In the latter, Night is shown as a full-length female figure, wearing a classicizing peplos with flowing folds. Draped in a half-moon billow above her is a cloth representing the starry night sky, just as is seen in the bust-length depiction of the first image. Night's left hand points down, and with it so does the long and elegant torch she is holding with its brilliant blue flame, signaling the waning of night. Night stands on Isaiah's left, while from the right a rosy-pink child springs into the scene carrying a torch with a dark-red flame. This child, like Night, is labeled— Dawn (*orthros*). His right hand gestures up toward Isaiah, who is raising both hands to the hand of God in the top-right corner of the frame. The two figures, Night and Dawn, manifest the opening of Isaiah's prayer: "I look for you during the night, my spirit within me seeks you at dawn" (Isaiah

26:9). Dark gray, rich blues, and muted purples are used for Night's body and garments, while a punchy red gives shape to the fleshy baby, matching the hues of his torch, and his body has a rich pink skin. Isaiah's flesh is a deeper red, as if darkened from years in the sun, but he is clad in a light-blue chiton and soft-pink himation whose tonalities parallel those of the two personifications beside him. The pink garment that wraps around the blue suggests the overtaking of night by day at the cusp of dawn. Isaiah thus comes to represent a figure on the edge of these two times of day, located as he is between the two.

That the eunuch's portrayal in the Menologion uses a visual language that is used elsewhere for personifications of night and darkness is telling. With that common language, Georgios is providing more than a commentary on the Ethiopian's darkness as being devoid of light. In depicting the eunuch as a figure between day and night, the artist is mediating between the pale and youthful iconography of court eunuchs and the dark skin suggested by their Ethiopian identity. It is possible that the unusual depiction of Night and Dawn in the Paris Psalter served as a prototype for the eunuch's depiction. The Paris miniatures are faithful copies of those commissioned by Constantine VII Porphyrogenitus in 952 for the fourteenth birthday of his son, the future Emperor Romanus II.[71] Romanus II would become the father of Basil II, for whom the Menologion was made around fifty years after the completion of the Psalter. The connection to the prayer of Isaiah would have been particularly compelling, for the Menologion scene unfolds after Philip hears the eunuch reading from the book of Isaiah, and later Philip would explicate the prophecy of Christ in Isaiah 53:7. Thus, the image of Isaiah caught between Night and Dawn seems to foreshadow the story of the eunuch, who is also caught between the iconographic stereotypes of the dainty paleness connected to their castration and the Ethiopian darkness of their black skin.

Eustathios Makrembolites's popular twelfth-century romance *Hysmine and Hysminias* provides evidence that personifications of night and dawn could be read racially in Byzantium. In a remarkable passage, the character Hysminias recounts the act of viewing a painting while working through and analyzing its iconography.[72] He marvels at two figures flanking a personification labeled as Eros:

One was like the sun and entirely white, with white hair, white eyes, white
tunic, face, hands, legs—everything white; the other was entirely black
[*melaina*]—hair, head, face and hands and feet, and tunic. They were identical

in age but different in colouring, identical in wrinkles but different in race
[*genos*], the one was as if she came from Achaia fair in women, the other as if
from scorched Ethiopia [*kekaumenēs Aithiopias*].[73]

The description of these figures matches the personifications of night and
day discussed previously. Crucially, Hysminias understands the depictions
as not simply allegorical or symbolic—the difference in skin color suggests
a difference in "race" (*genos*). Eventually, his companion Kratisthenes explains that these two figures are in fact "day and night" (*hēmera kai nyx*).[74]
Thus this text attests both to the popular understanding of this iconographic motif and to the possibility of reading such representations as images of racialized difference based on colorism and epidermal definitions
of race.

Even the dark blue of the eunuch's chlamys bears a complex and racialized history. In Byzantine color theory, the hues of blue and black were
deeply entangled and even conflated via overlapping terms and categories.[75]
The Greek word for "blue" (*kuaneos*) was consistently applied to the color
of the sky and the sea, but—just as in the ancient sources—its meaning
as "dark" was stressed.[76] For example, the tenth-century *Suda Lexicon* defines *kuaneoi* simply as "dark" (*melanes*).[77] The sixth-century lexicon of Hesychius has a variety of citations for blue, including the "water of the sea"
(*thalattion hydōr*) and the "perceptible color of the sky" (*eidos chrōmatos
ouranoeides*). Significantly, Hesychius's blue also covers the related *kuaneōn*
or "the blue ones" as referring to "the Dark Ones" (*Maurōn*)—whence the
term "Moors" derives—and "Ethiopians" (*Aithiopōn*).[78] Both in literary descriptions and in painting across the medieval world, artists and authors
regularly depict Ethiopians (and dark skin more broadly) as blue.[79] The interplay between blue and darkness in Byzantine color theories is a striking
conceptual parallel to what has been observed in the depiction of the Ethiopian eunuch.

The implications of blue—as signaling an absence of light, the color of
the sky, and the darkness of skin—have been present since antiquity. This
heritage makes blue (or, more accurately, *kuaneos*) the suitable color not
only for personifying Night, but also for conveying the color of the Ethiopian eunuch's skin in art. Gregorios seems to have had this logic in mind
when he illuminated the miniature of Philip and the Ethiopian eunuch in
the Menologion of Basil II. As we look at the eunuch's face, our gaze is led
down the outline of the chlamys over their left shoulder and arm, making it seem as if their face and cloak were of the same tone. Our eyes are

repeatedly deceived as to whether the eunuch's skin, as it fades into the richer blue of the chlamys with its dark shadowing, might be this same dark blue. And unlike what we see for the figure of Isaiah, the dark wraps over light, as the eunuch's pink tunic is covered by the blue chlamys.

This contrast is also made by Philip's clothing: he wears a pink chiton of the exact hue as that worn by the eunuch; the shading and contours of these pink garments are handled in the same way. Philip's beige himation, however, contrasts starkly with the eunuch's blue chlamys. Philip's is quite light yet equally varied in the hues and color saturations that compose it; there are dull white highlights on an olive-green color, while the fabric's folds and its outline over his left shoulder and arm are tawny ochre. The same dull white marks used for the himation's highlights are used for Philip's face, dull olive capturing the shading of his countenance—the shadowy right side of his face, the sides of his nose, the area around his eyes, and the curves of his neck—and ochre enlivening the lit left side of his face, particularly on his left temple, cheek, and neck. Thus, Georgios has deployed the same colors with surgical precision across garb and skin to articulate the racial difference between the two figures. While their outward skins may differ, the two are the same in their Christian faith, represented by the pink undertunics that unite the two figures.

While we have repeatedly encountered consistent beliefs in the fluidity of race, as defined by skin markers, we must also acknowledge and confront the radical disparities between the lives of the darkened transgender saints and the experiences of black men, such as Abba Moses the Ethiopian.[80] While the abbots and brothers seek to protect and guard transgender monks, lauding the supreme virtue of their trans brothers upon their death, similar abbots and brothers toss racial slurs at and dehumanize Abba Moses. Moses's virtue becomes reduced to his ability to maintain composure in spite of all this mistreatment. Rather than delight in his asceticism as such, the praise for the black man (when subjected to racial shaming and abuse) was based on his ability to keep silent.

White privilege thus apparently delights in the fantasy of becoming transracial, whereas the reality of a black person is that the same process is one of atonement and cleansing—whitewashing the Ethiopian, or purifying the primordial darkness of the soul. Thus, we see two vectors of identity at work in these authors. On the one hand, women become men, who are praised for their transgender ascent; white women become blackened men, who are praised for the asceticism demonstrated by their transracial transformation. But, within the same schema, men cannot become women lest they be corrupt effeminates; and black men can become white in spirit, only to be confronted with the futility of that change because their skin color remains the same. It is this double bind that Moses brings to the surface with his tongue-in-cheek statement that he had become wholly white, but only on the outside, playing on the colors of his garment and his skin.

In some regards, the myth of being transracial seems to be the last gasp of a culture that has momentarily deluded itself into believing itself to be postracial and color-blind despite failing to resolve its racial disparities, or the related brutalities and inequalities in its systems of oppression. Thus, the idea that one can be transracial emerges as an effort to performatively downplay the realities and dangers of racial inequality by culturally appropriating into oneself not elements of a culture but the whole idea of race itself, hoping to fully consume it by doing so. The commentaries on the Song of Songs actively seek to create a postracial utopia of inclusivity, but this attempt is ultimately held back by the systematics of racial prejudice. It is difficult to imagine a Byzantium in which there is no racial prejudice given that demons are depicted as black and their Roman heritage is replete with concerns about miscegenation, racial purity, and hypersexualized Ethiopian figures. Despite the marked differences in the Byzantine period from the West, texts like Nikephoros Basilakes's display pronounced antiblack and transphobic sentiments. Thus, the myth of a transracial possibility, while afforded to the nonblack transgender saints through their own racial privilege, is a phantasm for the black subject, reminded as they are that it is impossible to whiten them.

However, there is an important discussion to be had regarding the parallels, frictions, and intersectionality of race, gender, and sexual identity. As Kathryn Bond Stockton has argued, studying the contemporary interchange between race and queerness reveals the common trope of the poor, queer man of color (usually Latino, black, or both), who fashions himself through drag into the image of a white, wealthy woman, as in *Paris Is Burning* (dir. Jennie Livingston, 1990).[81] Yet, at the core of this impulse is the realization of an intersectional identity as the nonwhite, nonwealthy, nonheterosexual queer attempts to break through their own marginalization, an identity whose representation normative, homosexual communities and activism are often unable or unwilling to support. In other words, these recognitions of the enmeshments of race and sexuality, of race and gender demonstrate how identities, beyond their intersection, flow or switch into one another through the shared systematics of disadvantage, marginalization, and oppression.

IN THE MENOLOGION, while the martyrs are usually depicted in contemporary or more classicizing Byzantine garments, the torturers often wear richly embroidered pants, shirts with pseudo-Arabic script, and other such details that attempt to distinguish them from the martyrs. This differentiation does not always occur along the lines of skin color; in the few instances when skin color is involved, it is clear that these enemies are treated neither as a monolithic racialized other nor as *only* racially different. Nevertheless, these images contain an inherent murmur of racial tension, and I propose it is for this reason that the artist Georgios depicted the Ethiopian eunuch in a subtly yet distinctly different manner than the non-Christian foreigners of color. His aim was to remove the eunuch from the "ethnographic" portrayal of their facial features, garments, skin color, and so on. Faced with the task of presenting a Christian Ethiopian eunuch in a manner that would not confuse the viewer into understanding them as being somehow other to Philip, Georgios took extensive pains to ensure that all the eunuch's identities were conveyed favorably.

The eunuch is dressed in courtly attire with undertones of Byzantine military garb, clearly articulating that they are on Basil II's side. Their facial features are youthful, dainty, refined, and feminine, ensuring that they are properly interpreted as a eunuch cultivated in the fineries of the imperial court. In communicating their Ethiopian identity, the artist chose not to deploy the earthly tropes for portraying darker shades of skin color but instead to depict their form as a personification of Night. Rather than being dull and mottled, as are most human figures (both friends and foes) in the manuscript, the eunuch's skin radiates darkness, like the red glow of those fiery angels discussed previously. Georgios also had to ground the figure as a bodily, human form. Thus he paints the pulsating chlamys the color of the night sky, thereby simultaneously capturing the figure's origins as a personification and making them unquestionably earthly. In other words, the handling of the Ethiopian Christian eunuch's depiction is a visual metaphor for intersectionality as a method that seeks to represent the lived realities of a subject whose identity lies at the intersection of several marginalized groups. The fact that the eunuch cannot simply be a black Ethiopian, cannot simply be a white eunuch, cannot simply be a persecuted early Christian, but must develop a new system of representation altogether drives the methodological goals of this volume, which has sought to articulate new structures of representation to bring out the intersectional identities of Byzantine subjects.

The appearance of such a rich and complex depiction of the Ethiopian eunuch in a manuscript focused on the martyrdom of Christian subjects at the hands of barbaric others compels us to rethink blackness in Byzantium. Elsewhere in Byzantine art, persons of color appear when the evangelization of the various peoples of the earth is similarly stressed, such as the Pentecost scene.[82] Hence, the tenor of their depictions is usually positive, as they are welcomed into a broader Christian empire. The image of the Ethiopian eunuch requires that we confront the fact that, despite having inherited a long history of racial invective, the Byzantines repeatedly turned racist stereotypes on their heads. Moverover, in their identity as Roman subjects, the Byzantines had a different geopolitical position than did those the medieval West.

The Byzantines were not white. That a broad spectrum of skin tone was considered normative is evidence of that. Additionally, cosmopolitan conditions of a city such as Constantinople evidently created considerable room for "Ethiopian" figures to maneuver without prejudice in art, literature, and daily life. This does not mean that there was no racism or prejudice based on skin color. While we cannot accept the learned helplessness of viewing modern racism as a millennia-old phenomenon, immune to radical and immediate change, we must also ensure that we do not become apologists for ancient and medieval racism by somehow normalizing the systematic oppression and brutality against racial minorities in history. Black peoples in Byzantium merit further study, and so do the other racialized minorities and ethnic groups who fell under imperial brutality. In addition, we must turn to contemporary critical race studies to think of race beyond skin color, without underplaying or denying the role that it has in the subjugation and oppression of people of color.

Epilogue

IN 1992, MICHAEL CAMILLE ARGUED that "the margins add an extra dimension, a supplement, that is able to gloss, parody, modernize and problematize the text's authority while never totally undermining it."[1] The marginal identities discussed in this volume, however, do not form a strictly binary relationship with the center. In the Byzantine world, the ultimate recognition of the alterity of the so-called marginal is what always shocks those in the center into realizing their misgivings, their failures, and their own lacks. What we have seen here are figures who did not adhere to normative standards and who therefore actively challenged Byzantine culture to confront its privilege and entitlement. The praise enjoyed by transgender monks did not translate to a modern notion of equal rights. Transgender women, for example, are all but absent from the historical record. Nevertheless, because of trans monks, religious authors praised and venerated trans identities, despite legal and biblical prohibitions against their very existence. To consider the histories presented in this book is thus to glimpse the workings of a more ethical medieval past that neither fetishized otherness nor denigrated it, but rather sought to reevaluate its givens by learning from the subjectivities of these people.[2]

In looking at same-gender desire, slut-shaming, or gender identity in Byzantium, we find a world where gender and sexual practices that were nonnormative enjoyed a great deal of room to operate, even if, at times, it drew the ire of ecclesiastical figures or authorities who might have not approved of all the diverse practices in the various centers of the empire, from Constantinople to Alexandria. Camille's notion that the center is "dependent upon the margins for its continued existence"[3] rests on the assumption that it was by defining an othered and marginalized community that the center was able to retain its privilege and entitlement. Byzantium offers little evidence of this dynamic except in the most simplistic of forms. Byzantium's contact with others was always deeply personal; chances are that many people of any given identity—whether the focus is constructions of race, religious confession, or gender expression—existed in Constantinople as residents, tourists, or traders. There is no parallel in western Europe for Eustathios of Thessaloniki's praise for the eclectic and diverse Constantinopolitan court or Michael Psellus's boasts about their multicultural, multilingual, and multiethnic students.

In other words, in Byzantium the center does not depend on ostracizing the margins in order to forcefully exclaim and perpetually reclaim its centrality. Instead, the center depends on the margins for its continued existence in a quite different way; it worked more as an articulated hub in a broad network linked to various global and diverse centers than as a solitary colonial core. The saints' lives discussed here demonstrate an immense degree of mobility and circulation across the Mediterranean and Middle Eastern worlds, as fluid and permeable as the gender and sexual identities that unfold across those spaces. In describing the miraculous sacrifices of trans monks, the stories articulate what the center has to gain and learn from the marginalized, just as some Byzantine philosophers learned Arabic, spent time abroad, translated texts, and developed their ideas accordingly. When we examine figures like Procopius's Theodora, the homiletics on sexual consent, the various discussions on contraception and abortion, or offhand rules for dealing with same-gender desire in monastic spaces, we are forced to recognize the many discriminated against and disadvantaged figures who operated in the shadows of these centers.

Confronting the intersectionality of identity, we begin to perceive not only the struggles faced by disenfranchised identities but likewise the outlines of excised subjectivities who, owing to certain forms of privilege and entitlement, left a mark on the historical record even if many others like them were erased. Beyond illuminating the tentative and possible lives of medieval subjects, downtrodden because of their intersectional identities, the power of intersectionality as a method is to recognize the ability of privilege to compensate for a person's otherwise ill-regarded lives. Had Elagabalus or Theodora been just another person or performer in a late antique city, their identities would have been entirely expunged, existing only within the indiscriminately nameless mass of denigrated subjectivities compounded within the screeds of invective. Yet, as entitled and privileged figures who were nevertheless subjected to transphobia and slut-shaming, respectively, they managed to leave behind for us a ghostly image of such subjectivities in the premodern world.

My point here is certainly not that Elagabalus and Theodora enjoyed the privileges of the late antique equivalent of a straight white cis male, but rather that, because of the inordinate privileges of rank and wealth that they enjoyed, they were able to bypass the nameless obscurity of those whose identities placed them in positions of far less power. Just as intersectionality makes us aware that white feminism can be toxic to feminists of color whose suffering is radically different by the virtue of their intersecting identities, as historians we can use the privilege of recorded historical figures to excavate interstitial subjectivities that were denied to those less privileged. The relative privilege of a transgender monk, who is praised for his ascent from femininity to masculinity, converts misogynist rhetoric into a meagerly preserved identity in the historical record. Through them we can then obliquely consider the social, medical, and institutional possibilities for transgender women, for whom a transgender identity was met not with misogynistic praise but with transmisogynistic erasure.

Intersectionality thus makes Camille's center/periphery binary wholly irrelevant, redirecting our attention not to what lies at one place or the other, nor to the dialogic constitution of the two, but rather to the multiple states of marginality that repeatedly intersect. Rather than looking at the dynamics of marginality construed through power and authority, even when playfully subverted, we must question the institution of power directly. Despite his allusions to the flux between margins and centers, Camille's margin ultimately plays with glosses on identity without being able to flesh out the textures and messiness of identities in their individual pluralities. After all, as a gay white male scholar, marginal identity was monolithic and defined for Camille.[4] Camille's failures make us keenly aware that to uphold binary constructions of identity is ultimately to accede to the power structures that would rather keep center and periphery as valid classifications. As a retort to Michael Camille's *Image on the Edge*, this book is intended to stress the intersection, multiplicity, and ultimate erasure of the identities addressed.

Future scholarship must acknowledge that marginalization, oppression, and intersectionality are not modern constructs—they are methodologies. Even if such self-critical language is missing from our primary sources, we cannot state that the lived realities and experience of these subjectivities are not historically valid or present. To say that articulating and calling out these forces is anachronistic or contrary to the historian's project is to be complicit with oppression. The contemporary notion of being and becoming aware of these problems in our own society is captured by the word "woke," though its own complicities and self-satisfied hubris are also noted and rightly critiqued as virtue signaling. Even in a culture that has a developed language for articulating and fighting the inequalities of systematic oppression, one can far too easily be lulled into complacency and comfortable silence. Even today, to call out and argue for the realities of intersectionality often entails engaging with normalized power structures, ranging from governmental institutions to our friends and colleagues. As a method, intersectionality requires the articulation to each other of the patterns, actions, and mentalities of ingrained systematic oppression, for, as individuals, we often perpetuate these systematically normalized (yet no less violent) exercises of power without our own knowledge or intent.

In history, to write a truer, more ethical past requires a process of explanation that frequently is met with denial, retaliatory aggression, hurt feelings, and slow acceptance, even by those who are close to us. Despite this, to believe that our historical inquiries can begin only when our primary texts willingly offer up and display subjectivities is to be a crude apologist for social inequality and oppression. Furthermore, it is to delude ourselves into believing that we are taking a scholarly high ground in denying the existence of sexual violence, misogyny, transphobia, homophobia, and racism in the premodern world. If we are not willing to call out the distant historical past for its perpetuation of social inequality, then how will we ever be able to call out our neighbors and ourselves? Our past must be intersectional before our future can ever be—not just because our future depends on our past, but because if we are unwilling to give representation to the marginalized in our histories of the far-removed past, then we are certainly not able to undertake the systematic changes to our culture, infrastructures, and systems necessary to produce a livable reality for oppressed identities in the immediate present.

ACKNOWLEDGMENTS

ON 8 NOVEMBER 2016, I presented the first chapter of this book to our weekly Medieval Seminar meeting at the Institute for Advanced Study in Princeton. This project is indelibly marked by that time and place.

This project would not have been possible without the signature freedom that the Institute provided me as an Elizabeth and J. Richardson Dilworth Fellow. This is not the project I had set forth to do there, but it came to dominate most of my months in that idyllic place, surrounded by newfound friends and colleagues.

For me, the textures of this book are imbued with the mundanities of life in Princeton, which I relish the chance to recall and recount now—the countryside drives to the market with Columba Stewart; the dinners in odd suburban streetscapes with Jennifer Davis; the chats in the corridor of Fuld Hall with Daniel Sherman; the hauled caravans of books from the Princeton Theological Seminary with Rebecca Maloy; the many feasts shared with Charlie Barber and Beatrice Kitzinger; the impromptu hang with Katherine King when I sprained my back; the afternoon chats over tea and cookies with Nina Glibetić and Gabriel Radle; the nighttime stroll through the fireflies with Karen Engle; the making of mansaf and kanafeh for dinner with Lori Allen, Yezid Sayigh, and Vanja Hamzić; the joyful playtimes with Dilara, Emine Fetvacı, and Dan Star; the lunchtime seminars with Patrick Geary; the sunset visit to Yve-Alain Bois's farm in the late fall; the endless cooking with María Mercedes Tuya and Sabine Schmidtke for our massive dinner party; the chat in the hallway with Marian Zelazny on a gloomy afternoon as rain poured into my office; the chance coffee with Kelly McKowen; the wine hour in the Art Gallery with Serena Stein; the small farewell for Jane Hathaway and Suzanne Hakenbeck in one of our tiny studio apartments; the smile on Michelle Komie's face when I handed her the contract for this book; the phone calls with Samantha Jacobson where I recounted my day's work as they brimmed with pride; and the tears I wept when I crossed the border back into California on my way back home.

Amidst all this, there was also the quiet stillness of sunset in my Marcel Breuer apartment, when the sun glowed bright in a golden haze through the dirty windows. This event happened nearly all days, but, every time it felt unique and endless, somehow, at the same time. Precious eternities unfolded while deer and rabbits leaped across the evening grass, while my kitchen buzzed with whatever new recipe I was testing, and while I worried about tenure.

Those were the moments in the interstices of this book that truly mattered.

For Samantha Jacobson, this book is a testament to our eight years together, the youth we spent and the growth we shared. It was written to do its part, to make a better world for you.

There is a double-debt here, for this book also would not have happened without the early encouragement and support of Despina Stratigakos and Michelle Komie, who both latched onto this idea and believed it was not only worthwhile but necessary. Michelle has been the ideal editor in every capacity; she has spoiled me in her excellence.

For a project such as this, it has been the support and enthusiasm of colleagues and friends that has been the most significant. While a long list once stood here, I have opted not to dare list them all lest I forget a single one.

In reality, much of this project happened swiftly and in isolation, while being driven by the efforts of my exceptional friends and colleagues in the Medievalists of Color group. Particularly, Dorothy Kim has been a powerful beacon and harbor, both championing all that is good in the field and being to me a perfect colleague and friend. Furthermore, Adam Miyashiro, Jonathan Hsy, Cord Whittaker, Seeta Chaganti, and Vincent Van Gerven Oei have been there over the course of this project in various capacities— from Facebook to conferences—to provide their support, enthusiasm, and comradery in ways that are unrepayable. I also wish to highlight Shannon Steiner who, over the years, has continuously stood out for being an exemplary colleague in every respect, giving me hope and trust in the future of the field. She has lent support for this project in ways that were deeply meaningful when I needed it most.

Others have continually inspired me and encouraged me to demand more of myself and others. Gabrielle M. W. Bychowski and I have discussed methods and the Monk Marinos over the years with urgency and excitement. The writings of my high school friend Prisca Dorcas Mojica Rodríguez continue to inspire me, and I am so happy that we have come to be closer in recent years. Marianna Davison and Sharrissa Iqbal have been exceptional colleagues and interlocutors at a critical time and I am immensely grateful for their presence. Maggie Allen continues to mean a great deal to me, while Katie Allen Henderson's *Star Trek: Voyager* cross-stich has become my most prized possession. Marleny Mesa and Elaine Urdaneta continue to be lifelong friends, even if we rarely get to speak to or see each other. A special acknowledgement goes to Brantley Bryant, Sakina Bryant, and Lesley S. Curtis, who, in the months following November 2016, were continuous interlocutors as we reflected on family, belonging, and history.

In the past year and a half, I must duly acknowledge the warmth and care offered to me by Disneyland cast members as I finished and revised this book. I am grateful for all those who giddily and warmly welcomed me, particularly Sofia, Jordan, Jason, Mariah, Hunter, Raquel, Ashley, Patrick, Amanda, Meredith, and, of course, Sarah Sterrett, as well as for all the long lunches and endless dinners discussing both the contents of this book and the next.

My colleagues at UCI are exceptional in every capacity. I have been privileged to find myself amidst such a generous and supportive group of staff, faculty, and graduate students. I am convinced that our graduate students are the very best, offering the most rigorous intellectual stimulation. For them, I am deeply grateful.

In winter of 2018, I was graciously invited to present this work at the Pennsylvania State University as a Dickson Memorial Lecture, at the behest of Tony Cutler. And, in the summer of 2018, I was able to present parts of this work to the International Medieval Congress in Leeds as the inaugural New Directions lecture. I wish to thank the committees that allowed me the honor of sharing my work with such exceptional groups of colleagues. In Leeds, I also wish to thank Anna Klosowska and Catherine Karkov for their reparative company at such a crucial moment in my personal life. Our ventures "behind the curtain" are lifetime gems, eternal moments in which I often dwell. The company of Jennifer Timmons, Matthew Vanderpoel, and Sean Hannan during that visit also meant a great deal to me. An abridged version of chapter 5 appeared as "Imperial Brutality: Racial Difference and the Intersectionality of the Ethiopian Eunuch," in Bryan C. Keene (ed.), *Toward a Global Middle Ages: Encountering the World through Illuminated Manuscripts* (Los Angeles: J. Paul Getty Museum, 2019), 165–174.

Much goes into the finalization and production of a book. Financial support for this volume has been graciously provided by UCI's Humanities

Commons Publication Grant with the aid of Julia Lupton and Amanda Swain. The award of a generous Chancellor's Fellowship, spearheaded by our Dean Tyrus Miller, has not only provided necessary additional funds, but also served as a validation of my work that was deeply touching and motivating. Beth Pace, Heather Layton, and AJ Lipscomb have had the herculean task of processing countless image fees and reimbursements for this project. And I acknowledge all the librarians at UCI, the IAS, Princeton University, and across ILL and Borrow Direct who have helped make this project happen. Early on, Alexis May read a first draft of the manuscript and provided insightful comments as a potential undergrad reader. Subsequently, the book benefited from the insightful comments of the two readers, the line editing of Alice Falk, the proofreading of Aleah Hernandez, the exceptional copy editing of Michelle Hawkins, the work of Steven Sears as production manager, the text design and typesetting of Chris Crochetière, the cover design of Julie Allred, and the index of Kate Mertes.

To my mother, uncle, and aunt, there shall always be the debt of exile and the burden of gratitude, fueled by a healthy dose of Cuban guilt.

My dear friends Kate Durbin and Chloe LeGendre only become more and more important in my life as the years go by, for which I am immensely grateful and thankful.

And, finally, to Michael Kelleher who hobbled into my life one evening and has caused just about every person in these acknowledgements to remark on how happy I am. You have given a new life to my smile, made this luminous place a little more livable, and allowed me for once to relish the present, not just hunger for a future. My time with you continues to feel like ice cream on a warm summer's day. *Tap, tap, tap.*

NOTES

INTRODUCTION

1. The account is attributed to Sophronius of Jerusalem in the manuscript tradition, but this authorship has been unanimously rejected in the scholarly literature. See Bernard Flusin, "Palestinian Hagiography (Fourth–Eighth Centuries)," in *The Ashgate Companion to Byzantine Hagiography*, ed. Stephanos Efthymiadis, vol. 1 (Burlington, VT: Ashgate, 2011), 199–226, esp. 212.

2. Cyril of Scythopolis, *Life of Cyriacus* 233, trans. R. M. Price and John Binns, *Lives of the Monks of Palestine* (Kalamazoo, MI: Cistercian Publications, 1991), 257.

3. John Moschus, *The Spiritual Meadow* 179, trans. John Wortley, *The Spiritual Meadow of John Moschus* (Kalamazoo, MI: Cistercian Publications, 1992), 148–149.

4. *Life of Mary of Egypt* 10, trans. Maria Kouli, "The Life of St. Mary of Egypt," in *Holy Women of Byzantium: Ten Saints' Lives in English Translation*, ed. Alice-Mary Talbot (Washington, DC: Dumbarton Oaks, 1996), 76.

5. *Life of Mary of Egypt* 18, trans. Kouli, 80.

6. *Life of Mary of Egypt* 19–21, trans. Kouli, 81.

7. *Life of Mary of Egypt* 21, trans. Kouli, 81; ed. PG 87:3712.

8. See Angeliki Laiou, "Sex, Consent, and Coercion in Byzantium," in *Consent and Coercion to Sex and Marriage in Ancient and Medieval Societies*, ed. A. Laiou (Washington, DC: Dumbarton Oaks, 1998), 109–221.

9. On the clitoris's association with female sexuality in early modern thinking, see Valerie Traub, "The Psychomorphology of the Clitoris," *GLQ: A Journal of Lesbian and Gay Studies* 2 (1995): 81–113.

10. Aetius of Amida, *Tetrabiblos* 16.45–46, trans. James V. Ricci, *Aetios of Amida: The Gynaecology and Obstetrics of the VIth Century, A.D.* (Philadelphia: Blakiston Company, 1950), 50–51.

11. Paul of Aegina, *Medical Compendium* 6.70, trans. Francis Adam, *The Seven Books of Paulus Ægineta*, vol. 2 (London: Sydenham Society, 1846), 381.

12. See Jack Halberstam, *Female Masculinity* (Durham: Duke University Press, 1998), esp. 45–73.

13. On the frescoes of the Panagia Phorbiotissa at Asinou, see Annemarie Weyl Carr, "The Murals of the Bema and Naos: The Paintings of the Late Thirteenth and Fourteenth Centuries," in *Asinou Across Time: Studies in the Architecture and Murals of the Panagia Phorbiotissa, Cyprus*, eds. Annemarie Weyl Carr and Andréas Nicolaïdès (Washington, DC: Dumbarton Oaks, 2012), 211–312. On depictions of female piety for comparison, see Sharon E. J. Gerstel, "Painted Sources for Female Piety in Medieval Byzantium," *Dumbarton Oaks Papers* 52 (1998): 89–111.

14. *Life of Mary of Egypt* 10, trans. Kouli, 76.

15. *Life of Mary of Egypt* 12, trans. Kouli, 77.

16. See Marios Papadakis et al., "Gynaecomastia and Scrotal Rhacosis: Two Aesthetic Surgical Operations for Men in Byzantine Times," *Journal of Plastic, Reconstructive, & Aesthetic Surgery* 63:8 (2010): 600–604.

17. While the transgender monks are invariably commemorated in art as women in the Byzantine world, the figure of Mary of Egypt is often depicted in art with masculine features. Western depictions of these saints are far more varied. For a survey of these depictions in the later Middle Ages, see Andrea-Bianka Znorovzky, "Between Mary

and Christ: Depicting Cross-Dressed Saints in the Middle Ages (c. 1200–1600)," (PhD diss., Central European University, 2016). See also Idem, "Marinus Unveiled: A Transvestite Saint in Western Art and Literature" (MA thesis, Central European University, 2011); Idem, "Holy Female Monks-Patterns of Purity: A Comparative Approach of the Visual Representations of Saint Marina the Monk, Saint Eugenia of Rome, and Saint Euphrosyne," in *Il Genere Nella Ricerca Storica*, ed. S. Chemotti and C. La Rocca (Padua: Il Poligrafo, 2015), 1:151–170; Kirk Ambrose, "Two Cases of Female Cross-Undressing in Medieval Art and Literature," *Source: Notes in the History of Art* 23.3 (2004): 7–14.

18. *Suda Lexicon*, alphaiota 129 and alphaiota 138, ed. and trans. Catharine Roth and James Cousins, "*Aithiops*" and "*Aithops*," *Suda On Line*, ed. David Whitehead, www.stoa.org/sol-entries/alphaiota/129 and www.stoa.org/sol-entries/alphaiota/138.

19. Aetius of Amida, *Tetrabiblos*, 16.51, modified trans. James V. Ricci, *Aetios of Amida: The Gynaecology and Obstetrics of the VIth Century, A.D.* (Philadelphia: Blakiston, 1950), 55.

20. Eustathios of Thessaloniki, *Epitaphios for Manuel I Komnenos*, ed. and trans. Emmanuel C. Bourbouhakis, *Not Composed in a Chance Manner: The Epitaphios for Manuel I Komnenos by Eustathios of Thessaloniki* (Uppsala: Uppsala Universitet, 2017), 26–27.

21. *Life of Mary of Egypt* 10, trans. Kouli, 76.

22. Ibid.

23. See Kimberlé W. Crenshaw, "Demarginalizing the Intersection of Race and Sex: A Black Feminist Critique of Antidiscrimination Doctrine, Feminist Theory, and Antiracist Politics," *University of Chicago Legal Forum* 1:8 (1989): 139–167. See also Idem, "Mapping the Margins: Intersectionality, Identity Politics, and Violence against Women of Color," *Stanford Law Review* 43.6 (1991): 1241–1299. On intersectionality and method, see Ange-Marie Hancock, *Intersectionality: An Intellectual History* (Oxford: Oxford University Press, 2016); Sumi Cho, Kimberlé Williams Crenshaw, and Leslie McCall, "Toward a Field of Intersectionality Studies: Theory, Applications, and Praxis," *Signs* 38.4 (2013): 785–810. For a useful critique of the coloniality of intersectionality,

see María Lugones, "Toward a Decolonial Feminism," *Hypatia* 25.4 (2010): 742–759. Intersectionality in the medieval world was the focus of Medieval Intersectionality, a conference organized by Amanda Power and Robin Whelan at Oxford University, 15 March 2017. See also Jennifer C. Nash, *Black Feminism Reimagined: After Intersectionality* (Durham: Duke University Press, 2019).

24. On the state of the field on some of these matters, see Averil Cameron, *Byzantine Matters* (Princeton: Princeton University Press, 2014), esp. 26–67. For my response to this book, see Roland Betancourt, review of *Byzantine Matters*, by Averil Cameron, *Journal of Modern Greek Studies* 34.2 (2016): 401–404.

25. In mentioning neighbors of the Byzantine Empire, I am particularly thinking of the Coptic and Syriac spheres, for several reasons. First, sometimes Greek sources are better preserved in Syriac or Coptic translations, which also enable us to perceive how these stories persisted and changed as they were told. Second, at other times these close neighbors fill in the gaps of the historical record, corroborating details and nuances that Greek sources mention only in passing. Third, this capacious view of the Byzantine world accurately reflects the amount of contact, trade, and circulation across these spheres. It would be wrong to not include them in this dialogue when appropriate. Western European sources appear here only insofar as they directly elucidate the happenings of Constantinople or the Greek Mediterranean. In those cases, Western sources are used to emphasize contrasting viewpoints rather than internal Byzantine perspectives.

26. See Elizabeth Freeman, *Time Binds: Queer Temporalities, Queer Histories* (Durham, NC: Duke University Press, 2010), xvii.

27. Anjali Arondekar, *For the Record: On Sexuality and the Colonial Archive in India* (Durham, NC: Duke University Press, 2009), 1–25, at 4.

28. In calling these "minuscule histories," I am positioning this approach between the methodology of "microhistory" and that of "minor history." Microhistory closely scrutinizes one relatively small aspect of society in order to sketch out its implications, while a "minor history," as developed by Branden

Joseph (following Mike Kelley), is a history of all the so-called minor figures and actors that a so-called major history renders "a set of ancillary names and facts without impact," ultimately repressing or ignoring them by relegating these so-called minor figures to inconsequential contexts. See Branden W. Joseph, *Beyond the Dream Syndicate: Tony Conrad and the Arts after Cage (A "Minor" History)* (New York: Zone Books, 2008), esp. 47–51; quotation, 50. For a historiographic study of microhistory with a recent bibliography, see Sigurður Gylfi Magnússon and István M. Szíjártó, *What Is Microhistory? Theory and Practice* (London: Routledge, 2013). See also Carlo Ginzburg, "Microhistory: Two or Three Things That I Know about It," trans. John and Anne C. Tedeschi, *Critical Inquiry* 20.1 (1993): 10–35.

CHAPTER I: THE VIRGIN'S CONSENT

1. Emphasis in Mango. Photius, *Homily 5*, trans. Cyril Mango, *The Homilies of Photius Patriarch of Constantinople* (Cambridge, MA: Harvard University Press, 1958), 115; ed. Basileiou Laourda, OMILIAI (Thessaloniki: Hetaireia Makedonikōn Spoudōn, 1959), 55.

2. See Sebastian P. Brock, "Poetry and Hymnography (3): Syriac," in *The Oxford Handbook of Early Christian Studies*, ed. Susan Ashbrook Harvey and David G. Hunter (Oxford: Oxford University Press, 2008), 657–671, esp. 664–665, and also Idem, *Bride of Light: Hymns on Mary from the Syriac Churches* (Kerala, India: St. Ephrem Ecumenical Research Institute, 1994), esp. 12–13; see Germanus of Constantinople, *Homily on the Annunciation*, trans. Mary B. Cunningham, *Wider Than Heaven: Eighth-Century Homilies on the Mother of God* (Crestwood, NY: St. Vladimir's Seminary Press, 2008), 221–246.

3. See Mary B. Cunningham, "The Use of the *Protevangelion* of James in Eighth-Century Homilies on the Mother of God," in *The Cult of the Mother of God in Byzantium: Texts and Images*, ed. Leslie Brubaker and Mary B. Cunningham (Burlington, VT: Ashgate, 2011), 163–178.

4. Photius, *Homily 5*, trans. Mango, *The Homilies of Photius*, 114; ed. Basileiou Laourda, OMILIAI (Thessaloniki: Hetaireia Makedonikōn Spoudōn, 1959), 53–61.

5. See Robert B. Eno, "Mary and her Role in Patristic Theology," in *The One Mediator, the Saints, and Mary*, ed. H. G. Anderson, J. F. Stafford, and J. A. Burgess (Minneapolis: Augsburg, 1992), 159–176.

6. Gregory of Nazianzus, *First Letter to Cledonius* (Ep. 101), ed. P. Gallay, *Lettres théologiques*, Sources chrétiennes 208 (Paris: Éditions du Cerf, 1974), 36–68, at 39.

7. Photius, *Homily 9*, trans. Mango, *The Homilies*, 175.

8. See Nicholas Constas, *Proclus of Constantinople and the Cult of the Virgin in Late Antiquity* (Leiden: Brill, 2003), esp. 282–290.

9. Irenaeus, *Against Heresies* 3:22.4, trans. Alexander Roberts and James Donaldson *Ante-Nicene Fathers*, ed. Alexander Roberts and James Donaldson, vol. 1 (New York: Christian Literature Company, 1885), 455.

10. Narsai of Edessa, *Homily*, ed. A. Mingana, *Homiliae et carmina* (Mosul: Typis Fratrum praedicatorum, 1905), 353; Narsai of Edessa, *Homily on Creation* 1, ed. Philippe Gignoux, *Homélies de Narsaï sur la création*. Patrologia Orientalis 34 (Turnhout: Brepols, 1968), 3–4. See Taeke Jansma, "Narsai's Homilies on Creation: Remarks on a Recent Edition," *Muséon* 83 (1970): 209–235. See also Constas, *Proclus of Constantinople*, 284.

11. Proclus of Constantinople, *Homily 1*, ed. and trans. Constas, *Proclus of Constantinople*, 138–139.

12. Ps-Gregory Thaumaturgus, *Homily 1*, trans. S. D. F. Salmond, "Four Homilies," *Ante-Nicene Fathers*, ed. Alexander Roberts and James Donaldson, vol. 6 (New York: Christian Literature Company, 1890), 58–59.

13. On the erotic tension between Mary and Gabriel, see Thomas Arentzen, *The Virgin in Song: Mary and the Poetry of Romanos the Melodist* (Philadelphia: University of Pennsylvania Press, 2017), 46–86. See also Thomas Arentzen, "'Your Virginity Shines'— The Attraction of the Virgin in the *Annunciation Hymn* by Romanos the Melodist," in *Studia Patristica LXVII*, vol. 16, ed. Markus Vinzent (Leuven: Peeters, 2013), 125–132.

14. Romanus the Melodist, *Hymns*, 3.5–10, ed. and trans. Arentzen, *The Virgin in Song*, 177, 182.

15. Romanus the Melodist, *Hymns*, 7–8, 8.2, ed. and trans. Arentzen, *The Virgin in Song*, 175–184, 178.

16. Andrew of Crete, *Homily on the*

Annunciation; trans. Cunningham, *Wider Than Heaven*, 212.

17. Germanus, *Homily on the Annunciation*, trans. Cunningham, *Wider Than Heaven*, 228.

18. Ibid.

19. See Gedaliahu A. G. Stroumsa, *Another Seed: Studies in Gnostic Mythology* (Leiden: Brill, 1984), esp. 35–70.

20. *Apocryphon of John*, trans. Michael Waldstein and Frederik Wisse, *The Apocryphon of John* (Leiden: Brill, 1995), 47.

21. *The Hypostasis of the Archons*, trans. Bentley Layton, "The Hypostasis of the Archons," in *The Nag Hammadi Library in English*, ed. James M. Robinson, 3rd ed. (Leiden: Brill, 1990), 161–169, at 164.

22. *Protoevangelium of James*, trans. J. K. Elliott, *The Apocryphal New Testament* (Oxford: Oxford University Press, 1993), 62.

23. Emphasis in Arentzen. Romanus the Melodist, *Hymns* 12.4, ed. and modified trans. Arentzen, *The Virgin in Song*, 179, 185.

24. Romanus the Melodist, *Hymns* 13, 17.2, 17.4, ed. and trans. Arentzen, *The Virgin in Song*, 179–181, 185–187.

25. Justin Martyr, *First Apology*, trans. *Ante-Nicene Fathers*, 1:170.

26. Justin Martyr, *Dialogue with Trypho*, trans. *Ante-Nicene Fathers*, 1:237, ed. E. J. Goodspeed, *Die ältesten Apologeten* (Göttingen: Vandenhoeck & Ruprecht, 1915), 90–265.

27. James Brundage, "Rape and Marriage in the Medieval Canon Law," *Revue de droit canonique* 28 (1978): 62–75. See also Albrecht Classen, *Sexual Violence and Rape in the Middle Ages: A Critical Discourse in Premodern German and European Literature* (Berlin: De Gruyter, 2011).

28. Origen, *Against Celsus* 1.32, trans. Henry Chadwick, *Origen: Contra Celsum*, corrected ed. (Cambridge: Cambridge University Press, 1965), 31; ed. M. Borret, *Contre Celse*, vol. 1. Sources chrétiennes 132 (Paris: Éditions du Cerf, 1967), 64–476.

29. See Michael Meerson and Peter Schäfer, eds. and trans., *Toledot Yeshu: The Life Story of Jesus*, 2 vols. (Tübingen: Mohr Siebeck, 2014), 1:45–56. On the Talmud's approaches to this matter, see Peter Schäfer, *Jesus in the Talmud* (Princeton: Princeton University Press, 2007), 15–24.

30. Andrew of Crete, *Homily on the Annunciation*, trans. Cunningham, *Wider Than Heaven*, 213–216.

31. Cunningham, *Wider Than Heaven*, 216 n.68.

32. Germanus of Constantinople, *Homily on the Annunciation*, trans. Cunningham, *Wider Than Heaven*, 232.

33. Germanus of Constantinople, *Homily on the Annunciation*, ed. PG 98:328.

34. Germanus of Constantinople, *Homily on the Annunciation*, trans. Cunningham, *Wider Than Heaven*, 234; ed. PG 98:331.

35. Leontius of Neapolis, *Life of Symeon the Holy Fool*, trans. Derek Krueger, "Life of Symeon the Fool," in *Symeon the Holy Fool: Leontius's* Life *and the Late Antique City* (Berkeley: University of California Press, 1996), 121–170, at 156; ed. A.-J. Festugière and L. Rydén, *Léontios de Néapolis: Vie de Syméon le Fou et Vie de Jean de Chypre*, Bibliothèque archéologique et historique 95 (Paris: Geuthner, 1974), 85.

36. Romanus the Melodist, *Hymns*, 4.5–6, ed. and trans. Arentzen, *The Virgin in Song*, 177, 182–183.

37. Angeliki Laiou, "Sex, Consent, and Coercion in Byzantium," *Consent and Coercion to Sex and Marriage in Ancient and Medieval Societies*, ed. A. Laiou (Washington, DC: Dumbarton Oaks, 1998), 109–221, esp. 117–118.

38. See Patricia Karlin-Hayter, "Further Notes on Byzantine Marriage: Raptus—*hapargē* or *mnēsteiai*?," *Dumbarton Oaks Papers* 46 (1992): 133–154. See also Alexander Kazhdan, "Byzantine Hagiography and Sex in the Fifth to Twelfth Centuries," *Dumbarton Oaks Papers* 44 (1990): 131–143.

39. Angeliki Laiou, *Mariage, amour et parenté à Byzance aux XIe–XIIIe siècles* (Paris: De Boccard, 1993).

40. See P. Dalla-Vorgia, J. Lascaratos, P. Skiadas, and T. Garanis-Papadatos, "Is Consent in Medicine a Concept Only of Modern Times?" *Journal of Medical Ethics* 27:1 (2001): 59–61.

41. John Skylitzes, *Synopsis of Histories*, modified trans. Sigfús Blöndal, *The Varangians of Byzantium*, trans. Benedikt S. Benedikz (Cambridge: Cambridge University Press, 1978), 62–63; see also trans. John Wortley, *A Synopsis of Byzantine History, 811–1057* (Cambridge: Cambridge University Press, 2010), 372.

42. Laiou, "Sex, Consent, and Coercion,"
165.

43. John Skylitzes, *Synopsis of History*, ed.
J. Thurn, *Synopsis historiarum*, Corpus Fontium Historiae Byzantinae, Series Berolinensis 5 (Berlin: De Gruyter, 1973), 894.

44. In the popular imagination of Byzantium, this view of a woman's body as a be-
sieged city may be best captured by a line in
the Akathist Hymn, composed by Romanus
the Melodist in the sixth century, which was
a staple in liturgy and processions in later
centuries. There, the singer greets the Virgin,
"Hail, unsieged [*aporthēton*] wall of the kingdom." *Aporthēton* is a military term, often
translated here as "impregnable" or "unpene-
trated" to underline the sexual connotations.
Yet it denotes specifically that the city's walls
have not been compromised and that the
city remains unplundered, thus serving as a
model of an inviolate virginity. See Romanus
the Melodist, *Akathist Hymn* 23.13, modified
trans. and ed. Leena M. Peltomaa, *The Image
of the Virgin Mary in the Akathistos Hymn*
(Leiden: Brill, 2001), 18–19.

45. Nikephoros Basilakes, *Rhetorical Exercises* 56 (Ethiopoeiæ, 27), ed. and modified
trans. Jeffrey Beneker and Craig A. Gibson,
*The Rhetorical Exercises of Nikephoros Basi-
lakes*: Progymnasmata *from Twelfth-Century
Byzantium*, Dumbarton Oaks Medieval Library 43 (Cambridge, MA: Harvard University Press, 2016), 324–325.

46. Nikephoros Basilakes, *Rhetorical Exercises* 56 (Ethiopoeiæ, 27), ed. and trans.
Beneker and Gibson, *The Rhetorical Exercises*, 322–323.

47. Nikephoros Basilakes, *Rhetorical Exercises* 56 (Ethiopoeiæ, 27), ed. and trans.
Beneker and Gibson, *The Rhetorical Exercises*, 328–329.

48. Emphasis in Mango. Photius, *Homily 5*,
modified trans. Mango, *The Homilies*, 118–119;
ed. Laourda, OMIΛIAI, 53–61.

49. Eustathios Romaios, *Legal Opin-
ion*, trans. Denis Sullivan, "Appendix: Legal
Opinion of Eusthatios (Romaios) the Magis-
tros (after 1028)," in Laiou, "Sex, Consent, and
Coercion," 175–176, at 176; ed. A. Schminck,
"Vier eherechtliche Entscheidungen," *Fontes
Minores* 3 (1979): 224–228.

50. Sextus Empiricus, *Adversus mathematicos* 7.253–254, 257–258, ed. J. Mau and

H. Mutschmann, *Sexti Empirici opera*, vol. 2
(Leipzig: Teubner, 1914); trans. Long and Sedley, *The Hellenistic Philosophers*, vol. 1 (Cambridge: Cambridge University Press, 1987),
246.

51. Constas, *Proclus of Constantinople*,
273–313, esp. 279–282.

52. Terry Wilfong, "Reading the Disjointed
Body in Coptic: From Physical Modification to Textual Fragmentation," in *Changing Bodies, Changing Meanings: Studies on
the Human Body in Antiquity*, ed. Dominic
Montserrat (London: Routledge, 1998), 116–
136, esp. 123.

53. Jesper Svenbro, *Phrasikleia: An Anthro-
pology of Reading in Ancient Greece*, trans.
Janet Lloyd (Ithaca, NY: Cornell University
Press, 1993), esp. 187–216.

54. Pseudo-Demetrius of Antioch, *Homily*,
trans. E. A. Wallis Budge, "The Discourse by
Demetrius, Archbishop of Antioch, on the
birth, according to the flesh of God the Word,
and on the Virgin Mary," in *Miscellaneous
Coptic Texts in the Dialect of Upper Egypt*,
vol. 5 (London: British Museum, 1915), 687.

55. Pseudo-Epiphanius, *Homily*, trans.
Budge, "The Discourse of Apa Epiphanius,
Bishop of Cyprus, on the Holy Virgin, Mary
Theotokos," in *Miscellaneous Coptic Texts*,
712. Cyril of Rakote, *Homily*, trans. Budge,
"The Discourse of Saint Cyril, Archbishop of
Rakote, on the Virgin Mary," in ibid., 719.

56. *Martyrdom and Ascension of Isaiah*,
trans. M. A. Knibb, "Martyrdom and Ascension of Isaiah," in *The Old Testament Pseudepigrapha*, ed. James H. Charlesworth, vol. 1
(Peabody, MA: Hendrickson Publishers,
1983), 174.

57. On this matter, see Constas, *Proclus of
Constantinople*, 278–279.

58. Photius, *Homily 5*, modified trans.
Mango, *The Homilies*, 120.

59. See John Meyendorff, "Christian Marriage in Byzantium: The Canonical and Liturgical Tradition," *Dumbarton Oaks Papers*
44 (1990): 99–107.

60. John of Damascus, *Exposition of the
Faith*, trans. S. D. F. Salmond, "Exposition
of the Orthodox Faith," in *Nicene and Post-
Nicene Fathers*, Second Series, ed. Phillip
Schaff and Henry Wace, vol. 9 (New York:
Charles Scribner's Sons, 1902), 86.

61. Nicholas Mesarites, *Description of*

the Church of Holy Apostles*, trans. and ed. G. Downey, "Description of the Church of the Holy Apostles at Constantinople," *Transactions of the American Philosophical Society*, n.s., 47 (1957): 897–918, at 877, 905–906.

62. Nicholas Mesarites, *Description of the Church of Holy Apostles*, trans. Downey, "Description of the Church of Holy Apostles," 894.

63. See Roland Betancourt, *Sight, Touch, and Imagination in Byzantium* (Cambridge: Cambridge University Press, 2018).

64. Earlier, in a more cursory manner, Romanus the Melodist seems to have alluded to the same justification (though without as complex an excursus) when he wrote somewhat obliquely: "Such a greeting resounded in my hearing fully, and when it faded it had left me radiant and pregnant." Here, there is no mention of cognition or an articulation of consent, but conception comes about only as an aftereffect of the greeting ringing in Mary's hearing—perhaps deliberately reminding us of her careful debate and argument with the angel in the hymn. See Romanus the Melodist, *Hymns*, 17.1–2, ed. and modified trans. Arentzen, *The Virgin in Song*, 181, 187.

65. Michael Glykas, *Questions in the Holy Scripture* 34, ed. S. Eustratiades, *Eis tas aporias tēs Theias Graphēs* (Athens: P. D. Sakellarios, 1906), 373–375, at 374.

66. At the same time in the West, in the mid-twelfth century, Bernard of Clairvaux underscored the importance of the Virgin's consent in his homily on the Annunciation, given that it places Mary as a coworker in the salvation of humanity. See Bernard of Clairvaux, *In Praise of the Virgin Mother*, 4.7–11, trans. Marie-Bernard Saïd and Grace Perigo, *Magnificat: Homilies in Praise of the Blessed Virgin Mary* (Kalamazoo, MI: Cistercian Publications, 1979), 52–58.

67. Nicholas Cabasilas, *Homily on the Annunciation*, ed. M. Jugie, *Homélies mariales byzantines II*. Patrologia Orientalis 19:3 (Paris: Firmin-Didot et Companie, 1925–1926), 484–495, at 487.

68. Nicholas Cabasilas, *Homily on the Annunciation*, ed. Jugie, *Homélies mariales*, 487, 488.

69. Ibid., 488.

70. *Life of Mary of Egypt*, 21, trans. Maria Kouli, "The Life of St. Mary of Egypt," *Holy Women of Byzantium: Ten Saints' Lives in English Translation*, ed. Alice-Mary Talbot (Washington, DC: Dumbarton Oaks, 1996), 81; ed. PG 87:3712C.

71. Nicholas Cabasilas, *Homily on the Annunciation*, ed. Jugie, *Homélies mariales*, 487–488.

72. On images of rape in Byzantine art, see Mati Meyer, *An Obscure Portrait: Imagining Women's Reality in Byzantine Art* (London: Pindar Press, 2009), 260–281, 293–296.

73. On the word–image relations in the Kokkinobaphos homilies, see Kallirroe Linardou, "Reading Two Byzantine Illustrated Books: The Kokkinobaphos Manuscripts (Vaticanus graecus 1162 and Parisinus graecus 1208) and Their Illustration" (PhD thesis, University of Birmingham, 2004), esp. 123–151; Idem, "The Kokkinobaphos Manuscripts Revisited: The Internal Evidence of the Books," *Scriptorium* 61.2 (2007): 384–407. See also Henry Maguire, *The Icons of Their Bodies: Saints and Their Images in Byzantium* (Princeton: Princeton University Press, 1996), 161–166. I wish to thank Kelly Linardou for sharing her dissertation with me, and Elizabeth Jeffreys for sharing a draft of her translation of James Kokkinobaphos's fifth homily, dedicated to the subject of the Annunciation.

74. James Kokkinobaphos, *Homilies on the Virgin*, 5.9, trans. Maguire, *The Icons of Their Bodies*, 161.

75. James Kokkinobaphos, *Homilies on the Virgin*, 5.17, ed. PG 127:652A.

76. This timing is corroborated by Irmgard Hutter, see Irmgard Hutter and Paul Canart, *Marienhomiliar des Mönchs Jakobos von Kokkinobaphos* (Zurich: Belser Verlag, 1991), 67.

77. James Kokkinobaphos, *Homilies on the Virgin*, 5.19, ed. PG 127:653A.

78. Any direct attribution of this commission to Eirene must be made with caution. Nevertheless, the manuscript was certainly associated in some way with Eirene and her circle, at the very least the product of the same workshops, and it belongs to a broader network of female patronage in twelfth-century Constantinople. See Elizabeth Jeffreys, "The *sebastokratorissa* Irene as Patron," in *Female Founders in Byzantium and Beyond*, ed. Lioba Theis, Magaret Mullett, and Michael Grünbart (Vienna: Böhlau, 2014), 177–194, esp. 185–187.

79. I wish to thank Elizabeth Jeffreys for

sharing this observation with me over the course of her study of the homilies.

80. On the role of Mary in Early Christianity with a recent bibliography, see Stephen J. Shoemaker, *Mary in Early Christian Faith and Devotion* (New Haven: Yale University Press, 2016).

81. Amy Hollywood, "Kill Jesus," in *Mel Gibson's Bible: Religion, Popular Culture, and The Passion of the Christ*, ed. Timothy K. Beal and Tod Linafelt (Chicago: University of Chicago Press, 2006), 159–167, at 167.

82. See Christopher A. Beeley, "'Let This Cup Pass from Me' (*Matth.* 26:39): The Soul of Christ in Origen, Gregory Nazianzen, and Maximus the Confessor," *Studia Patristica* 63 (Leuven: Peeters, 2013), 29–43.

83. Maximus the Confessor, *Opusculum*, 6, modified trans. Paul M. Blowers and Robert Louis Wilken, "On the Two Wills of Christ in the Agony of Gethsemane," *On the Cosmic Mystery of Jesus Christ* (Yonkers, NY: St. Vladimir's Seminary Press, 2003), 173–176, at 174; ed. PG 91:65A–68D, at 68A.

CHAPTER II: SLUT-SHAMING AN EMPRESS

1. See Procopius, *Wars*, ed. and trans. H. B. Dewing, *History of the Wars*, 5 vols., Loeb Classical Library 48, 81, 107, 173, 217 (Cambridge, MA: Harvard University Press, 1914–1928); Procopius, *Buildings*, ed. and trans. H. B. Dewing and Glanville Downey, *On Buildings*, Loeb Classical Library 343 (Cambridge, MA: Harvard University Press, 1940); Procopius, *The Secret History*, trans. Anthony Kaldellis, *The Secret History with Related Texts* (Indianapolis: Hackett Publishing, 2010).

2. On the contemporary phenomenon, see Leora Tanenbaum, *I Am Not a Slut: Slut-Shaming in the Age of the Internet* (New York: Harper Collins, 2015). For an application of this phenomenon to the premodern world, see Lewis Webb, "Shame Transfigured: Slut-Shaming from Rome to Cyberspace," *First Monday* 20:4 (2015), https://doi.org/10.5210/fm.v20i4.5464.

3. On gender in the writings of Procopius, see Leslie Brubaker, "The Age of Justinian: Gender and Society," in *The Cambridge Companion to the Age of Justinian*, ed. Michael Maas (Cambridge: Cambridge University

Press, 2005), 427–447. See also Michael Grünbart, "Typisch Mann, Typisch Frau: Beschreibungen von Kaiserinnen in der byzantinischen Historiographie," *Byzantinoslavica* 74:1 (2016): 44–60. More generally, see Catia Galatariotou, "Holy Women and Witches: Aspects of Byzantine Conceptions of Gender," *Byzantine and Modern Greek Studies* 9 (1984): 55–94. For the most comprehensive survey and bibliography of the depiction of women and sexuality, see Mati Meyer, *An Obscure Portrait: Imagining Women's Reality in Byzantine Art* (London: Pindar Press, 2009).

4. For one of the more comprehensive and nuanced discussions of Theodora's sexual shaming in the *Secret History*, placed within the context of similar attacks against women across history, see Anne McClanan, *Representations of Early Byzantine Empresses: Image and Empire* (New York: Palgrave Macmillan, 2002), esp. 107–120. See also Leslie Brubaker, "Sex, Lies, and Textuality: The *Secret History* of Prokopios and the Rhetoric of Gender in Sixth-century Byzantium," in *Gender in the Early Medieval World: East and West, 300–900*, ed. Leslie Brubaker and Julia Smith (Cambridge: Cambridge University Press, 2004), 83–101; Pauline Allen, "Contemporary Portrayals of the Byzantine Empress Theodora (A.D. 527–548)," in *Stereotypes of Women in Power: Historical Perspectives and Revisionist Views*, ed. Barbara Garlick, Suzanne Dixon, and Pauline Allen (New York: Greenwood Press, 1992), 93–103; Harmut G. Ziche, "Abusing Theodora: Sexual and Political Discourse in Procopius," *Byzantiaka* 30 (2012–2013): 311–323; Michael Angold, "Procopius' Portrait of Theodora," *Philellēn: Studies in Honour of Robert Browning*, ed. C. N. Constantinides et al. (Venice: Istituto Ellenico di Studi Bizantini e Postbizantini di Venezia, 1996), 21–34; Liz James, *Empress and Power in Early Byzantium* (London: Leicester University Press, 2001), esp. 16–20; Lynda Garland, *Byzantine Empresses: Women and Power in Byzantium, AD 527–1204* (London: Routledge, 1999), 11–39.

5. Anthony Kaldellis, *Procopius of Caesarea: Tyranny, History, and Philosophy at the End of Antiquity* (Philadelphia: University of Pennsylvania Press, 2004), esp. 142–159; Averil Cameron, *Procopius and the Sixth Century* (Berkeley: University of California

Press, 1985), 49–83; McClanan, *Representations of Early Byzantine Empresses*, esp. 110–111; Kaldellis, *Secret History*, liv. On fictional accounts in ancient prosopography, see Janet Fairweather, "Fiction in the Biographies of Ancient Authors," *Ancient Society* 5 (1974): 231–275.

6. Hermogenes, *On Types of Style*, 2.3, trans. Cecil W. Wooten, *Hermogenes' On Types of Style* (Chapel Hill: University of North Carolina Press, 1987), 73. See Kaldellis, *Secret History*, liv.

7. Procopius, *Secret History* 9.20–21, trans. Kaldellis, 42.

8. See Ruth Webb, *Demons and Dancers: Performance in Late Antiquity* (Cambridge, MA: Harvard University Press, 2008); Juvenal, *Satires* 6.63, ed. and trans. Susanna Morton Braund, *Juvenal and Persius*, Loeb Classical Library 91 (Cambridge, MA: Harvard University Press, 2004), 238–239. See Barry Baldwin, "Sexual Rhetoric in Procopius," *Mnemosyne* 40:1/2 (1987): 150–152; Fritz Bornmann, "Su alcuni passi di Procopio," *Studi Italiani di filologia classica* 50 (1978): 27–37.

9. Procopius, *Secret History* 9.2–8, trans. Kaldellis, 40–41.

10. Ibid., 41.

11. Ibid., 43.

12. Ibid., 42.

13. Ibid., 68.

14. Ibid., 41–42.

15. Anonymous, *The Prose Salernitan Questions* B.10, ed. Brian Lawn, *The Prose Salernitan Questions* (London: Oxford University Press for the British Academy, 1979), 6.

16. For a comprehensive and nuanced overview, see John M. Riddle, *Contraception and Abortion from the Ancient World to the Renaissance* (Cambridge, MA: Harvard University Press, 1992). See also Keith Hopkins, "Contraception in the Roman Empire," *Comparative Studies in Society and History*, 8.1 (1965): 124–151; Evelyne Patlagean, "Birth Control in the Early Byzantine Empire," *Biology of Man in History*, ed. Robert Forster and Orest Ranum, trans. Elborg Forster and Patricia M. Ranum (Baltimore: Johns Hopkins University Press, 1975), 1–22; Anne L. McClanan, " 'Weapons to Probe the Womb': The Material Culture of Abortion and Contraception in the Early Byzantine Period," in *The Material Culture of Sex, Procreation, and Marriage*

in *Premodern Europe*, ed. Anne L. McClanan and Karen Rosoff Encarnación (New York: Palgrave Macmillan, 2002), 33–57; Marie-Hélène Congourdeau, "Un procès d'avortement à Constantinople au 14e siècle," *Revue des Études Byzantines* 40 (1982) : 103–115; Carolina Cupane and Ewald Kislinger, "Bemerkungen Zur Abtreibung in Byzanz," *Jahrbuch der Österreichischen Byzantinistik* 35 (1985): 21–49; S. N. Trojanos, "*Ē amblōsē sto buzantino dikaio*," *Byzantiaka* 4 (1984): 169–189; Zubin Misty, *Abortion in the Early Middle Ages, c. 500–900* (Rochester, NY: Boydell and Brewer, 2015); Jean Claude Bologne, *La naissance interdite: stérilité, avortement, contraception au Moyen Age* (Paris: O. Orban, 1988); and, to be used with caution: E. Poulakou-Rebelakou, J. Lascaratos, and S. G. Marketos; "Abortions in Byzantine Times (325–1453 A.D.)," *Vesalius* 2 (1996): 19–25.

17. See Wolfgang P. Müller, *The Criminalization of Abortion in the West: Its Origins in Medieval Law* (Ithaca, NY: Cornell University Press, 2012), esp. 20–44.

18. *Digest* 48.8.8, 47.11.4, 48.19.38.5, ed. and trans. Alan Watson, Theodor Mommsen, and Paul Krueger, *The Digest of Justinian*, vol. 4 (Philadelphia: University of Pennsylvania Press, 1985), 784, 820, 853.

19. *Digest* 48.19.39, ed. and trans. Watson, Mommsen, and Krueger, 854.

20. *Council of Ancyra* 21, trans. Henry Percival, "The Canons of the Council of Ancyra," in *Nicene and Post-Nicene Fathers*, Second Series, ed. Philip Schaff and Henry Wace, vol. 14 (Buffalo, NY: Christian Literature Publishing, 1900), 63–75, at 73.

21. Basil, *Letters* 188.2, ed. and trans. Roy J. Deferrari, *Letters*, vol. 3, Loeb Classical Library 243 (Cambridge, MA: Harvard University Press, 1930), 20–23.

22. Basil, *Letters* 188.8, ed. and trans. Deferrari, 34–35.

23. Sharon Gerstel, *Rural Lives and Landscapes in Late Byzantium: Art, Archaeology, and Ethnography* (Cambridge: Cambridge University Press, 2015), 87–90, at 87–88. The inclusion of this image in the realm of the damned may well be connected to the Greek *Apocalypse of Peter*, now preserved in full only in an Ethiopic translation, where a woman is condemned to a pit for an abortion. The pit is filled with pestilence and a certain "flow," which might even allude to

the woman being buried in her own aborted fetus, something to which the wall-painting seems to allude with the pale flux coming from her loins and engulfing her. In the *Apocalypse of Peter*, the woman is to be tortured for eternity by her unborn fetus, who shoots bolts of lightning from their eyes, drilling "the eye of those who by this adultery have brought about their destruction." Patrick Gray argues that this drilling lighting alludes to surgical abortion practices whereby a metal hook was inserted into the womb to remove the fetus through their ear or eye socket. This helps contextualize the odd depiction found in this Cretan wall-painting since the woman is suspended by a similar type of punishment as that which violated her womb. See *Apocalypse of Peter*, 8.1–4, ed. and trans. Dennis D. Buchholz, *Your Eyes Will Be Opened: A Study of the Greek (Ethiopic) Apocalypse of Peter* (Atlanta: Scholars Press, 1988), 316–317. See also Patrick Gray, "Abortion, Infanticide, and the Social Rhetoric of the *Apocalypse of Peter*," *Journal of Early Christian Studies* 9:3 (2001): 313–337, esp. 320. On surgical instruments used for abortions with relevant bibliography, see McClanan, "Weapons to Probe the Womb," 33–57.

24. For this iconography and relevant bibliography, see Meyer, *An Obscure Portrait*, 88–93.

25. Hippocrates of Cos, *The Oath*, ed. and trans. W. H. S. Jones, *Ancient Medicine*, Loeb Classical Library 147 (Cambridge, MA: Harvard University Press, 1923), 298–299.

26. See Riddle, *Contraception and Abortion*, 92.

27. See John Scarborough, "Teaching Surgery in Late Byzantine Alexandria," *Hippocrates and Medical Education*, ed. Manfred Horstmanshoff (Leiden: Brill, 2010), 235–260, esp. 240. See also with relevant bibliography, John Scarborough, "Theodora, Aetius of Amida, and Procopius: Some Possible Connections," *Greek, Roman, and Byzantine Studies* 53 (2013): 742–762, at 754 n. 34.

28. Soranus of Ephesus, *Gynecology* 1.60 (19), trans. Owsei Temkin, *Soranus' Gynecology* (Baltimore: Johns Hopkins University Press, 1956), 62.

29. Ibid., 62–64.

30. Ibid., 63.

31. Procopius, *Secret History* 15.6–9, trans. Kaldellis, 68.

32. Plato, *Republic* 461b–c, ed. and trans. Christopher Emlyn-Jones and William Preddy, *Republic*, vol. 1, Loeb Classical Library 237 (Cambridge, MA: Harvard University Press, 2013), 492–493; Aristotle, *Politics*, 1335b9–30, ed. and trans. H. Rackham, *Politics*, Loeb Classical Library 264 (Cambridge, MA: Harvard University Press, 1932), 622–625.

33. Plato, *Laws*, 740d–e, ed. and trans. R. G. Bury, *Laws*, vol. 1, Loeb Classical Library 187 (Cambridge, MA: Harvard University Press, 1926), 366–367. On infanticide in the Middle Ages, see Emily Coleman, "Infanticide in the Early Middle Ages," in *Women in Medieval Society*, ed. Susan Mosher Stuard (Philadelphia: University of Pennsylvania Press, 1976), 47–70.

34. Aetius of Amida, *Tetrabiblos*, 16.17 (18), modified trans. James V. Ricci, *Aetios of Amida: The Gynaecology and Obstetrics of the VIth Century, A.D.* (Philadelphia: Blakiston Company, 1950), 25; ed. Janus Cornarius, *Aetii Medici Graeci Contractae ex veteribus medicinae tetrabiblos* (Basel: Froben & Episcopius, 1542), 867–868; cf. ed. Skévos Zervos, *Gynaekologie des Aëtios* (Leipzig: Fock, 1901), 18–19. On the editions of the text, see Scarborough, "Theodora," 744 n. 6 and 7.

35. In Plato's *Theaetetus*, commenting on midwives' abilities with incantations and drugs (*pharmakia*) to induce or slow the pangs of labor "if they wish" (*boulontai*), Socrates states that these women are also able to "cause miscarriages if they think them desirable. Here, there is a clear sense of choice in the hands of a woman without the consultation of a physician, yet no specific regard is made for the choice of the patient herself." Plato, *Theaetetus*, 149d, ed. and trans. Harold North Fowler, *Theaetetus*, Loeb Classical Library 123 (Cambridge, MA: Harvard University Press, 1921), 32–33.

36. See Riddle, *Contraception and Abortion*, esp. 87–107.

37. See John M. Riddle, *Dioscorides on Pharmacy and Medicine* (Austin: University of Texas Press, 1985), 58–64.

38. For scattered references to male contraceptive drugs, see Riddle, *Contraception and Abortion*, 55, 84, 89, 97, 152.

39. See Riddle, *Contraception and Abortion*, 92–100.

40. Scarborough, "Theodora," 742–762.

41. Aetius of Amida, *Tetrabiblos*, 16.122, trans. Ricci, 119.

42. Holt N. Parker, "Women Doctors in Greece, Rome, and the Byzantine Empire" in *Women Healers and Physicians: Climbing a Long Hill*, ed. Lilian R. Furst (Lexington: University Press of Kentucky, 1997), 131–150. On the shift of gynecology from women to men in the later Middle Ages, see Monica H. Green, *Making Women's Medicine Masculine: The Rise of Male Authority in Pre-Modern Gynaecology* (Oxford: Oxford University Press, 2008).

43. Aetius of Amida, *Tetrabiblos* 16.14, 16.22, trans. Ricci, 23, 30–32.

44. See Roger Collins, *Visigothic Spain: 409–711* (Oxford: Blackwell Publishing, 2004), 213.

45. Paul the Deacon, *The Lives of the Fathers of Mérida*, 1.1–2.13, trans. A. T. Fear, *Lives of the Visigothic Fathers* (Liverpool: Liverpool University Press, 1997), 58–60, ed. A. Maya Sánchez, *Vitas Sanctorum Patrum Emeretensium*, Corpus Christianorum Series Latina 116 (Turnholt: Brepols, 1992), 25–30.

46. Gregory Tsoucalas et al., "Bishop Paul of Merida, and the First Known Caesarean Section on a Living Woman," *Journal of Obstetrics and Gynaecology* 35:2 (2015): 203.

47. Paul the Deacon, *The Lives of the Fathers of Mérida* 1.1, trans. Fear, 58; ed. Sánchez, 25. See Gregory of Tours, *History of the Franks* 10.15, trans. Ernest Brehaut, *History of the Franks* (New York: Columbia University Press, 1916), 238–239.

48. Paul the Deacon, *The Lives of the Fathers of Mérida* 2.11, trans. Fear, 60; Sánchez, 29.

49. Paul of Aegina, *Medical Compendium* 6.74, trans. Francis Adam, *The Seven Books of Paulus Ægineta*, vol. 2 (London: Sydenham Society, 1846), 387–392.

50. Aetius of Amida, *Tetrabiblos* 16.23, trans. Ricci, 32–34.

51. Gregory of Tours, *History of the Franks*, 10.15, trans. Ernest Brehaut, *History of the Franks* (New York: Columbia University Press, 1916), 238–239.

52. Niketas David Paphlagon, *The Life of Patriarch Ignatius* 86, ed. and modified trans. Andrew Smithies, *The Life of Patriarch Ignatius* (Washington, DC: Dumbarton Oaks, 2013), 114–115.

53. On the relationship between the depictions of Theodora and those of Antonina, see Elizabeth A. Fisher, "Theodora and Antonina in the *Historia Arcana*: History and/or Fiction?" *Arethusa* 11.1 (1978): 253–279.

54. Procopius, *Secret History* 1.11, trans. Kaldellis, 5; 1.12, modified trans. Kaldellis, 5; 22.27, trans. Kaldellis, 100; *Procopii Caesariensis opera omnia*, ed. G. Wirth, vol. 3 (Leipzig: Teubner, 1963), 138.

55. See Manfred Horstmanshoff, "Ancient Medicine between Hope and Fear: Medicament, Magic and Poison in the Roman Empire," *European Review* 7:1 (1999): 37–51. See also Michael A. Flower, "Religious Expertise," in *The Oxford Handbook of Ancient Greek Religion*, eds. Esther Eidinow and Julia Kindt (Oxford: Oxford University Press, 2015), 299–307, esp. 300.

56. See Gillian Clark, *Women in Late Antiquity: Pagan and Christian Lifestyles* (Oxford: Clarendon Press, 1993), 63–93. See also Henry Magoulias, "The Lives of Saints as Source Data for the History of Byzantine Medicine in the Sixth and Seventh Centuries," *Byzantinische Zeitschrift* 57 (1964): 127–150; Michael J. Harstad, "Saints, Drugs, and Surgery: Byzantine Therapeutics for Breast Diseases," *Pharmacy in History* 28:4 (1986): 175–180.

57. See Riddle, *Dioscorides*, esp. 1–24. See also Jerry Stannard, "Aspects of Byzantine Materia Medica," *Dumbarton Oaks Papers* 38 (1984): 205–211; John M. Riddle, "Byzantine Commentaries on Dioscorides," *Dumbarton Oaks Papers* 38 (1984): 95–102.

58. See Carmelo Capizzi, "Anicia Giuliana (462 ca.–530 ca.): Ricerche sulla sua famiglia e la sua vita," *Rivista di studi bizantini e neo-ellenici* 5 (1968): 191–226; John Martindale, ed., *The Prosopography of the Later Roman Empire*, vol. 2 (Cambridge: Cambridge University Press, 1980), 635–636; Carolyn L. Connor, *Women of Byzantium* (New Haven: Yale University Press, 2004), 94–116. See also Alan Cameron, "The House of Anastasius," *Greek, Roman, and Byzantine Studies* 19 (1978): 259–276, esp. 273–275.

59. Leslie Brubaker, "The Vienna Dioscurides and Anicia Juliana," *Byzantine Garden Culture*, ed. Antony Littlewood, Henry Maguire, and Joachim Wolschke-Bulmahn (Washington, DC: Dumbarton Oaks, 2002), 189–214, at 214.

60. See John Scarborough, "Drugs and

Drug Lore in the Time of Theophrastus: Folklore, Magic, Botany, Philosophy, and the Rootcutters," *Acta Classica* 49 (2006): 1–29, esp. 15–20.

61. See Gary Vikan, "Art, Medicine, and Magic in Early Byzantium," *Dumbarton Oaks Papers* 38 (1984): 65–86. See also John Scarborough, "Early Byzantine Pharmacology," *Dumbarton Oaks Papers* 38 (1984): 213–232.

62. Procopius, *Secret History* 4.37 and 5.18–23, trans. Kaldellis, 21 and 25.

63. Vivian Nutton, "Healers in the Medical Market Place: Towards a Social History of Greco-Roman Medicine," in *Medicine in Society: Historical Essays*, ed. A. Wear (Cambridge: Cambridge University Press, 1992), 15–58.

64. John Malalas, *Chronicles* 10.49, ed. and trans. Elizabeth Jeffreys, Michael Jeffreys, and Roger Scott, *The Chronicle of John Malalas* (Melbourne: Australian Association for Byzantine Studies, 1986), 139. John Lydus, *On Powers*, 1.20, ed. and trans. Anastasius Bandy, *On Powers: Or, the Magistracies of the Roman State* (Philadelphia: American Philosophical Society, 1983), 32–35.

65. Juvenal, *Satires* 6.592–601, ed. and modified trans. Braund, *Juvenal*, 288–289.

66. Procopius, *Secret History* 17.16–17, trans. Kaldellis, 77.

67. Aetius, *Tetrabiblos* 16.18, trans. Ricci, 27. Notable among these dangerous late procedures is embryotomy, to which Aetius devotes a lengthy chapter, attributed to Philumenos; see *Tetrabiblos* 16.23, trans. Ricci, 32–34.

68. Procopius, *Secret History*, 17.17–23, quotation, 21; trans. Kaldellis, 77–78, quotation 78.

69. Ibid., 78.

70. Ibid.

71. John Chrysostom, *Homily on Romans* 24, modified trans. J. B. Morris and W. H. Simcox, "Homily XXIV: Rom. XIII.II," in *Nicene and Post-Nicene Fathers*, First Series, ed. Philip Schaff, vol. 11 (Buffalo, NY: Christian Literature Publishing, 1889), 517–521, at 520; ed. PG 60:626–627.

72. Here, Chrysostom draws a disturbing causal chain from drunkenness to fornication (*porneia*), adultery (*moicheia*), and eventually murder (*phonos*); it is problematic for the modern reader because it is uncertain whether he is describing prostitution or some form of coupling at a tavern, where prostitution often occurred, or instead some form of drunken rape. The woman has little room for consent, since the rest of Chrysostom's statement makes clear that she is understood to be a sex worker. See Misty, *Abortion in the Early Middle Ages*, 52–53.

73. Chrysostom goes on to declare that the man's acts are crimes committed against the womb not only of the sex worker but also of his deceived wife: "for poisons [*pharmakeia*] are applied not upon the womb of the sex worker, but to the wife that has been done wrong." In causing the sex worker to become a murderer, the man also harms the wife on whom he has cheated. See John Chrysostom, *Homily on Romans* 24, modified trans. Morris and Simcox, 520; ed. PG 60:627.

74. Nemesius of Emesa, *On the Nature of Man* 25, trans. R. W. Sharples and P. J. van der Eijk, *On the Nature of Man* (Liverpool: Liverpool University Press, 2008), 157; ed. M. Morani, *De natura hominis* (Leipzig: Teubner, 1987), 87.

75. McClanan, *Representations of Early Byzantine Empresses*, 111.

76. Procopius, *Secret History* 9.17, trans. Kaldellis, 42; ed. Wirth, 59.

77. Procopius, *Secret History* 9.22, trans. Kaldellis, 43; ed. Wirth, 60.

78. Procopius, *Secret History* 9.14, trans. Kaldellis, 41; ed. Wirth, 58.

79. Procopius, *Secret History* 1.13, trans. Kaldellis, 5; ed. Wirth, 7.

80. See A. Daniel Frankforter, "Amalasuntha, Procopius, and a Woman's Place," *Journal of Women's History* 8:2 (1996): 41–57.

81. On *aidōs* in antiquity, see Douglas L. Cairns, *Aidōs: The Psychology and Ethics of Honour and Shame in Ancient Greek Literature* (Oxford: Clarendon Press, 1993).

82. See Elizabeth A. Clark, "Sex, Shame, and Rhetoric: En-gendering Early Christian Ethics," *Journal of the American Academy of Religion* 59 (1991): 221–245. See also Peter Brown, *The Body and Society: Men, Women, and Sexual Renunciation in Early Christianity* (New York: Columbia University Press, 1988); Virginia Burrus, *The Sex Lives of Saints: An Erotics of Ancient Hagiography* (Philadelphia: University of Pennsylvania Press, 2004), esp. 128–159.

83. Lucian, *Philosophies for Sale* 10, ed. and trans. A. M. Harmon, *Lucian*, vol. 2, Loeb

Classical Library 54 (Cambridge, MA: Harvard University Press, 1915), 468–469.

84. See Derek Krueger, "The Bawdy and Society: The Shamelessness of Diogenes in Roman Imperial Culture," in *The Cynics: The Cynic Movement in Antiquity and its Legacy*, eds. R. Bracht Branham and M.-O. Goulet Cazé (Berkeley: University of California Press, 1996), 222–239.

85. Ibid., esp. 227, 238.

86. See Derek Krueger, *Symeon the Holy Fool: Leontius' Life and the Late Antique City* (Berkeley: University of California Press, 1996), esp. 90–107.

87. Karmen MacKendrick, *Counterpleasures* (Albany: State University of New York Press, 1999); Virginia Burrus, *Saving Shame: Martyrs, Saints, and Other Abject Subjects* (Philadelphia: University of Pennsylvania Press, 2008); Niklaus Largier, *In Praise of the Whip: A Cultural History of Arousal* (Brooklyn, NY: Zone Books, 2007).

88. Burrus, *Saving Shame*, 8, 82.

89. To be able to construct an identity around shame requires the privilege of and entitlement to a stable identity, which can then be masochistically unfurled, creating passion plays staged for the tantalizing pleasure of those who are relatively marginalized but who still have a firm grasp on the social well-being afforded by privilege. To feel that one's entitlement to privilege has been denied is not the shame faced by queer people of color. To fetishize shame denies the reality of non-white, non-male, non-heteronormative, non-cisgendered, non-body-normative subjects for whom shame, shaming, and claims of shamelessness commonly end in injury and death. In the proceedings for a 2003 queer studies conference on the topic of "gay shame," which sought to consider what happens when the legitimization, dignity, acceptance, and assimilation of queer identity led to the "elimination of both the personal and the social shame attached to same-sex eroticism," David Halperin and Valeria Traub noted that the untenable ethical implications of the embrace of shame came to a head when it became clear that the emphasis on shame was structured on a gay white male subjectivity that overlooks the subjectivities of those who are shamed. The critiques of the event's whitewashing, as the one made by Hiram Pérez, were attacked as being prudish

oppositions to pornography and pleasure. The glorification of shame, as Jack Halberstam cautions, embraces the "awkward, undignified, and graceless childhoods" of marginalized subjects and ensures that they remain a part of our political future. Or, as another critic of the symposium wrote, this perspective results in "an invisible normative whiteness and assertiveness of empire which blanket everything except the shamed (brown? powder-white?) body." The fact that shame is not experienced the same way by people of different classes, races, ethnicities, and backgrounds creates a situation where white gay male shame not only served as a monolithic outlook, but similarly relished in the shaming of black and brown bodies without acknowledging the violence and privilege of such a position. As Halberstam notes, the gay white male subject encounters shame "from the experience of being denied access to privilege," a privilege which they as white males feel entitled to wield and possess. See David Halperin and Valerie Traub, eds., *Gay Shame* (Chicago: University of Chicago Press, 2009), 3 and 26. On the critiques, see J. Jack Halbertsam, "Shame and White Gay Masculinity," *Social Text* 23:3–4 (2005): 219–233; Hiram Pérez, *A Taste for Brown Bodies: Gay Modernity and Cosmopolitan Desire* (New York: New York University Press, 2015), 97–124.

90. Procopius, *Secret History* 9.12, trans. Kaldellis, 41.

91. See Harry J. Magoulias, "Bathhouse, Inn, Tavern, Prostitution, and the Stage as Seen in the Lives of the Saints in the Sixth and Seventh Centuries," *Epetēris Etaireias Byzantinōn Spoudōn* 38 (1971): 233–252, esp. 246–247.

92. *Theodosian Code* 15.7.12, trans. Clyde Pharr (Princeton: Princeton University Press, 1952), 435.

93. Procopius, *Secret History* 9.12, trans. Kaldellis, 41.

94. On dissidents under Justinian, see Anthony Kaldellis, "Identifying Dissident Circles in Sixth-Century Byzantium: The Friendship of Prokopios and Ioannes Lydos," *Florilegium* 21 (2004): 1–17.

95. Emphasis in Kaldellis. Procopius, *Secret History* 11.34–36, modified trans. Kaldellis, 55; ed. Wirth, 76.

96. On Justinian's ideological propaganda

and persecution, see Roger D. Scott, "Malalas, *The Secret History*, and Justinian's Propaganda," *Dumbarton Oaks Papers* 39 (1985): 99–109.

97. John Lydus, *On Powers*, 2.62, ed. and trans. Bandy, 230–231.

98. On same-gender desire under Justinian's rule, see Steven D. Smith, "Agathias and Paul the Silentiary: Erotic Epigram and the Sublimation of Same-Sex Desire in the Age of Justinian," in *Sex in Antiquity: Exploring Gender and Sexuality in the Ancient World*, ed. Mark Masterson, Nancy Sorkin Rabinowitz, and James Robson (London: Routledge, 2014), 500–516. See also Steven D. Smith, *Greek Epigram and Byzantine Culture: Gender, Desire, and Denial in the Age of Justinian* (Cambridge: Cambridge University Press, 2019); I thank the author for allowing me to consult the manuscript ahead of publication.

99. Procopius, *Secret History* 16.18–22, modified trans. Kaldellis, 74–75.

100. See Angold, "Procopius' Portrait of Theodora," 24.

101. Procopius, *Secret History*, 16.23–28, trans. Kaldellis, 75.

102. Procopius, *Secret History*, 20.9, trans. Kaldellis, 90–91.

103. Kaldellis, *Secret History*, lii; Stavroula Constantinou, "Violence in the Palace: Rituals of Imperial Punishment in Prokopios's *Secret History*," *Court Ceremonies and Rituals of Power in Byzantium and the Medieval Mediterranean*, eds. Alexander Beihammer, Stavroula Constantinou, and Maria Parani (Leiden: Brill, 2013), 376–387.

104. See Kaldellis, *Secret History*, xlix.

105. Cameron, *Procopius*, 68. For women patrons and founders with a recent bibliography, see Diliana Angelova, *Sacred Founders: Women, Men, and Gods in the Discourse of Imperial Founding, Rome through Early Byzantium* (Berkeley: University of California Press, 2015); Lioba Theis, Margaret Mullett, and Michael Grünbart, eds., *Female Founders in Byzantium and Beyond* (Vienna: Böhlau, 2014).

106. Charles Diehl, *Théodora: impératrice de Byzance*, 4th ed. (Paris: H. Piazza et Cie, 1904), 217–230.

107. On the afterlife of Theodora, particularly in the nineteenth century, see Elena Boeck, "Archaeology of Decadence: Uncovering Byzantium in Victorien Sardou's *Theodora*," in *Byzantium/Modernism: The Byzantine as Method in Modernity*, ed. Roland Betancourt and Maria Taroutina (Leiden: Brill, 2015), 102–132.

108. McClanan, *Representations of Early Byzantine Empresses*, 108.

109. Cameron, *Procopius*, 68.

CHAPTER III: TRANSGENDER LIVES

1. See Patricia Cox Miller, "Is There a Harlot in This Text? Hagiography and the Grotesque," *Journal of Medieval and Early Modern Studies* 33:3 (2003): 419–435; Stephen J. Davis, "Crossed Texts, Crossed Sex: Intertextuality and Gender in Early Christian Legends of Holy Women Disguised as Men," *Journal of Early Christian Studies* 10:1 (2002): 1–36; Evelyne Patlagean, "L'histoire de la femme déguisée en moine et l'évolution de la sainteté féminine a Byzance," *Studi Medievali*, series 3, 17 (1976): 597–623; John Anson, "The Female Transvestite in Early Monasticism: The Origin and Development of a Motif," *Viator* 5 (1974): 1–32; Kari Vogt, "'The Woman Monk': A Theme in Byzantine Hagiography," in *Greece and Gender*, ed. Brit Berggreen and Nanno Marinatos (Bergen: Norwegian Institute at Athens, 1995), 141–148; Crystal Lynn Lubinsky, *Removing Masculine Layers to Reveal a Holy Womanhood: The Female Transvestite Monks of Late Antique Eastern Christianity* (Turnhout: Brepols, 2013); Valerie R. Hotchkiss, *Clothes Make the Man: Female Cross Dressing in Medieval Europe* (New York: Garland Publishing, 1996); Stavroula Constantinou, "Holy Actors and Actresses: Fools and Cross-Dressers as the Protagonists of Saints' Lives," in *The Ashgate Research Companion to Byzantine Hagiography*, ed. Stephanos Efthymiadis, vol. 2 (Burlington, VT: Ashgate, 2014), 343–362; Vern L. Bullough, "Transvestites in the Middle Ages," *American Journal of Sociology* 79:6 (1974): 1381–1394; cf. Vern L. Bullough, "Transvestivism in the Middle Ages," in *Sexual Practices and the Medieval Church*, ed. Vern L. Bullough and James Brundage (Buffalo, NY: Prometheus Books, 1982), 43–54.

2. On transmission see, Patlagean, "L'histoire de la femme déguisée," 597–623. For more about the individual transmission and

translations of particular lives, see their respective editions and translations.

3. Hotchkiss, *Clothes Make the Man*, 131–142.

4. For an up-to-date glossary of appropriate terms and their definitions, see "GLAAD Media Reference Guide—Transgender," *GLAAD*, www.glaad.org /reference/transgender.

5. In her 2013 study on these "female transvestite monks," Crystal Lynn Lubinsky acknowledges that such stories "cannot be termed 'cross-dressing' because it oversimplifies the actions of these holy women," whom she simply genders as women. But Lubinsky also chooses to use the problematic term "transvestite," following Valerie Hotchkiss. Though Lubinsky claims that the expanded and metaphorical sense in which she employs the term avoids its "sexual or sensual connotations," she cites the very literature from the early twentieth century that shaped its pejorative, pathological definition. At the same time, she emphatically argues against the use of "transgender" or "transsexual" (without any attempt to distinguish between the two terms): "Also, the terms 'transgender' and 'transsexual' are not applicable because in these legends transvestism is a female enterprise that women utilize to safeguard their chastity and spiritual aspirations. These characters should not be considered humans who were male, but female bodied. Hagiographers do not describe these women as changing sex or as realizing their spiritual strengths within an opposite gender beyond the superficiality of a masculine disguise." A methodological tension immediately emerges, as Lubinsky simultaneously rejects the oversimplification implied by "cross-dressing" and advocates for the "superficiality of a masculine disguise." Ironically, Lubinsky's own book provides an eloquent argument precisely for a "transgender" identity—it demonstrates how masculine gender expression and identity were outwardly and inwardly manifested through the practices recounted in the narratives of these figures' lives. See Lubinsky, *Removing Masculine Layers*, 2, 109–217.

6. On the medicalization of being transgender and its problems, see Dean Spade, "Resisting Medicine, Re/modeling Gender," *Berkeley Journal of Gender, Law and Justice* 18:1 (2013): 15–37.

7. See David Valentine, *Imagining Transgender: An Ethnography of a Category* (Durham: Duke University Press, 2007), 1–65. See also Anne Bolin, "Transcending and Transgendering: Male-to-Female Transsexuals, Dichotomy, and Diversity," in *Third Sex, Third Gender: Beyond Sexual Dimorphism in Culture and History*, ed. Gilbert Herdt (New York: Zone Books, 1994), 447–485.

8. Valentine, *Imagining Transgender*, esp. 1–28.

9. Ibid., 26.

10. *Life of Marinos* 5, trans. Nicholas Constas, "Life of St. Mary/Marinos," in *Holy Women of Byzantium: Ten Saints' Lives in English Translation*, ed. Alice-Mary Talbot (Washington, DC: Dumbarton Oaks, 1996), 1–12.

11. *Life of Marinos* 9, 12, 14, trans. Constas, "Life of St. Mary/Marinos," 9, 10.

12. *Life of Matrona of Perge*, trans. Jeffrey Featherstone and Cyril Mango, "Life of St. Matrona of Perge," in *Holy Women of Byzantium*, ed. Talbot, 13–64. See Sarah Insley, "Dressing Up the Past: Fictional Narrative in the *Life of Matrona of Perge*," in *Medieval Greek Storytelling: Fictionality and Narrative in Byzantium*, ed. Panagiotis Roilos (Wiesbaden: Harrassowitz Verlag, 2014), 55–85.

13. *Life of Matrona of Perge*, 7, trans. Featherstone and Mango, "Life of St. Matrona of Perge," 26.

14. *Life of Dorotheos*, ed. James Drescher, *Three Coptic Legends* (Cairo: Institut Français d'Archéologie Orientale, 1947), 152–161.

15. *Life of Eugenia* 39a, trans. Agnes Smith Lewis, *Select Narratives of Holy Women: From the Syro-Antiochene or Sinai Palimpsest* (London: C. J. Clay, 1900), 20. On this story, see Robert Mills, "Visibly Trans?: Picturing Saint Eugenia in Medieval Art," *Transgender Studies Quarterly* 5:4 (2018): 540–564.

16. *Life of Matrona of Perge* 7, trans. Featherstone and Mango, "Life of St. Matrona of Perge," 26.

17. *Life of Eugenia* 33b, trans. Lewis, *Select Narratives*, 14.

18. This includes the cult around Aphrodite on Cyprus that entailed the cross-dressing of celebrants, and the Roman male-born eunuch priests known as the Galli who were referred to at times with she/her pronouns after their castration. See Hermann Usener, "Legenden der Pelagia," in *Vorträge*

und Aufsätze (Leipzig: Teubner, 1907), 190–215; see also Lynn E. Roller, "The Ideology of the Eunuch Priest," *Gender & History* 9:3 (1997): 542–559. *The Acts of Paul and Thecla* 25, 40, trans. J. K. Elliott, *The Apocryphal New Testament* (Oxford: Clarendon Press, 1993), 369, 371. On Thecla, see Davis, "Crossed Texts," esp. 15–21; Kim Haines-Eitzen, *The Gendered Palimpsest: Women, Writing, and Representation in Early Christianity* (Oxford: Oxford University Press, 2011), esp. 95–112, 124–127.

19. Cyril of Scythopolis, *Life of John the Hesychast* 219.20, trans. R. M. Price and John Binns, *Lives of the Monks of Palestine* (Kalamazoo, MI: Cistercian Publications, 1991), 238. *Martyrdom of Saints Perpetua and Felicitas*, 10, ed. and trans. Herbert Musurillo, *The Acts of the Christian Martyrs* (Oxford: Clarendon Press, 1972), 118–119.

20. See L. Stephanie Cobb, *Dying to Be Men: Gender and Language in Early Christian Martyr Texts* (New York: Columbia University Press, 2008), esp. 92–123. See also Elizabeth Castelli, "'I Will Make Mary Male': Pieties of the Body and Gender Transformation of Christian Women in Late Antiquity," in *Body Guards: The Cultural Politics of Gender Ambiguity*, ed. Julia Epstein and Kristina Straub (New York: Routledge, 1991), 29–49.

21. *Gospel of Thomas*, 114, trans. Elliott, *The Apocryphal New Testament*, 147.

22. See David Brakke, *Demons and the Making of the Monk: Spiritual Combat in Early Christianity* (Cambridge: Harvard University Press, 2006), esp. 182–212.

23. Sarah, *The Sayings of the Desert Fathers: The Alphabetical Collection* 4, 9, trans. Benedicta Ward (Kalamazoo, MI: Cistercian Publications, 1975), 230.

24. See Richard A. Baer, Jr., *Philo's Use of the Categories Male and Female* (Leiden: Brill, 1970), esp. 45–64.

25. Philo of Alexandria, *Questions and Answers on Exodus* I.8, trans. Ralph Marcus, *Questions on Exodus*, Loeb Classical Library 401 (Cambridge, MA: Harvard University Press, 1953), 15–16.

26. Philo of Alexandria, *On Abraham*, 149–151, ed. and modified trans. F. H. Colson, *Philo*, vol. 6 (Cambridge, MA: Harvard University Press, 1935), 76–77.

27. See Wayne A. Meeks, "The Image of the Androgyne: Some Uses of a Symbol in Earliest Christianity," *History of Religions* 13:3 (1974): 165–208.

28. Castelli, "I Will Make Mary Male," 32–33. See also Ra'anan Abusch, "Eunuchs and Gender Transformation: Philo's Exegesis of the Joseph Narrative," in *Eunuchs in Antiquity and Beyond*, ed. Shaun Tougher (London: Duckworth, 2002), 103–121.

29. This notion of the "male woman" differs strikingly from the toxic masculinity of today's idea that "boys will be boys," with its assumption that men are moved by their hot tempers and sexual desires through no fault of their own; women, in contrast, display tempered wiles and virginal asexuality. These stereotypes have their foundation in this early Christian literature that attempted to construct these characteristics as precisely the ideal for women to follow— characteristics that were then constituted as masculine, whereas today they are denigrated as feminine. However, male, masculinist privilege has selectively retained for itself the position of an objective, dispassionate arbiter in contrast to feminine hysteria and emotionality, both vestiges of these gender stereotypes. On the male woman, see Kerstin Aspegren, *The Male Woman: A Feminine Ideal in the Early Church*, ed. René Kieffer, Acta Universitatis Upsaliensis. Uppsala Women's Studies, A. Women in Religion 4 (Uppsala: Academia Ubsaliensis, 1990).

30. Susan Ashbrook Harvey, *Asceticism and Society in Crisis: John of Ephesus and the Lives of the Eastern Saints* (Berkeley: University of California Press, 1990), 116.

31. Caroline Walker Bynum, *Holy Feast and Holy Fast: The Religious Significance of Food to Medieval Women* (Berkeley: University of California Press, 1987), 291.

32. J. Jack Halberstam, *Female Masculinity* (Durham: Duke University Press, 1998), 6.

33. Bynum, *Holy Feast and Holy Fast*, 291.

34. *Council in Trullo*, 62, ed. and trans. George Nedungatt and Michael Featherstone, *The Council in Trullo Revisited* (Rome: Pontificio Istituto Orientale, 1995), 143.

35. *Council of Gangra*, 13 and 17, trans. Henry Percival, "The Council of Gangra," *Nicene and Post-Nicene Fathers*, Second Series, vol. 14, ed. Philip Schaff and Henry Wace (Buffalo, NY: Christian Literature Publishing, 1900), 89–101, at 97 and 99.

36. *Council of Gangra*, 17, modified trans. Percival, "The Council of Gangra," 97.

37. *Theodosian Code*, 16.2.27, trans. Clyde Pharr (Princeton: Princeton University Press, 1952), 445.

38. Basil of Ancyra, *On the True Purity of Virginity* 51, ed. PG 30:772B–C. See Teresa M. Shaw, *The Burden of the Flesh: Fasting and Sexuality in Early Christianity* (Minneapolis: Fortress Press, 1998), esp. 81–92, 235–238.

39. See Basil of Ancyra, *On the True Purity of Virginity* 18, 58, ed. PG 30:708D, 785B–788A; quotation, *On the True Purity of Virginity* 18, modified trans. Shaw, *The Burden of the Flesh*, 236.

40. *Life of Pelagius* 4, trans. Sebastian P. Brock and Susan Ashbrook Harvey, *Holy Women of the Syrian Orient* (Berkeley: University of California Press, 1987), 42.

41. *Life of Pelagius*, 5–6, trans. Brock and Harvey, *Holy Women*, 43.

42. *Life of Pelagius*, 6, trans. Brock and Harvey, *Holy Women*, 43.

43. See Charles H. Cosgrove, "A Woman's Unbound Hair in the Greco-Roman World, with Special Reference to the Story of the 'Sinful Woman' in Luke 7:36–50," *Journal of Biblical Literature* 124.4 (2005): 675–692. In Middle Assyrian law, unmarried sacred sex workers and common sex workers were commanded to leave their heads uncovered in the streets: "A sacred prostitute whom a man married must veil herself on the street, but one whom a man did not marry must have her head uncovered on the street; she must not veil herself. A harlot must not veil herself; her head must be uncovered; he who has seen a harlot veiled must arrest her, produce witnesses, (and) bring her to the palace tribunal." See *Middle Assyrian Laws*, Tablet A.40, trans. Theophile J. Meek, "The Middle Assyrian Laws," in *Ancient Near Eastern Texts: Relating to the Old Testament*, ed. James B. Pritchard, 3rd ed. (Princeton: Princeton University Press, 1969), 180–188, at 183. I wish to thank Gabriel Radle for this source and for allowing me to consult his work on hair-binding and veiling in Byzantium.

44. Throughout this text, I do not use the term "transition" casually. And I do not wish to unwittingly suggest that to be transgender requires a formal transition from one gender to another, since that requirement denies a place within the transgender spectrum to various kinds of gender-variant people, including those who do not wish to pursue hormone replacement therapy, gender confirmation surgery, or necessarily dress as or desire to present or "pass" as the opposite sex.

45. On fasting, asceticism, and gender, see Shaw, *The Burden of the Flesh*, esp. 235–253. See also Bynum, *Holy Feast and Holy Fast*, 287–291.

46. *Life of Anastasius*, 6, 7, trans. Brock and Harvey, *Holy Women*, 147.

47. For a useful comparison, see Tim Vivian, ed., *Witness to Holiness: Abba Daniel of Scetis: Translations of the Greek, Coptic, Ethiopic, Syriac, Armenian, Latin, Old Church Slavonic, and Arabic Accounts* (Kalamazoo, MI: Cistercian Publications, 2008), cf. 76, 132, 164, 193, 233, and 253.

48. See Vivian, *Witness to Holiness*, 132.

49. *Life of Anastasius*, 8, trans. Brock and Harvey, *Holy Women*, 147.

50. Ibid.

51. Ibid., 148.

52. Ibid.

53. *Life of Pelagius* 6, trans. Brock and Harvey, *Holy Women*, 43.

54. *Life of Dorotheos*, trans. Lubinsky, *Removing Masculine Layers*, 121.

55. Aetius of Amida, *Tetrabiblos* 16.51, modified trans. James V. Ricci, *Aetios of Amida: The Gynaecology and Obstetrics of the VIth Century, A.D.* (Philadelphia: Blakiston Company, 1950), 55.

56. Dio Cassius, *Roman History* 80.11–17, ed. and trans. Earnest Cary and Herbert B. Foster, *Roman History*, vol. 9, Loeb Classical Library 177 (Cambridge, MA: Harvard University Press, 1927), 460–471.

57. Dio Cassius, *Roman History*, 80.13–15, ed. and trans. Cary and Foster, *Roman History*, 462–467.

58. See Martijn Icks, *The Crimes of Elagabalus: The Life and Legacy of Rome's Decadent Boy Emperor* (Cambridge, MA: Harvard University Press, 2012), esp. 92–122.

59. See Leonardo de Arrizabalaga y Prado, *The Emperor Elagabalus: Fact or Fiction?* (Cambridge: Cambridge University Press, 2010).

60. See Fergus Millar, *A Study of Cassius Dio* (Oxford: Clarendon Press, 1964), esp. 1–4, 168–170, 195–203. See also Christopher Mallan, "The Style, Method, and Programme of Xiphilinus' *Epitome* of Cassius Dio's *Roman*

History," *Greek, Roman, and Byzantine Studies* 53 (2013): 610–644; Thomas M. Banchich and Eugene N. Lane, *The* History *of Zonaras: From Alexander Severus to the Death of Theodosius the Great* (London: Routledge, 2009), esp. 73–75; Iordanis Grigoriadis, *Linguistic and Literary Studies in the* Epitome Historion *of John Zonaras* (Thessalonike: Byzantine Research Center, 1998). John Xiphilinus's epitome, commissioned at the behest of Emperor Michael VII Doukas (1071–1078), specifically covered the chapters dealing with Elagabalus's reign and is preserved in a critical exemplar on Mount Athos. The Xiphilinus text is of particular importance because it attests to the enduring importance and popularity of Dio Cassius's work for Byzantine understandings of late antique Roman history. See B. C. Barmann, "The Mount Athos Epitome of Cassius Dio's Roman History," *Phoenix* 25:1 (1971): 58–67.

61. John of Antioch, *Fragments* 138, ed. K. Müller, *Fragmenta historicorum Graecorum*, vol. 4 (Paris: Didot, 1851), 592. George Synkellos, *Chronography* 437:12–14, modified trans. William Alder and Paul Tuffin, *The Chronography of George Synkellos: A Byzantine Chronicle of Universal History from the Creation* (Oxford: Oxford University Press, 2002), 515; ed. A. A. Mosshammer, *Georgius Syncellus. Ecloga chronographica* (Leipzig: Teubner, 1984), 437.

62. See Dio Cassius, *Roman History* 80.16, ed. and trans. Cary and Foster, *Roman History*, 470–471.

63. See Michael Glykas, *Chronicle*, 453:6–8, ed. I. Bekker, *Michaelis Glycae annals*, Corpus scriptorum historiae Byzantinae (Bonn: Weber, 1836), 453; Symeon Logothete (Leo Grammatikos), *Chronicle* 74:8–10, ed. I. Bekker, *Leonis Grammatici chronographia*, Corpus scriptorum historiae Byzantinae (Bonn: Weber, 1842), 74.

64. Dio Cassius, *Roman History* 80.9, ed. and trans. Cary and Foster, *Roman History*, 456–457.

65. Perhaps even more striking is that the late thirteenth-century Theodore Skoutariotes presented a wholly positive image of the emperor, writing that he was "righteous, sharp in war, gentle, thoughtful, servicing all, and loved by all." Skoutariotes's text suggests an erroneous understanding of Elagabalus or a purposeful revision of the narrative, with the detail of his gentleness or softness (*ēpios*) being the only remnants of the stereotypical charges of effeminacy lodged against the transgender Elagabalus. His work may be partially indebted to Herodian's *History of the Empire*, which featured a more neutral approach to Elagabalus's reign while nevertheless noting Elagabalus's dressing and adornment habits. Herodian's text was also known to Byzantine writers and is attested in Photius's *Bibliotheca*. See Theodore Skoutariotes, *Chronicle* 2:40, ed. R. Tocci, *Theodori Scutariotae chronica*, Corpus Fontium Historiae Byzantinae, Series Berolinensis 46 (Berlin: De Gruyter, 2015). See also Herodian, *History of the Empire* 5, ed. and trans. C. R. Whittaker, *History of the Empire*, vol. 2, Loeb Classical Library 455 (Cambridge, MA: Harvard University Press, 1970), 2–75; Photius, *Bibliotheca* 99, trans. J. H. Freese, *The Library of Photius*, vol. 1 (New York: Macmillan, 1920), 191–193.

66. Philostratus of Athens, *Lives of the Sophists* 625, ed. and trans. Wilmer C. Wright, *Lives of the Sophists*, Loeb Classical Library 134 (Cambridge, MA: Harvard University Press, 1921), 304–305.

67. *Epitome de Caesaribus* 23:3, ed. F. Pichlmayr, *Sextii Aurelii Victoris Liber de Caesaribus* (Leipzig: Teubner, 1911), 157.

68. The relevant text concerns a certain Syrian mime: evidence of a connection to Aelianus's attack on Elagabalus includes Elagabalus's Syrian origins, the fragment's derisive comments on the courtesan's wantonness and femininity, and the *Souda*'s attribution of these quotes to Aelianus himself. See Steven D. Smith, *Man and Animal in Severan Rome: The Literary Imagination of Claudius Aelianus* (Cambridge: Cambridge University Press, 2017), esp. 274–279.

69. See Shaun Tougher, *The Eunuch in Byzantine History and Society* (London: Routledge, 2008), esp. 26–35. See also Kathryn M. Ringrose, *The Perfect Servant: Eunuchs and the Social Construction of Gender in Byzantium* (Chicago: University of Chicago Press, 2003), esp. 15.

70. Tougher, *The Eunuch*, 32–34.

71. Basil of Caesarea, *Letters* 115, ed. and trans. Roy J. Deferrari, *Letters*, vol. 2, Loeb Classical Library 215 (Cambridge, MA: Harvard University Press, 1928), 230–231. Cf. Cyril of Alexandria, *Homilies* 19, ed. PG

77:1109B. See Kathryn M. Ringrose, "Living in the Shadows: Eunuchs and Gender in Byzantium," in *Third Sex, Third Gender: Beyond Sexual Dimorphism in Culture and History*, ed. G. Herdt (New York: Zone Books, 1994), 85–109, 507–518. Shaun Tougher and Charis Messis have qualified Ringrose's proposal, see Tougher, *The Eunuch*, 109–111; Charis Messis, *Les eunuques à Byzance, entre réalité et imaginaire* (Paris: Centre des Études Byzantines, 2014), 361–368.

72. Tougher, *The Eunuch*, 109–111.

73. Ringrose, *The Perfect Servant*, esp. 35–37.

74. Basil of Caesarea, *Letters* 115, ed. and trans. Deferrari, *Letters*, 230–231.

75. Aristotle, *Generation of Animals* 766a25, ed. and trans. A. L. Peck, *Generation of Animals*, Loeb Classical Library 366 (Cambridge, MA: Harvard University Press, 1942), 390–391.

76. Meletius the Monk, *On the Nature of Man* 24, ed. and modified trans. Holman, "On Phoenix and Eunuchs," 83–84. See Susan R. Holman, "On Phoenix and Eunuchs: Sources for Meletius the Monk's Anatomy of Gender," *Journal of Early Christian Studies* 16:1 (2008): 79–101.

77. Here, we have an image that resonates with Thomas Lacquer's argument that ancient Greek thought held to a "one-sex model": because the female was merely a differently constituted male, both sexes were essentially one. Lacquer's model has rightly been criticized for oversimplifying this unity. See Thomas Lacquer, *Making Sex: Body and Gender from the Greeks to Freud* (Cambridge, MA: Harvard University Press, 1990). For a different approach to this problem, see Joan Cadden, *Meanings of Sex Difference in the Middle Ages: Medicine, Science, and Culture* (Cambridge: Cambridge University Press, 1993). For critiques of Lacquer's theory, see Monica H. Green, "Bodily Essences: Bodies as Categories of Difference," in *A Cultural History of the Human Body in the Medieval Age*, ed. Linda Kalof (New York: Berg Publishers, 2010), 149–172, 264–268; Helen King, *The One-Sex Body on Trial: The Classical and Early Modern Evidence* (London: Routledge, 2016).

78. Michael Psellus, *Letters*, S 157, ed. and trans. Stratis Papaioannou, *Michael Psellos: Rhetoric and Authorship in Byzantium* (Cambridge: Cambridge University Press, 2013), 197.

79. Papaioannou, *Michael Psellos*, 201.

80. Paul of Aegina, *Medical Compendium* 6.46, trans. Francis Adam, *The Seven Books of Paulus Ægineta*, vol. 2 (London: Sydenham Society, 1846), 334.

81. Paul of Aegina, *Medical Compendium* 6.46, trans. Adam, 334. See Marios Papadakis et al., "Gynaecomastia and Scrotal Rhacosis: Two Aesthetic Surgical Operations for Men in Byzantine Times," *Journal of Plastic, Reconstructive and Aesthetic Surgery* 63 (2010): 600–604.

82. Aetius of Amida, *Tetrabiblos*, 16.103, 45–46, trans. Ricci, *The Gynaecology*, 107, 50–51.

83. Paul of Aegina, *Medical Compendium*, 6.70, 69, trans. Adam, *The Seven Books*, 381.

84. On these matters in the early modern period, see Valerie Traub, "The Psychomorphology of the Clitoris," *GLQ: A Journal of Lesbian and Gay Studies* 2 (1995): 81–113.

85. Paul of Aegina, *Medical Compendium*, 6.57, trans. Adam, *The Seven Books*, 349–350.

86. On mastectomies, see Aetius of Amida, *Tetrabiblos* 16.103, 16.43, trans. Ricci, *The Gynaecology*, 49, 107.

87. See John Lascaratos et al., "Plastic Surgery of the Face in Byzantium in the Fourth Century," *Plastic and Reconstructive Surgery* 102:4 (1998): 1274–1280; John Lascaratos, Christos Liapis, and Maria Kouvaraki, "Surgery on Varices in Byzantine Times (324–1453 CE)," *Journal of Vascular Surgery* 33:1 (2001): 197–203; Anastassios I. Mylonas et al., "Oral and Cranio-Maxillofacial Surgery in Byzantium," *Journal of Cranio-Maxillo-Facial Surgery* 42 (2014): 159–168. For a broad survey of plastic surgery, see Sander L. Gilman, *Making the Body Beautiful: A Cultural History of Aesthetic Surgery* (Princeton: Princeton University Press, 1999). See also Paolo Santoni-Rugiu and Philip J. Sykes, *A History of Plastic Surgery* (New York: Springer, 2007).

88. Michael Psellus, *Letters*, S 72, S 180, ed. and trans. Papaioannou, *Michael Psellos*, 207–208, 207.

89. Papaioannou, *Michael Psellos*, 215.

90. Ibid., 231.

91. Michael Psellus, *Letters*, S 157, ed. and trans. Papaioannou, *Michael Psellos*, 196–199.

92. Michael Psellus, *Encomium for Their Mother*, trans. Anthony Kaldellis,

"Encomium for his Mother," *Mothers and Sons, Fathers and Daughters: The Byzantine Family of Michael Psellos*, ed. and trans. Anthony Kaldellis (Notre Dame: University of Notre Dame, 2006), 51–109, at 55; ed. U. Criscuolo, *Autobiografia: ecomio per la madre* (Naples: M. D'Auria, 1989), 7.

93. On gender constructions in the work of Anna Komnene, see Leonora Neville, *Anna Komnene: The Life and Work of a Medieval Historian* (Oxford: Oxford University Press, 2016) and Idem, *Heroes and Romans in Twelfth-Century Byzantium: The "Material for History" of Nikephoros Bryennios* (Cambridge: Cambridge University Press, 2012).

94. Niketas Choniates, *Chronicle* 10, ed. J. van Dieten, *Nicetae Choniatae historia, pars prior*, Corpus Fontium Historiae Byzantinae, Series Berolinensis 11.1 (Berlin: De Gruyter, 1975), 10.

95. Nikephoros Basilakes, *Rhetorical Exercises* 27 (Refutation 1), ed. and trans. Jeffrey Beneker and Craig A. Gibson, *The Rhetorical Exercises of Nikephoros Basilakes: Progymnasmata from Twelfth-Century Byzantium*, Dumbarton Oaks Medieval Library 43 (Cambridge, MA: Harvard University Press, 2016), 96–99.

96. Ibid., 104–105.

97. Nikephoros Basilakes, *Rhetorical Exercises* 27 (Refutation 1), ed. and modified trans. Beneker and Gibson, *The Rhetorical Exercises*, 102–103.

98. Ibid., 98–101.

99. See Spade, "Resisting Medicine," esp. 15–19.

100. Nikephoros Basilakes, *Rhetorical Exercises*, 27 (Refutation, 1), ed. and modified trans. Beneker and Gibson, *The Rhetorical Exercises*, 98–101.

101. Ibid., 100–101.

CHAPTER IV: QUEER SENSATIONS

1. See Edward Gibbon, *The Decline and Fall of the Roman Empire*, new ed., 4 vols. (London: W. W. Gibbings, 1890), 2:278. On the association of Byzantium with queerness, see Roland Betancourt, "The Medium Is the Byzantine: Popular Culture and the Byzantine," in *The Middle Ages in the Modern World: Twenty-First Century Perspectives*, ed. Bettina Bildhauer and Chris Jones (Oxford: Oxford University Press, 2017), 305–336, plates 5–16.

2. Leonora Neville, *Byzantine Gender* (Leeds, UK: Arc Humanities Press, 2019), esp. 5–21, at 7.

3. For an assessment of the relationship between Michael III and Basil I and its modern (homophobic) historiography, see Shaun Tougher, "Michael III and Basil the Macedonian: Just Good Friends?" in *Desire and Denial in Byzantium*, ed. Liz James (Burlington, VT: Ashgate, 1999), 149–158.

4. Stratis Papaioannou, "Michael Psellos on Friendship and Love: Erotic Discourse in Eleventh-Century Constantinople," *Early Medieval Europe* 19:1 (2011): 43–61.

5. See Derek Krueger, "Between Monks: Tales of Monastic Companionship in Early Byzantium," *Journal of the History of Sexuality* 20:1 (2011): 28–61. See also Mark Masterson, "Impossible Translation: Antony and Paul the Simple in the *Historium Monachorum*," in *The Boswell Thesis: Essays on Christianity, Social Tolerance, and Homosexuality*, ed. Mathew Kuefler (Chicago: University of Chicago Press, 2006), 215–235; Margaret E. Mullet, "Byzantium: A Friendly Society?" *Past & Present* 118 (1988): 3–24. For a compendium of textual passages on same-gender intimacies in Byzantium, see Kōnstantinos G. Pitsakēs, "*Ē Thesē tōn omophulophilōn stē buzantinē koinōnia*," in *Praktika Ēmeridas*, ed. Chrysa A. Maltezou (Athens: Idruma Goulandrē, 1999), 171–269.

6. See Derek Krueger, "Homoerotic Spectacle and the Monastic Body in Symeon the New Theologian," in *Towards a Theology of Eros: Transfiguring Passion at the Limits of Discipline*, ed. Virginia Burrus and Catherine Keller (New York: Fordham University Press, 2006), 99–118. See also Stratis Papaioannou, "On the Stage of *Eros*: Two Rhetorical Exercises by Nikephoros Basilakes," in *Theatron: Rhetorische Kultur in Spätantike und Mittelalter*, ed. Michael Grünbart (Berlin: De Gruyter, 2007), 357–376.

7. John Boswell, *Rediscovering Gay History: Archetypes of Gay Love in Christian History* (London: Gay Christian Movement, 1982), 5–21; see also Idem, *Same-Sex Unions in Premodern Europe* (New York: Villard Books, 1994). Claudia Rapp, *Brother-Making in Late Antiquity and Byzantium: Monks, Laymen, and Christian Ritual* (Oxford: Oxford University Press, 2016).

8. See Charis Messis, "Des amitiés à

l'institution a'un lien social: l'*adelphopoiia à Byzance*," in *Corrispondenza d'amorosi sensi: L'omoerotismo nella letteratura medievale*, ed. Paul Odorico, N. Pasero, and M. P. Bachmann (Alessandria: Edizioni: dell'Orso, 2008), 31–64. See also Ruth J. Macrides, "Kinship by Arrangement: The Case of Adoption," *Dumbarton Oaks Papers* 44 (1990): 109–118, esp. 110.

9. Athanasius also attacks "brother-unions" (*adelphosunai*) with the same two terms in another entry. While Claudia Rapp discusses Athanasius's prohibitions against *adelphopoiēsis*, she neither cites these terms nor specifically addresses these accusations. The text has been published only in a French translation; the original Greek is unedited and unpublished. See Athanasius I, *Didaskaliai*, 1762 (cf. 1777), trans. V. Laurent, *Les regestes des actes du patriarcat de Constantinople*, I, vol. 4 (Paris: Institut Français d'Études Byzantines, 1971), 541, cf. 554; ed. Vat. gr. 2219, fol. 201r, cf. fol. 227v. See also Rapp, *Brother-Making*, 197–198, 238–240.

10. Albio Cesare Cassio, "Post-Classical Λέσβιαι," *The Classical Quarterly* 33:1 (1983): 296–297. See also Bernadette J. Brooten, *Love between Women: Early Christian Responses to Female Homoeroticism* (Chicago: University of Chicago Press, 1996), 337–338.

11. Hesychius, *Lexicon*, delta 1689, ed. Kurt Latte, *Hesychii Alexandrini lexicon*, vol. 1 (Copenhagen: Munksgaard, 1953), 451.

12. Lucian, *Dialogues of the Courtesans* 5.2.289, ed. and trans. M. D. MacLeod, *Lucian*, vol. 7, Loeb Classical Library 431 (Cambridge: Harvard University Press, 1961), 380–381. See Brooten, *Love between Women*, 17–26; see also Cassio, "Post-Classical Λέσβιαι," 296. See also Jeffrey Henderson, *The Maculate Muse: Obscene Language in Attic Comedy*, 2nd ed. (Oxford: Oxford University Press, 1991), 52, 156, 183.

13. See Eve Kosofsky Sedgwick, *Epistemology of the Closet*, updated ed. (Berkeley: University of California Press, 2008).

14. Emphasis in Sedgwick. Eve Kosofsky Sedgwick, *Tendencies* (Durham: Duke University Press, 1993), 8.

15. David M. Halperin, *How to Do the History of Homosexuality* (Chicago: University of Chicago Press, 2002), esp. 106.

16. These apt instructions come from Dion C. Smythe, "In Denial: Same-Sex Desire in Byzantium," in *Desire and Denial in Byzantium*, ed. Liz James (Burlington, VT: Ashgate, 1999), 139–148, at 148 and 139.

17. Krueger, "Between Monks," 58.

18. Shenoute of Atripe, *Canon 1* 90.27–29, trans. Caroline T. Schroeder, *Monastic Bodies: Discipline and Salvation in Shenoute of Atripe* (Philadelphia: University of Pennsylvania Press, 2007), 36. See also Heike Behlmer, "Koptische Quellen zu (männlicher) 'Homosexualität,'" *Studien zur altägyptischen Kultur* 28 (2000): 27–53.

19. See Schroeder, *Monastic Bodies*, esp. 35–44.

20. Pachomius, *Pachomian Koinonia: The Lives, Rules, and Other Writings of Saint Pachomius and His Disciples*, trans. Armand Veilleux, vol. 2 (Kalamazoo, MI: Cistercian Publications, 1981), 161–162.

21. John Climacus, *Heavenly Ladder* 26, modified trans. Colm Luibheid and Norman Russell, *The Ladder of Divine Ascent* (Mahwah, NJ: Paulist Press, 1982), 250; ed. PG 88:1065C–D.

22. Robert Mills, *Seeing Sodomy in the Middle Ages* (Chicago: University of Chicago Press, 2015), esp. 81–132.

23. *Life of Smaragdos* 81b, modified trans. Agnes Smith Lewis, *Select Narratives of Holy Women: From the Syro-Antiochene or Sinai Palimpsest* (London: C. J. Clay, 1900), 53.

24. Cyril of Scythopolis, *Life of Euthymius* 26, 50.1–5, trans. R. M. Price and John Binns, *Lives of the Monks of Palestine* (Kalamazoo, MI: Cistercian Publications, 1991), 21, 46.

25. *The Sayings of the Desert Fathers: The Alphabetical Collection*, Eudemon 1, trans. Benedicta Ward (Kalamazoo, MI: Cistercian Publications, 1975), 64.

26. *Acts of the Protaton*, ed. and trans. Denise Papachryssanthou, *Actes du Prôtaton* (Paris: P. Lethielleux, 1975), 213, 260.

27. For my choice on using female pronouns for Eugenia, see the discussion in chapter 3.

28. *Life of Eugenia*, 32b, 34b–36a, trans. Agnes Smith Lewis, *Select Narratives of Holy Women: From the Syro-Antiochene or Sinai Palimpsest* (London: C. J. Clay, 1900), 13, 16–17. On Eugenia, see chapter 2.

29. *Life of Eugenia*, 34b, trans. Lewis, *Select Narratives*, 16.

30. *Life of Athanasius*, ed. and modified trans. Britt Dahlman, *Saint Daniel of Sketis:*

A Group of Hagiographic Texts, Studia Byzantina Upsaliensia 10 (Uppsala: Uppsala University, 2007), 174–175.

31. *Life of Athanasius* 10, ed. and trans. Anne P. Alwis, *Celibate Marriages in Late Antique and Byzantine Hagiography: The Lives of Saints Julian and Basilissa, Andronikos and Athanasia, and Galaktion and Episteme* (London: Bloomsbury, 2011), 261.

32. Crystal Lynn Lubinsky, *Removing Masculine Layers to Reveal a Holy Womanhood: The Female Transvestite Monks of Late Antique Eastern Christianity* (Turnhout: Brepols, 2013), 199; Rapp, *Brother-Making*, 142.

33. On sex in Byzantine saint lives, see Alexander Kazhdan, "Byzantine Hagiography and Sex in the Fifth to Twelfth Centuries," *Dumbarton Oaks Papers* 44 (1990): 131–143.

34. *Life of Athanasius*, ed. and trans. Dahlman, *Saint Daniel of Sketis*, 176–177.

35. Lee Edelman, *No Future: Queer Theory and the Death Drive* (Durham: Duke University Press, 2004), 4. See also Leo Bersani, *Homos* (Cambridge: Harvard University Press, 1996). On responses to the antisocial thesis, see Robert L. Caserio, Lee Edelman, Judith Halberstam, José Esteban Muñoz, and Tim Dean, "The Antisocial Thesis in Queer Theory," *PMLA* 121:3 (2006): 819–828.

36. Edelman, *No Future*, 4.

37. See Leo Bersani, "Is the Rectum a Grave?" *October* 43 (1987): 197–222.

38. Krueger, "Between Monks," esp. 58–61; he is here following Eve Sedgwick.

39. See José Esteban Muñoz, *Cruising Utopia: The Then and There of Queer Futurity* (New York: New York University Press, 2009); Elizabeth Freeman, *Time Binds: Queer Temporalities, Queer Histories* (Durham: Duke University Press, 2010); Ann Cvetkovich, *An Archive of Feelings: Trauma, Sexuality, and Lesbian Public Cultures* (Durham: Duke University Press, 2003).

40. Muñoz, *Cruising Utopia*, 1.

41. See Sara Ahmed, *Queer Phenomenology: Orientations, Objects, Others* (Durham: Duke University Press, 2006), esp. 1–24.

42. On a queer theory not defined by sex and sexuality alone, see Janet Halley and Andrew Parker, eds., *After Sex? On Writing since Queer Theory* (Durham: Duke University Press, 2011).

43. See Rosanna Omitowoju, *Rape and the Politics of Consent in Classical Athens* (Cambridge: Cambridge University Press, 2002), 51–71.

44. The link of *proseggisai* to sexual intercourse is also attested to in the narrative of Athanasius and Andronicus from the hagiographic texts associated with Daniel of Sketis. After recounting the times they had sex and the children they conceived, the narrative continues that after the second child, "Andronikos did not approach her any more" (*ouketi prosetheto proseggisai autē*). The verb is unambiguously a euphemism for sex, just as the mention of their earlier intercourse uses the phrase "knew [*egnō*] the wife" in connection with conceiving their first child. See *Life of Athanasius*, ed. and trans. Dahlman, *Saint Daniel of Sketis*, 166–167.

45. Symeon the New Theologian, *Hymns* 15.160–164, trans. Daniel K. Griggs, *Divine Eros: Hymns of St. Symeon the New Theologian* (Yonkers, NY: St. Vladimir's Seminary Press, 2010), 87; ed. Athanasios Kambylis, *Symeon Neos Theologos, Hymnen*, Supplementa Byzantina 3 (Berlin: De Gruyter, 1976), 107.

46. See Derek Krueger, "Homoerotic Spectacle," esp. 113.

47. See Symeon the New Theologian, *Hymns* 24.75, modified trans. Griggs, *Divine Eros*, 184. It is difficult to ascertain if Symeon is confessing here to same-gender sexual acts, given that this phrase appears in the midst of a flurry of other historically dubious charges he makes against himself. This passage merits far closer scrutiny and attention than can be offered in the present text.

48. See Derek Krueger, *Liturgical Subjects: Christian Ritual, Biblical Narrative, and the Formation of the Self in Byzantium* (Philadelphia: University of Pennsylvania Press, 2014), 29–65, esp. 45–46.

49. Romanus the Melodist, *Hymns* 46.1, trans. Ephrem Lash, *On the Life of Christ: Kontakia* (New York: Harper Collins, 1995), 183–184.

50. Romanus the Melodist, *Hymns* 46.1, ed. Jean Grosdidier de Matons, *Romanos le Mélode. Hymnes*, vol. 5, Sources Chrétiennes 283 (Paris: Éditions du Cerf, 1981), 32.

51. Ibid.

52. Romanus the Melodist, *Hymns* 46.14, modified trans. Lash, *On the Life of Christ*, 189; ed. Matons, *Hymnes*, 52.

53. G. W. H. Lampe, *A Patristic Greek Lexicon* (Oxford: Clarendon Press, 1961), 724.

54. Symeon the New Theologian, *Hymns* 16.29, ed. Kambylis, *Hymnen*, 112.

55. Thomas Arentzen, *The Virgin in Song: Mary and the Poetry of Romanos the Melodist* (Philadelphia: University of Pennsylvania Press, 2017), 70–71.

56. Romanus the Melodist, *Hymns* 9.15, ed. and modified trans. Arentzen, *The Virgin in Song*, 180, 186.

57. On the rite of *zeon*, see Robert F. Taft, *The Precommunion Rites*, vol. 5 of *A History of the Liturgy of St. John Chrysostom* (Rome: Pontifico Istituto Orientale, 2000), 441–502.

58. See Taft, *The Precommunion Rites*, 444–445.

59. *Liturgical Poem* 30, trans. Roland Betancourt, "A Byzantine Liturgical Commentary in Verse: Introduction and Translation," *Orientalia Christiana Periodica* 81 (2015): 433–472, at 462.

60. Nicholas and Theodore of Andida, *Protheoria* 36, ed. PG 140:464B.

61. Romanus the Melodist, *Hymns* 46.16, modified trans. Lash, *On the Life of Christ*, 190.

62. Romanus the Melodist, *Hymns* 46.17, modified trans. Lash, *On the Life of Christ*, 190.

63. Pliny the Elder, *Natural History*, 35.36.65–66 (quotation, 65), ed. and trans. H. Rackham, *Natural History*, vol. 9, Loeb Classical Library 394 (Cambridge, MA: Harvard University Press, 1952), 308–311 (quotation, 309).

64. Philostratus the Elder, *Imagines*, 1.23.2, ed. and trans. Arthur Fairbanks, *Imagines*, Loeb Classical Library 256 (Cambridge: Harvard University Press, 1931), 88–91.

65. Diogenes Laertius, *Lives of Eminent Philosophers*, 7.6.177, ed. and trans. Hicks, *Lives of Eminent Philosophers*, 2 vols., Loeb Classical Library 184–185 (Cambridge, MA: Harvard University Press, 1925).

66. See Karl Thein, "Gods and Painters: Philostratus the Elder, Stoic Phantasia, and the Strategy of Describing," *Ramus* 31:1/2 (2002): 136–145.

67. Nemesius of Emesa, *On the Nature of Man* 7, trans. R. W. Sharples and P. J. van der Eijk, *On the Nature of Man* (Liverpool: Liverpool University Press, 2008), 108.

68. Ibid., 108–109.

69. On the problem of the phantasm and illusion in the Doubting Thomas in Late Antiquity, see Patrick R. Crowley, "Doubting Thomas and the Matter of Embodiment on Early Christian Sarcophagi," *Art History* 41:3 (2018): 566–591.

70. Nicholas Mesarites, *Description of the Church of Holy Apostles* 33.3, ed. and trans. Glanville Downey, "Nikolaos Mesarites: Description of the Church of Holy Apostles," *Transactions of the American Philosophical Society*, n.s., 47:6 (1957): 886, 912.

71. Nicholas Mesarites, *Description of the Church of Holy Apostles* 34.5, ed. and trans. Downey, "Description," 888, 913.

72. See Paul of Aegina, *Medical Compendium* 3.22, 2.4/3, trans. Francis Adam, *The Seven Books of Paulus Ægineta*, vol. 1 (London: Sydenham Society, 1846), 412, 190; ed. J. L. Heiberg, *Paulus Aegineta*, vol. 1, Corpus medicorum Graecorum 9.1 (Leipzig: Teubner, 1921), 75, 173–174.

73. Glenn W. Most, *Doubting Thomas* (Cambridge, MA: Harvard University Press, 2007), esp. 51–55, 69–73.

74. John Chrysostom, *On Genesis*, 16, ed. PG 53:127C.

75. John Chrysostom, *On Matthew*, 17, ed. PG 57:257.

76. Nicholas Mesarites, *Description of the Church of Holy Apostles* 33.3, ed. and modified trans. Downey, "Description," 888, 912.

77. Philo of Alexandria, *Questions and Answers on Exodus* I.8, trans. Ralph Marcus, *Questions on Exodus*, Loeb Classical Library 401 (Cambridge, MA: Harvard University Press, 1953), 15–16.

78. Philo of Alexandria, *On Abraham* 149–151, ed. and modified trans. F. H. Colson, *Philo*, vol. 6 (Cambridge, MA: Harvard University Press, 1935), 76–77.

79. Michael Psellus, *Letters* 16, trans. Papaioannou, "Michael Psellos on Friendship and Love," 55–56; ed. Paul Gautier, "Quelques lettres de Psellos inédites ou déjà éditées," *Revue des Études Byzantines* 44 (1986): 111–197, at 157.

80. Papaioannou, "Michael Psellos on Friendship and Love," 56.

81. Michael Psellus, *Chronographia* 6.46, ed. Diether Roderich Reinsch, *Chronographia*, vol. 1 (Berlin: De Gruyter, 2014), 125.

82. See Stratis Papaioannou, *Michael Psellos: Rhetoric and Authorship in Byzantium*

(Cambridge: Cambridge University Press, 2013), 192–231.

83. See Derek Krueger, "Mary at the Threshold: The Mother of God as Guardian in Seventh-Century Palestinian Miracle Accounts," *The Cult of the Mother of God in Byzantium: Texts and Images*, eds. Leslie Brubaker and Mary Cunningham (Burlington, VT: Ashgate, 2011), 31–38.

84. Romanus the Melodist, *Hymns* 9.16, modified trans. and ed. Arentzen, *The Virgin in Song*, 180–181, 186–187.

85. This connection is made explicit in Proclus of Constantinople's early fifth-century homily on the Theotokos. Musing on Mary's virginity after Christ's birth, Proclus states that he was indeed "wondrously born who also entered unhindered 'the doors having been closed,' whose union of natures was proclaimed by Thomas who said, 'My Lord and my God!'" See Proclus of Constantinople, *Homilies* 1.2, ed. and modified trans. Nicholas Constas, *Proclus of Constantinople and the Cult of the Virgin in Late Antiquity* (Leiden: Brill, 2003), 138–139.

86. See Charles Barber, "Icons, Prayer, and Vision in the Eleventh Century," *Byzantine Christianity*, ed. Derek Krueger (Minneapolis: Fortress Press, 2006), 149–163.

87. On the Doubting Thomas fresco in the crypt, the decorative program, and ritual context, see Carolyn L. Connor, *Art and Miracles in Medieval Byzantium: The Crypt at Hosios Loukas and Its Frescoes* (Princeton: Princeton University Press, 1991), esp. 39–40.

88. For an overview of the icon and its afterlife, along with the most recent bibliography, see Fani Gargova, "The Meteora Icon of the Incredulity of Thomas Reconsidered," in *Female Founders in Byzantium and Beyond*, ed. Lioba Theis, Margaret Mullet, and Michael Grünbart (Vienna: Böhlau Verlag, 2012), 369–381.

89. Nancy Patterson Ševčenko, "The Representation of Donors and Holy Figures on Four Byzantine Icons," *Deltion tēs Christianikēs Archaiologikēs Etairias* 17 (1993–1994): 157–164, esp. 163–164.

90. Monastery of the Theotokos Evergetis, *Synaxarion* P.08, ed. and trans. Robert H. Jordan, *The Synaxarion of the Monastery of the Theotokos Evergetis*, vol. 2 (Belfast: Queen's University Belfast, 2005), 536–543, at 538–539.

91. John Chrysostom, *Homilies on the Gospel of John* 87, trans. Philip Schaff, "Homily LXXXVII," *Nicene and Post-Nicene Fathers*, First Series, vol. 14, ed. Philip Schaff (Buffalo, NY: Christian Literature Publishing, 1889), 327–331, at 327; ed. PG 59:473.

92. John Chrysostom, *Homilies on the Gospel of John* 87, trans. Schaff, "Homily," 327; ed. PG 59:473.

93. John Chrysostom, *Homilies on the Gospel of John* 87, trans. Schaff, "Homily," 330; ed. PG 59:476

94. Ivan Drpić, *Epigram, Art, and Devotion in Later Byzantium* (Cambridge: Cambridge University Press, 2016), 12.

95. See Ibid., 312–314.

96. Ibid., 312.

97. See Averil Cameron, *Christianity and the Rhetoric of Empire: The Development of Christian Discourse* (Berkeley: University of California Press, 1991), 155–188, 228.

98. Gary Vikan, *Early Byzantine Pilgrimage Art*, rev. ed. (Washington, DC: Dumbarton Oaks, 2010), 64.

99. From early on, we see this same caption used for the scene as well as the choice to depict Christ grasping Thomas's wrist. For an example from around 600 see, the flask in the Treasury of the Cathedral of Saint John the Baptist in Monza (Monza, no. 9; cf. Bobbio, 10). See André Grabar, *Ampoules de Terre Sainte (Monza, Bobbio)* (Paris: C. Klincksieck, 1958), 24–26, pls. 14–15; cf. 37, pl. 42.

100. See Liz James, "Monks, Monastic Art, the Sanctoral Cycle and the Middle Byzantine Church," in *The Theotokos Evergetis and Eleventh-Century Monasticism*, ed. Margaret Mullett and Anthony Kirby (Belfast: Queen's University of Belfast, 1994), 162–175. See also Carolyn L. Connor, *Saints and Spectacle: Byzantine Mosaics in Their Cultural Setting* (Oxford: Oxford University Press, 2016), 11–50.

101. See Manolis Chatzidakis, *Hosios Loukas: Byzantine Art in Greece*, trans. Valerie Nunn (Athens: Melissa Publishing House, 1997), 28–29.

102. See Ljubomir Milanović, "On the Threshold of Certainty: The Incredulity of Thomas in the Narthex of the Katholikon of the Hosios Loukas Monastery," *Recueil des travaux de l'Institut d'études byzantines* 50 (2013): 367–388, esp. 380.

103. See Vasileios Marinis, *Architecture and Ritual in the Churches of Constantinople:*

Ninth to Fifteenth Centuries (Cambridge: Cambridge University Press, 2014), 71–73.

104. On mimesis and liturgical performance, see William Tronzo, "Mimesis in Byzantium: Notes toward a History of the Function of the Image," *Res: Anthropology and Aesthetics* 25 (1994): 61–76; Charles Barber, "Mimesis and Memory in the Narthex Mosaics at the Nea Moni, Chios," *Art History* 24:3 (2001): 323–337.

105. See Edelman, *No Future*, esp. 33–66. For a discussion of shame as an identity, see chapter 2; see also Virginia Burrus, *Saving Shame: Martyrs, Saints, and Other Abject Subjects* (Philadelphia: University of Pennsylvania Press, 2008).

106. Romanus the Melodist, *Hymns* 46.5, trans. Lash, *On the Life of Christ*, 185.

107. Maximus the Confessor, *Scholia on the Divine Names* 15, ed. PG 4:268C. In the writings of Maximus, *agapē* and *erōs* are critical factors in humanity's approach toward God and their fellow humankind, as in his "Four Hundred Chapters on Love." Andrew Louth states that, for Maximus, "Christianity is a training in love." See Andrew Louth, *Maximus the Confessor* (London: Routledge, 1996), 38–42, at 38. See also Maximus the Confessor, *Four Hundred Chapters on Love*, trans. George C. Berthold, *Maximus the Confessor: Selected Writings* (New York: Paulist Press, 1985), 35–98. On the problem of *agapē*, *erōs*, and chaste versus sexual desire, see Virginia Burrus, "Theology and Eros after Nygren," in *Toward a Theology of Eros: Transfiguring Passion at the Limits of Discipline*, eds. Virginia Burrus and Catherine Keller (New York: Fordham University Press, 2006), xiii–xxi; Daniel Boyarin, "What Do We Talk About When We Talk About Platonic Love?" in *Toward a Theology of Eros*, 3–22.

108. Maximus the Confessor, *Scholia on the Divine Names* 15, ed. PG 4:268D–269A.

CHAPTER V: THE ETHIOPIAN EUNUCH

1. On the Menologion of Basil II and its painters, see Ihor Ševčenko, "The Illuminators of the Menologium of Basil II," *Dumbarton Oaks Papers* 16 (1962): 245–276. See also Ihor Ševčenko, "On Pantoleon the Painter," *Jahrbuch der Österreichischen Byzantinistik* 21 (1972): 241–249.

2. See Maria Evangelatou, "Liturgy and the Illustration of the Ninth-Century Marginal Psalters," *Dumbarton Oaks Papers* 63 (2009): 59–116.

3. See Denise K. Buell, *Why This New Race: Ethnic Reasoning in Early Christianity* (New York: Columbia University, 2005).

4. Maria Parani, "Look Like an Angel: The Attire of Eunuchs and Its Significance within the Context of Middle Byzantine Court Ceremonial," in *Court Ceremonies and Rituals of Power in Byzantium and the Medieval Mediterranean*, ed. Alexander Beihammer, Stavroula Constantinou, and Maria Parani (Leiden: Brill, 2013), 433–463, esp. 439–440 n. 26.

5. On Byzantine attire and terminology, see Jennifer L. Ball, *Byzantine Dress: Representations of Secular Dress in Eighth- to Twelfth-Century Painting* (New York: Palgrave Macmillan, 2005).

6. Eustathios of Thessaloniki, *Orations* 16.2, trans. Andrew F. Stone "The Epiphany Oration of 1174," in *Eustathios of Thessaloniki. Secular Orations: 1167/8 to 1179* (Brisbane: Australian Association for Byzantine Studies, 2013), 11–130, at 19–21; ed. P. Wirth, *Eustathii Thessalonicensis opera minora (magnam partem inedita)*, Corpus Fontium Historiae Byzantinae, Series Berolinensis 32 (Berlin: De Gruyter, 1999), 261–288, at 263–264.

7. For a further breakdown of these various terms, see *The Oxford Dictionary of Byzantium*, ed. Alexander P. Kazhdan (Oxford: Oxford University Press, 1991).

8. On contact between Constantinople and India, see Cornelis Datema, "New Evidence for the Encounter Between Constantinople and 'India,'" in *After Chalcedon: Studies in Theology and Church History*, eds. C. Laga, J. A. Munitiz, and L. van Rompay (Leuven: Peeters, 1985), 57–65.

9. John Malalas, *Chronicle* 18:73, trans. Elizabeth Jeffreys, Michael Jeffreys, and Roger Scott, *The Chronicle of John Malalas* (Melbourne: Australian Association for Byzantine Studies, 1986), 282.

10. John Malalas, *Chronicle* 18:56, trans. Jeffreys et al., *The Chronicle of John Malalas*, 268–269.

11. Further contact with India is attested in later centuries via paths that included the exchange and translation of texts, as well as more cryptic allusions to the trade

goods from the subcontinent and its spheres of influence. For example, the mid-tenth-century *Life of Basil I* refers to the chapel of Saint Clement in the Great Palace of Constantinople as having been decorated with the "whole array of the wealth of India." See Constantine VII Porphyrogenitus, *Life of Basil I* 87, ed. and trans. Ihor Ševčenko, *Chronographiae quae Theophanus Continuati nomine fertur liber quo vita Basilii imperatoris amplectitur* (Berlin: De Gruyter, 2011), 284–285.

12. On *poikilia*, see Michael Roberts, *The Jeweled Style: Poetry and Poetics in Late Antiquity* (Ithaca, NY: Cornell University Press, 1989), esp. 38–65. See also Bissera Pentcheva, *The Sensual Icon: Space, Ritual, and the Senses in Byzantium* (University Park, PA: Pennsylvania State University Press, 2010), esp. 139–140.

13. Michael Psellus, *Letters to Michael Keroularios* 96–103, trans. Anthony Kaldellis and Ioannis Polemis, "Letter to the Patriarch Kyr Michael Keroullarios," in *Psellos and the Patriarchs: Letters and Funeral Orations for Keroullarios, Leichoudes, and Xiphilinos,* ed. Anthony Kaldellis and Ioannis Polemis (South Bend, IN: University of Notre Dame, 2015), 37–48, at 41–42.

14. On Psellus and his students, see Robert Volk, *Der medizinische Inhalt der Schriften des Michael Psellos* (Munich: Institut für Byzantinistik und neugriechische Philologie der Universität, 1990), 15–20. On his possible Georgian students, see B. Martin-Hisard, "Georgian Hagiography," in *The Ashgate Research Companion to Byzantine Hagiography,* vol. 1 (Burlington, VT: Ashgate, 2011), 285–298, esp. 288–289; L. Gigineishvili and G. Van Riel, "Ioane Petritsi: A Witness to Proclus' Works in the School of Psellus," in *Proclus et la théologie platonicienne,* ed. A.-Ph. Segonds and C. Steel (Leuven: Leuven University Press, 2000), 571–587.

15. See *Suda Lexicon,* alpha 86 and alpha 87, ed. and trans. Anne Mahoney, "*Habron*" and "*Habros,*" *Suda On Line,* ed. David Whitehead, www.stoa.org/sol-entries /alpha/86 and www.stoa.org/sol-entries /alpha/87.

16. See *Suda Lexicon,* gamma 77 and gamma 78, ed. and trans. Jennifer Benedict, "*Gauron*" and "*Gauros,*" *Suda On Line,* ed. David Whitehead, www.stoa.org/sol-entries /gamma/77 and www.stoa.org/sol-entries /gamma/78.

17. Robert de Clari, *The Conquest of Constantinople* 54, trans. Edgar Holmes McNeal, *The Conquest of Constantinople* (New York: Columbia University Press, 1936), 79–80.

18. See Bożena Rostkowska, "The Visit of a Nubian King to Constantinople in A.D. 1203," in *New Discoveries in Nubia: Proceedings of the Colloquium on Nubian Studies, The Hague, 1979,* ed. Paul van Moorsel (Leiden: Netherlands Instituut Voor Het Nabije Oosten, 1982), 113–116. See also B. Hendrickx, "Un roi Africain à Constantinople en 1203," *Byzantina* 13 (1985): 893–898; Gianfranco Fiaccadori, "Un re di Nubia a Constantinopoli nel 1203," *Scrinium* 1:1 (2005): 43–49.

19. Robert de Clari, *The Conquest of Constantinople* 54, trans. Charles Hope, *Chroniques Gréco-Romanes* (Berlin: Librairie de Weidmann, 1873), 45.

20. See Mokhtar Khalil and Catherine Miller, "Old Nubian and Language Uses in Nubia," *Égypte/Monde arabe* 27–28 (1996): 1–7, esp. 4.

21. Sharon Kinoshita, *Medieval Boundaries: Rethinking Difference in Old French Literature* (Philadelphia: University of Pennsylvania Press, 2006), 159–160.

22. See Henry Maguire, "Parodies of Imperial Ceremonial and their Reflections in Byzantine Art," in *Court Ceremonies and Rituals of Power in Byzantium and the Medieval Mediterranean,* ed. Alexander Beihammer, Stavroula Constantinou, and Maria Parani (Leiden: Brill, 2013), 417–432, esp. 421.

23. Niketas Choniates, *Chronicle* 86, modified trans. Henry J. Magoulias, *O City of Byzantium, Annals of Niketas Choniates* (Detroit: Wayne State University Press, 1984), 50–51; ed. J. van Dieten, *Nicetae Choniatae historia, pars prior,* Corpus Fontium Historiae Byzantinae, Series Berolinensis 11.1 (Berlin: De Gruyter, 1975), 86. He cites the Song of Songs 1:5–8.

24. Liutprand of Cremona, *The Embassy to Constantinople* 3, trans. F. A. Wright, *The Works of Liudprand of Cremona* (London: George Routledge and Sons, 1930), 236–237; ed. P. Chiesa, *Liudprandi Cremonensis. Opera omnia,* Corpus Christianorum 156 (Turnhout: Brepols, 1998), 188–189.

25. Christopher Mytilene, *Poems* 10:9–10, ed. and trans. Floris Bernard and Christopher

Livanos, *The Poems of Christopher Mytilene and John Mauropous* (Cambridge: Harvard University Press, 2018), 16–17.

26. For example, scholars have privileged ethnicity over race, overlooking the process of racialization, negating the validity of race as a historical concept, and even degrading processes of codeswitching and the fluidity of identity, see Anthony Kaldellis, *Romanland: Ethnicity and Empire in Byzantium* (Cambridge, MA: Harvard University Press, 2019), esp. 272–273. See also Anthony Kaldellis, *Ethnography after Antiquity: Foreign Lands and Peoples in Byzantine Literature* (Philadelphia: University of Pennsylvania Press, 2013). Alexander P. Kazhdan and Ann Wharton Epstein, *Change in Byzantine Culture in the Eleventh and Twelfth Centuries* (Berkeley: University of California Press, 1985), 167–196.

27. *Suda Lexicon*, alphaiota 129 and alphaiota 138, ed. and trans. Catharine Roth and James Cousins, "*Aithiops*" and "*Aithops*," *Suda On Line*, ed. David Whitehead, www.stoa.org/sol-entries/alphaiota/129 and www.stoa.org/sol-entries/alphaiota/138; *Suda Lexicon*, alphaiota 127 and alphaiota 128, ed. and trans. Roth and Cousins, "*Aithiopia*" and "*Aithopion*," *Suda On Line*, ed. Whitehead, www.stoa.org/sol-entries/alphaiota/127 and www.stoa.org/sol-entries/alphaiota/128.

28. Benjamin Isaac, *The Invention of Racism in Classical Antiquity* (Princeton: Princeton University Press, 2004), 49–50.

29. See Frank M. Snowden, Jr., *Blacks in Antiquity: Ethiopians in the Greco-Roman Experience* (Cambridge: Harvard University Press, 1970), and *Before Color Prejudice: The Ancient View of Blacks* (Cambridge: Harvard University Press, 1983). See also Martin Bernal, *Black Athena: The Afroasiatic Roots of Classical Civilization*, 3 vols. (New Brunswick: Rutgers University Press, 1987–2006).

30. For an exceptional bibliography, see Jonathan Hsy and Julie Orlemanski, "Race and Medieval Studies: A Partial Bibliography," *Postmedieval* 8:4 (2017): 500–513.

31. On the use of "race" in this study, see Buell, *Why This New Race*, 13–21.

32. Geraldine Heng, *The Invention of Race in the European Middle Ages* (Cambridge: Cambridge University Press, 2018), 27.

33. According to the *Suda Lexicon*, the phrase was used "in reference to those exerting vain efforts": *Suda Lexicon*, alphaiota 125, ed. and trans. Anne Mahoney, "*Aithiopa smēchein*," *Suda On Line*, ed. Whitehead, www.stoa.org/sol-entries/alpha/86 and www.stoa.org/sol-entries/alphaiota/125.

34. Anna Komnena, *The Alexiad* 9:6.4, ed. A. Kambylis and D. R. Reinsch, *Annae Comnenae Alexias*, Corpus Fontium Historiae Byzantinae, Series Berolinensis 60.1 (Berlin: De Gruyter, 2001), 271.

35. In the West Gregory the Great underscores the association with dirtiness; he builds on the proverb to say that an Ethiopian comes out of the bathhouse as black as they went in, yet nevertheless the proprietor receives their money; he thus articulated a play between blackness and uncleanliness that nevertheless reveals itself to be false. See Gregory the Great, *Letters* 3.67, ed. PL 77:668.

36. Basil of Caesarea, *Letters* 130, ed. and trans. Roy J. Deferrari, *Letters*, vol. 2, Loeb Classical Library 215 (Cambridge, MA: Harvard University Press, 1928), 292–293. Cf. John of Damascus, *Barlaam and Ioasaph*, 32, ed. and trans. G. R. Woodward and Harold Mattingly, *Barlaam and Ioasaph*, Loeb Classical Library 34 (Cambridge, MA: Harvard University Press, 1914), 490–491.

37. See Gay L. Byron, *Symbolic Blackness and Ethnic Difference in Early Christian Literature* (New York: Routledge, 2002).

38. David Brakke, *Demons and the Making of the Monk: Spiritual Combat in Early Christianity* (Cambridge, MA: Harvard University Press, 2006), esp. 156–157. See also Idem, "Ethiopian Demons: Male Sexuality, the Black-Skinned Other, and the Monastic Self," *Journal of the History of Sexuality* 10:3/4 (2001): 501–535.

39. Sarah, *The Sayings of the Desert Fathers: The Alphabetical Collection*, Heraclides 1, trans. Benedicta Ward (Kalamazoo, MI: Cistercian Publications, 1975), 72.

40. Pachomius, *Pachomian Koinonia: The Lives, Rules, and Other Writings of Saint Pachomius and His Disciples*, trans. Armand Veilleux, vol. 2 (Kalamazoo, MI: Cistercian Publications, 1981), 161–162.

41. The various mentions of Ethiopians across these sources seem to suggest another source of temptation or distraction for these desert ascetics, who might come into contact with "Ethiopian"—i.e., black, nomadic—persons in the desert in the course of their daily tasks. For example, in the life of

Arsenius, while the monk was approaching the river during his travels, a "little Ethiopian slave-girl came and touched his sheepskin." Later in the same story, the monk is shown an Ethiopian cutting wood and struggling to carry it, along with series of other figures, all serving as moralizing vignettes of daily life. Thus, Ethiopians also present how the other spheres of life that shared the desert terrain could intrude into the practices of late antique ascetics. See *The Sayings of the Desert Fathers*, Arsenius 32–33, trans. Ward, 15–16.

42. Brakke, *Demons and the Making of the Monk*, 171.

43. *Life of Eugenia* 36b, trans. Agnes Smith Lewis, *Select Narratives of Holy Women: From the Syro-Antiochene or Sinai Palimpsest* (London: C. J. Clay, 1900), 18.

44. Cord Whitaker has recently studied the importance of medieval metaphors of blackness in racialized thinking. See Cord J. Whitaker, *Black Metaphors: How Modern Racism Emerged from Medieval Race-Thinking* (Philadelphia: University of Pennsylvania Press, 2019).

45. Gregory of Elvira, *Explanation of the Song of Songs*, 1.23–24, trans. J. Robert Wright, *Proverbs, Ecclesiastes, Song of Solomon*, Ancient Christian Commentary on Scripture, Old Testament 9 (Downers Grove, IL: InterVarsity Press, 2005), 298.

46. Origen, *Commentary on the Song of Songs* 2.1, trans. R. P. Lawson, *Origen: The Song of Songs Commentary and Homilies*, Ancient Christian Writers 26 (Westminster, MD: Newman Press, 1957), 91. For a collection of similar commentaries, see Wright, *Proverbs, Ecclesiastes, Song of Solomon*, 296–300.

47. Origen, *Homilies on Jeremiah* 11.6.3, trans. John Clark Smith, *Origen: Homilies on Jeremiah and 1 Kings 28*, Fathers of the Church 97 (Washington, DC: Catholic University of America Press, 1998), 109.

48. See Penny Howell Jolly, *Made in God's Image? Eve and Adam in the Genesis Mosaics at San Marco, Venice* (Berkeley: University of California Press, 1997), esp. 21–27. See also Otto Demus, *The Mosaics of San Marco in Venice*, 2 vols. in 4 (Chicago: University of Chicago Press, 1984), 2.1:111–112.

49. Gregory of Nyssa, *Homilies on the Song of Songs*, 2, trans. Richard A. Norris, Jr., *Gregory of Nyssa: Homilies on the Song of Songs*

(Atlanta: Society of Biblical Literature, 2012), 52–55.

50. Theodoret of Cyrus, *Commentary on the Song of Songs* 1, trans. Robert C. Hill, *Theodoret of Cyrus: Commentary on the Song of Songs*, Early Christian Studies 2 (Brisbane: Australian Catholic University, 2001), 44–45.

51. *The Sayings of the Desert Fathers*, Moses 8, trans. Ward, 140.

52. *The Sayings of the Desert Fathers*, Moses 3, trans. Ward, 139.

53. *The Sayings of the Desert Fathers*, Moses 4, trans. Ward, 139.

54. See Catherine Holmes, *Basil II and the Governance of Empire (976–1025)* (Oxford: Oxford University Press, 2005), esp. 1–15.

55. See Paul Stephenson, *The Legend of Basil the Bulgar-Slayer* (Cambridge: Cambridge University Press, 2003), esp. 81–96.

56. See Stephenson, *The Legend of Basil the Bulgar-Slayer*, 49–65. See also Anthony Cutler, "A Psalter of Basil II (Part I)," *Arte Veneta* 30 (1976): 9–19. On the difficulty of identifying the figures, see Anthony Cutler, "A Psalter of Basil II (Part II)," *Arte Veneta* 31 (1977): 9–15, esp. 10–11.

57. *Psalter of Basil II*, modified trans. Ševčenko, "The Illuminators of the Menologium of Basil II," 272.

58. *'Menologion' of Basil II*, trans. Ševčenko, "The Illuminators of the Menologium of Basil II," 273.

59. *Digenis Akritis* 1.115, 1.32, ed. and trans. Elizabeth Jeffreys, *Digenis Akritis: The Grottaferrata and Escorial Versions* (Cambridge: Cambridge University Press, 1998), 4–5, 10–11.

60. *Life of Mary of Egypt* 10, trans. Maria Kouli, "The Life of St. Mary of Egypt," in *Holy Women of Byzantium: Ten Saints' Lives in English Translation*, ed. Alice-Mary Talbot (Washington, DC: Dumbarton Oaks, 1996), 65–93, at 76.

61. *Life of Athanasius*, ed. and modified trans. Britt Dahlman, *Saint Daniel of Sketis: A Group of Hagiographic Texts*, Studia Byzantina Upsaliensia 10 (Uppsala: Uppsala University, 2007), 174–175.

62. *Life of Theodore of Alexandria*, ed. Karl Wessely, "Zu den griechischen Papyri des Louvre und der Bibliothèque nationale," in *Fünfzehnter Jahresbericht des K. K. Staatsgymnasiums in Hernals* (Vienna: Verlag des K. K. Staatsgymnasiums in Hernals, 1889), 3–44, esp. 24–44, at 38. See Arietta

Papaconstantinou, "'Je suis noire, mais belle':
Le double langage de la *Vie de Théodora
d'Alexandrie, alias* Abba Théodore," *Lalies* 24
(2004): 63–86, esp. 78–79.

63. Eustathios of Thessaloniki, *Epitaphios
for Manuel I Komnenos*, ed. and trans. Emmanuel C. Bourbouhakis, *Not Composed in
a Chance Manner: The Epitaphios for Manuel I Komnenos by Eustathios of Thessaloniki*
(Uppsala: Uppsala Universitet, 2017), 26–27.

64. Chiara Thumiger, "'A Most Acute, Disgusting and Indecent Disease': Satyriasis and
Sexual Disorders in Ancient Medicine," in
Mental Illness in Ancient Medicine: From Celsus to Paul of Aegina, ed. Chiara Thumiger
and P. N. Singer (Leiden: Brill, 2018), 269–
284, esp. 280–281. See also Marke Ahonen,
Mental Disorders in Ancient Philosophy (Berlin: Springer, 2014), 217–222.

65. Nikephoros Basilakes, *Rhetorical Exercises*, 27 (Refutation, 1), ed. and trans. Jeffrey
Beneker and Craig A. Gibson, *The Rhetorical
Exercises of Nikephoros Basilakes*: Progymnasmata *from Twelfth-Century Byzantium*,
Dumbarton Oaks Medieval Library 43 (Cambridge, MA: Harvard University Press, 2016),
102–103.

66. For a comprehensive introductory
study, see Denise Eileen McCoskey, *Race: Antiquity and Its Legacy* (Oxford: Oxford University Press, 2012), 35–80.

67. Hippocrates of Cos, *Airs, Waters,
Places*, 18, 20, ed. and trans. W. H. S. Jones,
Hippocrates, vol. 1, Loeb Classical Library 147
(Cambridge, MA: Harvard University Press,
1923), 118–119, 124–125.

68. Pliny the Elder, *Natural History* 2:80
(189), ed. and trans. H. Rackham, *Natural
History*, vol. 1, Loeb Classical Library 330
(Cambridge, MA: Harvard University Press,
1938), 320–321.

69. Hippocrates of Cos, *Airs, Waters,
Places*, 22, ed. and modified trans. Jones,
Hippocrates, 126–127. See Charles Chiasson,
"Scythian Androgyny and Environmental Determinism in Herodotus and the Hippocratic *periaeron hudaton topon*," *Syllecta
Classica* 12 (2001): 33–73.

70. For an exceptional landmark study
of blackness and trans identity, albeit in the
modern world, see C. Reily Snorton, *Black
on Both Sides: A Racial History of Trans Identity* (Minneapolis: University of Minnesota
Press, 2017).

71. Hugo Buchthal, "The Exaltation of David," *Journal of the Warburg and Courtauld
Institutes* 37 (1974): 330–333, esp. 332. See also
Hugo Buchthal, *The Miniatures of the Paris
Psalter: A Study in Middle Byzantine Painting*, Studies of the Warburg Institute 2 (London: Warburg Institute, 1938).

72. On this unique depiction of the act of
viewing, see Paroma Chatterjee, "Viewing
and Description in *Hysmine and Hysminias*:
The Fresco of the Virtues," *Dumbarton Oaks
Papers* 67 (2013): 209–225.

73. Eustathios (or Eumathios) Makrembolites, *Hysmine and Hysminias* 2.9.2–3, trans.
Elizabeth Jeffreys, *Four Byzantine Novels*
(Liverpool: Liverpool University Press, 2012),
159–269, at 189; ed. M. Marcovich, *Eustathius
Macrembolites De Hysmines et Hysminiae
amoribus libri XI*, Bibliotheca scriptorum
Graecorum et Romanorum Teubneriana
(Munich-Leipzig: K. G. Saur, 2001).

74. Eustathios (or Eumathios) Makrembolites, *Hysmine and Hysminias* 2.11.3, trans.
Jeffreys, *Four Byzantine Novels*, 190; ed. Marcovich, *De Hysmines et Hysminiae*.

75. Liz James, *Light and Colour in Byzantine Art* (Oxford: Clarendon Press, 1996), esp.
49, 73.

76. James, *Light and Colour*, 77 and 119–121.

77. *Suda Lexicon*, kappa 2580, ed. and
trans. William Hutton, "*Kuaneoi*," *Suda On
Line*, ed. David Whitehead, www.stoa.org
/sol-entries/kappa/2580.

78. Hesychius, *Lexicon*, kappa 4350, 4348,
4347, ed. K. Latte, *Hesychii Alexandrini lexicon*, vol. 2 (Copenhagen: Munksgaard, 1966).

79. For textual descriptions, see Kathleen
Ann Kelly, "'Blue' Indians, Ethiopians, and
Saracens in Middle English Narrative Texts,"
Parergon 11:1 (1993): 35–52. For depictions in
art, see Debra Higgs Strickland, *Saracens,
Demons, and Jews: Making Monsters in Medieval Art* (Princeton: Princeton University
Press, 2003), esp. 89–90.

80. In the recent past, two events have
marked the popular perception of the intersection of gender variance and racial identity: the coming out of Caitlyn Jenner as a
transgender woman and the revelation that
Rachel Dolezal, the former president of the
NAACP chapter in Spokane, Washington,
was white despite having claimed to be and
having identified as African American. This
has led to an unsavory association between

transgender and transracial identities, as some assume that if it is possible to transition genders, then it is also possible to transition racial identities. However, such logic overlooks the fact that to be transgender is to desire to *affirm* one's gender, not to selectively *reassign* it. The entanglement of transgender and transracial is deeply problematic, as it fails in myriad ways to grapple with the realities of racial inequality: systematic oppression, white privilege, racial passing, the history of blackface as a form of racial "cross-dressing," and so on. For a somewhat flawed survey of this intermeshing and the germane arguments, see Rogers Brubaker, *Trans: Gender and Race in an Age of Unsettled Identities* (Princeton: Princeton University Press, 2016).

81. Kathryn Bond Stockton, "The Queerness of Race and Same-Sex Desire," in *The Cambridge Companion to Gay and Lesbian Writing*, ed. H. Stevens (Cambridge: Cambridge University Press, 2010), 116–131, esp. 118.

82. See André Grabar, "Le schéma iconographique de la Pentecôte," in *L'Art de la fin de l'Antiquité et du Moyen âge*, 3 vols. (Paris: Collège de France, 1968), 1:615–627. For a more generalist survey of this material, which is to be used with caution, see Jean Devisse, "The Black and His Color: From Symbols to Realities," in *The Image of the Black in Western Art*, ed. David Bindman and Henry Louis Gates, Jr., new ed., vol. 2.1 (Cambridge, MA: Belknap Press of Harvard University Press, 2010), 73–137.

EPILOGUE

1. Michael Camille, *Image on the Edge: The Margins of Medieval Art* (London: Reaktion Books, 1992), 10.

2. On ethics in medieval art history, see Roland Betancourt, "Beyond Foucault's Laugh: On the Ethical Practice of Medieval Art History," *Postcolonising the Medieval Image*, eds. Eva Frojmovic and Catherine Karkov (London: Routledge/Ashgate, 2017), 144–166.

3. Camille, *Image on the Edge*, 10.

4. On Michael Camille's respectability politics and professional failure, see Roland Betancourt, "Faltering Images: Failure and Error in Byzantine Manuscript Illumination," *Word & Image* 32:1 (2016): 1–20, esp. 16.

BIBLIOGRAPHY

ABBREVIATIONS

PG Jacques-Paul Minge, *Patrologia cursus completes. Series Graeca* (Paris: Migne, 1857–1866).

PL Jacques-Paul Minge, *Patrologia cursus completes. Series Latina* (Paris: Migne, 1844–1864).

PRIMARY SOURCES

The Acts of Paul and Thecla. Translated by J. K. Elliott, *The Apocryphal New Testament* (Oxford: Clarendon Press, 1993), 364–374.

Acts of the Protaton. Edited and translated by Denise Papachryssanthou, *Actes du Prôtaton* (Paris: P. Lethielleux, 1975).

Aetius of Amida, *Tetrabiblos*. Edited by Janus Cornarius, *Aetii Medici Graeci Contractae ex veteribus medicinae tetrabiblos* (Basel: Froben & Episcopius, 1542). Edited by Skévos Zervos, *Gynaekologie des Aëtios* (Leipzig: Fock, 1901). Partially translated by James V. Ricci, *Aetios of Amida: The Gynaecology and Obstetrics of the VIth Century, A.D.* (Philadelphia: Blakiston Company, 1950).

Andrew of Crete, *Homily on the Annunciation*. Translated by Mary B. Cunningham, "Oration on the Annunciation of the Supremely Holy Lady, Our Theotokos" in *Wider Than Heaven: Eighth-Century Homilies on the Mother of God* (Crestwood: St. Vladimir's Seminary Press, 2008), 197–219.

Apocalypse of Peter. Edited and translated by Dennis D. Buchholz, *Your Eyes Will Be Opened: A Study of the Greek (Ethiopic) Apocalypse of Peter* (Atlanta: Scholars Press, 1988).

Apocryphon of John. Translated by Michael Waldstein and Frederik Wisse (Leiden: Brill, 1995).

Aristotle, *Generation of Animals*. Edited and translated by A. L. Peck, Loeb Classical Library 366 (Cambridge: Harvard University Press, 1942).

———, *Politics*. Edited and translated by H. Rackham, Loeb Classical Library 264 (Cambridge: Harvard University Press, 1932).

Athanasius I, *Didaskaliai*, 1762 (cf. 1777). Text in Vat. Gr. 2219. Translated by V. Laurent, *Les regestes des actes du patriarcat de Constantinople*, I, vol. 4 (Paris: Institut Français d'Études Byzantines, 1971).

Basil of Ancyra, *On the True Purity of Virginity*. Edited by PG 30:670–810.

Basil of Caesarea, *Letters*. Edited and translated by Roy J. Deferrari, 4 vols., Loeb Classical Library 190, 215, 243, 270 (Cambridge: Harvard University Press, 1926–1934).

Basilakes, Nikephoros, *Rhetorical Exercises*. Edited and translated by Jeffrey Beneker and Craig A. Gibson, *The Rhetorical Exercises of Nikephoros Basilakes*: Progymnasmata *from Twelfth-Century Byzantium*, Dumbarton Oaks Medieval Library 43 (Cambridge: Harvard University Press, 2016).

Bernard of Clairvaux, *In Praise of the Virgin Mother*. Translated by Marie-Bernard Saïd and Grace Perigo, *Magnificat: Homilies in Praise of the Blessed Virgin Mary* (Kalamazoo: Cistercian Publications, 1979).

Cabasilas, Nicholas, *Homily on the Annunciation*. Edited by M. Jugie, *Homélies mariales byzantines*, vol. 2. Patrologia Orientalis 19:3 (Paris: Firmin-Didot, 1925–1926), 484–495.

Cassius, Dio, *Roman History*. Edited and translated by Earnest Cary and Herbert B. Foster, 9 vols., Loeb Classical Library 32, 37, 53, 66, 82–83, 175–177 (Cambridge: Harvard University Press, 1914–1927).

Choniates, Niketas, *Chronicle*. Edited by J. van Dieten, *Nicetae Choniatae historia, pars prior*, Corpus Fontium Historiae Byzantinae, Series Berolinensis 11:1 (Berlin: De Gruyter, 1975). Translated by Henry J. Magoulias, *O City of Byzantium, Annals of Niketas Choniates* (Detroit: Wayne State University Press, 1984).

Chrysostom, John, *Homilies on the Gospel of John*. Edited by PG 59:23–483. Translated by Philip Schaff, "Homilies on the Gospel of St. John" in *Nicene and Post-Nicene Fathers*, edited by Philip Schaff, First Series, vol. 14 (Buffalo, NY: Christian Literature Publishing, 1889), 1–334.

———, *Homilies on Matthew*. Edited by PG 57 and 58.

———, *Homilies on Romans*. Edited by PG 60:395–681. Translated by J. B. Morris and W. H. Simcox, "Homilies on Romans" in *Nicene and Post-Nicene Fathers*, edited by Philip Schaff, First Series, vol. 11 (Buffalo: Christian Literature Publishing, 1889), 335–566.

———, *On Genesis*. Edited by. PG 53:125–135.

Climacus, John, *Heavenly Ladder*, 26. Edited by PG 88:579–1211. Translated by Colm Luibheid and Norman Russell, *The Ladder of Divine Ascent* (Mahwah: Paulist Press, 1982).

Constantine VII Porphyrogenitus, *Life of Basil I*. Edited and translated by Ihor Ševčenko, *Chronographiae quae Theophanus Continuati nomine fertur liber quo vita Basilii imperatoris amplectitur* (Berlin: De Gruyter, 2011).

Council in Trullo. Edited and translated by George Nedungatt and Michael Featherstone, *The Council in Trullo Revisited* (Rome: Pontifico Instituto Orientale, 1995).

Council of Ancyra. Translated by Henry R. Percival, "The Canons of the Council of Ancyra" in *Nicene and Post-Nicene Fathers*, edited by Philip Schaff and Henry Wace, Second Series, vol. 14, reprint (Grand Rapids: Wm. B. Eerdmans Publishing, 1964), 63–75.

Council of Gangra. Translated by Henry R. Percival, "The Council of Gangra" in *Nicene and Post-Nicene Fathers*, edited by Philip Schaff and Henry Wace, Second Series, vol. 14, reprint (Grand Rapids: Wm. B. Eerdmans Publishing, 1964), 89–101.

Cyril of Alexandria, *Homilies*. Edited by PG 77:391–1119.

Cyril of Rakote, *Homily*. Edited and translated by E. A. Wallis Budge, "The Discourse of Saint Cyril, Archbishop of Rakote, on the Virgin Mary" in *Miscellaneous Coptic Texts in the Dialect of Upper Egypt*, vol. 5 (London: British Museum, 1915), 139–146, 717–724.

Cyril of Scythopolis, *Lives of the Monks of Palestine*. Translated by R. M. Price and John Binns (Kalamazoo: Cistercian Publications, 1991).

de Clari, Robert, *The Conquest of Constantinople*. Edited by Charles Hope, "La prise de Constantinople" in *Chroniques Gréco-Romanes* (Berlin: Librairie de Weidmann, 1873), 1–85. Translated by Edgar Holmes McNeal, *The Conquest of Constantinople* (New York: Columbia University Press, 1936).

Digenis Akritis. Edited and translated by Elizabeth Jeffreys, *Digenis Akritis: The Grottaferrata and Escorial Versions* (Cambridge: Cambridge University Press, 1998).

Digest. Edited and translated by Alan Watson, Theodor Mommsen, and Paul Krueger, *The Digest of Justinian*, 4 vols. (Philadelphia: University of Pennsylvania Press, 1985).

Empiricus, Sextus *Adversus mathematicos*. Edited by J. Mau and H. Mutschmann, *Sexti Empirici opera*, vol. 2 (Leipzig: Teubner, 1914). Translated by A. A. Long and D. N. Sedley, *The Hellenistic Philosophers*, vol. 1 (Cambridge: Cambridge University Press, 1987).

Epitome of Caesaribus. Edited by F. Pichlmayr, *Sextii Aurelii Victoris Liber de Caesaribus* (Leipzig: Teubner, 1911).

Eustathios of Thessaloniki, *Epitaphios for Manuel I Komnenos*. Edited and translated by Emmanuel C. Bourbouhakis, *Not Composed in a Chance Manner: The Epitaphios for Manuel I Komnenos by Eustathios of Thessaloniki* (Uppsala: Uppsala Universitet, 2017).

———, *Orations*. Edited by P. Wirth, *Eustathii Thessalonicensis opera minora (magnam partem inedita*), Corpus Fontium Historiae Byzantinae, Series Berolinensis 32 (Berlin: De Gruyter, 1999). Translated by Andrew F. Stone, *Eustathios of Thessaloniki. Secular Orations: 1167/8 to 1179* (Brisbane: Australian Association for Byzantine Studies, 2013).

Germanus of Constantinople, *Homily on the Annunciation* (or Homily 5). Edited by PG 98:319–339. Translated by Mary B. Cunningham, "Oration on the Annunciation of the Supremely Holy Theotokos" in *Wider Than Heaven: Eighth-Century Homilies on the Mother of God* (Crestwood: St. Vladimir's Seminary Press, 2008), 221–246.

Glykas, Michael, *Chronicle*. Edited by I. Bekker, *Michaelis Glycae annals*, Corpus scriptorum historiae Byzantinae (Bonn: Weber, 1836).

———, *Questions in the Holy Scripture*. Edited by S. Eustratiades, Εἰς τὰς ἀπορίας τῆς Θείας Γραφῆς (Athens: P. D. Sakellarios, 1906).

Gospel of Thomas. Translated by J. K. Elliott, in *The Apocryphal New Testament* (Oxford: Clarendon Press, 1993), 135–147.

Gregory of Elvira, *Explanation of the Song of Songs*. Translated by J. Robert Wright, *Proverbs, Ecclesiastes, Song of Solomon*, Ancient Christian Commentary on Scripture, Old Testament 9 (Downers Grove: InterVarsity Press, 2005).

Gregory of Nazianzus, *First Letter to Cledonius* (Ep. 101). Edited by P. Gallay, *Lettres théologiques*, Sources chrétiennes 208 (Paris: Éditions du Cerf, 1974), 36–68. Translated by Lionel Wickham, "Letter 101: The First Letter to Cledonius the Presbyter" in *On God and Christ: The Five Theological Orations and Two Letters to Cledonius* (Crestwood: St. Vladimir's Seminary Press, 2002), 155–166.

Gregory of Nyssa, *Homilies on the Song of Songs*. Translated by Richard A. Norris, Jr., *Gregory of Nyssa: Homilies on the Song of Songs* (Atlanta: Society of Biblical Literature, 2012).

Gregory of Tours, *History of the Franks*. Translated by Ernest Brehaut (New York: Columbia University Press, 1916).

Gregory the Great, *Letters*. Edited by PL 77:431–1327.

Hermogenes, *On Types of Style*. Translated by Cecil W. Wooten, *Hermogenes' On Types of Style* (Chapel Hill: University of North Carolina Press, 1987).

Herodian, *History of the Empire*. Edited and translated by C. R. Whittaker, 2 vols., Loeb Classical Library 454–455 (Cambridge: Harvard University Press, 1969–1970).

Hesychius, *Lexicon*. Edited by Kurt Latte, *Hesychii Alexandrini lexicon*, 2 vols. (Copenhagen: Munksgaard, 1953–1966).

Hippocrates of Cos, *Airs, Waters, Places*. Edited and translated by W. H. S. Jones, *Hippocrates*, vol. 1, Loeb Classical Library 147 (Cambridge: Harvard University Press, 1923), 65–137.

———, *The Oath*. Edited and translated by W. H. S. Jones, *Ancient Medicine*, Loeb Classical Library 147 (Cambridge: Harvard University Press, 1923), 298–301.

Hypostasis of the Archons, The. Translated by Bentley Layton, "The Hypostasis of the Archons," in *The Nag Hammadi Library in English*, edited by James M. Robinson, 3rd ed. (Leiden: Brill, 1990), 161–169.

Irenaeus, *Against Heresies*. Translated by Alexander Roberts and James Donaldson, "Against Heresies" in *Ante-Nicene Fathers*, vol. 1, reprint (Grand Rapids: Wm. B. Eerdmans Publishing, 1956), 315–567.

John of Antioch, *Fragments*. Edited by K. Müller, *Fragmenta historicorum Graecorum*, vol. 4 (Paris: Didot, 1851).

John of Damascus, *Barlaam and Ioasaph*. Edited and translated by G. R. Woodward and Harold Mattingly, Loeb Classical Library 34 (Cambridge: Harvard University Press, 1914).

———, *Exposition of the Faith*. Translated by S. D. F. Salmond, "Exposition of the Orthodox Faith" in *Nicene and Post-Nicene Fathers*. Edited by Philip Schaff and Henry Wace, Second Series, vol. 9, reprint (Grand Rapids: Wm. B. Eerdmans Publishing, 1963), 1–101.

Juvenal, *Satires*. Edited and translated by Susanna Morton Braund, *Juvenal and Persius*, Loeb Classical Library 91 (Cambridge: Harvard University Press, 2004).

Kokkinobaphos, James, *Homilies on the Virgin*. Edited by PG 127:543–700.

Komnena, Anna, *The Alexiad*. Edited by A. Kambylis and D. R. Reinsch, *Annae Comnenae Alexias*, Corpus Fontium Historiae Byzantinae, Series Berolinensis 60.1

(Berlin: De Gruyter, 2001). Translated by E. R. A. Sewter, *The Alexiad*, revised (New York: Penguin Books, 2009).

"La Vie Ancienne de Sainte Marie surnommée Marinos." Edited by Marcel Richard, in *Corona Gratiarum: Miscellanea Patristica, Historica et Liturgica Eligio Dekkers O. S. B. XII Lustra Complenti Oblata* (Bruges: Sint Pietersabdij, 1975), 83–115.

Laertius, Diogenes, *Lives of Eminent Philosophers*. Edited and translated by R. D. Hicks, 2 vols., Loeb Classical Library 184–185 (Cambridge, MA: Harvard University Press, 1925).

Leontius of Neapolis, *Life of Symeon the Holy Fool*. Edited by A.-J. Festugière and L. Rydén, *Vie de Syméon le Fou*, Bibliothèque archéologique et historique 95 (Paris: Geuthner, 1974). Translated by Derek Krueger, "Life of Symeon the Fool" in *Symeon the Holy Fool: Leontius' Life and the Late Antique City* (Berkeley: University of California Press, 1996), 121–170.

Life of Anastasius. Translated by Sebastian P. Brock and Susan Ashbrook Harvey, "Anastasia," in *Holy Women of the Syrian Orient* (Berkeley: University of California Press, 1987), 142–149.

Life of Athanasius. Edited and translated by Anne P. Alwis, "The *Vita* of Andronikos and Athanasia," in *Celibate Marriages in Late Antique and Byzantine Hagiography: The Lives of Saints Julian and Basilissa, Andronikos and Athanasia, and Galaktion and Episteme* (London: Bloomsbury, 2011), 249–277.

Life of Dorotheos. Edited and translated by James Drescher, "The Life of St. Apolinaria" in *Three Coptic Legends* (Cairo: Institut Français d'Archéologie Orientale, 1947), 152–161.

Life of Eugenia. Translated by Agnes Smith Lewis, "Eugenia" in *Select Narratives of Holy Women: From the Syro-Antiochene or Sinai Palimpsest* (London: C. J. Clay, 1900), 1–34.

Life of Euphemianos. Translated by Vasileios Marinis, "The Life of St. Anna/Euphemianos," *Journal of Modern Hellenism* 27 (2009–2010): 53–69.

Life of Hilarion. Edited and translated by James Drescher, "Hilaria" in *Three Coptic Legends* (Cairo: Institut Français d'Archéologie Orientale, 1947), 1–13, 69–82.

Life of Marinos. Translated by Nicholas Constas, "Life of St. Mary/Marinos" in *Holy Women of Byzantium: Ten Saints' Lives in English Translation*, edited by Alice-Mary Talbot (Washington, DC: Dumbarton Oaks, 1996), 1–12.

Life of Mary of Egypt. Edited by PG 87:3697–3725. Translated by Maria Kouli, "The Life of St. Mary of Egypt" in *Holy Women of Byzantium: Ten Saints' Lives in English Translation*, edited by Alice-Mary Talbot (Washington, DC: Dumbarton Oaks, 1996), 65–93.

Life of Matrona of Perge. Translated by Jeffrey Featherstone and Cyril Mango, "Life of St. Matrona of Perge" in *Holy Women of Byzantium: Ten Saints' Lives in English Translation*, edited by Alice-Mary Talbot (Washington, DC: Dumbarton Oaks, 1996), 13–64.

Life of Pelagius. Translated by Sebastian P. Brock and Susan Ashbrook Harvey, "Pelagia of Antioch" in *Holy Women of the Syrian Orient* (Berkeley: University of California Press, 1987), 40–62.

Life of Smaragdos (or *Life of Esmeraldus*). Translated by Agnes Smith Lewis, "Euphrosyne" in *Select Narratives of Holy Women: From the Syro-Antiochene or Sinai Palimpsest* (London: C. J. Clay, 1900), 46–59.

Life of Theodore of Alexandria. Edited by Karl Wessely, "Zu den griechischen Papyri des Louvre und der Bibliothèque nationale" in *Fünfzehnter Jahresbericht des K. K. Staatsgymnasiums in Hernals* (Vienna: Verlag des K. K. Staatsgymnasiums in Hernals, 1889), 3–44.

Liturgical Poem. Translated by Roland Betancourt, "A Byzantine Liturgical Commentary in Verse: Introduction and Translation," *Orientalia Christiana Periodica* 81 (2015): 433–472.

Liutprand of Cremona, *The Embassy to Constantinople*. Edited by P. Chiesa, *Liudprandi Cremonensis. Opera omnia*, Corpus Christianorum 156 (Turnhout: Brepols, 1998), 187–218. Translated by F. A. Wright, *The Works of Liudprand of Cremona* (London: George Routledge and Sons, 1930), 233–277.

Logothete, Symeon (Leo Grammatikos), *Chronicle*. Edited by I. Bekker, *Leonis Grammatici chronographia*, Corpus

Scriptorium historiae Byzantinae (Bonn: Weber, 1842).

Lucian, *Dialogues of the Courtesans*. Edited and translated by M. D. MacLeod, *Lucian*, vol. 7, Loeb Classical Library 431 (Cambridge: Harvard University Press, 1961), 355–467.

———, *Philosophies for Sale*. Edited and translated by A. M. Harmon, *Lucian*, vol. 2, Loeb Classical Library 54 (Cambridge: Harvard University Press, 1915), 449–511.

Lydus, John, *On Powers*. Edited and translated by Anastasius Bandy, *On Powers: Or, the Magistracies of the Roman State* (Philadelphia: American Philosophical Society, 1983).

Makrembolites, Eustathios (or Eumathios), *Hysmine and Hysminias*. Edited by M. Marcovich, *Eustathius Macrembolites De Hysmines et Hysminiae amoribus libri XI*, Bibliotheca Scriptorium Graecorum et Romanorum Teubneriana (Munich-Leipzig: K. G. Saur, 2001). Translated by Elizabeth Jeffreys, *Four Byzantine Novels* (Liverpool: Liverpool University Press, 2012), 159–269.

Malalas, John, *Chronicles*. Edited and translated by Elizabeth Jeffreys, Michael Jeffreys, and Roger Scott, *The Chronicle of John Malalas* (Melbourne: Australian Association for Byzantine Studies, 1986).

Martyr, Justin, *Dialogue with Trypho*. Edited by E. J. Goodspeed, *Die ältesten Apologeten* (Göttingen: Vandenhoeck & Ruprecht, 1915). Translated by Alexander Roberts and James Donaldson, "Dialogue with Trypho" in *Ante-Nicene Fathers*, vol. 1, reprint (Grand Rapids: Wm. B. Eerdmans Publishing, 1956), 194–270.

———, *First Apology*. Translated by Alexander Roberts and James Donaldson, "The First Apology" in *Ante-Nicene Fathers*, vol. 1, reprint (Grand Rapids: Wm. B. Eerdmans Publishing, 1956), 159–187.

Martyrdom and Ascension of Isaiah. Translated by M. A. Knibb, "Martyrdom and Ascension of Isaiah" in *The Old Testament Pseudepigrapha*, edited by James H. Charlesworth, vol. 1 (Peabody: Hendrickson Publishers, 1983), 174.

Martyrdom of Saints Perpetua and Felicitas. Edited and translated by Herbert Musurillo, in *The Acts of the Christian Martyrs* (Oxford: Clarendon Press, 1972), 106–131.

Maximus the Confessor, *Four Hundred Chapters on Love*. Translated by George C. Berthold, *Maximus the Confessor: Selected Writings* (New York: Paulist Press, 1985), 33–98.

———, *Opusculum*. Ed. PG 91:65A–68D. Translated by Paul M. Blowers and Robert Louis Wilken, "On the Two Wills of Christ in the Agony of Gethsemane" in *On the Cosmic Mystery of Jesus Christ* (Yonkers: St. Vladimir's Seminary Press, 2003), 173–176.

———, *Scholia on the Divine Names*. Edited by PG 4:185–415.

Mesarites, Nicholas, *Description of the Church of Holy Apostles*. Edited and translated by G. Downey, "Nikolaos Mesarites: Description of the Church of the Holy Apostles at Constantinople," *Transactions of the American Philosophical Society* n.s., 47:6 (1957): 855–924.

Middle Assyrian Laws, Tablet A.40. Translated by Theophile J. Meek, "The Middle Assyrian Laws" in *Ancient Near Eastern Texts: Relating to the Old Testament*, edited by James B. Pritchard, 3rd edition (Princeton: Princeton University Press, 1969), 180–188.

Monastery of the Theotokos Evergetis, *Synaxarion*. Edited and translated by Robert H. Jordan, *The Synaxarion of the Monastery of the Theotokos Evergetis*, 2 vols. (Belfast: Queen's University Belfast, 2000–2005).

Moschus, John, *The Spiritual Meadow*. Translated by John Wortley, *The Spiritual Meadow of John Moschus* (Kalamazoo: Cistercian Publications, 1992).

Mytilene, Christopher, *Poems*. Edited and translated by Floris Bernard and Christopher Livanos, *The Poems of Christopher Mytilene and John Mauropous* (Cambridge: Harvard University Press, 2018).

Narsai of Edessa, *Homilies on Creation*. Edited by Philippe Gignoux, *Homélies de Narsaï sur la création*. Patrologia Orientalis 34 (Turnhout: Brepols, 1968).

———, *Homily*. Edited by A. Mingana, *Homiliae et carmina* (Mosul: Typis Fratrum praedicatorum, 1905).

Nemesius of Emesa, *On the Nature of Man*. Edited by M. Morani, *De natura hominis* (Leipzig: Teubner, 1987). Translated by R. W. Sharples and P. J. van der Eijk, *On the Nature of Man* (Liverpool: Liverpool University Press, 2008).

Nicholas and Theodore of Andida, *Protheoria*. Edited by PG 140:413–468.

Origen, *Against Celsus*. Edited by M. Borret, *Contre Celse*, 5 vols., Sources chrétiennes 132, 136, 147, 150, 227 (Paris: Éditions du Cerf, 1967–1976). Translated by Henry Chadwick, *Origen: Contra Celsum*, corrected ed. (Cambridge: Cambridge University Press, 1965).

———, *Commentary on the Song of Songs*. Translated by R. P. Lawson, *Origen: The Song of Songs Commentary and Homilies*, Ancient Christian Writers 26 (Westminster, MD: Newman Press, 1957).

———, *Homilies on Jeremiah*. Translated by John Clark Smith, *Origen: Homilies on Jeremiah and 1 Kings 28*, Fathers of the Church 97 (Washington, DC: Catholic University of America Press, 1998).

Pachomius, *Pachomian Koinonia: The Lives, Rules, and Other Writings of Saint Pachomius and his Disciples*. Translated by Armand Veilleux, 3 vols. (Kalamazoo: Cistercian Publications, 1980–1982).

Paphlagon, Niketas David, *The Life of Patriarch Ignatius*. Edited and translated by Andrew Smithies (Washington, DC: Dumbarton Oaks, 2013).

Paul of Aegina, *Medical Compendium*. Edited by J. L. Heiberg, *Paulus Aegineta*, 2 vols., Corpus medicorum Graecorum 9.1–2 (Leipzig: Teubner, 1921–1924). Translated by Francis Adam, *The Seven Books of Paulus Aegineta*, 3 vols. (London: Sydenham Society, 1844–1847).

Paul the Deacon, *The Lives of the Fathers of Mérida*. Edited by A. Maya Sánchez, *Vitas Sanctorum Patrum Emeretensium*, Corpus Christianorum Series Latina 116 (Turnholt: Brepols, 1992). Translated by A. T. Fear, *Lives of the Visigothic Fathers* (Liverpool: Liverpool University Press, 1997), 45–105.

Pélagie la Pénitente: Métamorphoses d'une légende. Edited by Pierre Petitmengin et al., 2 vols. (Paris: Études Agustiniennes, 1981).

Philo of Alexandria, *On Abraham*. Edited and translated by F. H. Colson, *Philo. On Abraham*, vol. 6, Loeb Classical Library 289 (Cambridge: Harvard University Press, 1935).

———, *Questions and Answers on Exodus*. Edited and translated by Ralph Marcus, *Questions on Exodus*, Loeb Classical Library 401 (Cambridge: Harvard University Press, 1953).

Philostratus of Athens, *Lives of the Sophists*. Edited and translated by Wilmer C. Wright, Loeb Classical Library 134 (Cambridge: Harvard University Press, 1921).

Philostratus the Elder, *Imagines*. Edited and translated by Arthur Fairbanks, Loeb Classical Library 256 (Cambridge: Harvard University Press, 1931).

Photius, *Bibliotheca*. Translated by J. H. Freese, *The Library of Photius* (New York: Macmillan, 1920).

———, *Homilies*. Edited by Basileiou Laourda, OMIΛIAI (Thessaloniki: Hetaireia Makedonikōn Spoudōn, 1959). Translated by Cyril Mango, *The Homilies of Photius Patriarch of Constantinople* (Cambridge: Harvard University Press, 1958).

Plato, *Laws*. Edited and translated by R. G. Bury, 2 vols., Loeb Classical Library 187 and 192 (Cambridge: Harvard University Press, 1926).

———, *Republic*. Edited and translated by Christopher Emlyn-Jones and William Preddy, 2 vols., Loeb Classical Library 237 and 276 (Cambridge: Harvard University Press, 2013).

———, *Theaetetus*. Edited and translated by Harold North Fowler, Loeb Classical Library 123 (Cambridge: Harvard University Press, 1921).

Pliny the Elder, *Natural History*. Edited and translated by H. Rackham, 10 vols., Loeb Classical Library 330, 352–353, 370–371, 392–394, 418–419 (Cambridge: Harvard University Press, 1938–1962).

Proclus of Constantinople, *Homilies*. Edited and translated by Nicholas Constas, *Proclus of Constantinople and the Cult of the Virgin in Late Antiquity* (Leiden: Brill, 2003).

Procopius, *Buildings*. Edited and translated by H. B. Dewing and Glanville Downey, *On Buildings*, Loeb Classical Library 343 (Cambridge, MA: Harvard University Press, 1940).

———, *The Secret History*. Edited by G. Wirth, *Procopii Caesariensis opera omnia*, vol. 3 (Leipzig: Teubner, 1963). Translated by Anthony Kaldellis, *The Secret History with*

Related Texts (Indianapolis: Hackett Publishing, 2010).

———, *Wars*. Edited and translated by H. B. Dewing, *History of the Wars*, 5 vols., Loeb Classical Library 48, 81, 107, 173, 217 (Cambridge: Harvard University Press, 1914–1928).

The Prose Salernitan Questions. Edited by Brian Lawn (London: Oxford University Press for the British Academy, 1979).

Protoevangelium of James. Translated by J. K. Elliott, *The Apocryphal New Testament* (Oxford: Oxford University Press, 1993), 48–67.

Psellus, Michael, *Chronographia*. Edited by Diether Roderich Reinsch, 2 vols. (Berlin: De Gruyter, 2014).

———, *Encomium for their Mother*. Edited by U. Criscuolo, *Autobiografia: ecomio per la madre* (Naples: M. D'Auria, 1989). Translated by Anthony Kaldellis, "Encomium for his Mother" in *Mothers and Sons, Fathers and Daughters: The Byzantine Family of Michael Psellos*, edited and translated by Anthony Kaldellis, (Notre Dame: University of Notre Dame, 2006), 51–109.

———, *Letters*. Edited by Paul Gautier, "Quelques lettres de Psellos inédites ou déjà éditées," *Revue des Études Byzantines* 44 (1986): 111–197.

———, *Letters to Michael Keroularios*. Translated by Anthony Kaldellis and Ioannis Polemis, "Letter to the Patriarch Kyr Michael Keroullarios" in *Psellos and the Patriarchs: Letters and Funeral Orations for Keroullarios, Leichoudes, and Xiphilinos*, edited by Anthony Kaldellis and Ioannis Polemis (South Bend: University of Notre Dame, 2015), 37–48.

Pseudo-Demetrius of Antioch, *Homily*. Edited and translated by E. A. Wallis Budge, "The Discourse by Demetrius, Archbishop of Antioch, on the birth, according to the flesh of God the Word, and on the Virgin Mary" in *Miscellaneous Coptic Texts in the Dialect of Upper Egypt*, vol. 5 (London: British Museum, 1915), 74–119, 652–698.

Pseudo-Epiphanius, *Homily*. Edited and translated by Budge, "The Discourse of Apa Epiphanius, Bishop of Cyprus, on the Holy Virgin, Mary Theotokos" in *Miscellaneous Coptic Texts in the Dialect of Upper Egypt*, vol. 5 (London: British Museum, 1915), 120–138, 699–716.

Pseudo-Gregory Thaumaturgus, *Homilies*. Translated by S. D. F. Salmond, "Four Homilies" in *Ante-Nicene Fathers*, edited by Alexander Roberts and James Donaldson, vol. 6, reprint (Grand Rapids: Wm. B. Eerdmans Publishing, 1957), 58–71.

Romaios, Eustathios, *Legal Opinion*. Edited by A. Schminck, "Vier eherechtliche Entscheidungen," *Fontes Minores* 3 (1979): 224–228. Translated by Denis Sullivan, "Appendix: Legal Opinion of Eusthatios (Romaios) the Magistros (after 1028)" in A. Laiou, "Sex, Consent, and Coercion" in *Consent and Coercion to Sex and Marriage in Ancient and Medieval Societies*, edited by A. Laiou (Washington, DC: Dumbarton Oaks, 1998), 109–221.

Romanos the Melodist, *Akathist Hymn*. Edited and translated by Leena M. Peltomaa, *The Image of the Virgin Mary in the Akathistos Hymn* (Leiden: Brill, 2001).

———, *Hymns*. Edited by Jean Grosdidier de Matons, *Romanos le Mélode. Hymnes*, 5 vols., Sources Chrétiennes 99, 110, 114, 123, 283 (Paris: Éditions du Cerf, 1964–1981). Edited and translated by Thomas Arentzen, "On the Annunciation" in *The Virgin in Song: Mary and the Poetry of Romanos the Melodist* (Philadelphia: University of Pennsylvania Press, 2017), 175–187. Translated by Ephrem Lash, *On the Life of Christ: Kontakia* (New York: Harper Collins, 1995).

Saint Daniel of Sketis: A Group of Hagiographic Texts. Edited and translated by Britt Dahlman, Studia Byzantina Upsaliensia 10 (Uppsala: Uppsala University, 2007).

Sarah, *The Sayings of the Desert Fathers: The Alphabetical Collection*. Translated by Benedicta Ward (Kalamazoo: Cistercian Publications, 1975).

Skoutariotes, Theodore, *Chronicle*. Edited by R. Tocci, *Theodori Scutariotae chronica*, Corpus Fontium Historiae Byzantinae, Series Berolinensis 46 (Berlin: De Gruyter, 2015).

Skylitzes, John, *A Synopsis of Byzantine History*. Edited by J. Thurn, *Synopsis historiarum*. Corpus Fontium Historiae Byzantinae, Series Berolinensis 5 (Berlin: De Gruyter, 1973). Translated by John Wortley, *A Synopsis of Byzantine History, 811–1057* (Cambridge: Cambridge University Press, 2010).

Soranus of Ephesus, *Gynecology*. Translated by Owsei Temkin, *Soranus' Gynecology* (Baltimore: Johns Hopkins University Press, 1956).

Suda Lexicon. Edited and translated by David Whitehead, *Suda On Line*, www.stoa.org.

Symeon the New Theologian, *Hymns*. Edited by Athanasios Kambylis, *Symeon Neos Theologos, Hymnen*, Supplementa Byzantina 3 (Berlin: De Gruyter, 1976). Translated by Daniel K. Griggs, *Divine Eros: Hymns of St. Symeon the New Theologian* (Yonkers: St. Vladimir's Seminary Press, 2010).

Synkellos, George, *Chronography*. Edited by A. A. Mosshammer, *Georgius Syncellus. Ecloga chronographica* (Leipzig: Teubner, 1984). Translated by William Alder and Paul Tuffin, *The Chronography of George Synkellos: A Byzantine Chronicle of Universal History from the Creation* (Oxford: Oxford University Press, 2002).

Theodoret of Cyrus, *Commentary on the Song of Songs*. Translated by Robert C. Hill, *Theodoret of Cyrus: Commentary on the Song of Songs*, Early Christian Studies 2 (Brisbane: Australian Catholic University, 2001).

Theodosian Code, The. Translated by Clyde Pharr (Princeton: Princeton University Press, 1952).

SECONDARY SOURCES

Abusch, Ra'anan, "Eunuchs and Gender Transformation: Philo's Exegesis of the Joseph Narrative" in *Eunuchs in Antiquity and Beyond*, edited by Shaun Tougher (London: Duckworth, 2002), 103–121.

Ahmed, Sara, *Queer Phenomenology: Orientations, Objects, Others* (Durham: Duke University Press, 2006).

Ahonen, Marke, *Mental Disorders in Ancient Philosophy* (Berlin: Springer, 2014).

Allen, Pauline, "Contemporary Portrayals of the Byzantine Empress Theodora (A.D. 527–548)" in *Stereotypes of Women in Power: Historical Perspectives and Revisionist Views*, edited by Barbara Garlick, Suzanne Dixon, and Pauline Allen (New York: Greenwood Press, 1992), 93–103.

Ambrose, Kirk, "Two Cases of Female Cross-Undressing in Medieval Art and Literature," *Source: Notes in the History of Art* 23:3 (2004): 7–14.

Angelova, Diliana, *Sacred Founders: Women, Men, and Gods in the Discourse of Imperial Founding, Rome through Early Byzantium* (Berkeley: University of California Press, 2015).

Angold, Michael, "Procopius' Portrait of Theodora" in *Philellēn: Studies in Honour of Robert Browning*, edited by C. N. Constantinides et al. (Venice: Istituto Ellenico di Studi Bizantini e Postbizantini di Venezia, 1996), 21–34.

Anson, John, "The Female Transvestite in Early Monasticism: The Origin and Development of a Motif," *Viator* 5 (1974): 1–32.

Arentzen, Thomas, *The Virgin in Song: Mary and the Poetry of Romanos the Melodist* (Philadelphia: University of Pennsylvania Press, 2017).

———, "'Your Virginity Shines'—The Attraction of the Virgin in the *Annunciation Hymn* by Romanos the Melodist" in *Studia Patristica LXVII*, vol. 16, edited by Markus Vinzent (Leuven: Peeters, 2013), 125–132.

Arondekar, Anjali, *For the Record: On Sexuality and the Colonial Archive in India* (Durham: Duke University Press, 2009).

de Arrizabalaga y Prado, Leonardo, *The Emperor Elagabalus: Fact or Fiction?* (Cambridge: Cambridge University Press, 2010).

Aspegren, Kerstin, *The Male Woman: A Feminine Ideal in the Early Church*, edited by René Kieffer, Acta Universitatis Upsaliensis. Uppsala Women's Studies, A. Women in Religion 4 (Uppsala: Academia Ubsaliensis, 1990).

Baer, Jr., Richard A., *Philo's Use of the Categories Male and Female* (Leiden: Brill, 1970).

Baldwin, Barry, "Sexual Rhetoric in Procopius," *Mnemosyne* 40:1/2 (1987): 150–152.

Ball, Jennifer L., *Byzantine Dress: Representations of Secular Dress in Eighth- to Twelfth-Century Painting* (New York: Palgrave Macmillan, 2005).

Banchich, Thomas M. and Eugene N. Lane, *The History of Zonaras: From Alexander Servus to the Death of Theodosius the Great* (London: Routledge, 2009).

Barber, Charles, "Icons, Prayer, and Vision in the Eleventh Century" in *Byzantine Christianity*, edited by Derek Krueger (Minneapolis: Fortress Press, 2006), 149–163.

———, "Mimesis and Memory in the Narthex

Mosaics at the Nea Moni, Chios," *Art History* 24:3 (2001): 323–337.

Barmann, B. C., "The Mount Athos Epitome of Cassius Dio's Roman History," *Phoenix* 25:1 (1971): 58–67.

Beeley, Christopher A., "'Let This Cup Pass from Me' (*Matth.* 26:39): The Soul of Christ in Origen, Gregory Nazianzen, and Maximus the Confessor," *Studia Patristica* 63 (Leuven: Peeters, 2013): 29–43.

Behlmer, Heike, "Koptische Quellen zu (männlicher) 'Homosexualität,'" *Studien zur altägyptischen Kultur* 28 (2000): 27–53.

Bernal, Martin, *Black Athena: The Afroasiatic Roots of Classical Civilization*, 3 vols. (New Brunswick: Rutgers University Press, 1987–2006).

Bersani, Leo, *Homos* (Cambridge: Harvard University Press, 1996).

———, "Is the Rectum a Grave?" *October* 43 (1987): 197–222.

Betancourt, Roland, "Beyond Foucault's Laugh: On the Ethical Practice of Medieval Art History" in *Postcolonising the Medieval Image*, edited by Eva Frojmovic and Catherine Karkov (London: Routledge/Ashgate, 2017), 144–166.

———, "Faltering Images: Failure and Error in Byzantine Manuscript Illumination," *Word & Image* 32:1 (2016): 1–20.

———, "The Medium Is the Byzantine: Popular Culture and the Byzantine" in *The Middle Ages in the Modern World: Twenty-First Century Perspectives*, edited by Bettina Bildhauer and Chris Jones (Oxford: Oxford University Press, 2017), 305–336.

———, "Review of Averil Cameron, *Byzantine Matters*," *Journal of Modern Greek Studies* 34:2 (2016): 401–404.

———, *Sight, Touch, and Imagination in Byzantium* (Cambridge: Cambridge University Press, 2018).

Blöndal, Sigfús, *The Varangians of Byzantium*, translated by Benedikt S. Benedikz (Cambridge: Cambridge University Press, 1978).

Boeck, Elena, "Archaeology of Decadence: Uncovering Byzantium in Victorien Sardou's *Theodora*" in *Byzantium/Modernism: The Byzantine as Method in Modernity*, edited by Roland Betancourt and Maria Taroutina (Leiden: Brill, 2015), 102–132.

Bolin, Anne, "Transcending and Transgendering: Male-to-Female Transsexuals, Dichotomy, and Diversity" in *Third Sex, Third Gender: Beyond Sexual Dimorphism in Culture and History*, edited by Gilbert Herdt (New York: Zone Books, 1994), 447–485.

Bologne, Jean Claude, *La naissance interdite: stérilité, avortement, contraception au Moyen Age* (Paris: O. Orban, 1988).

Bornmann, Fritz, "Su alcuni passi di Procopio," *Studi Italiani di filologia classica* 50 (1978): 27–37.

Boswell, John, *Rediscovering Gay History: Archetypes of Gay Love in Christian History* (London: Gay Christian Movement, 1982).

———, *Same-Sex Unions in Premodern Europe* (New York: Villard Books, 1994).

Boyarin, Daniel, "What Do We Talk About When We Talk About Platonic Love?" in *Toward a Theology of Eros: Transfiguring Passion at the Limits of Discipline*, edited by Virginia Burrus and Catherine Keller (New York: Fordham University Press, 2006), 3–22.

Brakke, David, *Demons and the Making of the Monk: Spiritual Combat in Early Christianity* (Cambridge: Harvard University Press, 2006).

———, "Ethiopian Demons: Male Sexuality, the Black-Skinned Other, and the Monastic Self," *Journal of the History of Sexuality* 10:3/4 (2001): 501–535.

Brock, Sebastian P., *Bride of Light: Hymns on Mary from the Syriac Churches* (Kerala: St. Ephrem Ecumenical Research Institute, 1994).

———, "Poetry and Hymnography (3): Syriac" in *The Oxford Handbook of Early Christian Studies*, edited by Susan Ashbrook Harvey and David G. Hunter (Oxford: Oxford University Press, 2008), 657–671.

Brooten, Bernadette J., *Love Between Women: Early Christian Responses to Female Homoeroticism* (Chicago: University of Chicago Press, 1996).

Brown, Peter, *The Body and Society: Men, Women, and Sexual Renunciation in Early Christianity* (New York: Columbia University Press, 1988).

Brubaker, Leslie, "The Age of Justinian: Gender and Society" in *The Cambridge Companion to the Age of Justinian*, edited by Michael Maas (Cambridge: Cambridge University Press, 2005), 427–447.

———, "Sex, Lies, and Textuality: The

Secret History of Prokopios and the Rhetoric of Gender in Sixth-century Byzantium" in *Gender in the Early Medieval World: East and West, 300–900*, edited by Leslie Brubaker and Julia Smith (Cambridge: Cambridge University Press, 2004), 83–101.

———, "The Vienna Dioscurides and Anicia Juliana" in *Byzantine Garden Culture*, edited by Antony Littlewood, Henry Maguire, and Joachim Wolschke-Bulmahn (Washington, DC: Dumbarton Oaks, 2002), 189–214.

Brubaker, Rogers, *Trans: Gender and Race in an Age of Unsettled Identities* (Princeton: Princeton University Press, 2016).

Brundage, James, "Rape and Marriage in the Medieval Canon Law," *Revue de droit canonique* 28 (1978): 62–75.

Buchthal, Hugo, "The Exaltation of David," *Journal of the Warburg and Courtauld Institutes* 37 (1974): 330–333.

———, *The Miniatures of the Paris Psalter: A Study in Middle Byzantine Painting*, Studies of the Warburg Institute 2 (London: The Warburg Institute, 1938).

Buell, Denise K., *Why This New Race: Ethnic Reasoning in Early Christianity* (New York: Columbia University, 2005).

Bullough, Vern L., "Transvestites in the Middle Ages," *American Journal of Sociology* 79:6 (1974): 1381–1394.

———, "Transvestivism in the Middle Ages" in *Sexual Practices and the Medieval Church*, edited by Vern L. Bullough and James Brundage (Buffalo: Prometheus Books, 1982), 43–54.

Burrus, Virginia, *Saving Shame: Martyrs, Saints, and Other Abject Subjects* (Philadelphia: University of Pennsylvania Press, 2008).

———, *The Sex Lives of Saints: An Erotics of Ancient Hagiography* (Philadelphia: University of Pennsylvania Press, 2004).

———, "Theology and Eros after Nygren" in *Toward a Theology of Eros: Transfiguring Passion at the Limits of Discipline*, edited by Virginia Burrus and Catherine Keller (New York: Fordham University Press, 2006), xiii–xxi.

Bynum, Caroline Walker, *Holy Feast and Holy Fast: The Religious Significance of Food to Medieval Women* (Berkeley: University of California Press, 1987).

Byron, Gay L., *Symbolic Blackness and Ethnic Difference in Early Christian Literature* (New York: Routledge, 2002).

Cadden, Joan, *Meanings of Sex Difference in the Middle Ages: Medicine, Science, and Culture* (Cambridge: Cambridge University Press, 1993).

Cairns, Douglas L., *Aidōs: The Psychology and Ethics of Honour and Shame in Ancient Greek Literature* (Oxford: Clarendon Press, 1993).

Cameron, Alan, "The House of Anastasius," *Greek, Roman, and Byzantine Studies* 19 (1978): 259–276.

Cameron, Averil, *Byzantine Matters* (Princeton: Princeton University Press, 2014).

———, *Christianity and the Rhetoric of Empire: The Development of Christian Discourse* (Berkeley: University of California Press, 1991).

———, *Procopius and the Sixth Century* (Berkeley: University of California Press, 1985).

Camille, Michael, *Image on the Edge: The Margins of Medieval Art* (London: Reaktion Books, 1992).

Capizzi, Carmelo, "Anicia Giuliana (462 ca.–530 ca.): Ricerche sulla sua famiglia e la sua vita," *Rivista di studi bizantini e neoellenici* 5 (1968): 191–226.

Carr, Annemarie Weyl, "The Murals of the Bema and Naos: The Paintings of the Late Thirteenth and Fourteenth Centuries" in *Asinou Across Time: Studies in the Architecture and Murals of the Panagia Phorbiotissa, Cyprus*, edited by Annemarie Carr and Andréas Nicolaïdès (Washington, DC: Dumbarton Oaks, 2012), 211–312.

Caserio, Robert L., Lee Edelman, Judith Halberstam, José Esteban Muñoz, and Tim Dean, "The Antisocial Thesis in Queer Theory," *PMLA* 121:3 (2006): 819–828.

Cassio, Albio Cesare, "Post-Classical Λέσβιαι," *The Classical Quarterly* 33:1 (1983): 296–297.

Castelli, Elizabeth, "'I Will Make Mary Male': Pieties of the Body and Gender Transformation of Christian Women in Late Antiquity" in *Body Guards: The Cultural Politics of Gender Ambiguity*, edited by Julia Epstein and Kristina Straub (New York: Routledge, 1991), 29–49.

Chatterjee, Paroma, "Viewing and Description in *Hysmine and Hysminias*: The

Fresco of the Virtues," *Dumbarton Oaks Papers* 67 (2013): 209–225.

Chatzidakis, Manolis, *Hosios Loukas: Byzantine Art in Greece*, translated by Valerie Nunn (Athens: Melissa Publishing House, 1997).

Chiasson, Charles, "Scythian Androgyny and Environmental Determinism in Herodotus and the Hippocratic *periaeron hudaton topon*," *Syllecta Classica* 12 (2001): 33–73.

Cho, Sumi, Kimberlé Williams Crenshaw, and Leslie McCall, "Toward a Field of Intersectionality Studies: Theory, Applications, and Praxis," *Signs* 38:4 (2013): 785–810.

Clark, Elizabeth A., "Sex, Shame, and Rhetoric: En-gendering Early Christian Ethics," *Journal of the American Academy of Religion* 59 (1991): 221–245.

Clark, Gillian, *Women in Late Antiquity: Pagan and Christian Lifestyles* (Oxford: Clarendon Press, 1993).

Classen, Albrecht, *Sexual Violence and Rape in the Middle Ages: A Critical Discourse in Premodern German and European Literature* (Berlin: De Gruyter, 2011).

Cobb, L. Stephanie, *Dying to Be Men: Gender and Language in Early Christian Martyr Texts* (New York: Columbia University Press, 2008).

Coleman, Emily, "Infanticide in the Early Middle Ages" in *Women in Medieval Society*, edited by Susan Mosher Stuard (Philadelphia: University of Pennsylvania Press, 1976), 47–70.

Collins, Roger, *Visigothic Spain: 409–711* (Oxford: Blackwell Publishing, 2004).

Congourdeau, Marie-Hélène, "Un procès d'avortement à Constantinople au 14e siècle," *Revue des Études Byzantines* 40 (1982): 103–115.

Connor, Carolyn L., *Art and Miracles in Medieval Byzantium: The Crypt at Hosios Loukas and its Frescoes* (Princeton: Princeton University Press, 1991).

———, *Saints and Spectacle: Byzantine Mosaics in their Cultural Setting* (Oxford: Oxford University Press, 2016).

———, *Women of Byzantium* (New Haven: Yale University Press, 2004).

Constantinou, Stavroula, "Holy Actors and Actresses: Fools and Cross-Dressers as the Protagonists of Saints' *Lives*" in *The Ashgate Research Companion to Byzantine Hagiography*, vol. 2, edited by Stephanos Efthymiadis (Burlington: Ashgate, 2014), 343–362.

———, "Violence in the Palace: Rituals of Imperial Punishment in Prokopios's *Secret History*" in *Court Ceremonies and Rituals of Power in Byzantium and the Medieval Mediterranean*, edited by Alexander Beihammer, Stavroula Constantinou, and Maria Parani (Leiden: Brill, 2013), 376–387.

Constas, Nicholas, *Proclus of Constantinople and the Cult of the Virgin in Late Antiquity* (Leiden: Brill, 2003).

Cosgrove, Charles H., "A Woman's Unbound Hair in the Greco-Roman World, with Special Reference to the Story of the 'Sinful Woman' in Luke 7:36–50," *Journal of Biblical Literature* 124:4 (2005): 675–692.

Crenshaw, Kimberlé Williams, "Demarginalizing the Intersection of Race and Sex: A Black Feminist Critique of Antidiscrimination Doctrine, Feminist Theory, and Antiracist Politics," *University of Chicago Legal Forum* 1:8 (1989): 139–167.

———, "Mapping the Margins: Intersectionality, Identity Politics, and Violence Against Women of Color," *Stanford Law Review* 43:6 (1991): 1241–1299.

Crowley, Patrick R., "Doubting Thomas and the Matter of Embodiment on Early Christian Sarcophagi," *Art History* 41:3 (2018): 566–591.

Cunningham, Mary B., "The Use of the *Protevangelion* of James in Eighth-Century Homilies on the Mother of God" in *The Cult of the Mother of God in Byzantium: Texts and Images*, edited by Leslie Brubaker and Mary B. Cunningham (Burlington: Ashgate, 2011), 163–178.

———, *Wider Than Heaven: Eighth-Century Homilies on the Mother of God* (Crestwood: St. Vladimir's Seminary Press, 2008).

Cupane, Carolina and Ewald Kislinger, "Bemerkungen Zur Abtreibung in Byzanz," *Jahrbuch der Österreichischen Byzantinistik* 35 (1985): 21–49.

Cutler, Anthony, "A Psalter of Basil II (Part I)," *Arte Veneta* 30 (1976): 9–19.

———, "A Psalter of Basil II (Part II)," *Arte Veneta* 31 (1977): 9–15.

Cvetkovich, Ann, *An Archive of Feelings: Trauma, Sexuality, and Lesbian Public*

Cultures (Durham: Duke University Press, 2003).

Dalla-Vorgia, P., J. Lascaratos, P. Skiadas, and T. Garanis-Papadatos, "Is Consent in Medicine a Concept Only of Modern Times?" *Journal of Medical Ethics* 27:1 (2001): 59–61.

Datema, Cornelis, "New Evidence for the Encounter Between Constantinople and 'India'" in *After Chalcedon: Studies in Theology and Church History*, edited by C. Laga, J. A. Munitiz, and L. van Rompay (Leuven: Peeters, 1985), 57–65.

Davis, Stephen J., "Crossed Texts, Crossed Sex: Intertextuality and Gender in Early Christian Legends of Holy Women Disguised as Men," *Journal of Early Christian Studies* 10:1 (2002): 1–36.

Demus, Otto, *The Mosaics of San Marco in Venice*, 2 vols. in 4 (Chicago: University of Chicago Press, 1984).

Devisse, Jean, "The Black and His Color: From Symbols to Realities" in *The Image of the Black in Western Art*, new ed., vol. 2.1, edited by David Bindman and Henry Louis Gates, Jr. (Cambridge: Belknap Press, 2010), 73–137.

Diehl, Charles, *Théodora: impératrice de Byzance*, 4th edition (Paris: H. Piazza et Cie, 1904).

Drpić, Ivan, *Epigram, Art, and Devotion in Later Byzantium* (Cambridge: Cambridge University Press, 2016).

Edelman, Lee, *No Future: Queer Theory and the Death Drive* (Durham: Duke University Press, 2004).

Eno, Robert B., "Mary and her Role in Patristic Theology" in *The One Mediator, the Saints, and Mary*, edited by H. G. Anderson, J. F. Stafford, and J. A. Burgess (Minneapolis: Augsburg, 1992), 159–176.

Evangelatou, Maria, "Liturgy and the Illustration of the Ninth-Century Marginal Psalters," *Dumbarton Oaks Papers* 63 (2009): 59–116.

Fairweather, Janet, "Fiction in the Biographies of Ancient Authors," *Ancient Society* 5 (1974): 231–275.

Fiaccadori, Gianfranco, "Un re di Nubia a Constantinopoli nel 1203," *Scrinium* 1:1 (2005): 43–49.

Fisher, Elizabeth A., "Theodora and Antonina in the *Historia Arcana*: History and/or Fiction?" *Arethusa* 11:1 (1978): 253–279.

Flower, Michael A., "Religious Expertise" in *The Oxford Handbook of Ancient Greek Religion*, edited by Esther Eidinow and Julia Kindt (Oxford: Oxford University Press, 2015), 299–307.

Flusin, Bernard, "Palestinian Hagiography (Fourth-Eighth Centuries)" in *The Ashgate Companion to Byzantine Hagiography*, vol. 1, edited by Stephanos Efthymiadis (Burlington: Ashgate, 2011), 199–226.

Frankforter, A. Daniel, "Amalasuntha, Procopius, and a Woman's Place," *Journal of Women's History* 8:2 (1996): 41–57.

Freeman, Elizabeth, *Time Binds: Queer Temporalities, Queer Histories* (Durham: Duke University Press, 2010).

Galatariotou, Catia, "Holy Women and Witches: Aspects of Byzantine Conceptions of Gender," *Byzantine and Modern Greek Studies* 9 (1984): 55–94.

Gargova, Fani, "The Meteora Icon of the Incredulity of Thomas Reconsidered" in *Female Founders in Byzantium and Beyond*, edited by Lioba Theis, Margaret Muller, and Michael Grünbart (Vienna: Böhlau Verlag, 2012), 369–381.

Garland, Lynda, *Byzantine Empresses: Women and Power in Byzantium, AD 527–1204* (London: Routledge, 1999).

Gerstel, Sharon E. J., "Painted Sources for Female Piety in Medieval Byzantium," *Dumbarton Oaks Papers* 52 (1998): 89–111.

———, *Rural Lives and Landscapes in Late Byzantium: Art, Archaeology, and Ethnography* (Cambridge: Cambridge University Press, 2015).

Gibbon, Edward, *The Decline and Fall of the Roman Empire*, new ed., 4 vols. (London: W. W. Gibbings, 1890).

Gigineishvili, L., and G. Van Riel, "Ioane Petritsi: A Witness to Proclus' Works in the School of Psellus" in *Proclus et la théologie platonicienne*, edited by A.-Ph. Segonds and C. Steel (Leuven: Leuven University Press, 2000), 571–587.

Gilman, Sander L., *Making the Body Beautiful: A Cultural History of Aesthetic Surgery* (Princeton: Princeton University Press, 1999).

Ginzburg, Carlo, "Microhistory: Two or Three Things That I Know about It," translated by John and Anne C. Tedeschi, *Critical Inquiry* 20:1 (1993): 10–35.

"GLAAD Media Reference Guide—

Transgender," *GLAAD*, www.glaad.org
/reference/transgender.

Grabar, André, *Ampoules de Terre Sainte
(Monza, Bobbio)* (Paris: C. Klincksieck,
1958).

———, "Le schéma iconographique de la
Pentecôte," *L'Art de la fin de l'Antiquité et
du Moyen âge*, 3 vols. (Paris: Collège de
France, 1968), 1: 615–627.

Gray, Patrick, "Abortion, Infanticide, and the
Social Rhetoric of the *Apocalypse of Peter*," *Journal of Early Christian Studies* 9:3
(2001): 313–337.

Green, Monica H., "Bodily Essences: Bodies
as Categories of Difference" in *A Cultural
History of the Human Body in the Medieval Age*, edited by Linda Kalof (New York:
Berg Publishers, 2010), 149–172.

———, *Making Women's Medicine Masculine:
The Rise of Male Authority in Pre-Modern
Gynaecology* (Oxford: Oxford University
Press, 2008).

Grigoriadis, Iordanis, *Linguistic and Literary
Studies in the* Epitome Historion *of John
Zonaras* (Thessalonike: Byzantine Re-
search Center, 1998).

Grünbart, Michael, "Typisch Mann, Typisch
Frau: Beschreibungen von Kaiserinnen in
der byzantinischen Historiographie," *Byzantinoslavica* 74:1 (2016): 44–60.

Haines-Eitzen, Kim, *The Gendered Palimpsest: Women, Writing, and Representation
in Early Christianity* (Oxford: Oxford University Press, 2011).

Halberstam, J. Jack, *Female Masculinity*
(Durham: Duke University Press, 1998).

———, "Shame and White Gay Masculinity,"
Social Text 23:3–4 (2005): 219–233.

Halley, Janet, and Andrew Parker, eds. *After Sex?: On Writing since Queer Theory*
(Durham: Duke University Press, 2011).

Halperin, David M., *How to Do the History
of Homosexuality* (Chicago: University of
Chicago Press, 2002).

Halperin, David, and Valerie Traub, eds. *Gay
Shame* (Chicago: University of Chicago
Press, 2009).

Hancock, Ange-Marie, *Intersectionality: An
Intellectual History* (Oxford: Oxford University Press, 2016).

Harstad, Michael J., "Saints, Drugs, and Surgery: Byzantine Therapeutics for Breast
Diseases," *Pharmacy in History* 28:4 (1986):
175–180.

Harvey, Susan Ashbrook, *Asceticism and
Society in Crisis: John of Ephesus and the
Lives of the Eastern Saints* (Berkeley: Uni-
versity of California Press, 1990).

Henderson, Jeffrey, *The Maculate Muse: Obscene Language in Attic Comedy*, 2nd ed.
(Oxford: Oxford University Press, 1991).

Hendrickx, B., "Un roi Africain à Constantinople en 1203," *Byzantina* 13 (1985):
893–898.

Heng, Geraldine, *The Invention of Race in the
European Middle Ages* (Cambridge: Cambridge University Press, 2018).

Hollywood, Amy, "Kill Jesus" in *Mel Gibson's Bible: Religion, Popular Culture,
and* The Passion of the Christ, edited by
Timothy K. Beal and Tod Linafelt (Chicago: University of Chicago Press, 2006),
159–167.

Holman, Susan R., "On Phoenix and Eu-
nuchs: Sources for Meletius the Monk's
Anatomy of Gender," *Journal of Early
Christian Studies* 16:1 (2008): 79–101.

Holmes, Catherine, *Basil II and the Governance of Empire (976–1025)* (Oxford: Oxford University Press, 2005).

Hopkins, Keith, "Contraception in the Roman Empire," *Comparative Studies in Society and History*, 8:1 (1965): 124–151.

Horstmanshoff, Manfred, "Ancient Medi-
cine between Hope and Fear: Medicament,
Magic and Poison in the Roman Empire,"
European Review 7:1 (1999): 37–51.

Hotchkiss, Valerie R., *Clothes Make the
Man: Female Cross Dressing in Medieval
Europe* (New York: Garland Publishing,
1996).

Hsy, Jonathan, and Julie Orlemanski, "Race
and Medieval Studies: A Partial Bibliography," *Postmedieval* 8:4 (2017): 500–513.

Hutter, Irmgard, and Paul Canart, *Marienhomiliar des Mönchs Jakobos von Kokkinobaphos* (Zurich: Belser Verlag, 1991).

Icks, Martijn, *The Crimes of Elagabalus: The
Life and Legacy of Rome's Decadent Boy
Emperor* (Cambridge: Cambridge Univer-
sity Press, 2012).

Insley, Sarah, "Dressing Up the Past: Fictional Narrative in the *Life of Matrona
of Perge*" in *Medieval Greek Storytelling:
Fictionality and Narrative in Byzantium*,
edited by Panagiotis Roilos (Wiesbaden:
Harrassowitz Verlag, 2014), 55–85.

Isaac, Benjamin, *The Invention of Racism in*

Classical Antiquity (Princeton: Princeton University Press, 2004).

James, Liz, *Empress and Power in Early Byzantium* (London: Leicester University Press, 2001).

———, *Light and Colour in Byzantine Art* (Oxford: Clarendon Press, 1996).

———, "Monks, Monastic Art, the Sanctoral Cycle and the Middle Byzantine Church" in *The Theotokos Evergetis and Eleventh-Century Monasticism*, edited by Margaret Mullett and Anthony Kirby (Belfast: Queen's University of Belfast, 1994), 162–175.

Jansma, Taeke, "Narsai's Homilies on Creation: Remarks on a Recent Edition," *Muséon* 83 (1970): 209–235.

Jeffreys, Elizabeth, "The *sebastokratorissa* Irene as Patron" in *Female Founders in Byzantium and Beyond*, edited by Lioba Theis, Magaret Mullett, and Michael Grünbart (Vienna: Böhlau, 2014), 177–194.

Jolly, Penny Howell, *Made in God's Image? Eve and Adam in the Genesis Mosaics at San Marco, Venice* (Berkeley: University of California Press, 1997).

Joseph, Branden W., *Beyond the Dream Syndicate: Tony Conrad and the Arts after Cage (A "Minor" History)* (New York: Zone Books, 2008).

Kaldellis, Anthony, *Ethnography after Antiquity: Foreign Lands and Peoples in Byzantine Literature* (Philadelphia: University of Pennsylvania Press, 2013).

———, "Identifying Dissident Circles in Sixth-Century Byzantium: The Friendship of Prokopios and Ioannes Lydos," *Florilegium* 21 (2004): 1–17.

———, *Procopius of Caesarea: Tyranny, History, and Philosophy at the End of Antiquity* (Philadelphia: University of Pennsylvania Press, 2004).

———, *Romanland: Ethnicity and Empire in Byzantium* (Cambridge: Harvard University Press, 2019).

Karlin-Hayter, Patricia, "Further Notes on Byzantine Marriage: Raptus—ἁρπαγή or μνηστεῖαι?" *Dumbarton Oaks Papers* 46 (1992): 133–154.

Kazhdan, Alexander, "Byzantine Hagiography and Sex in the Fifth to Twelfth Centuries," *Dumbarton Oaks Papers* 44 (1990): 131–143.

———, ed. *The Oxford Dictionary of Byzantium* (Oxford: Oxford University Press, 1991).

Kazhdan, Alexander P., and Ann Wharton Epstein, *Change in Byzantine Culture in the Eleventh and Twelfth Centuries* (Berkeley: University of California Press, 1985).

Kelly, Kathleen Ann, "'Blue' Indians, Ethiopians, and Saracens in Middle English Narrative Texts," *Parergon* 11:1 (1993): 35–52.

Khalil, Mokhtar, and Catherine Miller, "Old Nubian and Language Uses in Nubia," *Égypte/Monde arabe* 27–28 (1996): 1–7.

King, Helen, *The One-Sex Body on Trial: The Classical and Early Modern Evidence* (London: Routledge, 2016).

Kinoshita, Sharon, *Medieval Boundaries: Rethinking Difference in Old French Literature* (Philadelphia: University of Pennsylvania Press, 2006).

Krueger, Derek, "The Bawdy and Society: The Shamelessness of Diogenes in Roman Imperial Culture" in *The Cynics: The Cynic Movement in Antiquity and its Legacy*, edited by R. Bracht Branham and M.-O. Goulet Cazé (Berkeley: University of California Press, 1966), 222–239.

———, "Between Monks: Tales of Monastic Companionship in Early Byzantium," *Journal of the History of Sexuality* 20:1 (2011): 28–61.

———, "Homoerotic Spectacle and the Monastic Body in Symeon the New Theologian" in *Towards a Theology of Eros: Transfiguring Passion at the Limits of Discipline*, edited by Virginia Burrus and Catherine Keller (New York: Fordham University Press, 2006), 99–118.

———, *Liturgical Subjects: Christian Ritual, Biblical Narrative, and the Formation of the Self in Byzantium* (Philadelphia: University of Pennsylvania Press, 2014).

———, "Mary at the Threshold: The Mother of God as Guardian in Seventh-Century Palestinian Miracle Accounts" in *The Cult of the Mother of God in Byzantium: Texts and Images*, edited by Leslie Brubaker and Mary Cunningham (Burlington, VT: Ashgate, 2011), 31–38.

———, *Symeon the Holy Fool: Leontius' Life and the Late Antique City* (Berkeley: University of California Press, 1996).

Lacquer, Thomas, *Making Sex: Body and*

Gender from the Greeks to Freud (Cambridge: Harvard University Press, 1990).

Laiou, Angeliki, *Mariage, amour et parenté à Byzance aux XIe–XIIIe siècles* (Paris: De Boccard, 1993).

———, "Sex, Consent, and Coercion in Byzantium" in *Consent and Coercion to Sex and Marriage in Ancient and Medieval Societies*, edited by A. Laiou (Washington, DC: Dumbarton Oaks, 1998): 109–221.

Lampe, G. W. H., *A Patristic Greek Lexicon* (Oxford: Clarendon Press, 1961).

Largier, Niklaus, *In Praise of the Whip: A Cultural History of Arousal* (Brooklyn: Zone Books, 2007).

Lascaratos, John, Christos Liapis, and Maria Kouvaraki, "Surgery on Varices in Byzantine Times (324–1453 CE)," *Journal of Vascular Surgery* 33:1 (2001): 197–203.

Lascaratos, John et al., "Plastic Surgery of the Face in Byzantium in the Fourth Century," *Plastic and Reconstructive Surgery* 102:4 (1998): 1274–1280.

Lewinsky, Monica, "The Price of Shame," filmed March 2015 in Vancouver, Canada, *TED2015: Truth and Dare*, https://www.ted.com/talks/monica_lewinsky_the_price_of_shame/.

Linardou, Kallirroe, "The Kokkinobaphos Manuscripts Revisited: The Internal Evidence of the Books," *Scriptorium* 61:2 (2007): 384–407.

———, "Reading Two Byzantine Illustrated Books: The Kokkinobaphos Manuscripts (Vaticanus graecus 1162 and Parisinus graecus 1208) and their Illustrations," unpublished PhD thesis, University of Birmingham (2004).

Louth, Andrew, *Maximus the Confessor* (London: Routledge, 1996).

Lubinsky, Crystal Lynn, *Removing Masculine Layers to Reveal a Holy Womanhood: The Female Transvestite Monks of Late Antique Eastern Christianity* (Turnhout: Brepols, 2013).

Lugones, Maria, "Toward a Decolonial Feminism," *Hypatia* 25:4 (2010): 742–759.

MacKendrick, Karmen, *Counterpleasures* (Albany: State University of New York Press, 1999).

Macrides, Ruth J., "Kinship by Arrangement: The Case of Adoption," *Dumbarton Oaks Papers* 44 (1990): 109–118.

Magnússon, Sigurður Gylfi, and István M. Szíjártó, *What is Microhistory? Theory and Practice* (London: Routledge, 2013).

Magoulias, Henry, "Bathhouse, Inn, Tavern, Prostitution, and the Stage as Seen in the Lives of the Saints in the Sixth and Seventh Centuries," Ἐπετηρὶς Ἑταιρείας Βυζαντινῶν Σπουδῶν 38 (1971): 233–252.

———, "The Lives of Saints as Source Data for the History of Byzantine Medicine in the Sixth and Seventh Centuries," *Byzantinische Zeitschrift* 57 (1964): 127–150.

Maguire, Henry, *The Icons of their Bodies: Saints and their Images in Byzantium* (Princeton: Princeton University Press, 1996).

———, "Parodies of Imperial Ceremonial and their Reflections in Byzantine Art" in *Court Ceremonies and Rituals of Power in Byzantium and the Medieval Mediterranean*, edited by Alexander Beihammer, Stavroula Constantinou, and Maria Parani (Leiden: Brill, 2013), 417–432.

Mallan, Christopher, "The Style, Method, and Programme of Xiphilinus' *Epitome* of Cassius Dio's *Roman History*," *Greek, Roman, and Byzantine Studies* 53 (2013): 610–644.

Marinis, Vasileios, *Architecture and Ritual in the Churches of Constantinople: Ninth to Fifteenth Centuries* (Cambridge: Cambridge University Press, 2014).

Martindale, John, ed. *The Prosopography of the Later Roman Empire*, vol. 2 (Cambridge: Cambridge University Press, 1980).

Martin-Hisard, B., "Georgian Hagiography" in *The Ashgate Research Companion to Byzantine Hagiography*, vol. 1 (Burlington, VT: Ashgate, 2011), 285–298.

Masterson, Mark, "Impossible Translation: Antony and Paul the Simple in the *Historium Monachorum*" in *The Boswell Thesis: Essays on Christianity, Social Tolerance, and Homosexuality*, edited by Mathew Kuefler (Chicago: University of Chicago Press, 2006), 215–235.

McClanan, Anne, *Representations of Early Byzantine Empresses: Image and Empire* (New York: Palgrave Macmillan, 2002).

———, "'Weapons to Probe the Womb': The Material Culture of Abortion and Contraception in the Early Byzantine Period" in *The Material Culture of Sex, Procreation, and Marriage in Premodern Europe*, edited by Anne L. McClanan and Karen Rosoff

Encarnación (New York: Palgrave Macmillan, 2002), 33–57.

McCoskey, Denise Eileen, *Race: Antiquity and Its Legacy* (Oxford: Oxford University Press, 2012).

Meeks, Wayne A., "The Image of the Androgyne: Some Uses of a Symbol in Earliest Christianity," *History of Religions* 13:3 (1974): 165–208.

Meerson, Michael and Peter Shäfer, eds. *Toledot Yeshu: The Life Story of Jesus*, 2 vols. (Tübingen: Mohr Siebeck, 2014).

Messis, Charis, "Des amitiés à l'institution a'un lien social: l'*adelphopoiia* à Byzance" in *Corrispondenza d'amorosi sensi: L'omoerotismo nella letteratura medieval*, edited by Paul Odorico, N. Pasero, M. P. Bachmann (Alessandria: Edizioni: dell'Orso, 2008), 31–64.

———, *Les eunuques à Byzance, entre réalité et imaginaire* (Paris: Centre des Études Byzantines, 2014).

Meyendorff, John, "Christian Marriage in Byzantium: The Canonical and Liturgical Tradition," *Dumbarton Oaks Papers* 44 (1990): 99–107.

Meyer, Mati, *An Obscure Portrait: Imagining Women's Reality in Byzantine Art* (London: The Pindar Press, 2009).

Milanović, Ljubomir, "On the Threshold of Certainty: The Incredulity of Thomas in the Narthex of the Katholikon of the Hosios Loukas Monastery," *Recueil des travaux de l'Institut d'études byzantines* 50 (2013): 367–388.

Millar, Fergus, *A Study of Cassius Dio* (Oxford: Clarendon Press).

Miller, Patricia Cox, "Is There a Harlot in This Text? Hagiography and the Grotesque," *Journal of Medieval and Early Modern Studies* 33:3 (2003): 419–435.

Mills, Robert, *Seeing Sodomy in the Middle Ages* (Chicago: University of Chicago Press, 2015).

———, "Visibly Trans?: Picturing Saint Eugenia in Medieval Art," *Transgender Studies Quarterly* 5:4 (2018): 540–564.

Misty, Zubin, *Abortion in the Early Middle Ages, c. 500–900* (Rochester: Boydell and Brewer, 2015).

Most, Glenn W., *Doubting Thomas* (Cambridge: Harvard University Press, 2007).

Müller, Wolfgang P., *The Criminalization of Abortion in the West: Its Origins in Medieval Law* (Ithaca, NY: Cornell University Press, 2012).

Mullet, Margaret E., "Byzantium: A Friendly Society?" *Past & Present* 118 (1988): 3–24.

Muñoz, José Esteban, *Cruising Utopia: The Then and There of Queer Futurity* (New York: New York University Press, 2009).

Mylonas, Anastassios I. et al., "Oral and Cranio-Maxillofacial Surgery in Byzantium," *Journal of Cranio-Maxillo-Facial Surgery* 42 (2014): 159–168.

Nash, Jennifer C., *Black Feminism Reimagined: After Intersectionality* (Durham: Duke University Press, 2019).

Neville, Leonora, *Anna Komnene: The Life and Work of a Medieval Historian* (Oxford: Oxford University Press, 2016).

———, *Byzantine Gender* (Leeds: Arc Humanities Press, 2019).

———, *Heroes and Romans in Twelfth-Century Byzantium: The "Material for History" of Nikephoros Bryennios* (Cambridge: Cambridge University Press, 2012).

Nutton, Vivian, "Healers in the Medical Market Place: Towards a Social History of Greco-Roman Medicine" in *Medicine in Society: Historical Essays*, edited by A. Wear (Cambridge: Cambridge University Press, 1992), 15–58.

Omitowoju, Rosanna, *Rape and the Politics of Consent in Classical Athens* (Cambridge: Cambridge University Press, 2002).

Papaconstantinou, Arietta, "'Je suis noire, mais belle': Le double langage de la *Vie de Théodora d'Alexandrie, alias* Abba Théodore," *Lalies* 24 (2004): 63–86.

Papadakis, Marios et al., "Gynaecomastia and Scrotal Rhacosis: Two Aesthetic Surgical Operations for Men in Byzantine Times," *Journal of Plastic, Reconstructive and Aesthetic Surgery* 63 (2010): 600–604.

Papaioannou, Stratis, "Michael Psellos on Friendship and Love: Erotic Discourse in Eleventh-Century Constantinople," *Early Medieval Europe* 19:1 (2011): 43–61.

———, "On the Stage of *Eros*: Two Rhetorical Exercises by Nikephoros Basilakes" in *Theatron: Rhetorische Kultur in Spätantike und Mittelalter*, edited by Michael Grünbart (Berlin: De Gruyter, 2007), 357–376.

———, *Michael Psellos: Rhetoric and Authorship in Byzantium* (Cambridge: Cambridge University Press, 2013).

Parani, Maria, "Look Like an Angel: The

Attire of Eunuchs and Its Significance within the Context of Middle Byzantine Court Ceremonial" in *Court Ceremonies and Rituals of Power in Byzantium and the Medieval Mediterranean*, edited by Alexander Beihammer, Stavroula Constantinou, and Maria Parani (Leiden: Brill, 2013), 433–463.

Parker, Holt N., "Women Doctors in Greece, Rome, and the Byzantine Empire" in *Women Healers and Physicians: Climbing a Long Hill*, edited by Lilian R. Furst (Lexington: University Press of Kentucky, 1997), 131–150.

Patlagean, Evelyne, "Birth Control in the Early Byzantine Empire" in *Biology of Man in History*, edited by Robert Forster and Orest Ranum, translated by Elborg Forster and Patricia M. Ranum (Baltimore: Johns Hopkins University Press, 1975), 1–22.

———, "L'histoire de la femme déguisée en moine et l'évolution de la sainteté féminine a Byzance," *Studi Medievali*, series 3, 17 (1976): 597–623.

Pentcheva, Bissera, *The Sensual Icon: Space, Ritual, and the Senses in Byzantium* (University Park: Pennsylvania State University Press, 2010).

Pérez, Hiram, *A Taste for Brown Bodies: Gay Modernity and Cosmopolitan Desire* (New York: New York University Press, 2015).

Pitsakēs, Kōnstantinos G., "*Ē Thesē tōn omophulophilōn stē buzantinē koinonia*" in *Praktika Ēmeridas*, edited by Chrysa A. Maltezou (Athens: Idruma Goulandrē, 1999), 171–269.

Poulakou-Rebelakou, E., J. Lascaratos, and S. G. Marketos, "Abortions in Byzantine Times (325–1453 A.D.)," *Vesalius* 2 (1996): 19–25.

Power, Amanda, and Robin Whelan (organizers), *Medieval Intersectionality*, conference at Oxford University, March 15, 2017.

Rapp, Claudia, *Brother-Making in Late-Antiquity and Byzantium: Monks, Laymen, and Christian Ritual* (Oxford: Oxford University Press, 2016).

Riddle, John M., "Byzantine Commentaries on Dioscorides," *Dumbarton Oaks Papers* 38 (1984): 95–102.

———, *Contraception and Abortion from the Ancient World to the Renaissance* (Cambridge: Harvard University Press, 1992).

———, *Dioscorides on Pharmacy and Medicine* (Austin: University of Texas Press, 1985).

Ringrose, Kathryn M., "Living in the Shadows: Eunuchs and Gender in Byzantium" in *Third Sex, Third Gender: Beyond Sexual Dimorphism in Culture and History*, edited by G. Herdt (New York: Zone Books, 1994), 85–109.

———, *The Perfect Servant: Eunuchs and the Social Construction of Gender in Byzantium* (Chicago: University of Chicago Press, 2003).

Roberts, Michael, *The Jeweled Style: Poetry and Poetics in Late Antiquity* (Ithaca: Cornell University Press, 1989).

Roller, Lynn E., "The Ideology of the Eunuch Priest," *Gender & History* 9:3 (1997): 542–559.

Rostkowska, Bożena, "The Visit of a Nubian King to Constantinople in A.D. 1203" in *New Discoveries in Nubia: Proceedings of the Colloquium on Nubian Studies, The Hague, 1979*, edited by Paul van Moorsel (Leiden: Netherlands Instituut Voor Het Nabije Oosten, 1982), 113–116.

Santoni-Rugiu, Paolo and Philip J. Sykes, *A History of Plastic Surgery* (New York: Springer, 2007).

Scarborough, John, "Drugs and Drug Lore in the Time of Theophrastus: Folklore, Magic, Botany, Philosophy, and the Rootcutters," *Acta Classica* 49 (2006): 1–29.

———, "Early Byzantine Pharmacology," *Dumbarton Oaks Papers* 38 (1984): 213–232.

———, "Teaching Surgery in Late Byzantine Alexandria" in *Hippocrates and Medical Education*, edited by Manfred Horstmanshoff (Leiden: Brill, 2010), 235–260.

———, "Theodora, Aetius of Amida, and Procopius: Some Possible Connections," *Greek, Roman, and Byzantine Studies* 53 (2013): 742–762.

Schroeder, Caroline T., *Monastic Bodies: Discipline and Salvation in Shenoute of Atripe* (Philadelphia: University of Pennsylvania Press, 2007).

Scott, Roger D., "Malalas, *The Secret History*, and Justinian's Propaganda," *Dumbarton Oaks Papers* 39 (1985): 99–109.

Sedgwick, Eve Kosofsky, *Epistemology of the Closet*, updated edition (Berkeley: University of California Press, 2008).

———, *Tendencies* (Durham: Duke University Press, 1993).

Ševčenko, Ihor, "The Illuminators of the Menologium of Basil II," *Dumbarton Oaks Papers* 16 (1962): 245–276.

———, "On Pantoleon the Painter," *Jahrbuch der Österreichischen Byzantinistik* 21 (1972): 241–249.

Ševčenko, Nancy Patterson, "The Representation of Donors and Holy Figures on Four Byzantine Icons," *Deltion tēs Christianikēs Archaiologikēs Etairias* 17 (1993–1994): 157–164.

Shäfer, Peter, *Jesus in the Talmud* (Princeton: Princeton University Pres, 2007).

Shaw, Teresa M., *The Burden of the Flesh: Fasting and Sexuality in Early Christianity* (Minneapolis: Fortress Press, 1998).

Shoemaker, Stephen J., *Mary in Early Christian Faith and Devotion* (New Haven: Yale University Press, 2016).

Smith, Steven D., "Agathias and Paul the Silentiary: Erotic Epigram and the Sublimation of Same-Sex Desire in the Age of Justinian" in *Sex in Antiquity: Exploring Gender and Sexuality in the Ancient World*, edited by Mark Masterson, Nancy Sorkin Rabinowitz, and James Robson (London: Routledge, 2014), 500–516.

———, *Greek Epigram and Byzantine Culture: Gender, Desire, and Denial in the Age of Justinian* (Cambridge: Cambridge University Press, 2019).

———, *Man and Animal in Severan Rome: The Literary Imagination of Claudius Aelianus* (Cambridge: Cambridge University Press, 2017).

Smythe, Dion C., "In Denial: Same-Sex Desire in Byzantium" in *Desire and Denial in Byzantium*, edited by Liz James (Burlington, VT: Ashgate, 1999), 139–148.

Snorton, C. Reily, *Black on Both Sides: A Racial History of Trans Identity* (Minneapolis: University of Minnesota Press, 2017).

Snowden, Jr., Frank M., *Before Color Prejudice: The Ancient View of Blacks* (Cambridge: Harvard University Press, 1983).

———, *Blacks in Antiquity: Ethiopians in the Greco-Roman Experience* (Cambridge: Harvard University Press, 1970).

Spade, Dean, "Resisting Medicine, Re/modeling Gender," *Berkeley Journal of Gender, Law and Justice* 18:1 (2013): 15–37.

Stannard, Jerry, "Aspects of Byzantine Materia Medica," *Dumbarton Oaks Papers* 38 (1984): 205–211.

Stephenson, Paul, *The Legend of Basil the Bulgar-Slayer* (Cambridge: Cambridge University Press, 2003).

Stockton, Kathryn Bond, "The Queerness of Race and Same-Sex Desire" in *The Cambridge Companion to Gay and Lesbian Writing*, edited by H. Stevens (Cambridge: Cambridge University Press, 2010), 116–131.

Strickland, Debra Higgs, *Saracens, Demons, and Jews: Making Monsters in Medieval Art* (Princeton: Princeton University Press, 2003).

Stroumsa, Gedaliahu A. G., *Another Seed: Studies in Gnostic Mythology* (Leiden: Brill, 1984).

Svenbro, Jesper, *Phrasikleia: An Anthropology of Reading in Ancient Greece*, translated by Janet Lloyd (Ithaca, NY: Cornell University Press, 1993).

Szarmach, Paul E., "St. Euphrosyne: Holy Transvestite" in *Holy Men and Holy Women: Old English Prose Saints' Lives and Their Contexts*, edited by Paul E. Szarmach (Albany: SUNY Press, 1996), 353–365.

Taft, Robert F., *A History of the Liturgy of St. John Chrysostom*, vol. 5: The Precommunion Rites (Rome: Pontifico Istituto Orientale, 2000).

Tanenbaum, Leora, *I Am Not a Slut: Slut-Shaming in the Age of the Internet* (New York: Harper Collins, 2015).

Thein, Karl, "Gods and Painters: Philostratus the Elder, Stoic Phantasia, and the Strategy of Describing," *Ramus* 31:1/2 (2002): 136–145.

Theis, Lioba, Margaret Mullett, and Michael Grünbart, eds. *Female Founders in Byzantium and Beyond* (Wien: Böhlau, 2014).

Thumiger, Chiara, " 'A Most Acute, Disgusting and Indecent Disease': Satyriasis and Sexual Disorders in Ancient Medicine" in *Mental Illness in Ancient Medicine: From Celsus to Paul of Aegina*, edited by Chiara Thumiger and P. N. Singer (Leiden: Brill, 2018): 269–284.

Tougher, Shaun, *The Eunuch in Byzantine History and Society* (London: Routledge, 2008).

———, "Michael III and Basil the Macedonian: Just Good Friends?" in *Desire and Denial in Byzantium*, edited by Liz James (Burlington, VT: Ashgate, 1999), 149–158.

Traub, Valerie, "The Psychomorphology of the Clitoris," *GLQ: A Journal of Lesbian and Gay Studies* 2 (1995): 81–113.

Trojanos, S. N., "Η άμβλωσή στο βυζαντινό δίκαιο," *Byzantiaka* 4 (1984): 169–189.

Tronzo, William, "Mimesis in Byzantium: Notes toward a History of the Function of the Image," *Res: Anthropology and Aesthetics* 25 (1994): 61–76.

Tsoucalas, Gregory, Konstantinos Laios, Marianna Karamanou, and Markos N. Sgantzos, "Bishop Paul of Merida, and the First Known Caesarean Section on a Living Woman," *Journal of Obstetrics and Gynaecology* 35:2 (2015): 203.

Usener, Hermann, "Legenden der Pelagia," *Vorträge und Aufsätze* (Leipzig: Teubner, 1907), 190–215.

Valentine, David, *Imagining Transgender: An Ethnography of a Category* (Durham: Duke University Press, 2007).

Vikan, Gary, "Art, Medicine, and Magic in Early Byzantium," *Dumbarton Oaks Papers* 38 (1984): 65–86.

———, *Early Byzantine Pilgrimage Art*, revised ed. (Washington, DC: Dumbarton Oaks, 2010).

Vogt, Kari, "'The Woman Monk': A Theme in Byzantine Hagiography" in *Greece and Gender*, edited by Brit Berggreen and Nanno Marinatos (Bergen: Norwegian Institute at Athens, 1995), 141–148.

Volk, Robert, *Der medizinische Inhalt der Schriften des Michael Psellos* (Munich: Institut für Byzantinistik und neugriechische Philologie der Universität, 1990).

Webb, Lewis, "Shame Transfigured: Slut-Shaming from Rome to Cyberspace," *First Monday* 20:4 (2015), https://doi.org/10.5210/fm.v20i4.5464.

Webb, Ruth, *Demons and Dancers: Performance in Late Antiquity* (Cambridge: Harvard University Press, 2008).

Whitaker, Cord J., *Black Metaphors: How Modern Racism Emerged from Medieval Race-Thinking* (Philadelphia: University of Pennsylvania Press, 2019).

Wilfong, Terry, "Reading the Disjointed Body in Coptic: From Physical Modification to Textual Fragmentation" in *Changing Bodies, Changing Meanings: Studies on the Human Body in Antiquity*, edited by Dominic Montserrat (London: Routledge, 1998), 116–136.

Ziche, Harmut G., "Abusing Theodora: Sexual and Political Discourse in Procopius," *Byzantiaka* 30 (2012–2013): 311–323.

Znorovzky, Andrea-Bianka, "Between Mary and Christ: Depicting Cross-Dressed Saints in the Middle Ages (c. 1200–1600)," unpublished PhD thesis, Central European University (2016).

———, "Holy Female Monks—Patterns of Purity: A Comparative Approach of the Visual Representations of Saint Marina the Monk, Saint Eugenia of Rome, and Saint Euphrosyne" in *Il Genere Nella Ricerca Storica*, 2 vols., edited by S. Chemotti and C. La Rocca (Padua: Il Poligrafo, 2015), 1: 151–170.

———, "Marinus Unveiled: A Transvestite Saint in Western Art and Literature," unpublished MA thesis, Central European University (2011).

INDEX

Page numbers in *italics* indicate illustrations.

abortion and contraception: aristocratic use of, 72, 73–79, 80; death of woman due to, 64, 66–67; Dorotheos, divinely sanctioned abortion in life of, 95; effectiveness of medieval methods, 75, 76; legal and religious views on, 64–67, *67*, 220–21n23; *pharmaka* and *pharmakeusi*, 73–74; prescriptions and methods in medical texts, 67–70; Procopius's accusations of, 63–64, 68, 73–77; surgical procedures (embryotomy and late-term abortion), 70–72, 221n23, 223n67; threat to life of woman without, 66, 68, 70, 71, 72; timing of, 76; women's choice regarding, 74–76, 78–79, 221n35; women's knowledge of, 64, 69–70, 221n35
Abraham of Ephesus, 33
Adam: Christological narrative undoing sin of, 56; Eve as rib "stolen" from, 39–40, 56; Joseph (husband of Virgin Mary) as New Adam, 24
adelphopoiēsis and *adelphosunai*, 123, 129, 232n9
adultery and fornication: in aristocratic Constantinopolitan society, 77–78; drunkenness, adultery, and murder, John Chrysostom drawing causal chain between, 223n72; illegitimate children and, 75, 76–77; Juvenal, *Satires* on, 74–77, 80; rape, developing distinction from, 25, 28; touch, sight's temptation toward, 142; Virgin Mary's consent to become Mother of God, pre-Iconoclasm concerns regarding, 22–26. *See also* slut-shaming
Aeglippis of Ethiopia, 164, *167*
Aelianus (Claudius), 108–9, 229n68
Aetius of Amida, 5, 7, 69, 71, 76, 105, 112–13, 117, 192, 223n67
agapē and *erōs*, 159, 236n107

Saint Agatha, 7–11, *10*
Agios Vasilios, Crete, church of Saint John Prodromos, damned woman, 66
Akathist Hymn (Romanus the Melodist), 217n44
Alexius IV Angelos (emperor), 174
Amnon, rape of Tamar by, 43, *45*, 48
ampullae with Doubting Thomas narrative, 152–54, *153*, 235n99
anal sex, 59, 62
Ananias of Persia, 186, *plate 4*
Anastasius (trans monk), 103–4
Anastasius of Antioch, 33
Ancyrus, Council of (314), 65
Andrew of Crete, 19, 23, 26, 27, 33
Andronicus and Athanasius, 127–29, 192, 233n44
Anicia Juliana, 73, 74
Anna Komnene (empress), 115–16, 178
Anno Vianno, Crete, church of St. Pelagia, female sinners in hell, 66, *67*
Annunciation. *See* Virgin Mary's consent to become Mother of God
Antonina wife of Belisarius, 73–74, 75, 81, 88
Antoninus, 64
Apocalypse of Peter, 220–21n23
Apocryphon of John, 24
Arentzen, Thomas, 136
Arethas of Caesarea, 123
Aristotle, 68, 120
Arius and Arianism, 178
Arondekar, Anjali, 16
Arsenius, 239–39n41
ascetic life and transmasculinity, 92, 100, 102–6
Asinou, Cyprus, Church of the Panagia Phorbiotissa: John the Baptist and Virgin Mary, 6, *9*; Mary of Egypt, 6, *8*, 12
Aspasia, 69–70, 71, 76
Aspergen, Kerstin, 98
Atalanta, 116–19, 193–94

revenge porn, 59–60, 82
Ringrose, Kathryn, 109
Robert de Clari, 173–75
Roman History (Dio Cassius), 106–9, 229n60
Romanus II (emperor), 198
Romanus III (emperor), 28
Romanus the Melodist: *Akathist Hymn,*
    217n44; on consent of Virgin Mary, 19,
    22–25, 27, 33, 217n44, 218n64; same-gender
    desire and, 135–38, 145, 152, 158, 160

Sabas, 126
Sacra Parallela, 43–46, *45, 46,* 48
St. Catherine's Monastery, Mount Sinai. *See*
    Mount Sinai
St. Clement, chapel of, Great Palace, Con-
    stantinople, 237n11
salvation history and consent, 54–57, 218n66
same-gender desire, 17, 121–60; *adelpho-
    poiēsis* and *adelphosunai,* 123, 129, 232n9;
    castration as penalty for, 84, 85; conflation
    of male effeminacy and female masculinity
    with, 125; demons depicted as black,
    feminized, and hypersexual, 179–81;
    Doubting Thomas narratives and, 121–22,
    131–34, *133, 134,* 135–39, 148–52, *155,* 156–58,
    160; homoerotic hymns and homilies on
    union with God, 134–39, 159; Justinian's
    law prohibiting, Procopius on political
    use of, 83–86; *malthakos* (softness) as
    medical term for pathologization of, 193;
    monastic community and, 124–25, 157–60;
    perception/sensation and, 121–22, 139–57
    (*see also* perception and sensation); queer
    theory and, 129–31; queerness of Byzan-
    tium and, 122–25; from same-sex desire
    to, 120, 125–29; sexual intercourse, moving
    queer intimacy beyond, 128, 129–31;
    shame/shaming and, 224n89; slut-shaming
    of Theodora by Procopius likening her
    to male sodomite, 62; terms for women
    experiencing, 123–24; transgender monks
    and, 125–29, 181; Washing of the Feet of the
    Apostles narrative and, 154–57, *155*
San Marco, Church of, Venice. *See* Venice,
    Church of San Marco
San Vitale, Church of, Ravenna, Theodora
    mosaic, *60*
Sarah (desert ascetic), 97, 100
The Sayings of the Desert Fathers, 179–81
scrotal rhacosis, 113
Secret History. See Procopius, *Secret History*
Sedgwick, Eve, 124
sensation. *See* perception and sensation

Ševčenko, Nancy Patterson, 150
Severus, 64
sex workers: abortion/contraception and, 15,
    63–64, 72, 75, 77, 79; empress Theodora
    regarded as, 59, 62–64, 83, 86, 160; Mary
    of Egypt described as, 2; mimes equated
    with, 83; Pelagius (transgender monk) as,
    101–2, 104, 106; socioeconomic status of, 15;
    transgender lives/identities and, 101–2, 104,
    106; uncovered heads, association with,
    228n43
sexual dimorphism, Byzantine theories
    about, 110–11, 230n77
sexuality and sexual consent, 2–5; clitoral
    enlargement, 5, 111–13; demons depicted
    as black, feminized, and hypersexual,
    14, 168, 179–82; developing distinction of
    adultery versus rape, 25; Dio Cassius on
    sexual voracity of Elagabalus, 106–9. *See
    also* adultery and fornication; rape; same-
    gender desire; slut-shaming; Virgin Mary's
    consent to become Mother of God
shame and shaming: queer rejection of,
    158–60; queer shame, 224n89; racial
    shaming and racial prejudice, 175–76,
    184–85, 200; recovery/rehabilitation of, 82,
    224n89. *See also* slut-shaming
Shenoute of Artipe, 125
Sinai. *See* Mount Sinai
skin color. *See* race and racial difference
Skoutariotes, Theodore, 229n65
Skylitzes, John, *Synopsis of Histories,* 28–30, *29*
slut-shaming: of Antonina wife of Belisarius,
    73–74, 75, 81; in art, 66, *67;* defined, 2,
    59–60; of empress Theodora by Procopius,
    3–4, 59, 60, 61–64, 74, 76–78, 82, 83, 86;
    empress Theodora using as political
    weapon, 83, 85; in *Life of Mary of Egypt,*
    2–5; as political weapon, 83–86; rape and,
    29, 116–17; revenge porn and, 59–60, 82; as
    rhetorical practice, 60, 80–83; socioeco-
    nomic status, intersectionality with, 61–62,
    73, 80, 83; of Virgin Mary, 25–26, 53–54
Smaragdos, 126
Smith, Steven, 109
Snowden, Frank M., Jr., 177
socioeconomic status: abortion and contra-
    ception, aristocratic use of, 72, 73–79, 80;
    privacy created by privilege, 15–16; of sex
    workers, 15; shame, rehabilitation/recovery
    of, 224n89; slut-shaming, intersectionality
    with, 61–62, 73, 80, 83; transracial myth of
    white privilege and, 200–201
soghyatha, 19

Virgin Mary's consent to become Mother of
God, 16, 19–57; art, iconography of consent
in, 46–54, *47, 49, 50, 52, 53*; art, parallels
between depictions of rape and Annunciation in, 40–46, *41, 42, 44–46*; conception
and consent, 32–34; Doubting Thomas
narrative and, 145–46; Gabriel and, 22–23,
27, 34, 40, *41*, 46–48, *47*, 52–53, *53*; Joseph
and, 24–25, 26, 27; in later Byzantine
writings, 35–40; pagan/Jewish critiques of
Christianity and, 25–26; perception, consent, and conception, 33–38, 144, 146–47,
218n64; post-iconoclasm narratives of rape
and forced marriage, consent issues in,
28–32, *29*; post-Iconoclasm stress on consent, 4–5, 16, 19–20, 32–35; pre-Iconoclasm
accounts denying possibility of consent,
26–27; pre-Iconoclasm concerns regarding
adultery and rape, 22–26; prudence of
Mary and, 20–22, 32; rape, relationship
to, 22–27, 40–46, *41, 42, 44–46*; salvation
history and consent, 54–57, 218n66; will
and consent, in later Byzantium, 38–40
Vitae. See specific subjects by name

Wars and Buildings (Procopius), 59, 81
Washing of the Feet of the Apostles narrative,
154–57, *155*
Whitaker, Cord J., 239n44
will and consent, 38–40

Xiphilinus, John, 107, 229n60

Yaldabaoth (archon), 24

zeon, 137
Zeus (pagan deity), 20, 25, 61
Zeuxis, 139
Zonaras, John, 107–8
Zosimas and Mary of Egypt, 1–7, 191–92

PHOTO CREDITS

The Byzantine Institute and Dumbarton Oaks fieldwork records and papers, Dumbarton Oaks, Trustees for Harvard University, Washington, D. C. (figs. 0.1–2); Vat. gr. 1613 is reproduced by permission of Biblioteca Apostolica Vaticana, with all rights reserved (figs. 0.4, 0.9, 3.1–2, 5.1, 5.11, plates 1, 4, 5, 7); Add. Ms. 19352 is reproduced by permission of the British Library Board, with all rights reserved (figs. 0.3, 4.4, 5.3); Courtesy of C. S. Osborne and Company (fig. 0.5); Courtesy of Staatsbibliothek Bamberg, Creative Commons (fig. 0.6); Drawings after Marios Papadakis et al. "Gynaecomastia and Scrotal Rhacosis: Two Aesthetic Surgical Operations for Men in Byzantine Times," *Journal of Plastic, Reconstructive, & Aesthetic Surgery* 63:8 (2010): 600–604, at 601–602 (figs. 0.7–8); Matritensis gr. vitr. 26–2 is reproduced by permission of the Biblioteca Nacional de España, with all rights reserved (fig. 1.1); Courtesy of Father Justin Sinaites and St. Catherine's Monastery on Mount Sinai (figs. 1.2–3, 5.8); Courtesy of the Esphigmenou Monastery on Mount Athos, after S. M. Pelekanidis et al., *The Treasures of Mount Athos: Illuminated Manuscripts*, vol. 2 (Athens: Ekdotikē Athēnōn, 1975), 249, fig. 401 (fig. 1.4); Par. gr. 923 is reproduced by permission of Bibliothèque Nationale de France, with all rights reserved (figs. 1.5–6); Vat. gr. 1162 is reproduced by permission of Biblioteca Apostolica Vaticana, with all rights reserved (figs. 1.7–14); Photograph by author (fig. 2.1); Courtesy of the Ephorate of Antiquities of Heraklion, Greek Ministry of Culture and Sports (fig. 2.2); Courtesy of Taylor Hostetter, after W. Taylor Hostetter, *In the Heart of Hilandar: An Interactive Presentation of the Frescoes in the Main Church of the Hilandar Monastery on Mt. Athos*, CD–ROM (Tuskegee: Digital Byzantium, 1999), n.p.; Ekkehard Ritter, Corpus for Wall Mosaics in the North Adriatic Area, Dumbarton Oaks, Trustees for Harvard University, Washington, D. C. (figs. 4.2, 5.5, 5.6 7, 5.9–10, 5.14); Erich Lessing / Art Resource, NY (figs. 4.3 and 4.8); Courtesy of Hosios Loukas, after Manolis Chatzidakis, *Hosios Loukas: Byzantine Art in Greece*, translated by Valerie Nunn (Athens: Melissa Publishing House,

1997), 82, fig. 83 (fig. 4.5); Courtesy of the Ephorate of Antiquities of Trikala, Greek Ministry of Culture and Sports (fig. 4.6); Courtesy of the British Museum, Creative Commons (fig. 4.7); ГИМ gr. 129 is reproduced by permission of the State Historical Museum, Moscow, with all rights reserved (plate 2); Pantokrator, cod. 61 is reproduced by permission of Pantokrator Monastery, Mount Athos, with all rights reserved (fig. 5.2); Courtesy of the BLAGO Fund, www.srpskoblago.org (fig. 5.4); Courtesty of Docheiariou Monastery, after S. M. Pelekanidis et al., *Hoi Thēsauroi tou Hagiou Orous: Eikonographēmena Cheirographa*, vol. 3 (Athens: Ekdotikē Athēnōn, 1979), 166, fig. 258 (plate 3); Marciana gr. 17 is reproduced by permission of the Ministero per i Beni e la Attività Culturali, Biblioteca Nazionale Marciana, with all rights reserved (fig. 5.12); Vat. Reg. gr. 1B is reproduced by permission of Biblioteca Apostolica Vaticana, with all rights reserved (plate 6); Vat. gr. 747 is reproduced by permission of Biblioteca Apostolica Vaticana, with all rights reserved (fig. 5.13); Par. gr. 139 is reproduced by permission of Bibliothèque Nationale de France, with all rights reserved (fig. 5.15, plate 8).